How to
EXTEND
your Victorian terraced house

RIBA Publishing

JACQUELINE GREEN

© Jacqueline Green, 2020

Published by RIBA Publishing, 66 Portland Place, London, W1B 1AD

ISBN 9781 85946 902 6

The right of Jacqueline Green to be identified as the Author of this Work has been asserted in accordance with the Copyright, Designs and Patents Act 1988 sections 77 and 78.

British Library Cataloguing-in-Publication Data
A catalogue record for this book is available from the British Library.

Commissioning Editor: Ginny Mills
Assistant Editor: Clare Holloway
Production: Richard Blackburn
Designed and typeset by Sara Miranda Icaza
Printed and bound by Short Run Press, Exeter
Cover image © Chris Snook

www.ribapublishing.com

Thank you to my husband, Tom, for my morning cups of tea and to Mum and Dad for always being there for me. Thanks to Victoria, Linda and Sam for their encouragement right from the start, and thanks to all of the contributors to the book, who let me use their material without charge, and to Ginny, for spotting its potential.

For Aasta and Lachlann, for being who they are.

TABLE
OF CONTENTS

FOREWORD

If you are considering extending or remodelling a Victorian terraced house and are uninspired by the options available, this is the book for you. Through elegant hand-drawn plans and in-situ images, this book explores unusual ways of making a traditional Victorian terrace work, bringing all the advantages of modern architecture to a traditional house.

I have worked on more Victorian houses than any other type in my career – and in fact I live in one. They are invariably well proportioned and generous in space. *En masse*, they make a very successful townscape and they get the balance of public and private just right. The transition from street to private living spaces is handled by devices such as bay windows and level changes that allow these to be very close – even in high density areas. They are infinitely adaptable and I've been consistently surprised by how they seem to be able to be constantly reinvented.

In this beautiful and accessible book, filled with plans, sections and photographs of real projects, Jacqueline Green shows you how to get the best out of any Victorian house. Her step by step approach and the use of plenty of examples through beautiful hand drawn plans makes for a treasure trove of ideas that will be of great use either for a resident thinking about altering their home or a professional architect looking for inspiration. She looks at multiple configurations of a selection of Victorian house typologies, showing how these houses can be adapted for many different users, lifestyles and budgets.

Paul Archer, Director, Paul Archer Design

ABOUT THE AUTHOR

JACQUELINE GREEN, ARCHITECT, GREEN & TEGGIN ARCHITECTS, UK.
Jacqueline studied architecture at the University of Liverpool, where she gained a BA (Hons) and a BArch. During this time, she also studied at the University of Washington in Seattle, helped design and build a school for a squatter community near Cuernavaca in Mexico and worked in an architectural office in Berlin. She moved to London in 1997, becoming a registered architect in 1999. In 2010, she and her husband — also an architect — started their own company, concentrating mainly on residential projects, where enhancing quality of life, rather than making money, is the primary goal.

Having worked mainly with private residential clients for a number of years, Jacqueline has devised an 'Ideas Consultation' to show clients the full potential of their property. She visits the property; discusses the clients' requirements; and, after measuring up the areas that they would like to change, draws some plan options (to scale) of what could be possible. These plans are discussed and left with the client at the end of the consultation. Experience with these consultations forms the basis for this book.

INTRODUCTION

Victorian terraced houses make up a large percentage of the UK housing stock and – due to their character, durability and flexibility – are generally thought of as desirable places to live. However, with more emphasis being placed on natural light, open planning, flexible living and a connection to the outdoors, the typical layout of this type of dwelling often no longer caters for our modern lifestyles. With the cost of moving house increasing year on year, not forgetting the value of neighbourhood bonds built up over time, more and more people are choosing to extend rather than relocate.

There are a number of resources available to help visualise what might be possible, but many of the examples shown are quite similar in layout and do not take into account differing briefs, budgets or house sizes. A good architect should be able to take these variables into consideration when remodelling a house in order to come up with a solution that may be more daring or unique than usual – or, equally, may be as simple as moving a door position to create more useable space.

This book includes examples of a wide range of different Victorian terraced houses and reveals, floor by floor, the various options available for extending and/or rearranging their spaces. Each option plan is accompanied by a small-scale existing plan with the areas affected by that proposal indicated in red. Care has been taken to avoid replicating ideas in different case studies, so an element of 'mix and match' across the examples is encouraged: an idea from one case study may well work on another. The front part of one proposal could work with the rear of another, which immediately provides many more options than the ones shown in this book. The following pages also include photographs of completed projects in order to further explain certain ideas. In some cases, the plans depicting these actual projects have been tweaked to fit within the base plan of the appropriate case study – so photographs of these examples may not match exactly to the corresponding plans. The options have been arranged in ascending cost order.

In order to get started, you must first ask yourself what you want out of your house. It may be that remodelling is a cost-effective alternative to extending that meets all your needs. Once you have established your brief, you will need to work out which of the seven case studies best represents your house. You will need a ruler and a tape measure for this. The case studies cover a wide range of houses of different widths, heights and lengths – and on different levels. The head height that you have in your loft and the size, level and orientation of your garden will make a difference to the options that you can use – as will the form of the adjacent properties, as mentioned in the Rules of Thumb section.

Once you have identified which case study best suits your house (and remember that options from other case studies may also be appropriate), you can start to narrow down your choices. It is important to understand that all the proposed plans are drawn at a scale of 1:100 – so that if you measure 1cm on the drawing it equates to 1m in reality, with 1mm equating to 10cm.

It is hoped that this book will provide you with all the inspiration required to start you on the path to turning your house into a home that suits all your needs.

GLOSSARY
AND KEY

Amenity – the benefit enjoyed from physical space that is part of a private home. The benefit enjoyed depends on the quality of space based on factors such as location, size, orientation, enclosure and light.

Beam-to-ridge-height – the measurement in loft from the loft floor up to the underside of the ridge beam that spans across the building to support the apex of the roof.

Bespoke – made to measure.

Boundary wall – a wall that is constructed adjacent to the boundary but wholly on the land of the owner.

Butterfly roof – also referred to as a London roof, the butterfly roof has two pitched sections of roof rising from a central gutter, which runs from front to back to parapet party walls on either side.

Circulation space – the space required for access from one area to another, such as a corridor, stair, landing or a route through a room. It is not considered useable space, as it cannot be used to place furniture.

Clerestory glazing – high-level glazing

Curtilage – the area of land surrounding, and belonging to, a given property.

Dado rail – a rail located at waist height often found in Victorian terraced houses. The wall underneath this rail used to be clad in timber to protect the wall and mask any rising damp.

Dormer – a window that projects vertically from a pitched roof. These can vary in size, depending on requirements and restrictions. Many loft conversions include a full width dormer to create the greatest internal volume.

Eaves – the portion of roof that meets or overhangs the walls of a building, and includes the triangular section of interior space underneath the pitched roof that is too low to stand up in.

Elevation – the side, or façade, of a building. It is usually depicted as a two-dimensional drawing.

Falls – the slope of the roof.

Gable end – the triangle of side wall between the edges of intersecting pitched roofs.

Galley kitchen – a kitchen that has units on both sides, with a circulation route between.

Headroom – the floor to ceiling height at any given point.

Hipped roof – a roof form in which gable is replaced with a pitched roof sloping from the ridge level down to the eaves level of the front and back sections of pitched roof.

Juliet balcony – a very shallow balcony (often, just a railing across an opening door) that doesn't project beyond the external skin of a building.

Oriel window – a protruding window that cantilevers above ground level. It originally referred to windows serving floors above ground level, but is used here to mean any protruding window that is suspended above the ground.

Orientation – the direction in which a building or garden faces.

Outrigger – the narrower, rear section of the house that usually accommodates the kitchen at ground floor level.

Party wall – a common wall that sits astride a boundary and belongs to the buildings on both sides of it.

Picture rail – a rail located at door head height (or higher) that can be used to hang pictures from.

Protected means of escape – a route through a building that is enclosed by fire rated walls and doors and terminates at an external exit door.

Riser – the vertical section of the step.

Side return – the external area adjacent to the outrigger that allows light and air into the rear reception room.

Tread – the horizontal step of a step.

Cooker		Wash hand basin	
Sink		Shower	
Washing machine		Bath	
Single bed		Wood burning stove	
Double bed		New brick wall	
Sofa		Sliding pocket door	
Arm chair		Stairs going up	
Built in seat		Stairs one above the other	
Coat cupboard		Boundary line	
Dining table		Skylight	
WC		Void	

WHAT TO CONSIDER WHEN DESIGNING AN EXTENSION

BRIEF

The brief is one of the most important considerations in any building project. Many people approach an architect with a design in mind before they have really considered what they want an extension for. Extending a newly acquired house has become almost as essential to the personalisation of a property as is choosing the curtain material.

It is common for alterations to be made to suit old habits rather than trying to adjust habits to fit an existing environment. So, ideally, you should live in the property for a while before embarking on such a project. That way, you can work out what you like about your house – you will probably find more things than you initially thought you would. Once you have worked out what you like and dislike, you need to consider what you want from any improvement works. You can then work with an architect to create the least intrusive, most cost-effective way of meeting your requirements. It may be that you can fulfil your brief without the need to extend at all: it could be as simple as changing a door position in order to consolidate circulation space, thus creating a more efficient layout.

When creating the brief, some questions to consider are:
- What is your budget?
- How many people will be living there?
- If there are children, what ages are they?
- How many years do you hope to be there?
- How many bedrooms are there currently, and how many would you like?
- How many bathrooms are there currently, and how many would you like?
- How many reception rooms are there currently, and how many would you like?
- Do you prefer an open-plan layout or separate rooms, or a mixture of both?
- Do you have and/or would you like a utility room?
- Do you have and/or would you like a downstairs WC?
- Do you have and/or would you like a study area?

- What size of dining area would you like?
- How much storage are you likely to need, both now and in the future?
- What do you like about the property?
- What do you dislike about the property?
- Are there any special requirements, such as accommodating disability?

DURATION OF STAY

It is important to create spaces that will accommodate your changing requirements, so that they continue to work for you as your situation changes. For example, it may be cute for two or more young children to share a room now – but when they are teenagers, it could be a different story! Conversely, if you are only going to be living in the property for two or three years, bearing in mind that a full extension project will usually take at least 12 months, you need to ask yourself if it's going to be worth doing at all.

SITE CONSTRAINTS

The physical characteristics of the property and its surroundings are equally as important as the brief.

Some of the things you should consider are:
- the height, depth and proximity of neighbouring properties
- orientation
- structural constraints
- the condition of the property
- the size of the garden
- the location of trees and bushes
- noise from the street
- interesting architectural features.

Some of these are considered in more detail in the Rules of Thumb section.

Handwritten margin notes:
- Quality of some reservation:
  - floors
  - Doors
- Loss of original features / layout.
  - large / dingy rooms.
- Lack of storage:
  - toys, coats.
    - kitchen?
- Noise / privacy – bedroom, garden
- Not a white box
- utility?
- Use of every dining room
- More space
- By board area

LEGISLATIVE CONSTRAINTS

PLANNING

If you are intending to carry out external alterations to your house, you will require either planning permission or a Certificate of Lawfulness gained through a permitted development application. Although this certificate is not strictly required until you sell your property, it is highly recommended that you submit the application before carrying out the works. Your local planning department will deal with both of these applications. If you live in a flat or if your property is in a Conservation Area, you will not have permitted development rights and will need to submit a householder planning application. Your local planning website should have a map of its Conservation Areas and a list of locally listed properties.

Every local council will have its own Supplementary Planning Guidance or Residential Design Standards, usually available on its website, that go into detail about the kind of developments that are likely to be granted permission. Each council has different guidelines, and you will probably need a local architect to translate and navigate these for you. However, it should be noted that there are four main areas of concern that a planner must consider when making a decision:
- loss of light
- loss of amenity
- overlooking
- overdevelopment

Nonetheless, aesthetics, however subjective, can also influence a decision.

Searching through recent planning applications in your vicinity on your council's website will give you a good idea of what is likely to be granted permission, and there are documents available to help explain permitted development guidance.[1] Looking on Bing Maps, Apple Maps and Google Maps can also give you an idea of what has been built around you, although these resources will not necessarily be up to date.

Once a proposal gains planning permission, you must begin construction within a three-year period – after which time, you will need to reapply. However, it is worth noting that if works have begun, and that can be as little as starting to dig foundations, your planning permission will not run out. It is with this in mind that architects usually advise any client wanting to undertake works in two or more phases to apply for planning permission for all phases together. It is not only more cost efficient in terms of architect's fees but also means that once you have built phase one, planning permission for all other phases will not run out. Therefore, even if you decide not to carry out the subsequent phases, you can sell your property with a valid planning permission.

BUILDING CONTROL

Building Control deals with issues such as structural design, construction, drainage design, energy efficiency and fire protection. Although usually not considered in detail until a proposal has been granted planning permission, your architect should have a sound knowledge of the building regulations when coming up with the initial planning drawings. These can dictate the depth of construction and the location of stairs, to name just a couple of issues that can alter an internal layout and that will often impact on the external appearance of a proposal as well.

PARTY WALLS

If you are doing work to a party wall – including raising it or supporting off it, building a new party or boundary wall, or digging foundations near to a boundary – you will need to serve a Party Wall or Boundary Wall Notice. You will need to appoint a party wall surveyor who will advise on and prepare the appropriate notices. Depending on which type is required, it is necessary to serve notice between one and two months prior to construction works commencing, unless an agreement can be reached during this time period. You can learn more about the Party Wall Act by looking on the government website, GOV.UK.[2] It is important to be aware of the fact that that you require your neighbour's consent to build astride the boundary but not to build up to it, even though a notice is required in both instances.

FREEHOLDER CONSENT

If you do not own the entire freehold of the property, you will be required to secure freeholder consent from all freeholders of the property. If any of the freeholders withhold consent, you will be unable to carry out the works. Therefore, it is imperative that this is dealt with early on in the project.

TIMINGS

It is common for clients to approach an architect at around Easter time, hoping to start work in the summer. However, it usually takes much longer than this to get from appointment to site. Every architect's practice works differently, so you would need to ask your architect for their usual timescales – but as a rule of thumb, you should expect the following:

SURVEY *(4 weeks)*

It is strongly recommended that you get a professional, who has the appropriate equipment, to carry this section of the works out for you. This usually takes about four weeks.

DESIGN *(4 weeks)*

Drafting and finalising a design usually takes about four weeks, depending on the complexity of the client's brief.

PLANNING SUBMISSION *(8 weeks)*

Once the design is agreed and it has been submitted to the planning department, the planners have eight weeks in which to make their decision from the date of validation. Note that this is not necessarily the date of submission. If more information is required, the application will not be validated until all the information is received. So your architect should chase up an application a few days after submission to check that the planners have everything they require rather than waiting to hear back from them, which should take up to ten days but often takes longer.

BUILDING CONTROL INFORMATION *(4–6 weeks)*

To avoid unnecessary risk, it is recommended that you only commence this section of work once planning permission has been granted. It is at this stage that, if appropriate to the design, the architect would require input from other consultants such as a structural engineer and an energy assessor. It is also at this stage that the architect will recommend consulting a party wall surveyor to deal with any notices, as it can sometimes be difficult to track down owners of adjacent properties. Architects can often suggest a surveyor and will supply any information requested to deal with the notices, but the latter are usually directly appointed by the homeowner. If drainage works are included in the design, you will also require a drainage survey, which your architect can usually organise. The time needed to compile the necessary information depends on the time it takes the other consultants to supply their information. However, on average, this section of work usually takes between four and six weeks.

BUILDING CONTROL SUBMISSION *(4 weeks)*

The information submitted by the consultants above (not including the party wall surveyor) is then submitted for Full Plans approval, together with architectural drawings showing construction, to the building control department (or independent, approved inspector) for comments and conditional approval. Once submitted, it usually takes another four weeks to get a conditional approval back from the building control department. An approved inspector may be able to respond more quickly, but often costs a bit more.

It is possible to start work on the next stage prior to receiving conditional approval – in fact, some architects would skip this stage altogether, preferring to submit a Building Notice a few days before commencing construction. However, this does come with the risk of proposals not complying with the regulations. All parts of the building regulations, called the Approved Documents, can be found on the Planning Portal website.

TENDER INFORMATION *(6–8 weeks)*

Together with the information compiled during the building control stage, you will require electrical and plumbing/drainage design; large-scale, detailed drawings of any tricky junctions; and a detailed specification covering the entire works. It is at this stage that you should choose the fixtures and fittings to be included in the specification. Depending on the size and complexity of the project, this stage usually takes between six and eight weeks.

TENDER STAGE *(4 weeks)*

Once the tender information is complete, it is usually sent off to three contractors for pricing. Pricing normally takes about four weeks.

TENDER NEGOTIATION *(2–4 weeks)*

Once all three tender returns are received, a comparison is made between them and it is at this stage that a contractor is chosen, often after a period of negotiation. Depending on the degree of negotiation required, this usually takes between two and four weeks.

SITE SET-UP *(2 weeks)*

Following the appointment of a contractor, it will usually take about two weeks to mobilise the site – applying for the necessary permits, ordering materials and getting a team together. During this time, if not already completed, the architect can produce a set of construction drawings that includes dimensions.

Altogether, this adds up to between 38 and 44 weeks to get to site from the point at which an architect is appointed.

FINANCIAL CONSTRAINTS

Although clients can be understandably wary about giving out financial information, it is important for an architect to know what budget there is to work to in order to avoid designing unrealistic projects. The options in this book start at the least expensive, working up to the most expensive option for each floor of each case study. Cost will obviously depend greatly on your location and on the materials that you decide to use. Generally, the larger and more complicated the scheme and the more structural work required, the greater the cost. Adding a loft is usually the least expensive way to get more space, and digging a basement is usually the costliest.

If you have a very tight budget, it would be worth employing a quantity surveyor after gaining planning permission, and again at building control stage, to give you a more accurate cost estimate. Quantity surveyors deal solely with project costs, and usually on a more regular basis than the architect. This means that they will have more up-to-date information.

BUDGET, TIMESCALE AND QUALITY

There is a direct link between these three elements. It is very difficult to get a good-quality job done cheaply and quickly – in the end, one of these three elements (quality, cost and time) has to 'give'. It is therefore important to establish at the outset what you most value so that you can prioritise accordingly. It is advisable to include for a 10% contingency sum, and to remember that most cost estimates exclude value added tax (VAT) and fees.

---

1 In England, it is the September 2019 document 'Permitted development rights for householders', issued by the Ministry of Housing, Communities and Local Government. In Wales, the Welsh Government's Technical Guidance document 'Permitted development for householders', Version 2 of April 2014 should be consulted. Scotland has the Scottish Government's Circular 1/2012: 'Guidance on Householder Permitted Development Rights'. In Northern Ireland, the relevant document is 'Your Home and Planning Permission: A guide for householders in Northern Ireland' of March 2011.

2 'Party walls and building work', www.gov.uk/party-walls-building-works

RULES OF THUMB

GENERAL

- Design for flexible living. Even if you are intending to move houses in a few years, it's always good to plan for a growing family – not least because plans often change, but also because it will make your property more attractive to future potential buyers. Open-plan living might work well for a young family, but you may find that you want separate spaces as your family grows, or to accommodate a spare room or study.
- Always consider the path of the sun. Orientation can be very important, both for the overall design and daylight levels and in terms of the kind of schemes that are likely to be granted planning permission. Shading a neighbour's north facing window will be more likely to gain permission than one that faces south, east or west.
- The function of the room that the overshadowed window serves will influence a planning decision. Reducing the levels of natural light to a kitchen or bathroom is not usually considered as detrimental as reducing levels to a bedroom, study, living room or dining room.
- The size of your garden will, to a certain extent, dictate what you can do. Building over more than 50% of your garden will generally be rejected at planning stage. If you have a small curtilage, it would be more sensible to look at options that do not extend to the rear.
- The height and depth of the adjacent buildings will have a direct influence on the scale of any proposed extension permitted at planning stage. Case Study 5, the Tall Terrace, is a good example of this.
- Taking the ceiling out of a room directly under a roof, so that the new ceiling follows the pitch of the roof, gives more headroom and a grander feel.
- Always take depth of construction into account. A cavity wall is usually about 0.35m thick and a flat roof is at least 0.3m deep, plus whatever depth is necessary to create the required slope to drain (1 in 60 falls minimum), which depends on the length of the roof.
- Consider where the existing drainage is. It is not acceptable to have an internal manhole, so if there is one positioned within the footprint of the proposed extension, it must be relocated externally. Avoiding this will reduce build cost.

Mapledene Road by Platform 5 Architects, Hackney, London, 2008. Window seat.

STRUCTURAL

- It is always good to try and work with the existing structure of a building, especially if you have a limited budget.
- Keeping the external corner of an outrigger reduces the extent of structural alterations significantly.
- A cheaper alternative to removing a chimneybreast is to retain its side sections, removing the central section up to ceiling level. This space can be used to accommodate a cooker or built-in storage.
- If there are trees near to the area that you'd like to develop, even if they are not in your garden, you may need to consider deeper foundations than usual.

KITCHEN

- A galley kitchen represents the most efficient arrangement.
- Leave at least 1.2m of circulation space between kitchen units.
- Base units are about 0.6m deep and 0.9m tall.
- Wall units are about 0.4m deep, and should be positioned at least 0.5m above the worktop.
- Island units are at least 0.8m wide, and require more space around them than any other kitchen layout.

DINING ROOM

- A four-person dining table is usually around 1m square.
- A six-person dining table is usually around 1.6m long by 0.9m wide.
- An eight-person dining table is around 1.8m long by 0.9m wide.
- A dining table should have at least 0.6m around it for space for chairs, or 1m if you want to walk behind the chairs.
- To create more space, consider designing a window seat or oriel window. (See image above).
- Placing the dining table immediately behind a kitchen island will consolidate circulation space, enabling more to be fitted into the available space.

LIVING ROOM

- Sofas are usually around 0.9m wide and 1.8–2.2m long.
- Built-in seating can be much more space efficient, but less flexible, than freestanding furniture.

BATHROOMS AND WCS

- Bathroom width should be at least the length of a standard bath (1.7m), shower rooms 1.3m in width, and both at least 2.2m long.

- If you have a choice between installing an en-suite or an independently accessed bathroom, it is often preferable to choose independently accessed to give greater flexibility.
- If you are thinking of slotting in a WC under the stairs, there are no regulations governing the size of these unless you are planning for a disabled occupant. Tuck toilets and basins into areas with less headroom. The front of your toilet should have at least 1.8m headroom above it, but the toilet seat needs less height above it.
- If WCs in lofts are positioned behind the stairs, it is likely that you will need a pump and macerator.

BEDROOM
- A standard single bed is 0.9m wide and 2m long.
- A standard double bed is 1.4m wide by 2m long, and should have at least 0.6m around it for access.
- Wardrobes are usually 0.6m deep.

CORRIDORS
- Corridors should be at least 0.8m wide.

LOFT DESIGN
- Outrigger extensions are often only allowed to be constructed under permitted development, which means that the entire loft extension must not exceed 40m³ in volume (50m³ for a detached house). This will restrict the size of extension permissible over the outrigger. This volume is calculated using the external dimensions of the new build. Refer to permitted development rights guidance for more information (see the note in What to Consider When Designing an Extension, in this book).
- Extending a butterfly roof is not allowed under permitted development, as any construction would need to extend above the highest point of the original roof. This is only rarely given planning permission, depending on location, precedent, quality of design, the council in question and sometimes even the planning officer assigned to the job. It is more likely to be given permission if it is stepped back from the front of the building.
- There are companies that take advantage of the fact that homeowner clients often can't interpret plans as well as their commercial counterparts. Make sure that you understand how much of the room shown on the plans is space that you can actually stand up in. It's often much smaller than anticipated. Get your designer to draw a line depicting the edge of where you can stand.

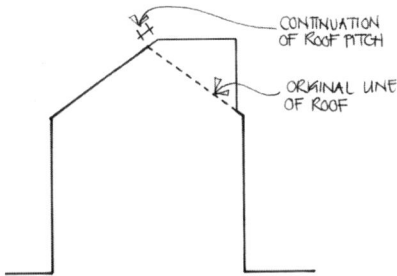

Diagram to show continuation of roof pitch above ridge.

- It is likely that you will need to replace your roof membrane to avoid condensation build-up if you are insulating within the rafters. You will need to remove all your roof tiles and battens to get to the membrane. Many of the cheaper loft companies fail to do this, resulting in mould growth down the line.
- More often than not, the depth of your loft floor will need to be increased to meet the current structural requirements (assume an additional 0.1m). Likewise, a pitched roof will usually require additional insulation underneath the rafters, which also increases the depth of construction (again, assume an additional 0.1m). If you have less than 2.1m headroom in your existing loft space, you are unlikely to achieve the 2m headroom at the top of the stairs required by the building regulations without lowering the ceilings of the rooms below or raising the roof ridge.
- To gain extra height in the loft, some local authorities will now permit continuation of the roof pitch up at the front by a few centimetres, keeping the same gradient. (See diagram above).
- Carefully positioned roof lights can provide invaluable headroom in tight loft spaces. Placing roof lights either side of a bed that is tucked into the eaves can make getting in and out of bed much more comfortable. (See the Half House, Loft Option 3).
- Party walls can be extended up above the roof in brickwork, but must be built inside the boundary if cladding the sidewalls.
- Remember to include space for 70mm of insulation to party walls at loft level if adjacent properties have not converted their lofts. If you do not wish to see a step where the insulation stops, it is a good idea to continue this insulation down the new stairwell to meet the new treads. This additional width should be considered when designing your stairs.
- If your new loft room is more than 7.5m above ground level (on the second floor or above), a protected means of escape will be required from the loft-room door all the way to the entrance door of the house. This often means that you will need to replace the existing doors (except bathroom doors, but including cupboard doors) that face onto your stairwell with fire doors.
- If you cannot achieve a protected means of escape, or you prefer not to have a door serving your new loft space, a full-house sprinkler system may be installed as an alternative.
- To satisfy building regulations, you will require a landing at the top of the new stair at least as deep as the stairs are wide (usually at least 0.7m), which can often cut awkwardly into the new loft space. Alternatively, you can position the door to the loft room at the bottom of the stairs (again, with a landing the width of the stair) to give a greater sense of space above.

Turney Road by Green & Teggin Architects, Dulwich, London, 2013. Slot window.

- Overheating and noise pollution can be a problem in new loft extensions. Adding extra insulation and openable roof lights can help to tackle these issues. If you live adjacent to a noisy road or under a flight path, it might also be worth considering an acoustic ceiling.

WINDOWS AND DOORS

- When considering which windows and doors to choose, it's important to note that sliding doors and pivot doors come in larger pane sizes, which means less frame, but sliding, folding doors are the only option to give a full-width opening.
- A slot window inserted in the roof at the junction of the extension and the main building provides light to deepest part of the house. (See adjacent image).
- To satisfy planning guidelines, side windows in outriggers should be frosted and fixed below a level of 1.7m to avoid overlooking. Glazing above this level can be transparent and openable.
- When designing a window seat, if you want an oriel window it's best to have fixed glazing to avoid a bulky structure. If you want openable windows, it's best to build your window seat from the ground.
- Consider solar gain when choosing your windows. If your windows face south-west or west, low-level sun can penetrate deep into your room and can cause overheating – especially if this room is at the top of the house, where warm air rises naturally. One way of reducing solar gain would be to install external blinds that can be operated remotely.

ENERGY-SAVING IDEAS

- Installing insulation – whether it is under your floorboards, on your walls or in your roof – is the most cost-effective way of reducing your energy bills. Depending on your house and your area, you could insulate your walls externally (and then overclad or render them) to avoid internal disruption and reduction of floor space. Make sure that you consult a professional, though, as badly or inappropriately installed insulation can result in trapped moisture and mould growth.
- Replacing your windows with double-glazing or installing secondary glazing can greatly reduce heat loss and help to keep out noise.
- Draughtproofing around external doors and windows can reduce heat loss and noise. Installing heavy curtains can also help with this.
- Installing a chimney balloon will stop warm air being lost up the chimney.

- If your boiler is more than 10 years old, it is likely that replacing it with a more efficient, modern one will lower your energy bills. There is now a shift away from gas heating towards electrically powered heat pumps. It should be noted that a bulky compressor, which will probably accompany a pump, would need to be accommodated externally – so it would be worth allowing for this early on in the design stage.
- Other 'quick fixes' in order to save energy include insulating your hot-water tank and replacing your lighting with low-energy bulbs. Installing a heat-recovery system can also be an effective way to save energy, but only in a relatively airtight home.

RENEWABLE-ENERGY SOLUTIONS

- Solar Water Heating:
  This option won't directly heat your home, but it is a very energy-efficient way of producing hot water during the sunnier months. You will need to install thermal panels on your roof and an insulated water cylinder to store the hot water. The panels absorb heat directly from the sun to produce hot water by means of heat transfer, which is then stored in the insulated cylinder. This system is compatible with most boilers that have a two-coil water cylinder.
- Air Source Heat Pumps:
  This system works by absorbing the warmth from the outside air and converting it to heat, which can then be used for heating your home and, in some instances, your hot water as well. The pumps can be installed in most locations, as they are not dependent on direct sunlight and they are relatively small. However, they are quite noisy and not particularly attractive, so you may not want them in full view or near a bedroom window. You may have to install a compatible heating system with this option.
- Ground Source Heat Pumps:
  This system involves installing pipework in the ground, either vertically or in a trench horizontally, and transferring heat stored in the soil, using a pump, to heat radiators or underfloor heating. It is one of the most expensive renewable-energy systems to install, but it also has one of the lowest running costs and carbon emissions of all the systems.
- Biomass Boilers:
  This is most similar to a conventional heating system, and so is more likely to be compatible with your existing central-heating system. Sustainable fuel such as pellets, chips or logs are burnt to run the boiler, making it relatively labour intensive. Fuel storage must also be considered.

Reighton Road by Poulsom/Middlehurst Architects, Clapton, London, 2014. Storage space behind mirrors makes the most of the eaves space.

Power House by Paul Archer Design, Islington, London, 2012. Seat with storage under built-in alcove.

High-level shelves free up space below to create an uncluttered appearance.

- Photovoltaic (PV) Panels:
  This system involves installing PV panels on your roof, much like you would with thermal water-heating panels. These panels convert sunlight to electricity. The electricity produced can be used to heat your home but, unlike the options above, it can also be used to run household appliances and lighting. Any surplus energy can be sold back to the grid. It's also worth noting that the effectiveness of PV panels is limited to certain times of the day and year.
- Wind Turbines:
  Wind turbines harness the power of the wind and convert it to electricity. They can either be mounted directly onto your house or are freestanding on poles. Pole-mounted turbines are generally larger than their building-mounted alternatives. As with PV systems, any surplus electricity can be sold back to the grid or stored in batteries. It should be noted that batteries require storage space. Maintenance for these systems is relatively high, and they are best suited to less urban, more exposed sites.

It is usually worth employing the services of a domestic-energy assessor, who would be able to advise you on which type of system is most suitable for your home and make you aware of any potential subsidies available for your chosen system.

STORAGE

- There are many companies now offering under-stair storage solutions for houses that don't have a cellar. To make the most of the depth under the stair, most companies will suggest a series of different-sized pull-out drawers, although simple cupboard doors work well too.
- Similar to under-stair storage, bespoke cupboards make the most of the awkward triangular space in the eaves.
- Planning perpendicular storage either side of a roof light can also exhibit efficient use of space. (See: the Three Up Three Down, Loft Option 3)
- If you are installing a bench seat, whether in a dining area or in a bay window, it makes sense to use the space underneath as storage – either in the form of drawers or top-opening.
- A wall of books can sometimes appear to dominate a room. If you have a lot of books and you would prefer to store them slightly more discreetly, it might be worth making the most of tall Victorian ceilings by putting up bookshelves at picture-rail height, which keeps the walls at eye height clear to exhibit artwork.

'Our House', Lausanne Road (Phase Two) by Green & Teggin Architects, Peckham, London, 2017. Furniture built around shop-bought storage boxes.

Slim, off-the- floor storage near the entrance to contain outdoor wear.

Brokesley Street by Poulsom/Middlehurst, Tower Hamlets, London, 2016. Mezzanine bed space.

- There are plenty of off-the-shelf storage boxes on offer, of varying sizes – so if your bed does not already come with built-in storage, you can usually find something that will fit well.
- When designing drawers within a bespoke cupboard or wardrobe, it is worth looking at the ready-made drawers available on the high street to build your cupboard around, to reduce costs.
- Victorian terraced houses tend to have quite narrow corridors, but there are a few solutions available to maximise storage space in corridors. Using the whole length of the corridor to store coats avoids having an overloaded clump at the entrance. This can be at picture-height level, with a shelf over, or at dado level (you may need to replace a standard radiator with a vertical one to accommodate this). There are also off-the-shelf shoe-storage solutions designed for narrow spaces.
- Constructing a mezzanine bed can free up a great deal of space in the bedroom below.

THE HALF HOUSE

'Half houses' share the same street door but then have their own front door at the end of a shared corridor that enters the house in the centre of the plan, reducing circulation space. The house in this case study is built on a 4.3m-wide plot and, although not split-level, is built on a hill. There is therefore a large drop down from the house to the garden at the rear. It has a small, single-storey outrigger that houses the bathroom. As it is similar in size to the houses shown in Central Stair and Two Up Two Down, many of the plans shown in these two case studies can be used in this one and vice versa.

GROUND FLOOR

In the existing plan, the front door opens into the kitchen, which leads to a separate front reception room, to the bathroom at the rear, out to the garden and up the stairs to the first floor.

OPTION 1

This option seeks to retain as much of the existing structure as possible to minimise costs. In order to do this, the bedrooms have been positioned on the ground floor with the existing bathroom. This creates an 'upside-down house', affording the opportunity to create a grander living area upstairs. A new partition has been erected to create a small bedroom where the existing kitchen had been located and the bathroom remains unchanged, accommodated in the existing outrigger. The area underneath the existing stairs has been enclosed to create a store area, and a small coat cupboard has been positioned adjacent to the front door. This plan can be read in conjunction with First-floor Option 4 and Loft Option 4.

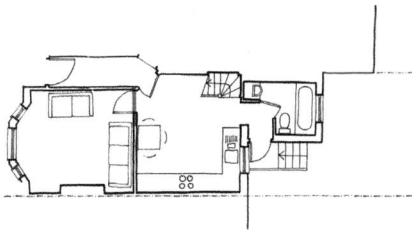

COAT CUPBOARD AND
STORE CUPBOARD
SLOTTED UNDER STAIRS

OUTRIGGER ACCOMMODATING
BATHROOM RETAINED AS EXISTING

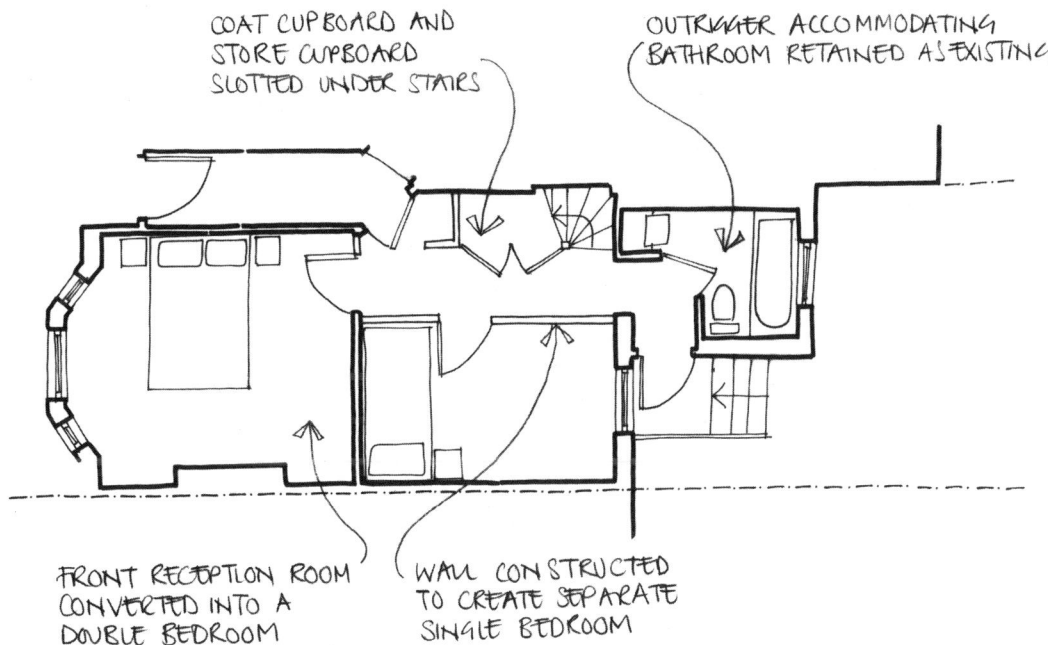

FRONT RECEPTION ROOM
CONVERTED INTO A
DOUBLE BEDROOM

WALL CONSTRUCTED
TO CREATE SEPARATE
SINGLE BEDROOM

OPTION 2

This option, which assumes an upstairs bathroom, retains a separate living room and existing kitchen location. A new niche provides visual screening between entrance door and kitchen – and a coat cupboard.

The outrigger has been rebuilt full width to the depth of the neighbouring building. Its living/dining area sits four steps down, reducing the height and impact of the extension. It also gives level access to the garden and a clerestory view from the kitchen over the extension. The clerestory also brings light deeper into the dwelling's footprint.

Part of the rear kitchen wall has been removed to enhance connection with the dining area. A small WC sits adjacent to the dining area – alternatively, this could be a store or utility room. Built-in dining-area bench seating links in with the height and width of the new steps. The built-in sofa fits snugly beside the WC, forming a window seat overlooking the garden. Both these fittings optimise available space while allowing more storage.

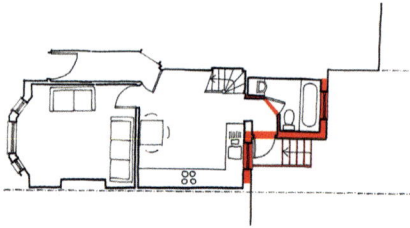

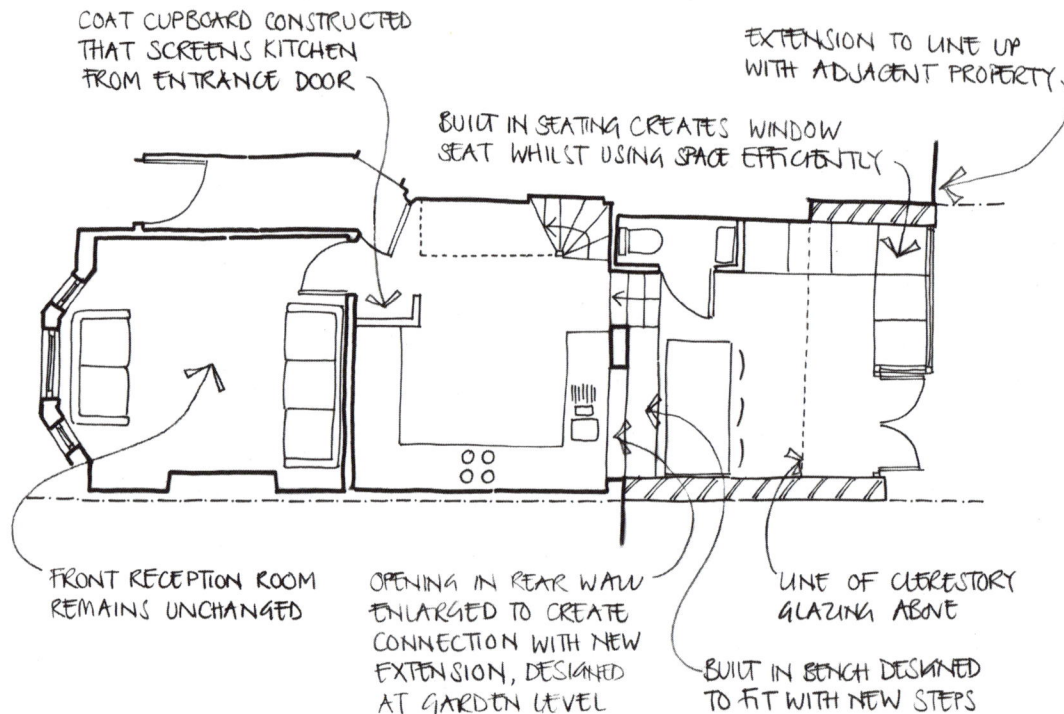

COAT CUPBOARD CONSTRUCTED THAT SCREENS KITCHEN FROM ENTRANCE DOOR

BUILT IN SEATING CREATES WINDOW SEAT WHILST USING SPACE EFFICIENTLY

EXTENSION TO LINE UP WITH ADJACENT PROPERTY

FRONT RECEPTION ROOM REMAINS UNCHANGED

OPENING IN REAR WALL ENLARGED TO CREATE CONNECTION WITH NEW EXTENSION, DESIGNED AT GARDEN LEVEL

BUILT IN BENCH DESIGNED TO FIT WITH NEW STEPS

LINE OF CLERESTORY GLAZING ABOVE

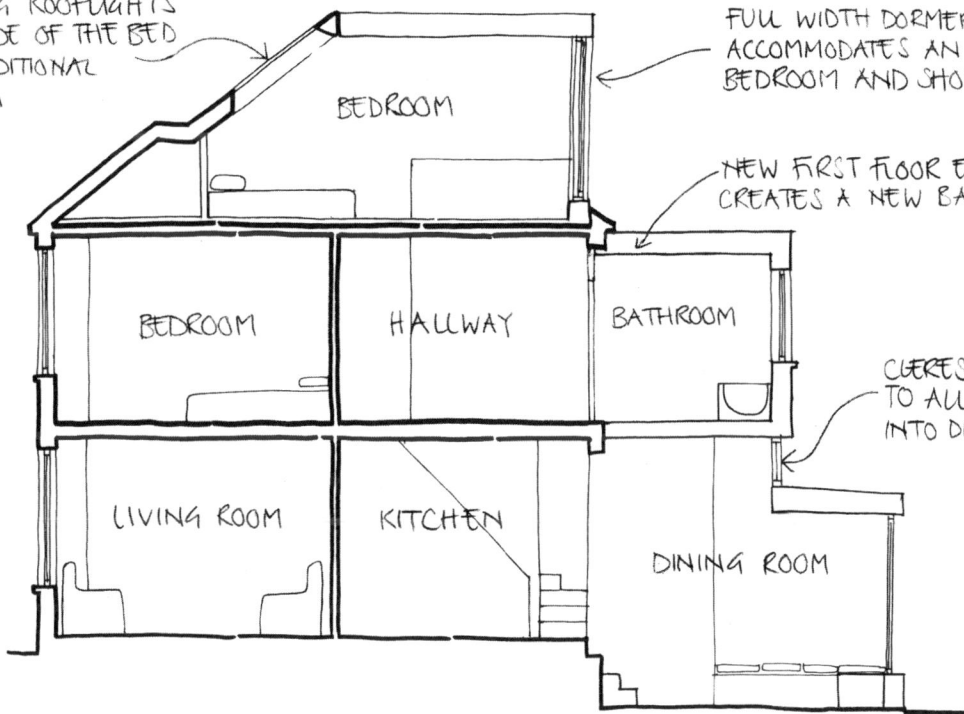

POSITIONING ROOFLIGHTS EITHER SIDE OF THE BED CREATES ADDITIONAL HEAD ROOM

FULL WIDTH DORMER EXTENSION ACCOMMODATES AN ADDITIONAL BEDROOM AND SHOWER ROOM

NEW FIRST FLOOR EXTENSION CREATES A NEW BATHROOM

CLERESTORY GLAZING TO ALLOW LIGHT INTO DINING AREA

BEDROOM

BEDROOM

HALLWAY

BATHROOM

LIVING ROOM

KITCHEN

DINING ROOM

OPTION 3

In this option, the front reception room has been converted into a dining room adjacent to the kitchen. The existing entrance into this room has been retained and new sliding doors installed to close off the kitchen. This provides a protected means of escape from the upper floors. A section of the central, internal wall has been removed to create a connection between the kitchen and dining room. A breakfast bar has been positioned in this gap.

A small WC has been positioned under the stairs and, again, the existing single-storey outrigger has been replaced with a full-width rear extension that here accommodates a living room and small study area. The existing openings in the house's rear wall have been retained to minimise structural alterations. A sliding door has been positioned here to complete the protected means of escape, enabling a loft conversion without the need for a sprinkler system. The extension makes use of the level drop between house and garden – with built-in furniture maximising the use of space, allowing a storeroom to be positioned adjacent to the stairs. This option assumes an upstairs bathroom.

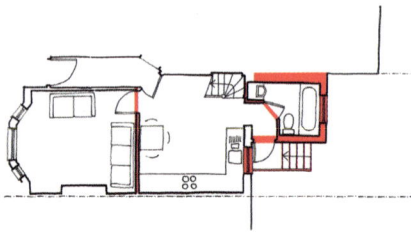

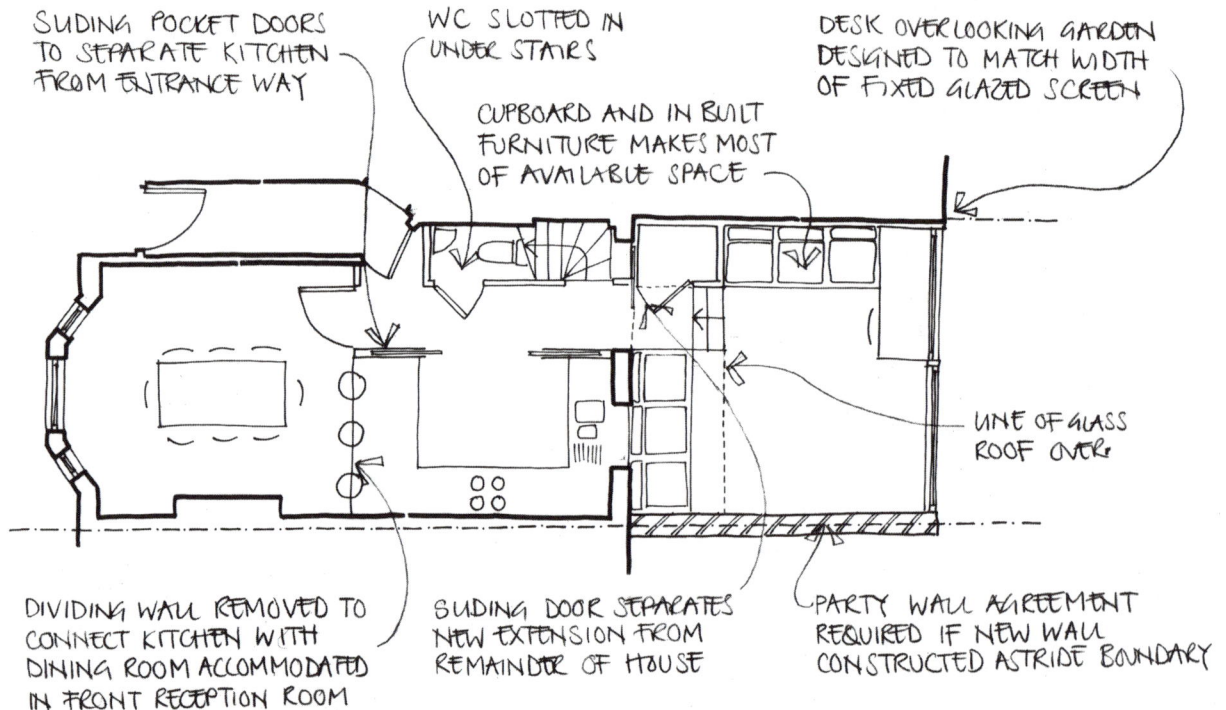

SLIDING POCKET DOORS TO SEPARATE KITCHEN FROM ENTRANCE WAY

WC SLOTTED IN UNDER STAIRS

DESK OVERLOOKING GARDEN DESIGNED TO MATCH WIDTH OF FIXED GLAZED SCREEN

CUPBOARD AND IN BUILT FURNITURE MAKES MOST OF AVAILABLE SPACE

LINE OF GLASS ROOF OVER

DIVIDING WALL REMOVED TO CONNECT KITCHEN WITH DINING ROOM ACCOMMODATED IN FRONT RECEPTION ROOM

SLIDING DOOR SEPARATES NEW EXTENSION FROM REMAINDER OF HOUSE

PARTY WALL AGREEMENT REQUIRED IF NEW WALL CONSTRUCTED ASTRIDE BOUNDARY

Section B

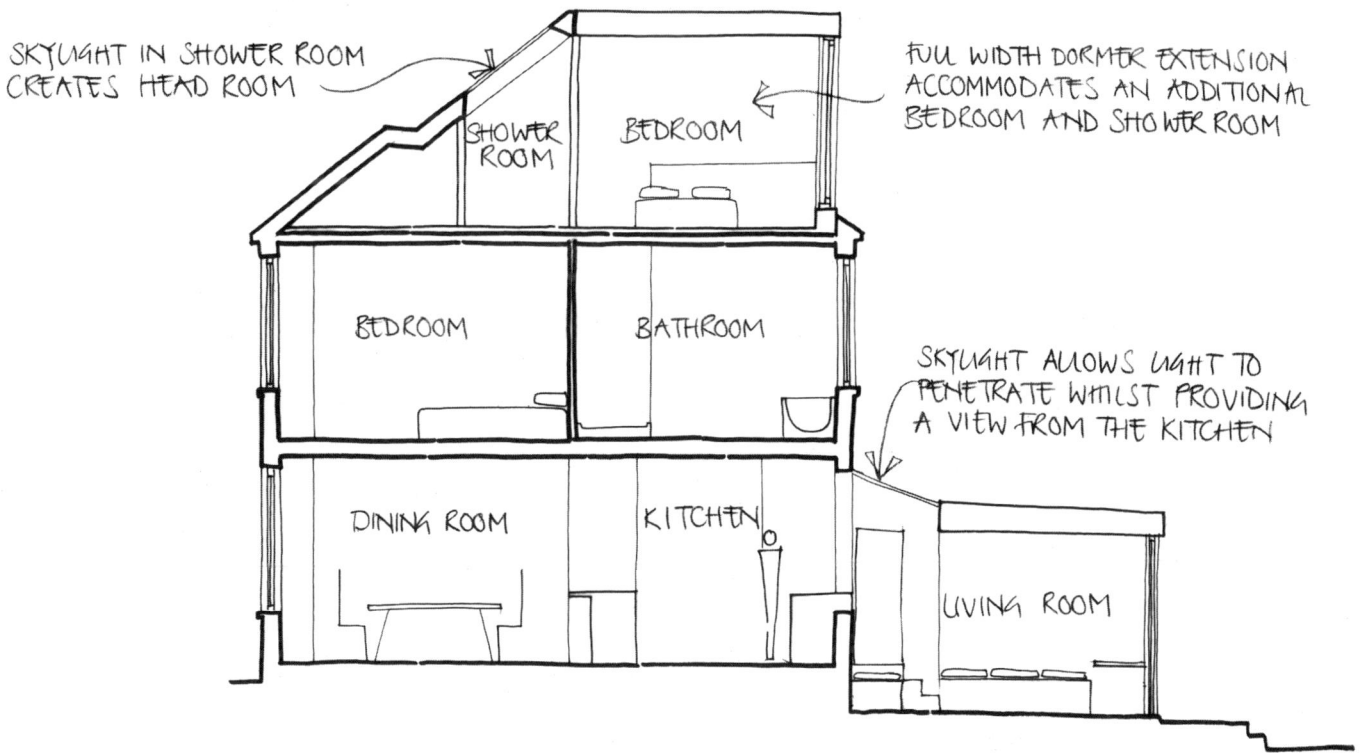

SKYLIGHT IN SHOWER ROOM
CREATES HEAD ROOM

SHOWER ROOM

BEDROOM

FULL WIDTH DORMER EXTENSION
ACCOMMODATES AN ADDITIONAL
BEDROOM AND SHOWER ROOM

BEDROOM

BATHROOM

SKYLIGHT ALLOWS LIGHT TO
PENETRATE WHILST PROVIDING
A VIEW FROM THE KITCHEN

DINING ROOM

KITCHEN

LIVING ROOM

OPTION 4

This option, like Ground-floor Option 1, creates an upside-down house with the bedrooms on the ground floor, enabling a grand, two-storey living area upstairs, as shown in First floor option 4 and Loft option 4. The front reception room remains intact, creating a good-sized double bedroom. The rear reception room is carved up to accommodate a large bathroom and ample storage. The existing outrigger is extended sideways and backwards to create a second, good-sized double bedroom with a window seat and access to the garden.

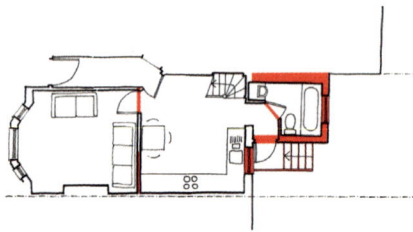

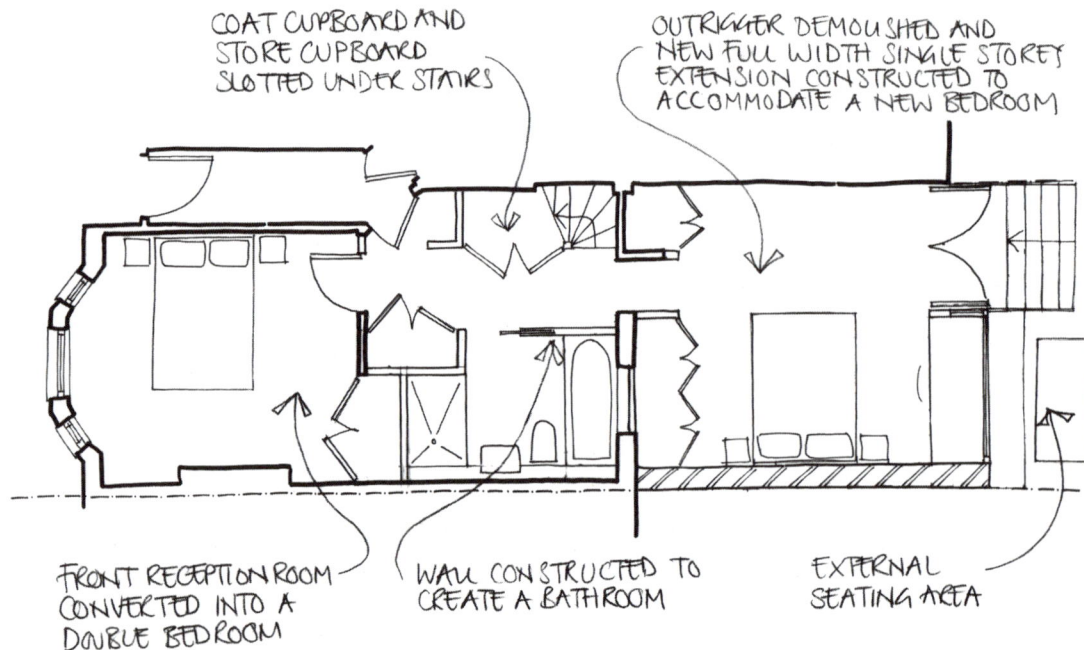

COAT CUPBOARD AND STORE CUPBOARD SLOTTED UNDER STAIRS

OUTRIGGER DEMOLISHED AND NEW FULL WIDTH SINGLE STOREY EXTENSION CONSTRUCTED TO ACCOMMODATE A NEW BEDROOM

FRONT RECEPTION ROOM CONVERTED INTO A DOUBLE BEDROOM

WALL CONSTRUCTED TO CREATE A BATHROOM

EXTERNAL SEATING AREA

Section C

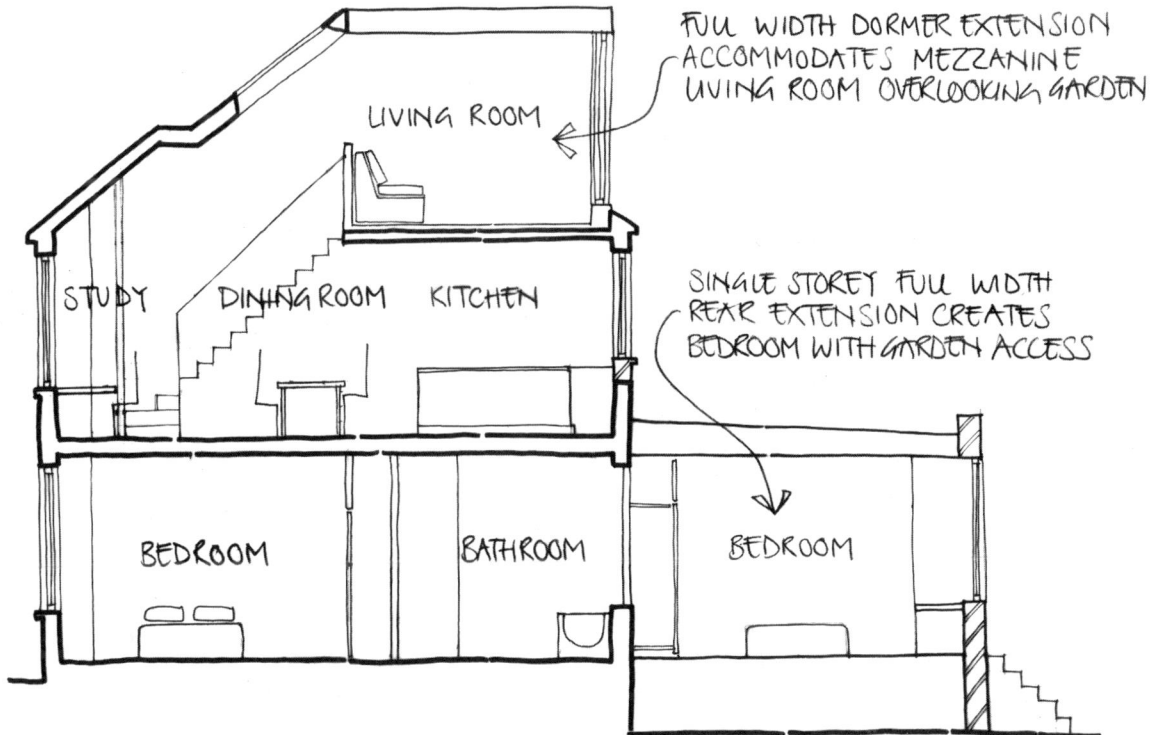

FULL WIDTH DORMER EXTENSION
ACCOMMODATES MEZZANINE
LIVING ROOM OVERLOOKING GARDEN

LIVING ROOM

STUDY   DINING ROOM   KITCHEN

SINGLE STOREY FULL WIDTH
REAR EXTENSION CREATES
BEDROOM WITH GARDEN ACCESS

BEDROOM   BATHROOM   BEDROOM

OPTION 5

(Based on the Landells Road project by Alma-nac)

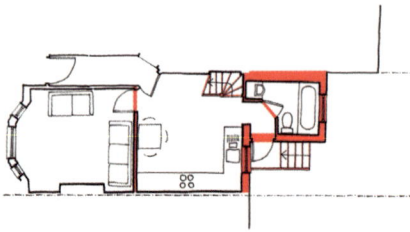

By reconfiguring the stairs to start at the entrance, the circulation space previously required to access the upper floors can be eliminated. Double doors into the kitchen area create an entrance lobby that acts as a protected means of escape, and access to the rear extension is now through the kitchen. Separation to the front reception room is retained using pocket doors, but access to this is also now via the kitchen.

As with Ground-floor Options 2, 3 and 4, the existing outrigger has been replaced with a full-width extension set down a number of steps – in this case, three broad steps. This capitalises on the level change with a high ceiling, and is built to the line of the neighbouring extension. This extension serves as a spacious dining area with direct, level access to the garden via a large, single door. A small WC is tucked under the new stair. This option assumes an upstairs bathroom. To be read in conjunction with First Floor Option 2 and Loft Option 3.

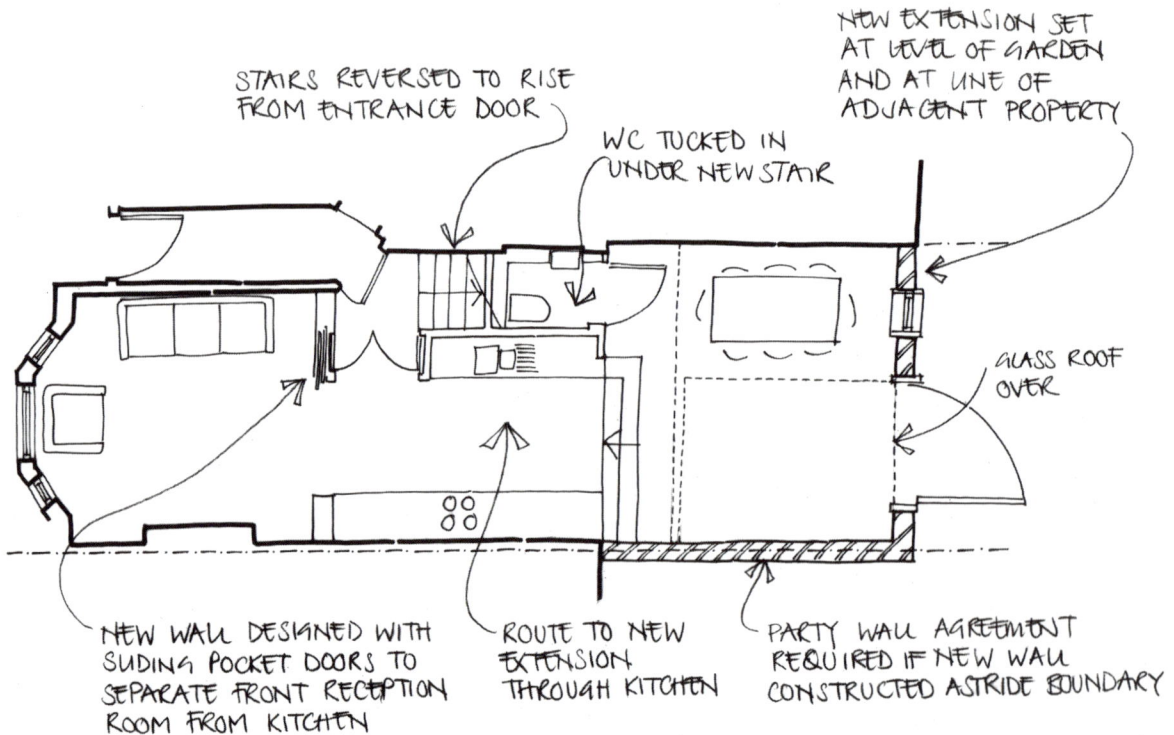

STAIRS REVERSED TO RISE FROM ENTRANCE DOOR

WC TUCKED IN UNDER NEW STAIR

NEW EXTENSION SET AT LEVEL OF GARDEN AND AT LINE OF ADJACENT PROPERTY

GLASS ROOF OVER

NEW WALL DESIGNED WITH SLIDING POCKET DOORS TO SEPARATE FRONT RECEPTION ROOM FROM KITCHEN

ROUTE TO NEW EXTENSION THROUGH KITCHEN

PARTY WALL AGREEMENT REQUIRED IF NEW WALL CONSTRUCTED ASTRIDE BOUNDARY

Landells Road by Alma-nac, East Dulwich, London, 2014. Changing the stair direction consolidates circulation space. Image mirrored to reflect plan.

Next page. Landells Road by Alma-nac, East Dulwich, London, 2014. Glass slot in roof brings light deep into plan. Image mirrored to reflect plan.

Landells Road by Alma-nac, East Dulwich, London, 2014. Extra large door and unusual roof formation give visual interest to this small extension. Image mirrored to reflect plan.

OPTION 6

*(Based on A Wide Illusion
by Scenario Architecture)*

A large kitchen has been positioned in the front reception room in this option. The existing outrigger has been replaced by a full-width extension that accommodates the living room and connects to the garden via sliding, folding doors. The floor level of the extension matches that of the front of the house, so a terrace will need to be constructed with steps down to the garden level. The foot of the stairs has been reconfigured to give a more discreet entrance from the living room. A glass roof allows light to permeate into the living room and dining area.

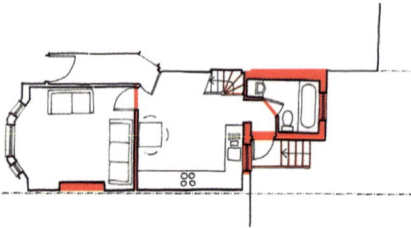

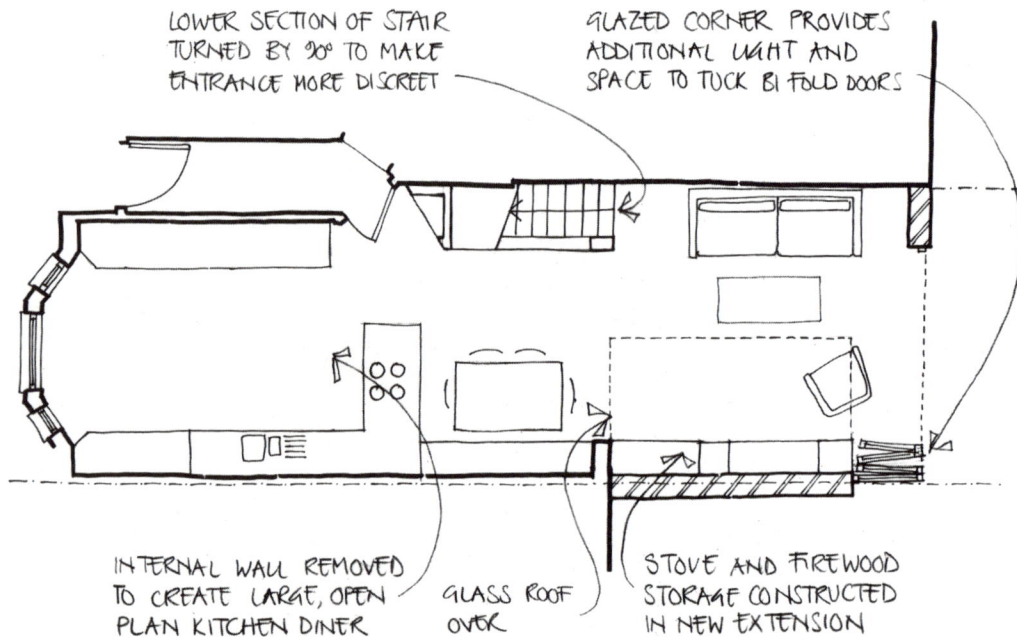

LOWER SECTION OF STAIR TURNED BY 90° TO MAKE ENTRANCE MORE DISCREET

GLAZED CORNER PROVIDES ADDITIONAL LIGHT AND SPACE TO TUCK BI FOLD DOORS

INTERNAL WALL REMOVED TO CREATE LARGE, OPEN PLAN KITCHEN DINER

GLASS ROOF OVER

STOVE AND FIREWOOD STORAGE CONSTRUCTED IN NEW EXTENSION

A Wide Illusion by Scenario Architecture , Islington, London, 2014. View from new extension through open-plan living room/kitchen/diner.

A Wide Illusion by Scenario Architects, Islington, London, 2014. View from kitchen through open-plan dining room into new extension.

FIRST FLOOR

OPTION 1
(As depicted in Section B)

In the existing plan, the first floor accommodates two double bedrooms and does not extend over the outrigger.

This option assumes no extension at first-floor level. A spacious bathroom is created in the smaller, rear bedroom and a new staircase is shown leading to the loft. There is a door positioned at the foot of this stair to enable the loft room to be completely open plan, as shown in Loft Options 1 and 2.

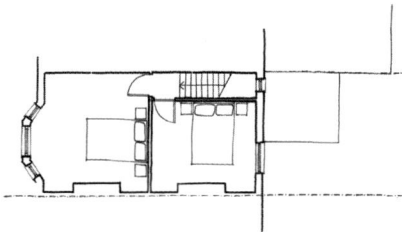

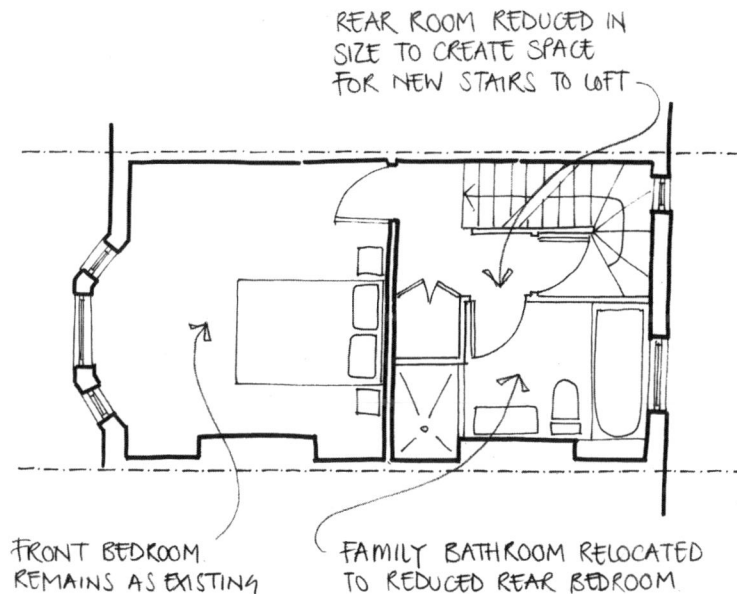

REAR ROOM REDUCED IN SIZE TO CREATE SPACE FOR NEW STAIRS TO LOFT

FRONT BEDROOM REMAINS AS EXISTING

FAMILY BATHROOM RELOCATED TO REDUCED REAR BEDROOM

OPTION 2

In this option, the stairs have been reorientated to finish towards the rear of the house. There is no extension at first-floor level, so the rear bedroom has been divided up to accommodate a bathroom and small study area. The door to the front bedroom has been moved to accommodate a stair that continues up to loft level. This option is to be read in conjunction with Ground-floor Option 5 and Loft Option 3.

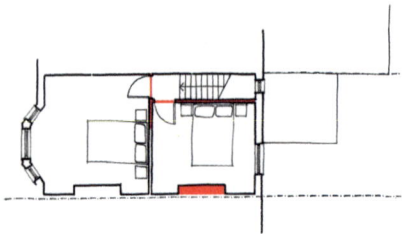

FRONT BEDROOM DOOR REPOSITIONED
TO MAKE WAY FOR NEW REORIENTATED
STAIR FROM GROUND TO LOFT

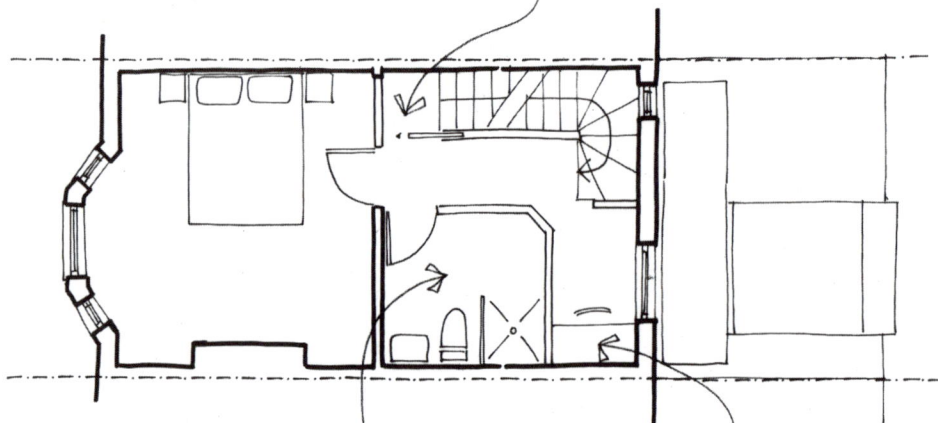

REAR ROOM REDUCED IN SIZE
TO MAKE WAY FOR NEW STAIR.
SHOWER ROOM ACCOMMODATED
IN REMAINING SPACE

SMALL STUDY AREA
CREATED AT TOP OF
REORIENTATED STAIR

OPTION 3

(As depicted in Section A)

A small first-floor rear extension, accommodating a new bathroom, is shown here above the outrigger. A new wall is constructed to form a corridor to access this bathroom without the need to walk through the rear bedroom. The plan also shows a new staircase to access the loft.

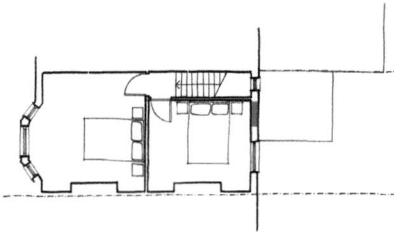

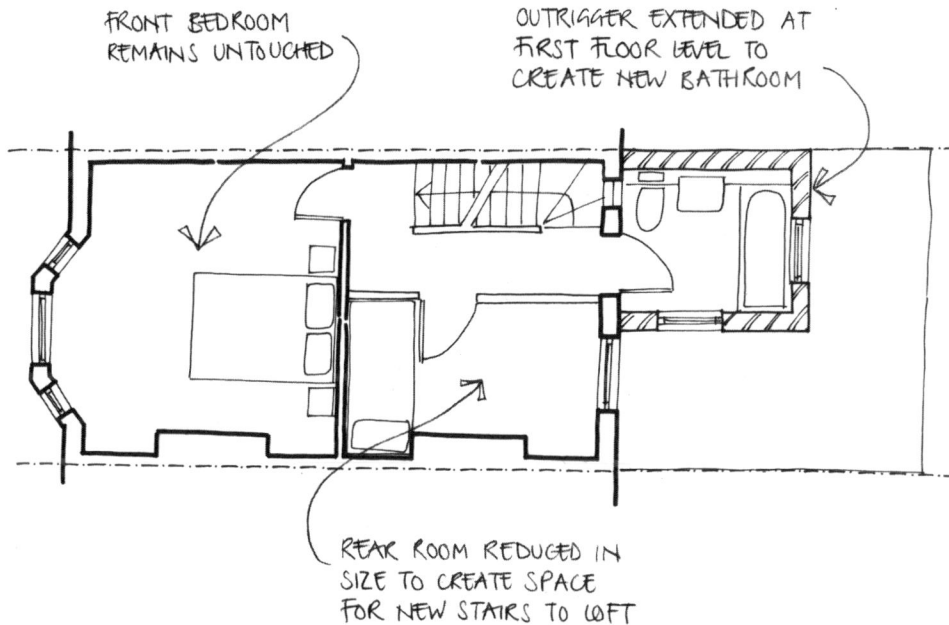

FRONT BEDROOM REMAINS UNTOUCHED

OUTRIGGER EXTENDED AT FIRST FLOOR LEVEL TO CREATE NEW BATHROOM

REAR ROOM REDUCED IN SIZE TO CREATE SPACE FOR NEW STAIRS TO LOFT

OPTION 4

(As depicted in Section C)

In this option, a kitchen/diner is shown at first-floor level, providing an opportunity to create a mezzanine level in the loft. The bedrooms would be located on the ground floor, as shown in Ground-floor Options 1 and 4. The ceiling in the front part of this open-plan room follows the gradient of the roof to give a grander-than-usual feel. The mezzanine could be used as a living area or a study as shown in Loft Option 4 – or enclosed and used as a bedroom, if the appropriate sprinkler system is installed.

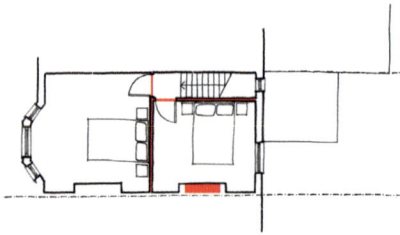

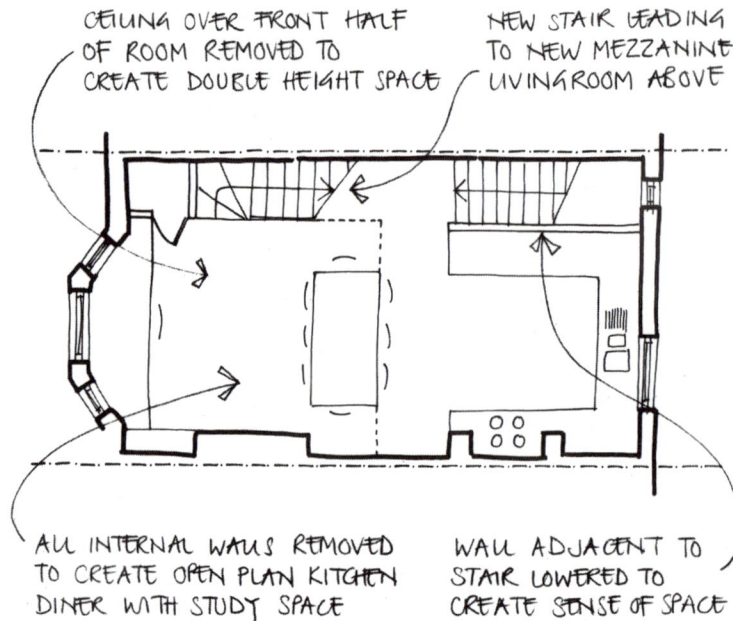

CEILING OVER FRONT HALF OF ROOM REMOVED TO CREATE DOUBLE HEIGHT SPACE

NEW STAIR LEADING TO NEW MEZZANINE LIVINGROOM ABOVE

ALL INTERNAL WALLS REMOVED TO CREATE OPEN PLAN KITCHEN DINER WITH STUDY SPACE

WALL ADJACENT TO STAIR LOWERED TO CREATE SENSE OF SPACE

Artist's impression of mezzanine living room
above kitchen.

LOFT

The loft, which has a beam-to-ridge height of 2.5m, has not yet been extended. If extending, provision should be made for additional insulation in the roof and additional structure in the floor.

OPTION 1
(As depicted in Section B)

This option shows a full-width, rear dormer extension that accommodates a double bedroom. A shower room and dressing area are tucked into the eaves. It assumes a door at the bottom of the stairs (as in First-floor Option 1). Alternatively, a door could be installed at the top of the stair (making it compatible with First-floor Option 3) and a protected escape route provided (as in Ground-floor Option 3) – or a suitable sprinkler system installed.

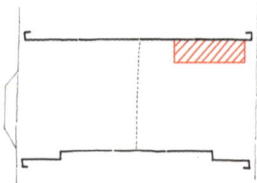

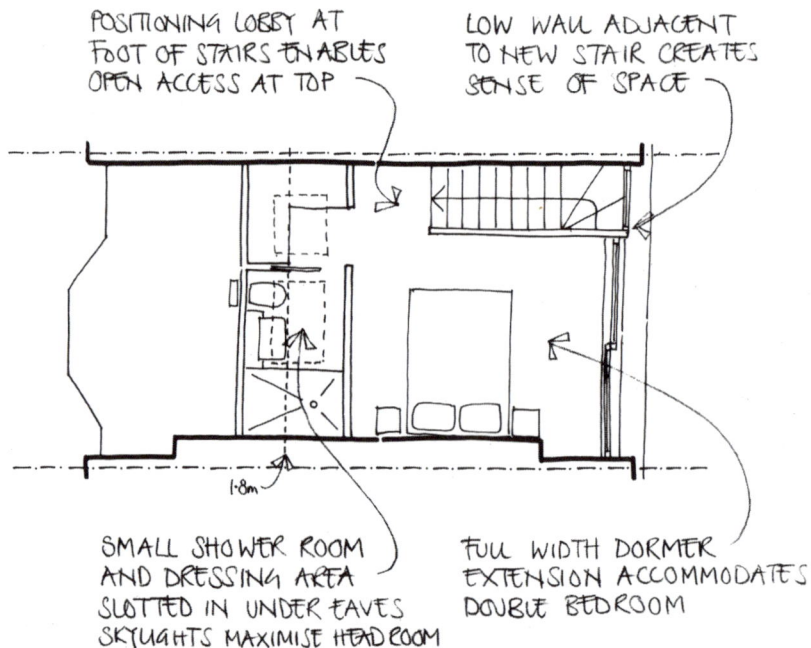

POSITIONING LOBBY AT FOOT OF STAIRS ENABLES OPEN ACCESS AT TOP

LOW WALL ADJACENT TO NEW STAIR CREATES SENSE OF SPACE

1·8m

SMALL SHOWER ROOM AND DRESSING AREA SLOTTED IN UNDER EAVES SKYLIGHTS MAXIMISE HEAD ROOM

FULL WIDTH DORMER EXTENSION ACCOMMODATES DOUBLE BEDROOM

OPTION 2

The low wall shown around the stair enhances the sense of space in this option. Tucking the slim shower room in alongside the stairs frees up the rest of the space to create a spacious double bedroom within a full-width, rear dormer extension. The wardrobe space is positioned under the front eaves. However, this could be relocated to free up the eaves area, further enhancing the sense of space. It again assumes a door at the bottom of the stair, as shown in First-floor Option 1, and a protected escape route or the installation of an appropriate sprinkler system.

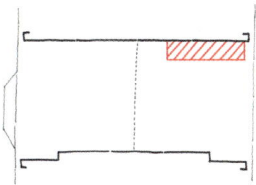

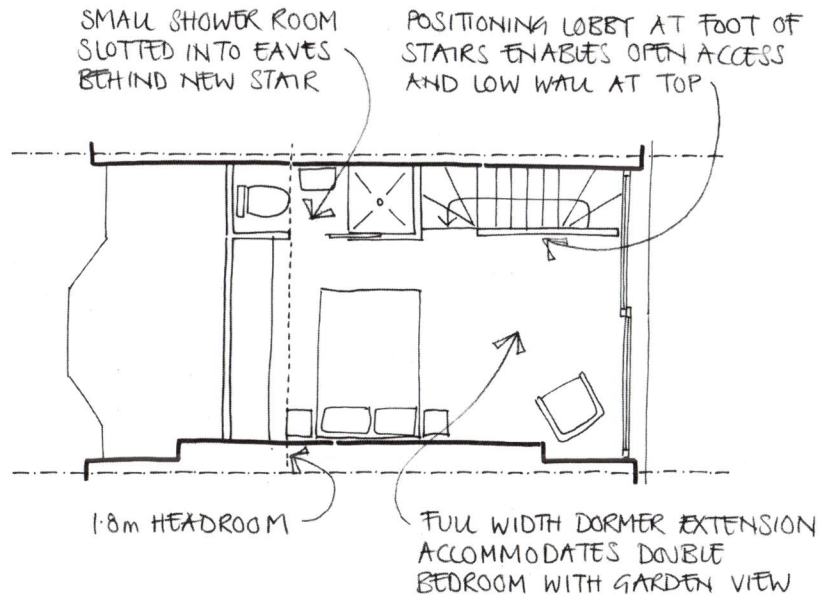

SMALL SHOWER ROOM SLOTTED INTO EAVES BEHIND NEW STAIR

POSITIONING LOBBY AT FOOT OF STAIRS ENABLES OPEN ACCESS AND LOW WALL AT TOP

1.8m HEADROOM

FULL WIDTH DORMER EXTENSION ACCOMMODATES DOUBLE BEDROOM WITH GARDEN VIEW

OPTION 3

(Based on the Barnes Brick House by Yard Architects)
(As depicted in Section A)

This option also shows a full-width, rear dormer extension. It is to be read in conjunction with First-floor Option 2 and Ground-floor Option 5, in which the existing stairs have been reconfigured. Positioning the door at the bottom of the stairs enables them to open out directly into the loft room without the need for a sprinkler system. This option shows front eaves storage and no en-suite bathroom, but the front-area layouts shown in Loft Options 1 and 2 could be used here. Alternatively, the eaves storage could be omitted. This would continue the ceiling slope down to the floor at the front, which would make the room feel less enclosed.

This option also shows skylights either side of the bed to provide additional headroom and exposed beams increase the sense of space.

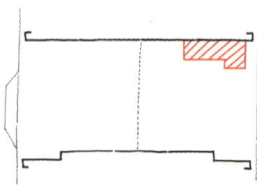

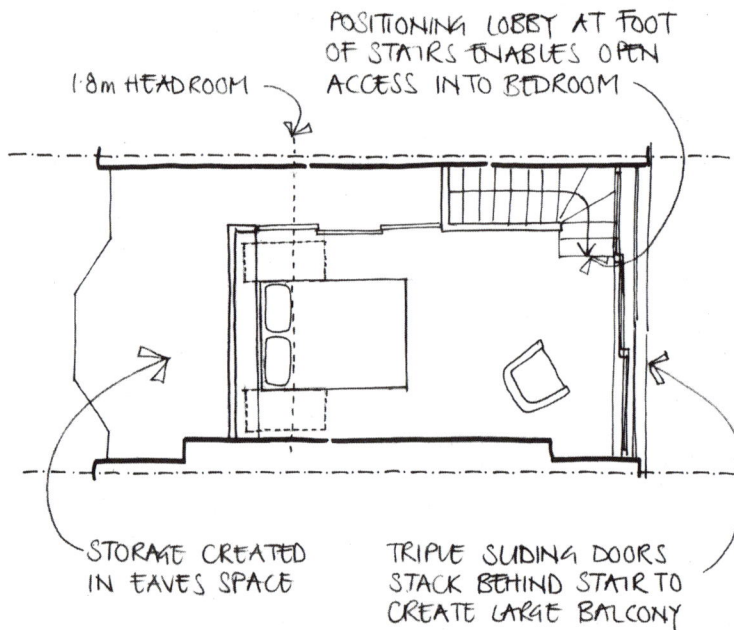

POSITIONING LOBBY AT FOOT OF STAIRS ENABLES OPEN ACCESS INTO BEDROOM

1.8m HEADROOM

STORAGE CREATED IN EAVES SPACE

TRIPLE SLIDING DOORS STACK BEHIND STAIR TO CREATE LARGE BALCONY

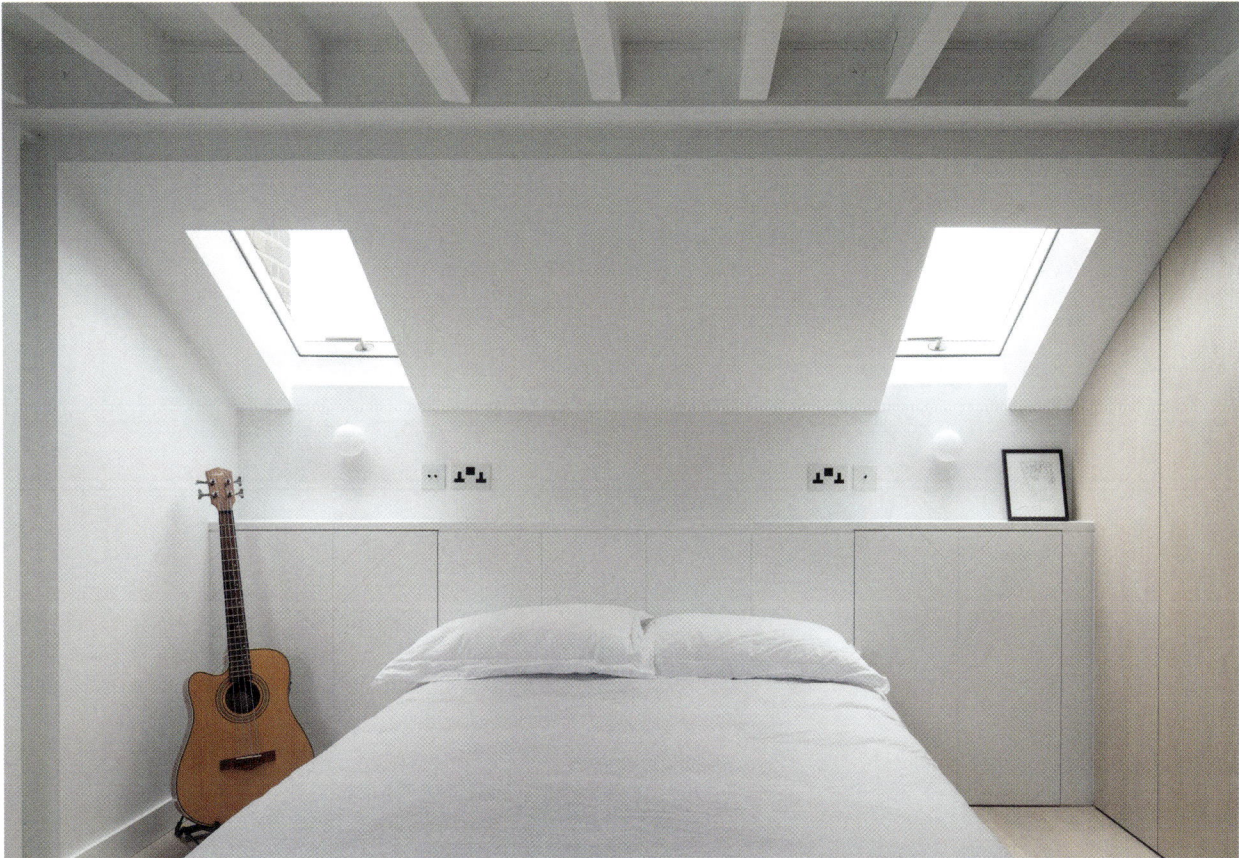

Barnes Brick House by Yard Architects, Barnes,
London, 2019. Skylights either side of bed provide
additional headroom. Image mirrored to reflect plan.

Next page: Brick Barnes House by Yard Architexts,
Barnes, 2019. Storage tucked in behind stairs.
Image mirrored to reflect plan.

OPTION 4

(As depicted in Section C)

This option is to be read in conjunction with First-floor Option 4 and Ground-floor Options 1 or 4, in which the living space is located at the top of the house and the bedrooms are on the ground floor. The full-width, rear dormer extension creates enough space to accommodate a mezzanine living room that looks down into the dining/study area.

This mezzanine could also be used as a study area or, if a wall and door were added, it could be used as a separate bedroom.

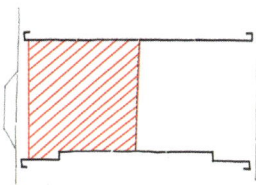

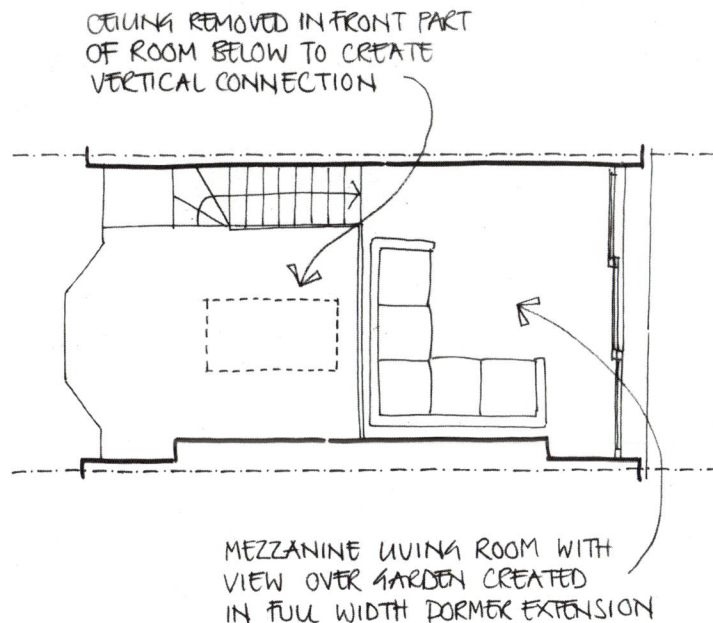

CEILING REMOVED IN FRONT PART OF ROOM BELOW TO CREATE VERTICAL CONNECTION

MEZZANINE LIVING ROOM WITH VIEW OVER GARDEN CREATED IN FULL WIDTH DORMER EXTENSION

THE CENTRAL STAIR

This case study features a small, two-storey terraced house constructed on a 4.2m-wide plot. Unlike any of the other examples in this book, it has a central stair separating the front and rear reception areas. It has a small, west-facing garden. Many of these plans can be used on houses with more traditional, front-to-back staircases by simply relocating the stairs.

GROUND FLOOR

The front door opens directly into the front reception room, with a second reception room and small outrigger, housing a kitchen, located at the rear of the property, behind the central staircase.

OPTION 1

This option rearranges the existing space without needing to extend. The central stair is reorientated so that it is accessed from the dining area. The advantage of doing this lies in the reduction of circulation space achieved above and the opportunity for the first-floor bathroom to be accessed independently of the rear bedroom, as in First-floor Option 1. The stair is open on both sides to maximise connection between living room and dining area.

The living room is located at the front of the house, to give it an element of separation from the kitchen/diner. The dining table in the rear reception room is positioned centrally, as this space requires the most circulation.

Aside from this, the only other changes proposed are replacing the kitchen door with a window to provide more wall space against which to fit units, and removing a section of the wall between the main house and the outrigger to create a greater connection between kitchen and dining room.

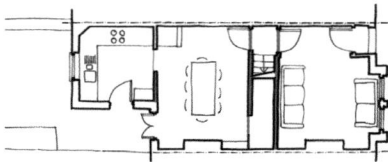

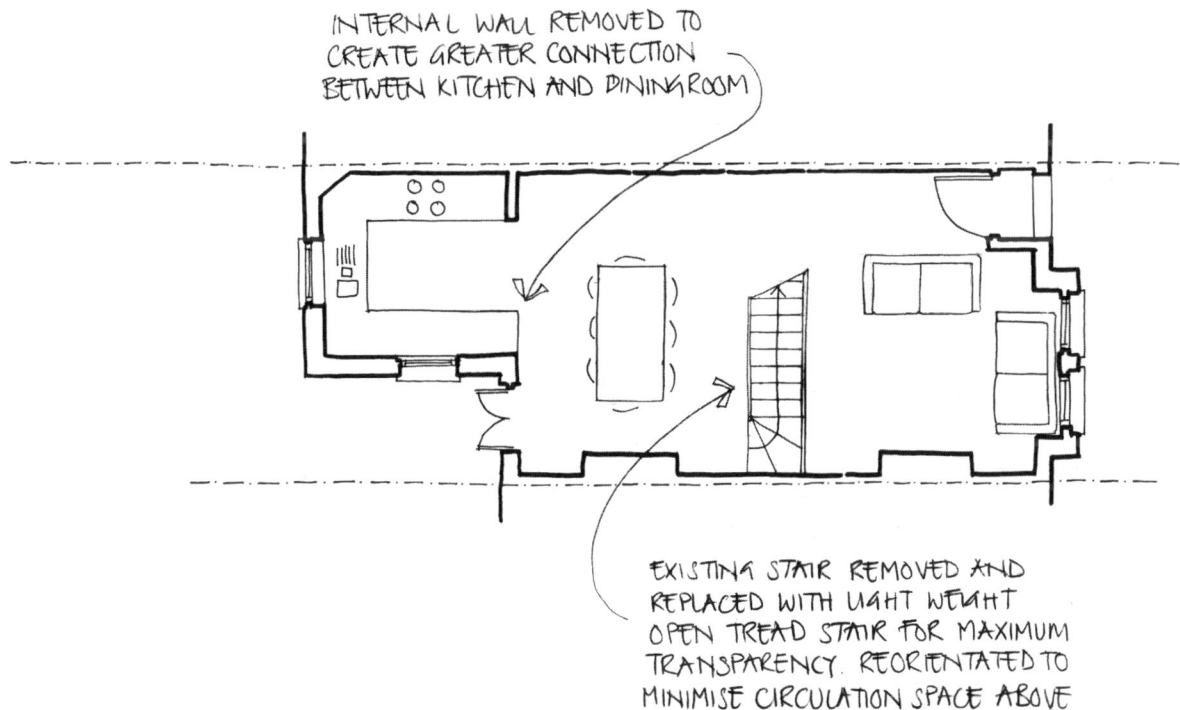

INTERNAL WALL REMOVED TO CREATE GREATER CONNECTION BETWEEN KITCHEN AND DINING ROOM

EXISTING STAIR REMOVED AND REPLACED WITH LIGHT WEIGHT OPEN TREAD STAIR FOR MAXIMUM TRANSPARENCY. REORIENTATED TO MINIMISE CIRCULATION SPACE ABOVE

OPTION 2

This option also flips the staircase round and positions the living room at the front of the house. It, too, is to be read in conjunction with First-floor Option 1.

In this case, however, the walls flanking the stairs have been retained to preserve a separate living room. Extending to the rear provides a larger kitchen area and accommodates a dining area. This enables the existing rear reception room to be used as a second, more informal family living room.

Positioning the garden door in the side wall of the extension, rather than at the end, shortens the internal circulation route. It also frees up the whole width of the rear of the extension to be used for dining.

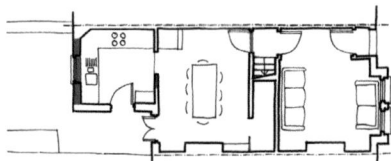

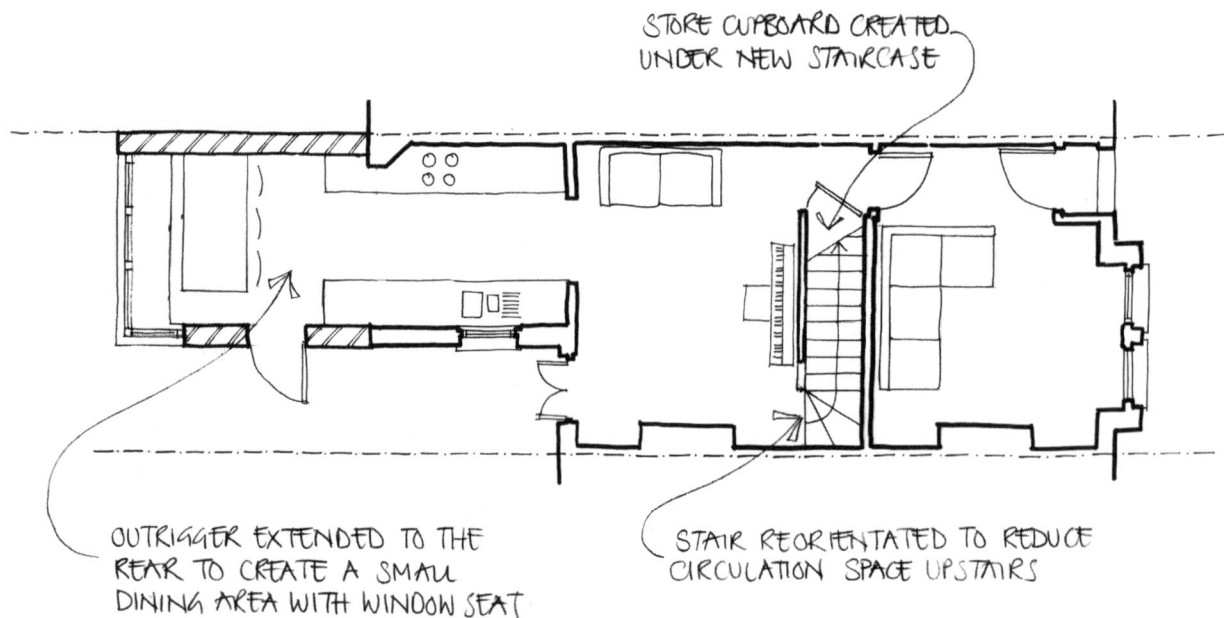

STORE CUPBOARD CREATED
UNDER NEW STAIRCASE

OUTRIGGER EXTENDED TO THE
REAR TO CREATE A SMALL
DINING AREA WITH WINDOW SEAT

STAIR REORIENTATED TO REDUCE
CIRCULATION SPACE UPSTAIRS

Waveney Avenue by MW Architects, Peckham, London, 2017. Garden view and side access retained.

OPTION 3

(Based on the Waveney Avenue project by MW Architects)

The stairs are also flipped and accessed via the rear reception room in this option. Again, the wall between the stair and the living room is retained to preserve the separate living room. By extending the kitchen into the central living area, which is open to the stairs, the rear extension can be used solely to accommodate the dining room. Building out part-way into the side return gives enough room to position a dining table to one side in this space and provides circulation space to reach the garden via a rear door. External access is retained from the rear reception room through the remaining side return to the garden.

The opening in the wall between the main section of the house and the outrigger has been enlarged to create a greater link between the kitchen and the informal family living room. This should be read in conjunction with First-floor Option 1.

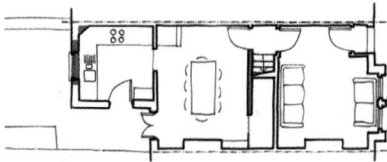

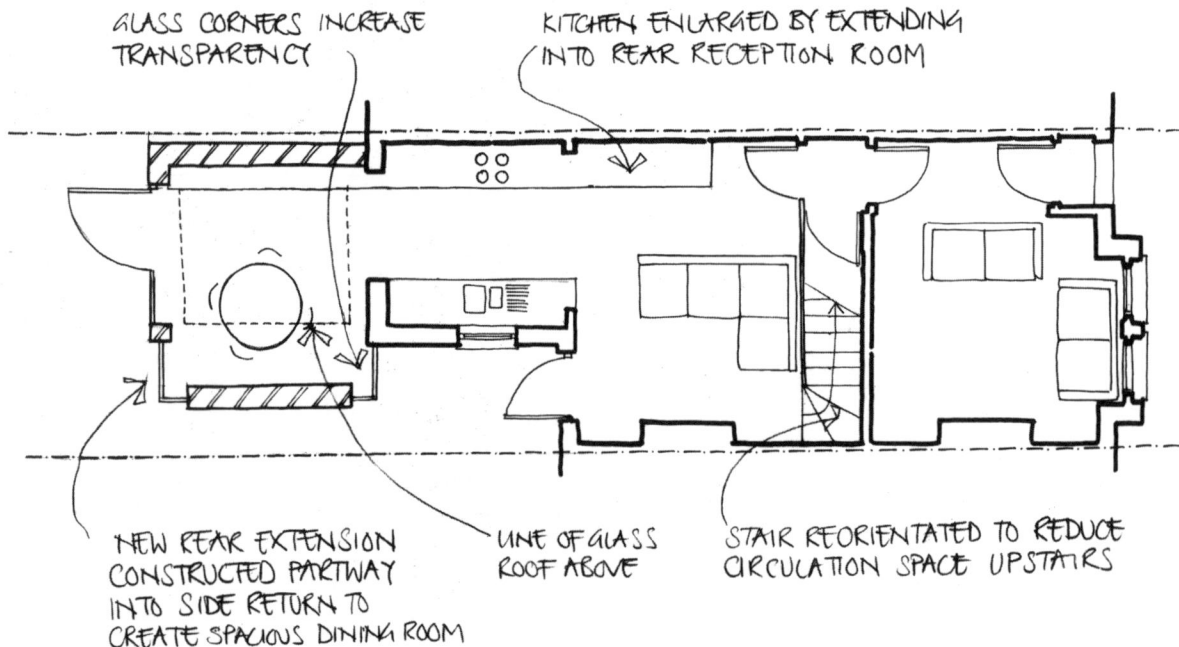

GLASS CORNERS INCREASE TRANSPARENCY

KITCHEN ENLARGED BY EXTENDING INTO REAR RECEPTION ROOM

NEW REAR EXTENSION CONSTRUCTED PARTWAY INTO SIDE RETURN TO CREATE SPACIOUS DINING ROOM

LINE OF GLASS ROOF ABOVE

STAIR REORIENTATED TO REDUCE CIRCULATION SPACE UPSTAIRS

Waveney Avenue by MW Architects, Peckham,
London, 2017. New kitchen/diner.

OPTION 4

This option involves removing most of the existing internal walls. The stairs have been flipped and are accessed via the living room, which is located at the front of the house. The second stair wall is retained and the doorway that previously accessed the under-stair store blocked to act as separation between the living room and the kitchen/dining area.

The kitchen has been positioned in the rear reception room and the outrigger extended into the side return, which is used as a spacious dining area that connects directly to the garden. This should be read in conjunction with First-floor Option 1.

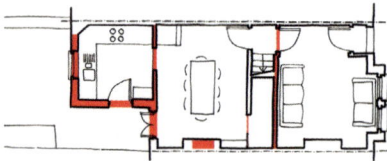

EXTERNAL WALLS AT REAR OF HOUSE REMOVED AND OUTRIGGER EXTENDED INTO SIDE RETURN TO CREATE OPEN PLAN KITCHEN DINER CONNECTED TO GARDEN

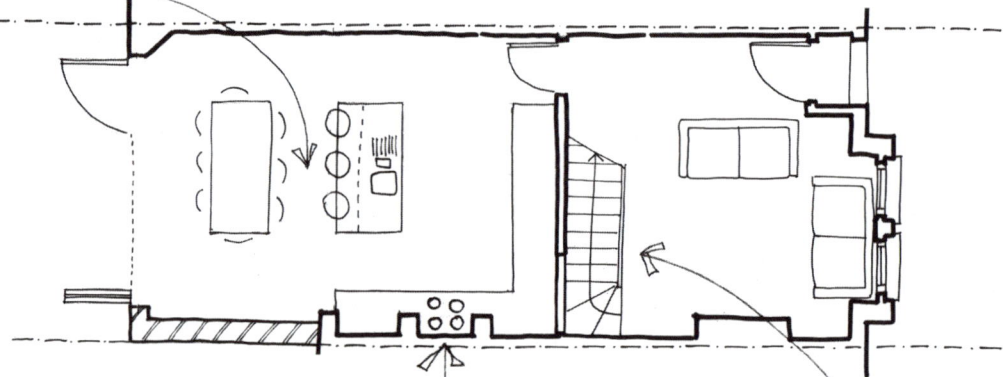

COOKER ACCOMMODATED IN EXISTING CHIMNEY BREAST

STAIRS REORIENTATED TO REDUCE CIRCULATION SPACE UPSTAIRS, OPEN TO THE LIVING ROOM TO CREATE A GREATER SENSE OF SPACE

OPTION 5

Similarly to Ground-floor Option 4, many of the existing internal walls have been removed, maximising connections between the different spaces in this option. The kitchen is located at the front of the property to free up the rear for a more flexible space. This is shown here accommodating a dining and living room, with direct garden access.

A small coat cupboard adjacent to the front door provides a degree of separation between entranceway and kitchen. The stairs have been flipped and are accessed via the rear reception room, and should therefore be read in conjunction with First-floor Option 1. The stair walls have been removed to create a visual connection between the kitchen and dining area.

The outrigger has been extended out to the side only, creating enough room to accommodate a living space. The living and dining rooms can be swapped to give a cosier living area and a dining area that opens up to the garden.

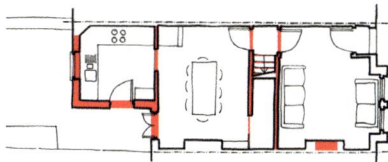

EXTERNAL WALLS REMOVED AT REAR AND OUTRIGGER EXTENDED INTO SIDE RETURN TO CREATE AN OPEN PLAN LIVING AND DINING ROOM

COAT CUPBOARD CONSTRUCTED ADJACENT TO FRONT ENTRANCE

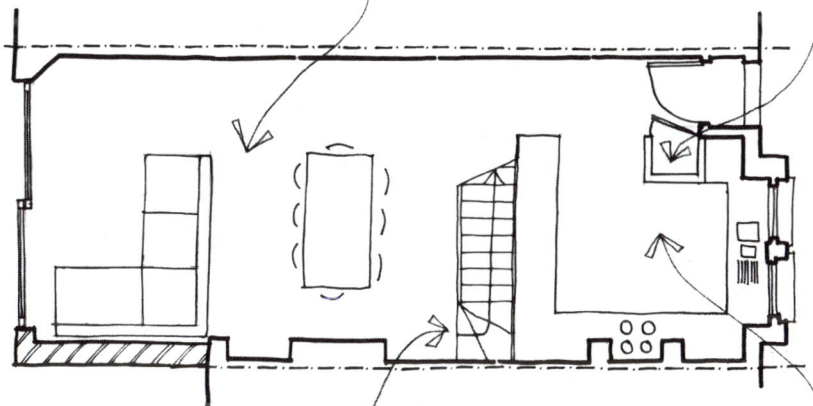

STAIR REORIENTATED TO REDUCE CIRCULATION SPACE ON FIRST FLOOR

KITCHEN RELOCATED TO FRONT OF HOUSE TO ENABLE LIVING ROOM TO BE POSITIONED WITH DIRECT ACCESS TO GARDEN

OPTION 6

All the internal walls and the stairs are removed in this option. The outrigger is extended out to the side to create a single, open-plan room with the kitchen at the rear to give greater flexibility in the living/dining area. The direction of the new stairs has been changed to enable two separate bedrooms and a bathroom to be created on the first floor, as in First-floor Option 1.

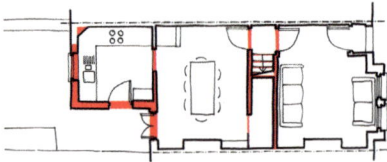

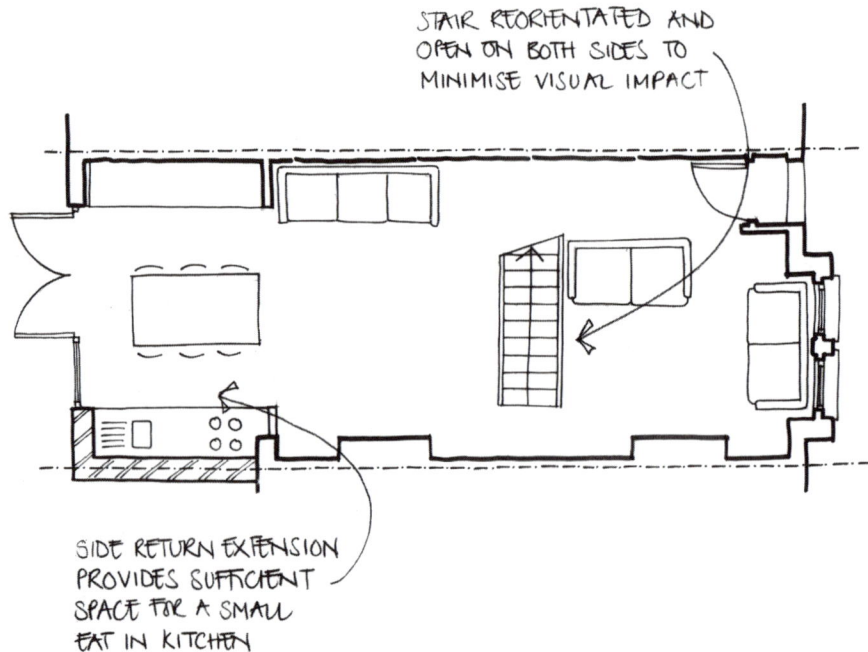

STAIR REORIENTATED AND OPEN ON BOTH SIDES TO MINIMISE VISUAL IMPACT

SIDE RETURN EXTENSION PROVIDES SUFFICIENT SPACE FOR A SMALL EAT IN KITCHEN

Artist's impression of view through stairs to
rear extension.

OPTION 7

This option also shows the removal of all internal walls, and incorporates a complete redesign of the stair. This plan can be read in conjunction with First-floor Option 3 and Loft Option 4. Designing the stair in this way also creates enough space to accommodate a WC and a coat cupboard that faces the entrance door. The living room is again located at the front of the house, providing access to a separate kitchen/diner at the rear.

The rear reception room has been used here to accommodate the kitchen, whilst the existing outrigger has had internal walls and a corner section of the external walls removed at ground floor level to create a dining room that connects both with the kitchen and the garden to the rear. There is no extension required in this option.

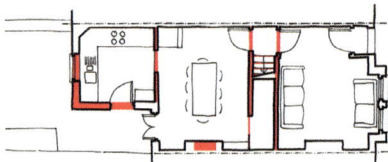

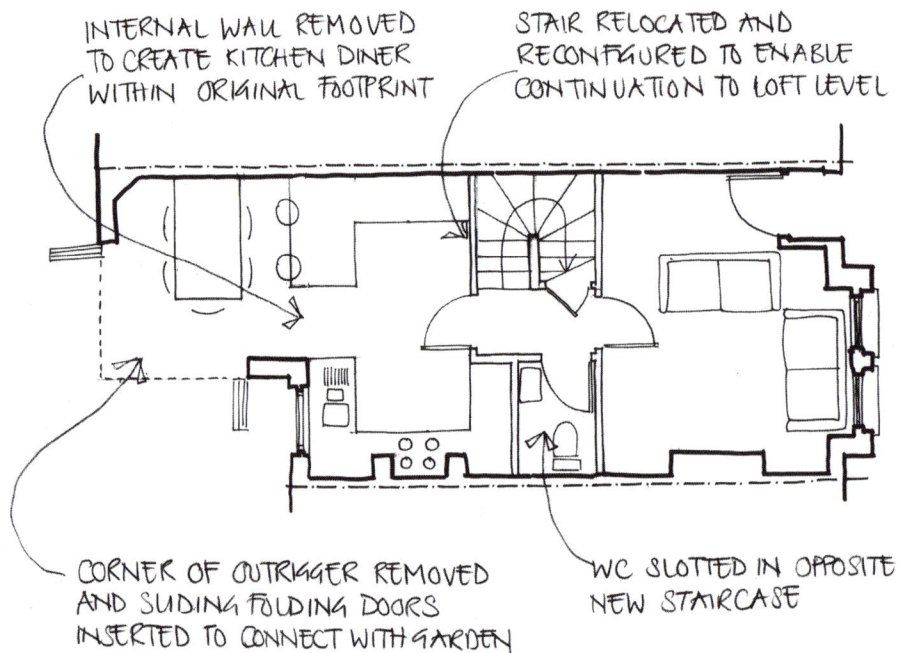

INTERNAL WALL REMOVED TO CREATE KITCHEN DINER WITHIN ORIGINAL FOOTPRINT

STAIR RELOCATED AND RECONFIGURED TO ENABLE CONTINUATION TO LOFT LEVEL

CORNER OF OUTRIGGER REMOVED AND SLIDING FOLDING DOORS INSERTED TO CONNECT WITH GARDEN

WC SLOTTED IN OPPOSITE NEW STAIRCASE

OPTION 8

This option retains the existing stair arrangement but opens up underneath the first-floor landing to create a link between the kitchen and the dining room. It can be read in conjunction with First-floor Option 2. A wall has been erected to separate the entranceway from the kitchen, and to provide more wall space against which to fit the kitchen units.

The wall between the main section of the house and the outrigger has been largely removed – as have the outrigger's side and part of the rear walls. This opens up the rear of the house and allows the insertion of a glazed courtyard that will bring additional light into the dining room. The circulation route through the outrigger has been moved to create enough space to accommodate a downstairs WC and a utility room.

A full-width rear extension has been shown beyond the outrigger that mirrors the proportions of the first-floor front bedroom. This creates a living area that connects, through sliding glass doors, both to the garden and the dining area.

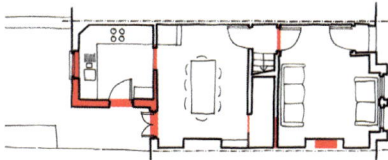

NEW FULL WIDTH EXTENSION ACCOMMODATES A LIVING ROOM SEPARATED BY SLIDING DOORS

WC AND UTILITY ROOM ACCOMMODATED IN ORIGINAL OUTRIGGER

CONSTRUCTING A CORRIDOR WALL SEPARATES THE KITCHEN FROM THE HALL AND STAIR

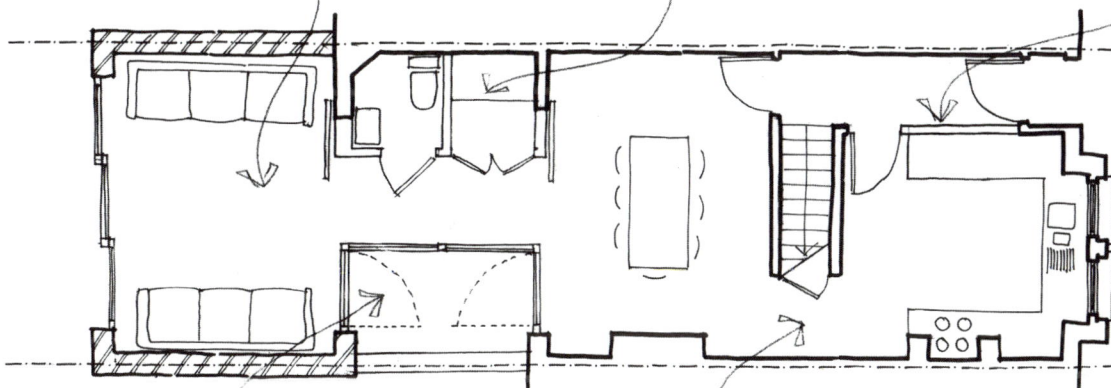

CREATING A COURTYARD AREA RETAINS LIGHT AND VENTILATION TO THE DINING AREA DOORS CAN FOLD BACK TO INCORPORATE THE COURTYARD INTO THE SPACE

OPENING CREATED UNDER EXISTING STAIR TO CONNECT THE RELOCATED KITCHEN WITH THE DINING ROOM

FIRST FLOOR

In the existing plan, the central stair leads up to two double bedrooms – one at the front, one at the rear. The bathroom, which is accommodated in the outrigger, is accessed through the rear bedroom.

OPTION 1

This option can be used in conjunction with any of the Ground-floor Options 1–6. It shows the most obvious and conventional arrangement once the stair is flipped to consolidate circulation space on the first floor. It enables enclosure of the rear bedroom, to separate it from the bathroom to the rear.

Access to the front bedroom must be changed to suit the new stair arrangement – as must the access into the now-separate bathroom. Adding loft stairs would seriously compromise the bedroom space, so none are shown in this option.

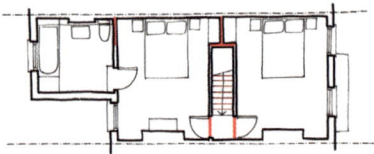

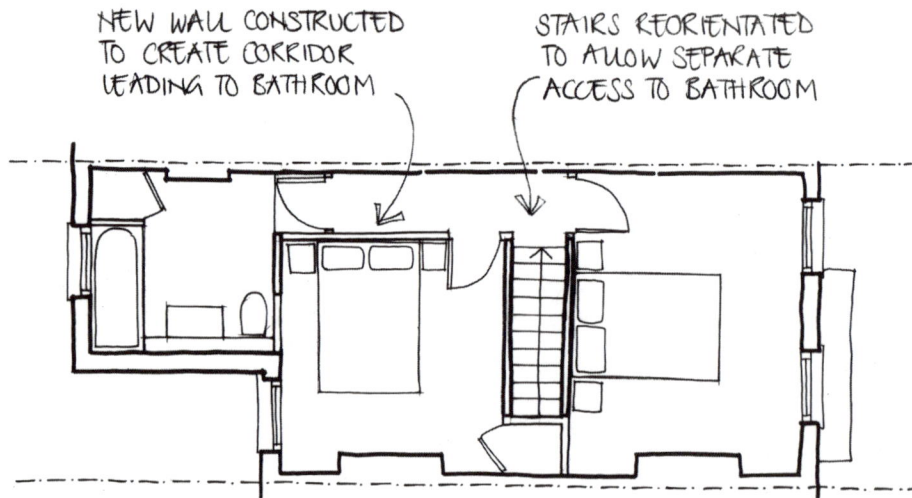

NEW WALL CONSTRUCTED TO CREATE CORRIDOR LEADING TO BATHROOM

STAIRS REORIENTATED TO ALLOW SEPARATE ACCESS TO BATHROOM

OPTION 2

This option allows for the addition of a second stair flight to access the loft. It is to be used in conjunction with the original stair option, shown in Ground-floor Option 8, or, by retaining the orientation of the stair, in any of the first six Ground-floor Options. Positioning a door at the bottom of the loft stair enables direct, open access to the loft room without the need for a door at the top of the stairs. This makes the plan most compatible with Loft Options 1 and 3, but it can also work with Loft Option 2, omitting the requirement for a door at the foot of the stair.

The front bedroom remains almost untouched. The rear bedroom and outrigger have been rearranged to make best use of the space and to minimise circulation. This creates a small shower room where the second bedroom was originally located and a long, narrow bedroom that extends into the outrigger. The latter keeps the step down in floor level to retain existing headroom.

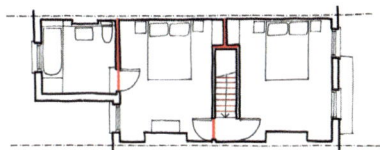

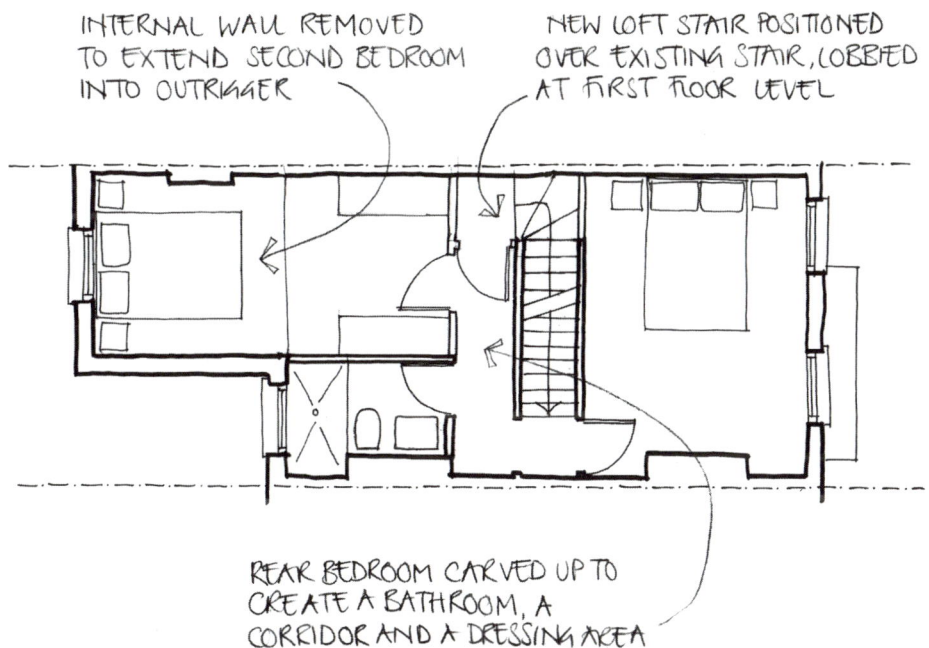

INTERNAL WALL REMOVED
TO EXTEND SECOND BEDROOM
INTO OUTRIGGER

NEW LOFT STAIR POSITIONED
OVER EXISTING STAIR, LOBBIED
AT FIRST FLOOR LEVEL

REAR BEDROOM CARVED UP TO
CREATE A BATHROOM, A
CORRIDOR AND A DRESSING AREA

OPTION 3

In this option, all of the internal walls have been removed. The stairs follow on from those shown in Ground-floor Option 7 and continue up to those shown in Loft Option 4. As the stairs arrive at the centre of the first floor, circulation space can be minimised.

This stair arrangement allows for the insertion of a large shower room and the creation of a wardrobe space in the front bedroom. Having no door at the bottom of the stair means that one must be installed at the top.

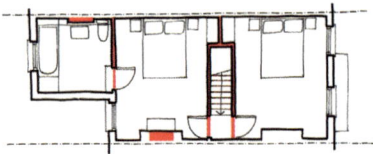

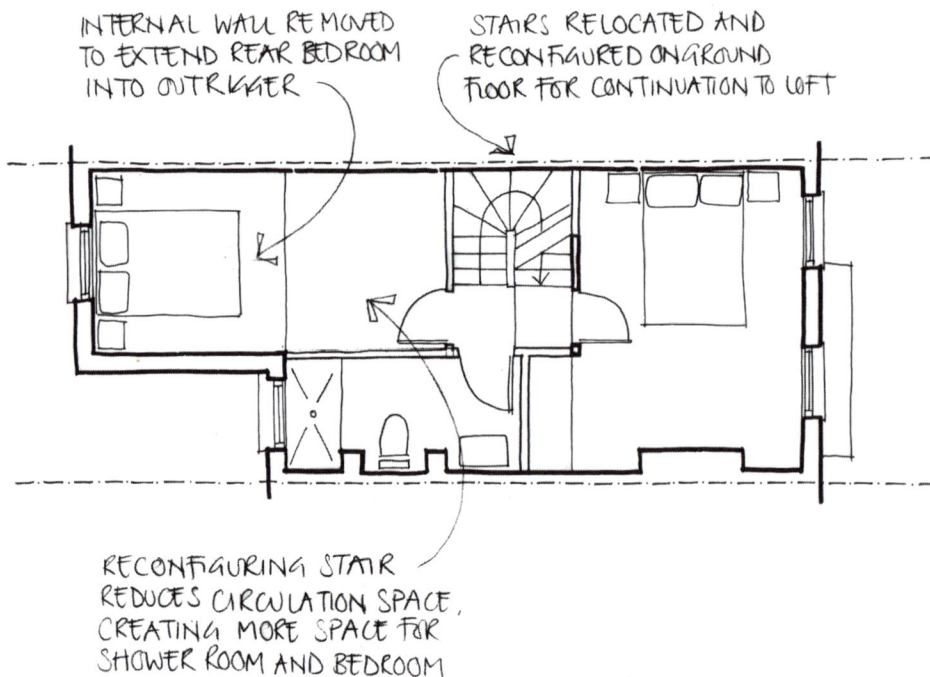

INTERNAL WALL REMOVED
TO EXTEND REAR BEDROOM
INTO OUTRIGGER

STAIRS RELOCATED AND
RECONFIGURED ON GROUND
FLOOR FOR CONTINUATION TO LOFT

RECONFIGURING STAIR
REDUCES CIRCULATION SPACE,
CREATING MORE SPACE FOR
SHOWER ROOM AND BEDROOM

LOFT

The loft, which in the original house has not yet been converted, has a beam-to-ridge height of 2.4m. As noted in the Rules of Thumb section, you should make allowance for 10cm of insulation in the roof and 10cm of additional structure in the floor when calculating final headroom.

OPTION 1

This option, to be read in conjunction with First-floor Option 2, shows a stair coming up centrally into an open-plan space. The walls around the stair are designed to be low to add to the sense of openness. A full-width dormer above the main section of the house creates a spacious bedroom with an unobstructed view of the garden. Skylights in the front pitch of the roof provide light into the front half of the room and views to the east.

There is not enough headroom under the slope of the front section of the roof to create a shower room, and the bedroom would be very small if a shower room were to be installed at the rear. As a result, neither has been shown in this option.

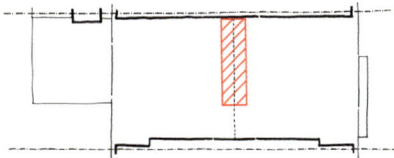

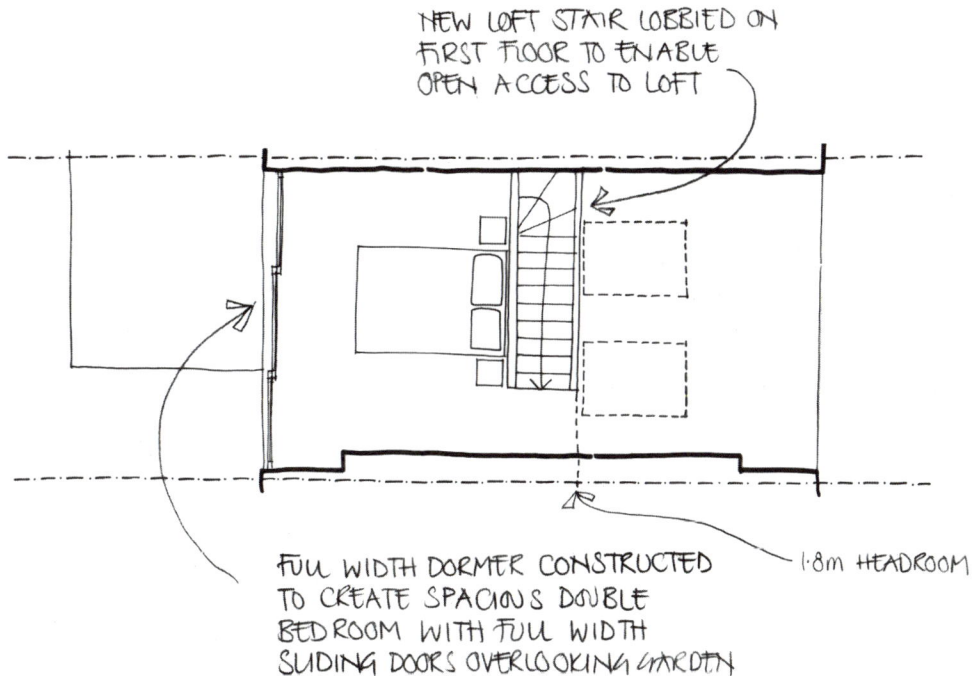

NEW LOFT STAIR LOBBIED ON FIRST FLOOR TO ENABLE OPEN ACCESS TO LOFT

FULL WIDTH DORMER CONSTRUCTED TO CREATE SPACIOUS DOUBLE BEDROOM WITH FULL WIDTH SLIDING DOORS OVERLOOKING GARDEN

1.8m HEADROOM

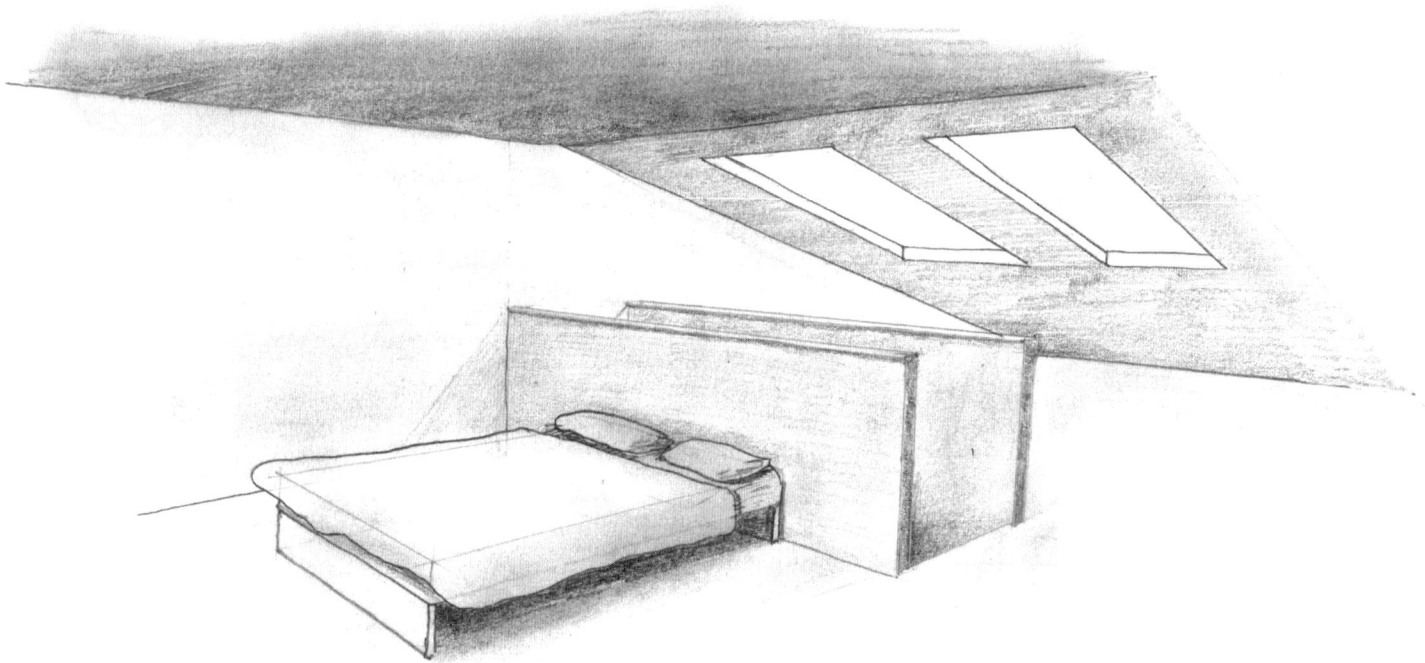

Artist's impression of bed against low
stair walls. Based on option 1.

OPTION 2

In this option, the loft extends into the rear of the main loft space by use of a full-width dormer, and over the outrigger to accommodate a large double bedroom and shower room. Outrigger extensions at loft level are often more likely to gain permission under permitted development rights than with a planning application.

This option can be used in conjunction with First-floor Option 2. The plan also shows a corner glazed window seat to make the most of the southwest sun. The ceiling above the front bedroom on the first floor is open to the roof, and two skylights have been inserted into the front roof pitch.

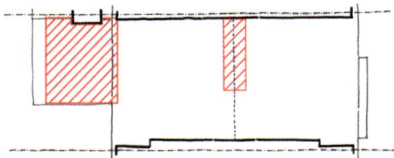

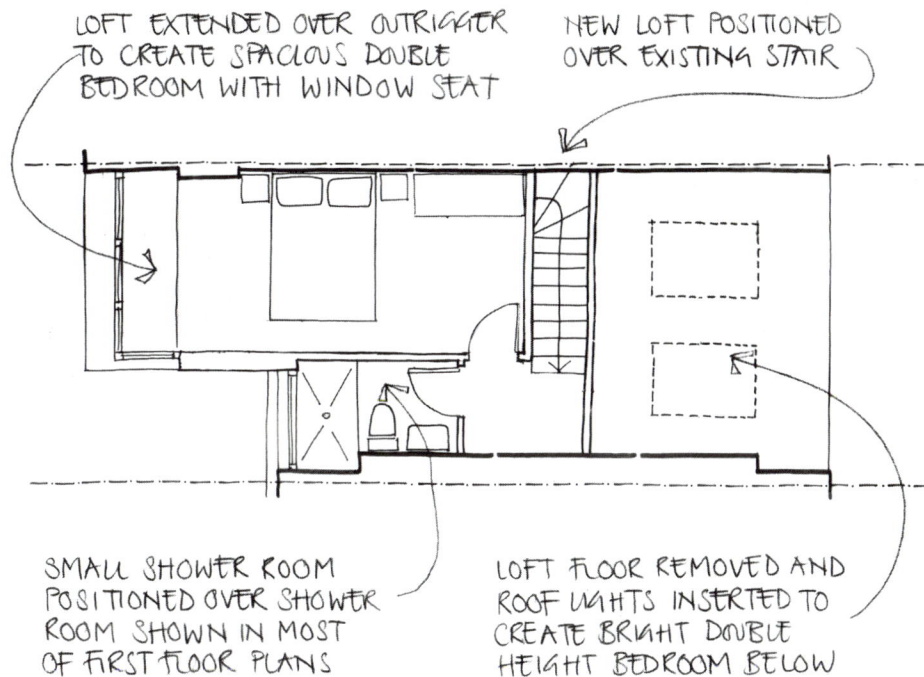

LOFT EXTENDED OVER OUTRIGGER TO CREATE SPACIOUS DOUBLE BEDROOM WITH WINDOW SEAT

NEW LOFT POSITIONED OVER EXISTING STAIR

SMALL SHOWER ROOM POSITIONED OVER SHOWER ROOM SHOWN IN MOST OF FIRST FLOOR PLANS

LOFT FLOOR REMOVED AND ROOF LIGHTS INSERTED TO CREATE BRIGHT DOUBLE HEIGHT BEDROOM BELOW

OPTION 3

The stairs are open to the loft room in this option, too, and a full-width dormer creates a spacious bedroom, but the outrigger has also been built out over to accommodate a bathroom. This does compromise the view from the bedroom out over the garden, but it gives a great view from the bath. If the existing outrigger is only single storey, it is less likely that an extension over it at loft level would gain planning permission. To be read in conjunction with First-floor Option 2.

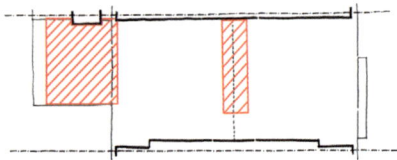

EXTENDING OUT OVER OUTRIGGER CREATES BATHROOM WITH GARDEN VIEW

NEW LOFT STAIR LOBBIED AT FIRST FLOOR LEVEL TO ENABLE OPEN ACCESS TO LOFT

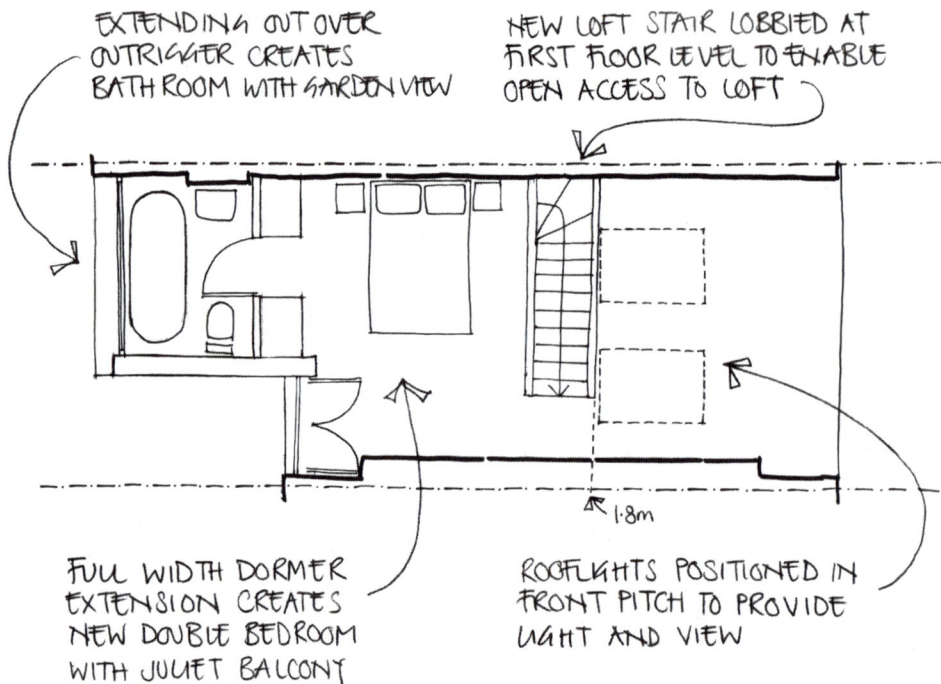

1·8m

FULL WIDTH DORMER EXTENSION CREATES NEW DOUBLE BEDROOM WITH JULIET BALCONY

ROOFLIGHTS POSITIONED IN FRONT PITCH TO PROVIDE LIGHT AND VIEW

OPTION 4

Again, this option involves the construction of a full-width dormer and the extension out over the outrigger at loft level. The dormer extension accommodates the bedroom and the outrigger extension accommodates a seating area with a great view over the garden.

The stairs follow on from those shown in First-floor Option 3, and there is a door between the stair and the bedroom. The area at the front of the loft is open to the stair and there is space for a small shower room at the top of the stair, but it could be enclosed if preferred.

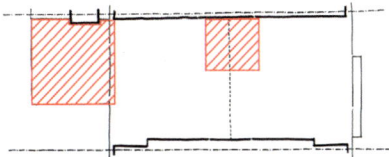

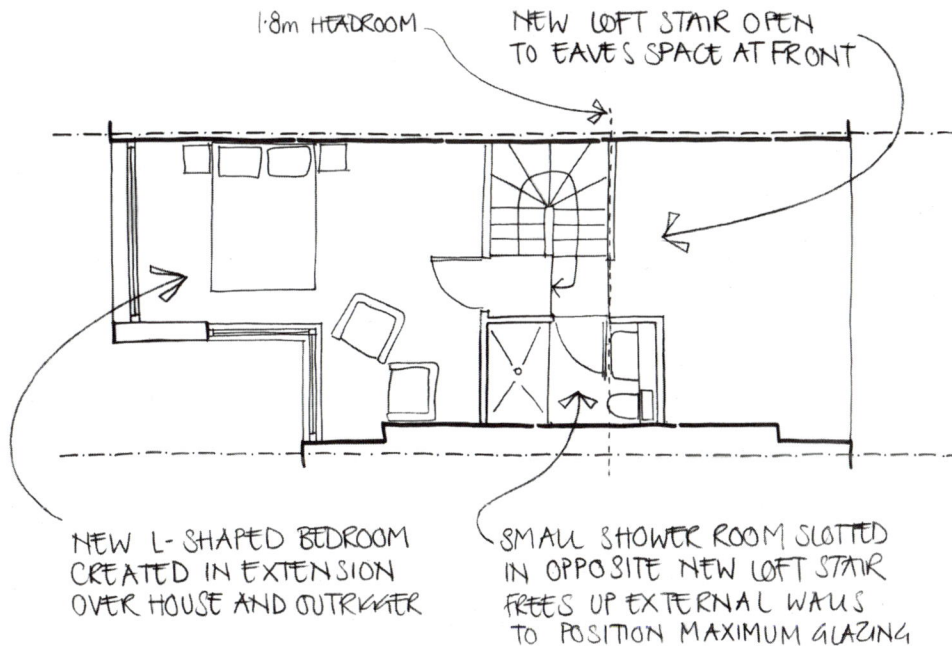

1·8m HEADROOM

NEW LOFT STAIR OPEN TO EAVES SPACE AT FRONT

NEW L-SHAPED BEDROOM CREATED IN EXTENSION OVER HOUSE AND OUTRIGGER

SMALL SHOWER ROOM SLOTTED IN OPPOSITE NEW LOFT STAIR FREES UP EXTERNAL WALLS TO POSITION MAXIMUM GLAZING

THE TWO UP TWO DOWN

At 4.2m, this house is similar in width to that in the Central Stair case study. However, it has a longer, single-storey outrigger and has more traditional, front-to-back stairs. In all of the following options, the stair location remains as existing. Many of the options shown in the Central Stair are also possible here if the stairs are reconfigured and relocated.

GROUND FLOOR

As with many narrower terraced houses, in the existing plan the front door opens directly into the front room to make the most of the available space. This leads to a separate rear reception room and, via a corridor, to the outrigger, which accommodates a small galley kitchen and a bathroom accessed through the kitchen. If extending into the loft, a sprinkler system must be installed to retain the open-plan arrangement on the ground floor.

OPTION 1

In this option, the front and rear reception rooms have been amalgamated to create one large living area with a cupboard to retain an element of separation.

Most of the walls of the outrigger are retained, with a corner section being removed from the existing bathroom and extended out to accommodate a corner window seat. Concertina windows enable this seat to be used externally as well as internally.

Retaining the existing rear-door location allows the positioning of a dining table at the far end of the outrigger without the need to squeeze past it to reach the garden.

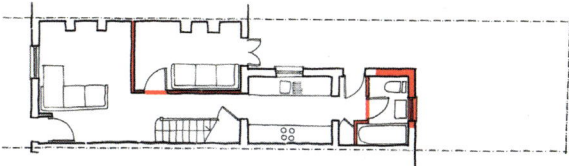

INTERNAL WALLS REMOVED TO
CREATE OPEN PLAN LIVING SPACE
STORAGE PROVIDES VISUAL SCREEN

REAR DOOR TO GARDEN RETAINED

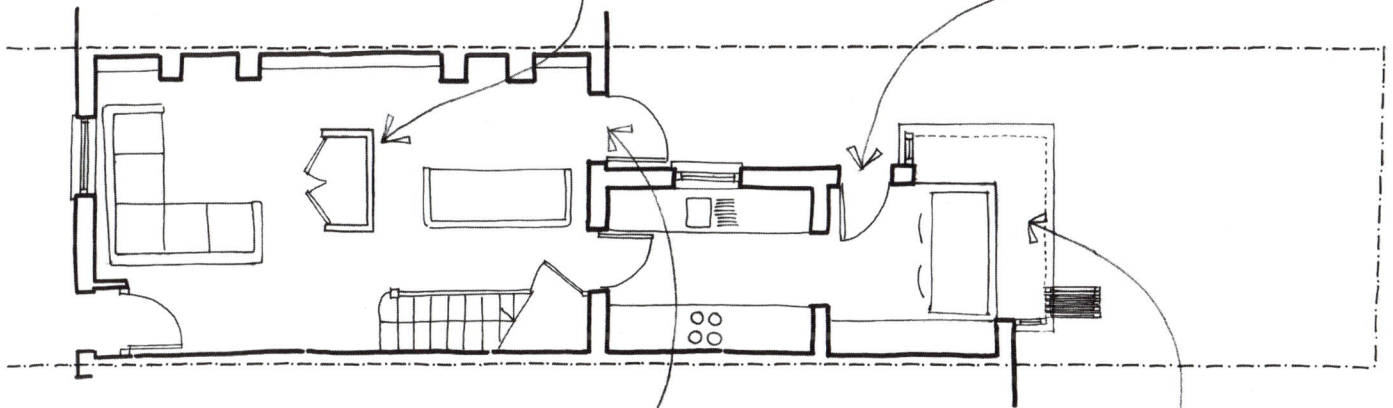

KITCHEN RETAINED AS EXISTING
TO MINIMISE COST AND RETAIN
LIGHT AND VENTILATION VIA
EXISTING WINDOW AND REAR DOOR.

BATHROOM RELOCATED UPSTAIRS.
CORNER OF OUTRIGGER REMOVED
AT GROUND FLOOR LEVEL AND SMALL
EXTENSION CONSTRUCTED TO CREATE
WINDOW SEAT AND DINING AREA
WITH CONCERTINA WINDOWS

OPTION 2

The internal walls in the main section of the house have been removed to create a large living room, and a small WC has been positioned under the stairs.

This option retains the footprint of the outrigger while removing its internal walls and enlarging the rear opening to create a stronger connection with the garden. The roof height of the outrigger's rear section has been increased to give a greater sense of space and light. The ceiling height over the kitchen has been retained to enable a small, first-floor extension to be constructed above – as in First-floor Option 2.

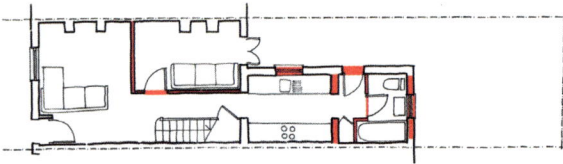

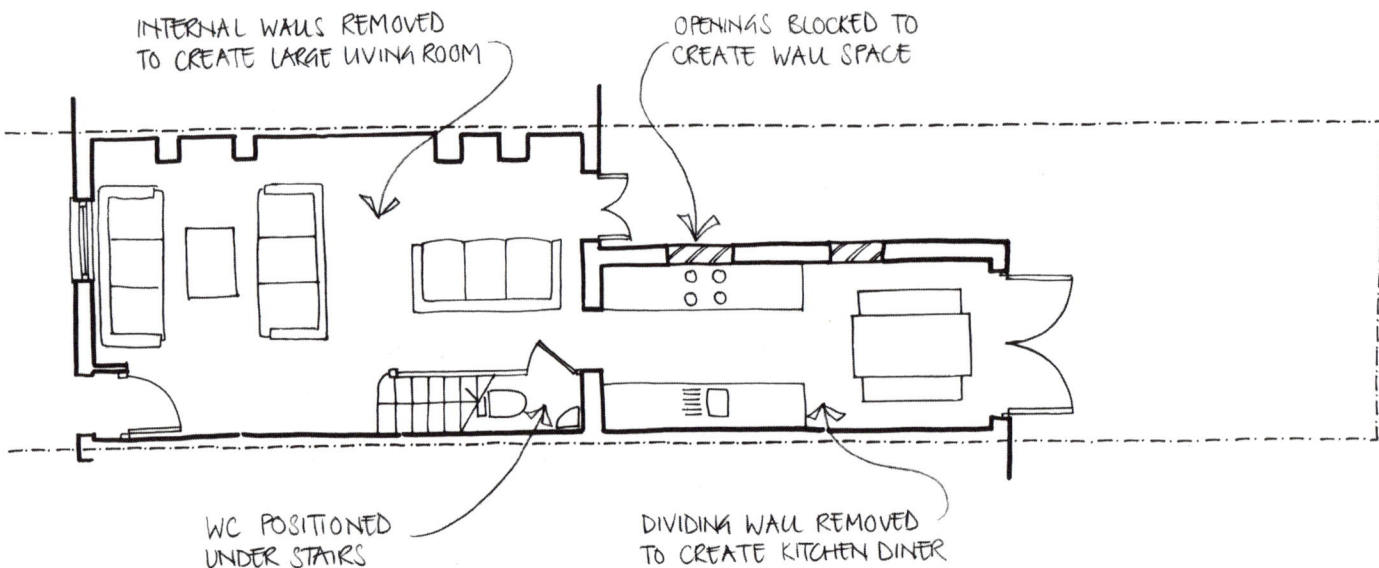

INTERNAL WALLS REMOVED TO CREATE LARGE LIVING ROOM

OPENINGS BLOCKED TO CREATE WALL SPACE

WC POSITIONED UNDER STAIRS

DIVIDING WALL REMOVED TO CREATE KITCHEN DINER

Slim House by Alma-nac, Clapham, London, 2012.
Galley kitchen and new dining-room extension.

OPTION 3

(Based on the Barnes Brick House project by Yard Architects)

The internal walls in the main section of the house have been removed to create a large living room, and a wall has been constructed adjacent to the front door to give some privacy to the front part of the room.

This option retains part of the outrigger while extending into the side return to create a kitchen/diner. It accommodates storage and a WC in the existing outrigger, and creates a small courtyard in the remaining side return. If no extension was permitted at first-floor level, this WC could be enlarged to create a bathroom.

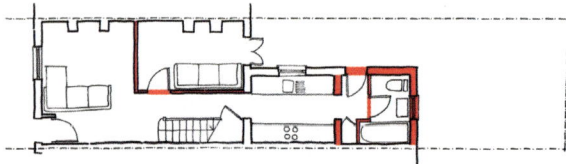

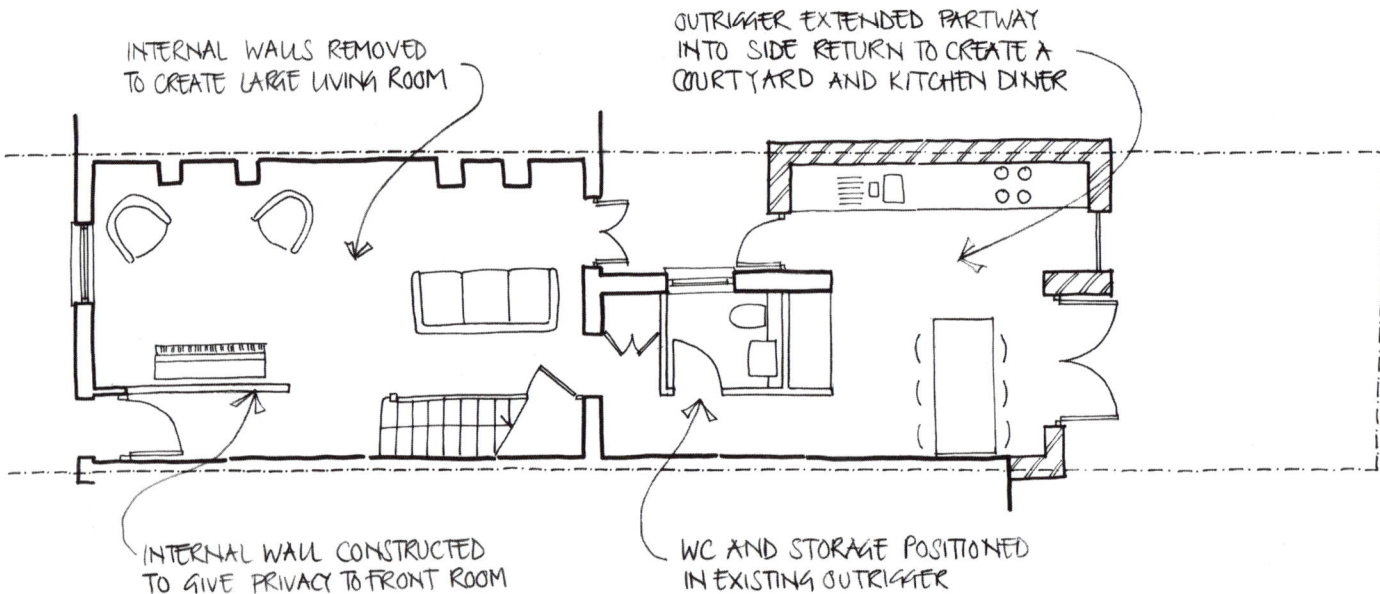

INTERNAL WALLS REMOVED TO CREATE LARGE LIVING ROOM

OUTRIGGER EXTENDED PARTWAY INTO SIDE RETURN TO CREATE A COURTYARD AND KITCHEN DINER

INTERNAL WALL CONSTRUCTED TO GIVE PRIVACY TO FRONT ROOM

WC AND STORAGE POSITIONED IN EXISTING OUTRIGGER

The Barnes Brick House by Yard Architects, Barnes,
London, 2019. Garden design creates outside room.

The Barnes Brick House by Yard Architects, Barnes,
London, 2019. View of open plan living room looking
into courtyard beyond.

The Barnes Brick House by Yard Architects, Barnes, London, 2019. Rooflight in extension creates bright and airy kitchen.

OPTION 4

(Based on the Larch Extension project by Yard Architects)

The internal walls have been removed from the main section of the house to create a large living room. A wall has been constructed adjacent to the front door to provide screening to the living room.

This option removes the outrigger completely, replacing it with a full-width, rear extension that extends into the whole of the side return. The existing opening into the outrigger has been blocked off to create more wall space against which to position furniture. The original window opening of the rear reception room has been enlarged to provide access into the new extension, and a large sliding door has been designed to separate front from rear.

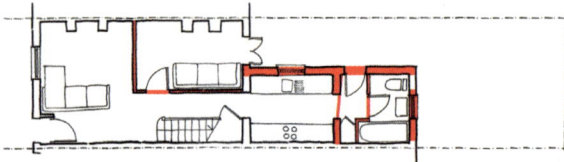

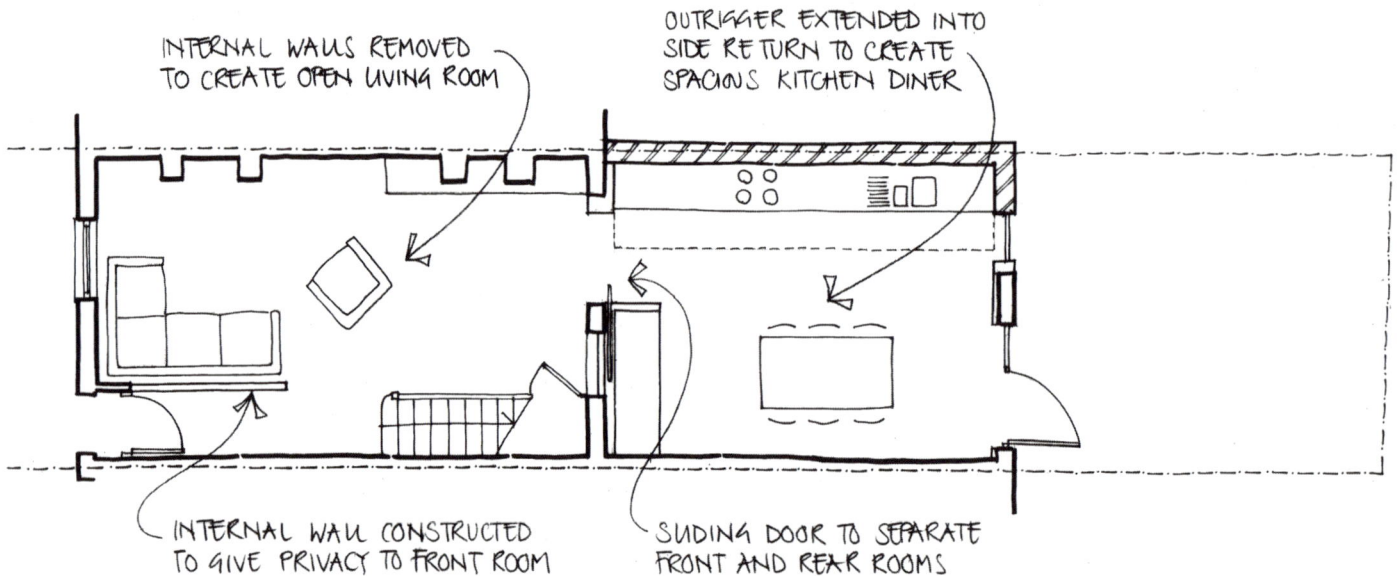

INTERNAL WALLS REMOVED
TO CREATE OPEN LIVING ROOM

OUTRIGGER EXTENDED INTO
SIDE RETURN TO CREATE
SPACIOUS KITCHEN DINER

INTERNAL WALL CONSTRUCTED
TO GIVE PRIVACY TO FRONT ROOM

SLIDING DOOR TO SEPARATE
FRONT AND REAR ROOMS

The Larch Extension by Yard Architects, Mortlake, London, 2019. Retaining part of rear wall simplifies structural design.

Next page. The Larch Extension by Yard Architects, Mortlake, London, 2019. Glazed roof over extension maximises light penetration.

OPTION 5

In this option, the stairs have been flipped to create a coat cupboard opposite the front door and to reduce circulation space on the floor above (to be read in conjunction with First-floor Option 1). The walls of the small, rear reception room have been removed to create a larger open-plan space. This accommodates a lounge at the front of the property and a study area adjacent to the outrigger.

The walls of the outrigger are retained to minimise costs. The kitchen location has not changed, but the opening in the side wall has provided an opportunity to create a breakfast bar area in the new side-return extension. A new window seat at the end of the outrigger provides enough space to create a dining area, which is connected to the extension by removing a section of the side wall. This extension provides an alternative, rear access to the house – and the garden is reached via a large pivot door.

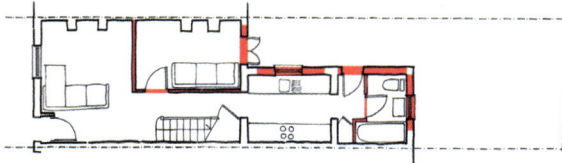

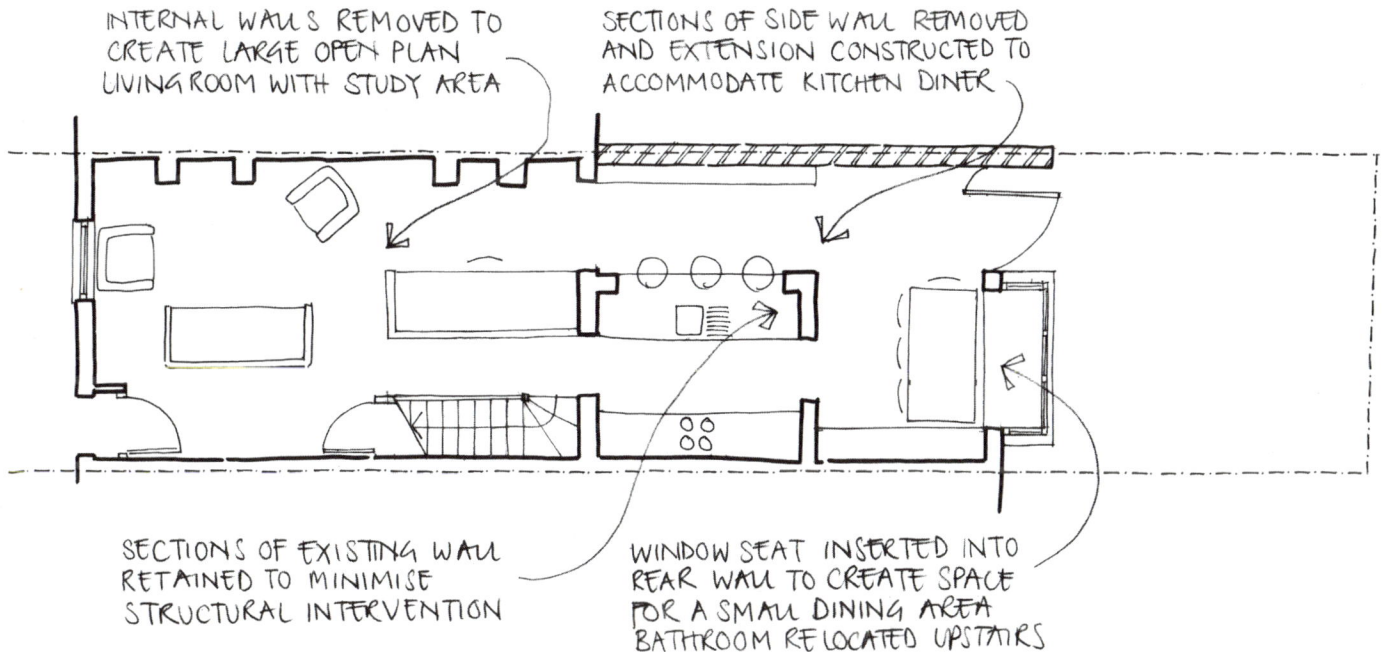

INTERNAL WALLS REMOVED TO CREATE LARGE OPEN PLAN LIVING ROOM WITH STUDY AREA

SECTIONS OF SIDE WALL REMOVED AND EXTENSION CONSTRUCTED TO ACCOMMODATE KITCHEN DINER

SECTIONS OF EXISTING WALL RETAINED TO MINIMISE STRUCTURAL INTERVENTION

WINDOW SEAT INSERTED INTO REAR WALL TO CREATE SPACE FOR A SMALL DINING AREA
BATHROOM RELOCATED UPSTAIRS

OPTION 6

The living area is, again, situated at the front of the property. The rear reception room is divided to accommodate a bathroom and utility cupboard. This is a great option if it is not possible to locate a bathroom at first-floor level. By relocating the bathroom to the centre of the property, removing the outrigger walls and extending into the side return, the rear of the property is freed up. It can now accommodate a large, open-plan kitchen/diner with a good connection to the garden via large, sliding doors.

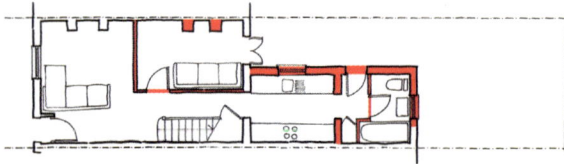

SIDE AND REAR WALLS OF OUTRIGGER REMOVED AT GROUND FLOOR LEVEL AND EXTENSION CONSTRUCTED INTO SIDE RETURN TO CREATE KITCHEN DINER

LARGE SLIDING DOORS CONNECT KITCHEN DINER TO GARDEN

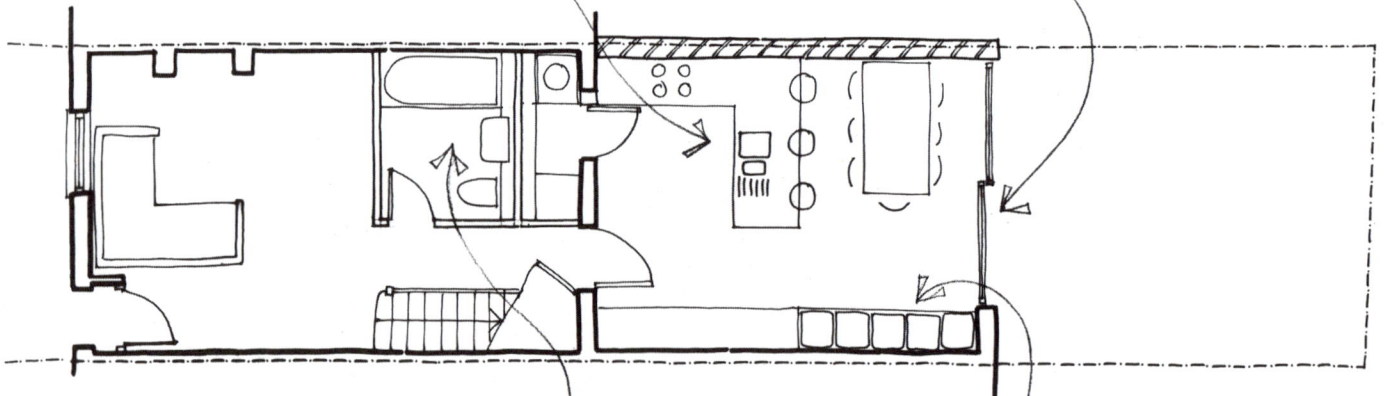

REAR RECEPTION ROOM DIVIDED UP TO ACCOMMODATE A BATHROOM AND UTILTY WHILST ENLARGING THE FRONT ROOM

BUILT IN SEATING MAKES THE MOST OF AVAILABLE SPACE

OPTION 7

The kitchen in this option has been relocated to the front of the plan. The last three treads of the stair have been reconfigured to create space to accommodate a WC and coat cupboard opposite the entrance. A wall has been positioned to create a hall and give a degree of separation between the kitchen and WC. The walls of the rear reception room have been removed to create an open-plan dining area.

The rear wall of the main section of the house has been removed, and the outrigger has been rebuilt and extended. This creates a large living room with a study area at the end looking out over the garden. The width of this study area matches that of the existing side return, echoing the proportions of the house.

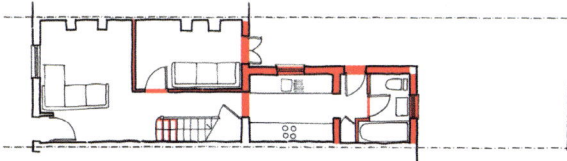

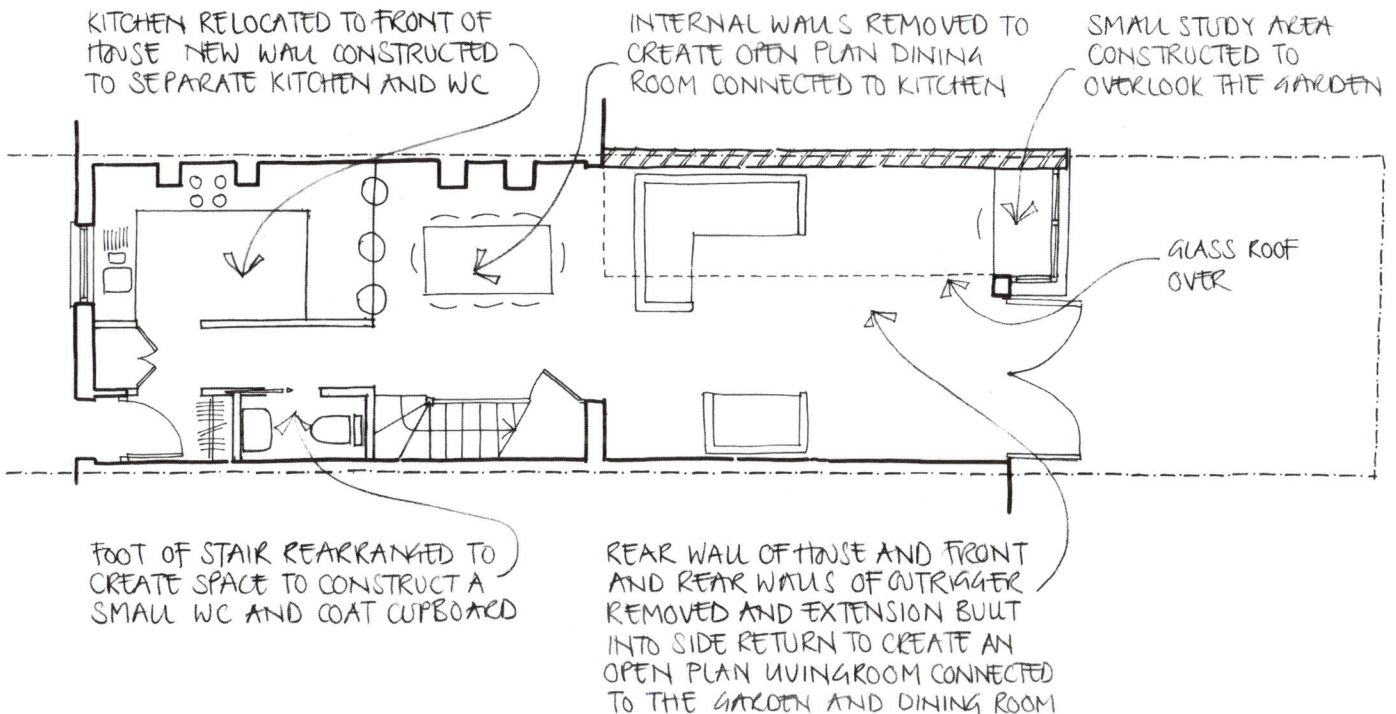

KITCHEN RELOCATED TO FRONT OF HOUSE NEW WALL CONSTRUCTED TO SEPARATE KITCHEN AND WC

INTERNAL WALLS REMOVED TO CREATE OPEN PLAN DINING ROOM CONNECTED TO KITCHEN

SMALL STUDY AREA CONSTRUCTED TO OVERLOOK THE GARDEN

GLASS ROOF OVER

FOOT OF STAIR REARRANGED TO CREATE SPACE TO CONSTRUCT A SMALL WC AND COAT CUPBOARD

REAR WALL OF HOUSE AND FRONT AND REAR WALLS OF OUTRIGGER REMOVED AND EXTENSION BUILT INTO SIDE RETURN TO CREATE AN OPEN PLAN LIVINGROOM CONNECTED TO THE GARDEN AND DINING ROOM

OPTION 8

In this option, too, the kitchen is relocated to the front of the house with the creation of an open-plan dining area where the existing rear reception room has been opened up. The rear wall of the main section of the house has been removed to make room for a glass-enclosed courtyard. This opens up to give greater connection between the dining area and rear living room. A WC has been tucked in behind the stair, accessed via the link adjacent to the courtyard. The rear living room connects to the garden via sliding, folding doors. To be read in conjunction with First-floor Option 4.

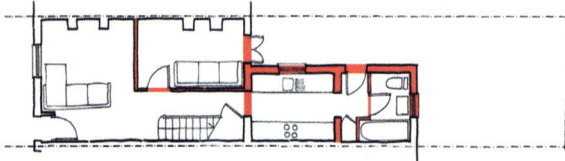

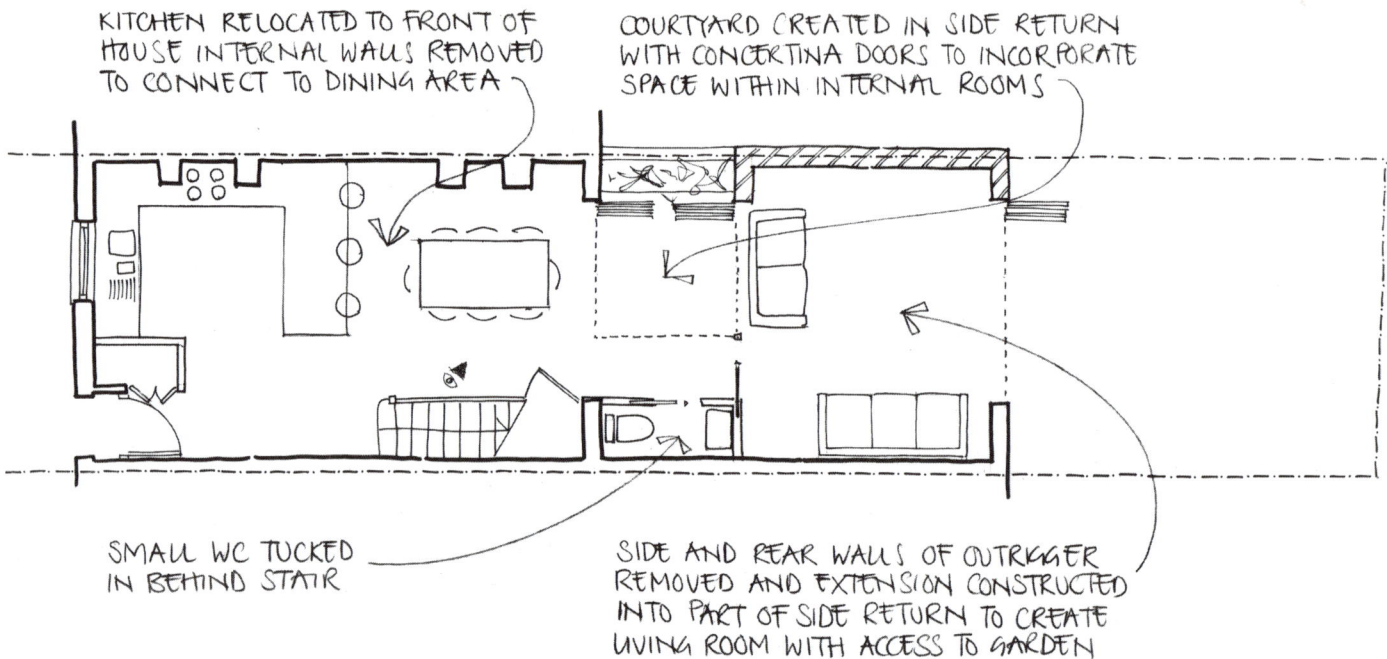

KITCHEN RELOCATED TO FRONT OF HOUSE INTERNAL WALLS REMOVED TO CONNECT TO DINING AREA

COURTYARD CREATED IN SIDE RETURN WITH CONCERTINA DOORS TO INCORPORATE SPACE WITHIN INTERNAL ROOMS

SMALL WC TUCKED IN BEHIND STAIR

SIDE AND REAR WALLS OF OUTRIGGER REMOVED AND EXTENSION CONSTRUCTED INTO PART OF SIDE RETURN TO CREATE LIVING ROOM WITH ACCESS TO GARDEN

Artist's impression of glass-enclosed courtyard.

FIRST FLOOR

In the existing plan for this house the first floor, which accommodates a double and a single bedroom, does not extend over the outrigger.

OPTION 1

If, for some reason, it is not possible to extend over the outrigger at first-floor or loft level, this option provides a double and single bedroom and a shower room by flipping the stair to reduce circulation space at this level. This plan should be read in conjunction with Ground-floor Option 5.

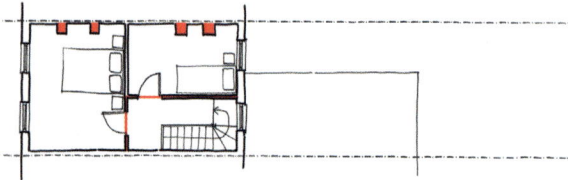

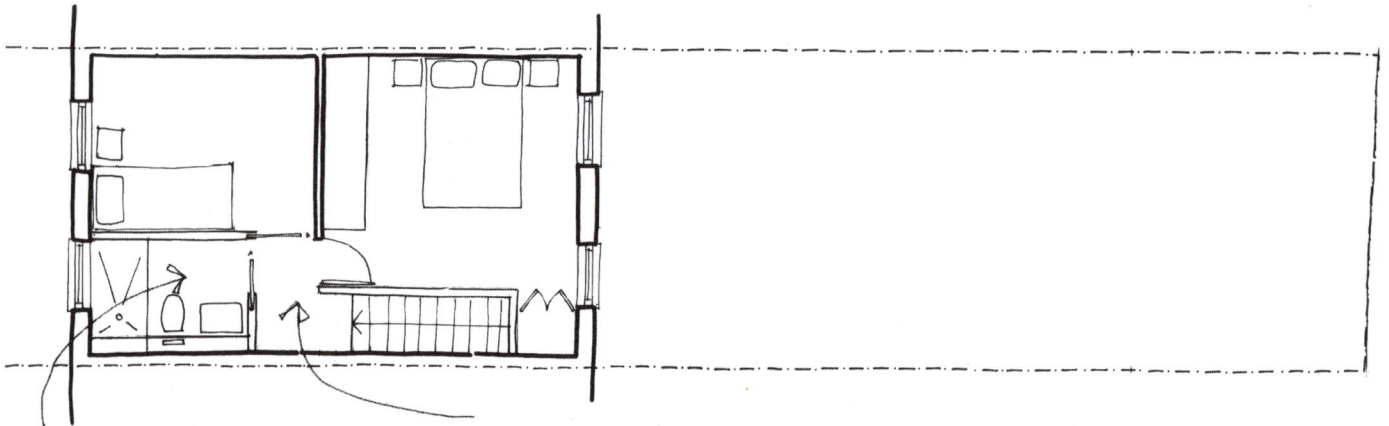

FRONT BEDROOM DIVIDED TO
CREATE A SINGLE BEDROOM
AND SMALL BATHROOM

DIRECTION OF STAIRS REVERSED
TO REDUCE CIRCULATION SPACE

OPTION 2

This is the most traditional arrangement, in which the outrigger can be extended at first-floor level – at least enough to accommodate a new bathroom. This frees up space downstairs purely for the living, dining or kitchen area. The two existing bedrooms remain the same. The loft is not extended in this option.

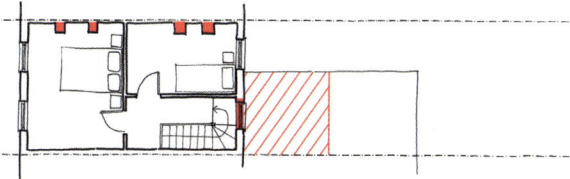

CHIMNEY BREASTS REMOVED FROM BOTH BEDROOMS TO CREATE MORE SPACE

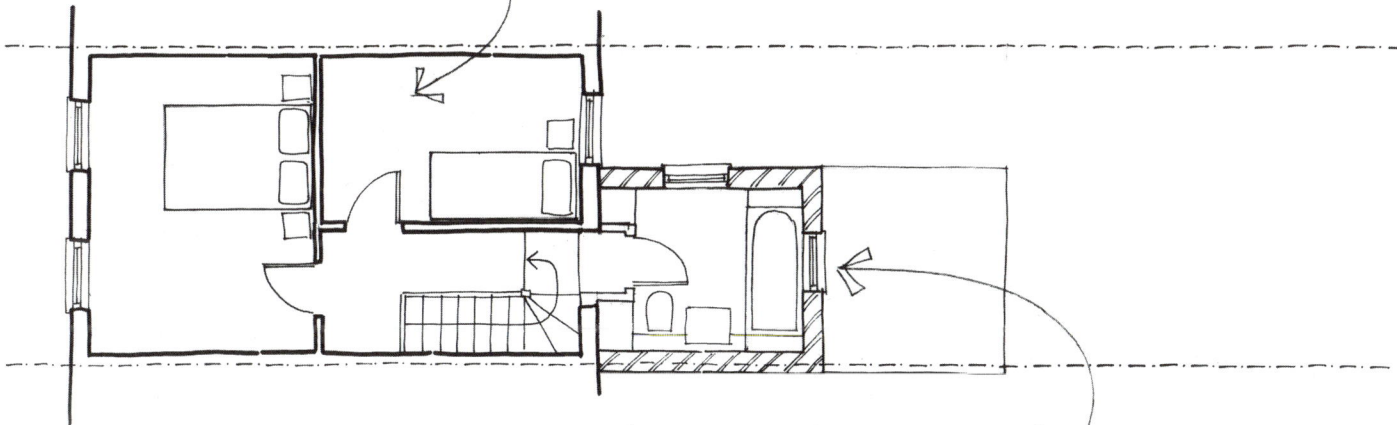

SMALL EXTENSION CONSTRUCTED OVER PART OF EXISTING OUTRIGGER TO CREATE A BATHROOM

OPTION 3

In this option, the entire outrigger has been extended up a storey to create a new bedroom. The existing, smaller bedroom has been carved up to create a bathroom and a dressing room for the larger front bedroom. In this option, the bedroom door has been moved to make room for a new staircase connecting to the loft. The door at the bottom of the staircase enables these stairs to arrive directly into the new loft room, as in Loft Option 1. This plan can also be read in conjunction with Loft Options 2 and 3, removing the door at the foot or the top of the stair.

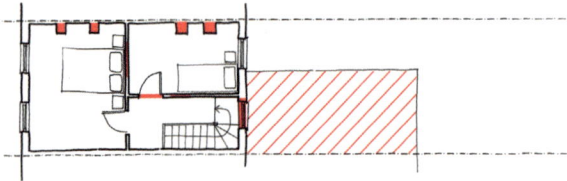

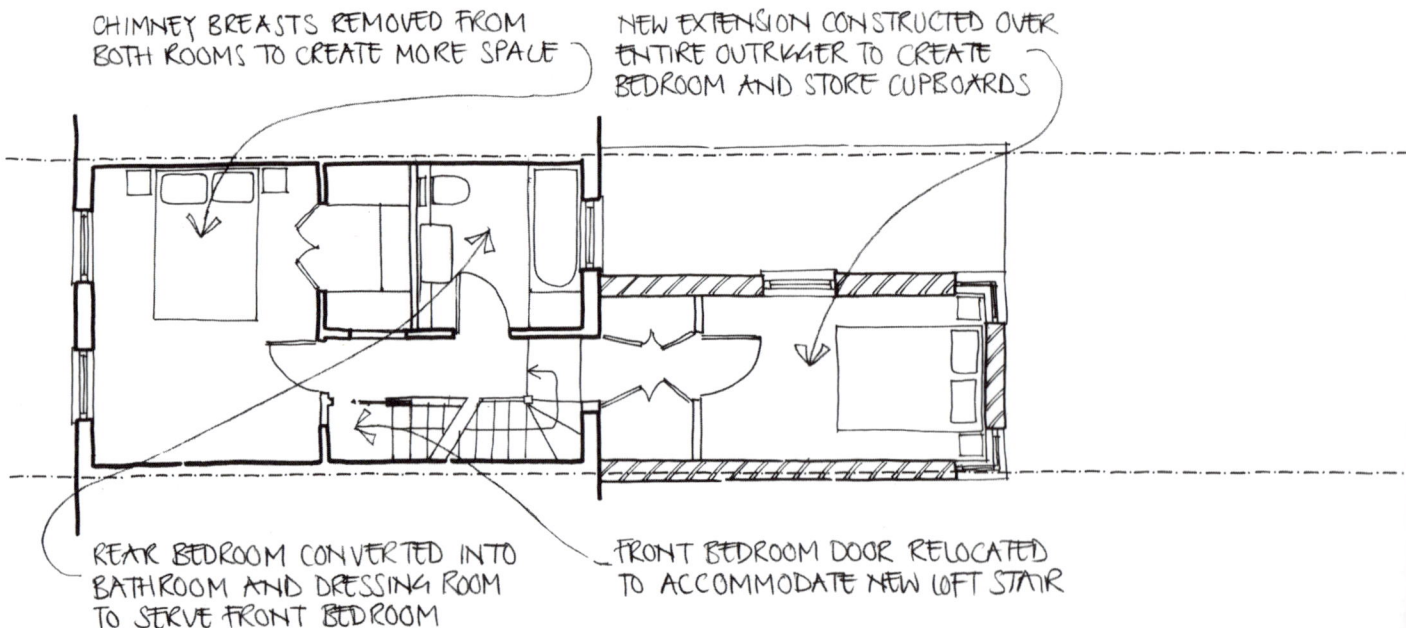

CHIMNEY BREASTS REMOVED FROM BOTH ROOMS TO CREATE MORE SPACE

NEW EXTENSION CONSTRUCTED OVER ENTIRE OUTRIGGER TO CREATE BEDROOM AND STORE CUPBOARDS

REAR BEDROOM CONVERTED INTO BATHROOM AND DRESSING ROOM TO SERVE FRONT BEDROOM

FRONT BEDROOM DOOR RELOCATED TO ACCOMMODATE NEW LOFT STAIR

OPTION 4

This option is to be read in conjunction with Ground-floor Option 8, in which a section of the outrigger has been removed to create a large courtyard area at ground-floor level. A bathroom is created above the rear section of the existing outrigger. The existing bedrooms remain untouched apart from the relocation of the door to the larger bedroom to make space for a new staircase leading to the loft. This staircase is open at the bottom, which means that there should be an enclosed lobby at loft level – as in Loft Options 2 and 3.

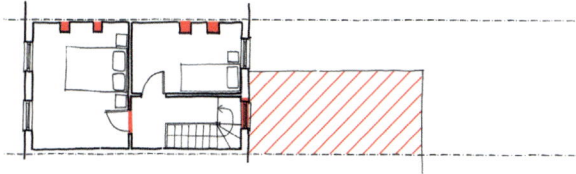

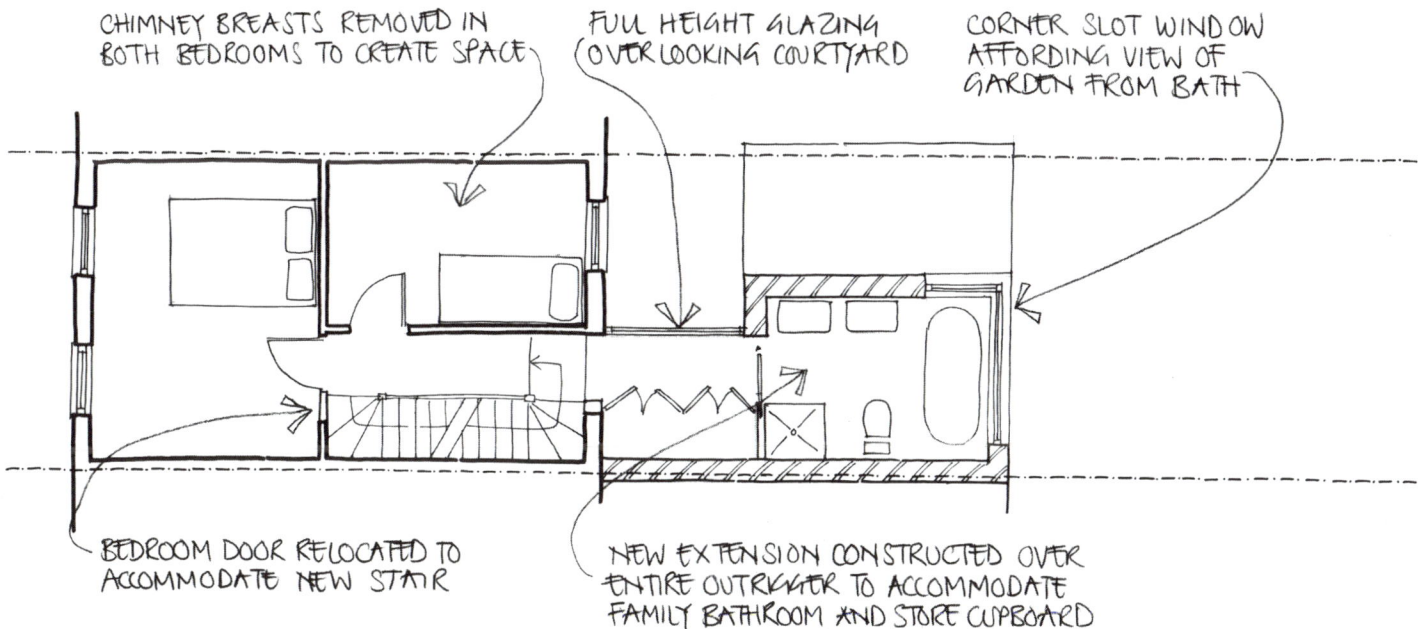

CHIMNEY BREASTS REMOVED IN BOTH BEDROOMS TO CREATE SPACE

FULL HEIGHT GLAZING OVERLOOKING COURTYARD

CORNER SLOT WINDOW AFFORDING VIEW OF GARDEN FROM BATH

BEDROOM DOOR RELOCATED TO ACCOMMODATE NEW STAIR

NEW EXTENSION CONSTRUCTED OVER ENTIRE OUTRIGGER TO ACCOMMODATE FAMILY BATHROOM AND STORE CUPBOARD

LOFT

The loft is being used for storage in the existing property, and is insulated at floor level. If converting the loft, insulation will need to be added to the underside of the roof instead. The floor will also need to be strengthened. This will, as a result, reduce the head height by approximately 20cm.

OPTION 1

This is the simplest option. A full-width dormer extension creates a large, open-plan bedroom with an unobstructed view of the garden through sliding glass doors that open to a Juliet balcony. To create a sense of space, the stairs are open to the room. Therefore, there should be a door at the bottom of the stairs, as in First-floor Option 3.

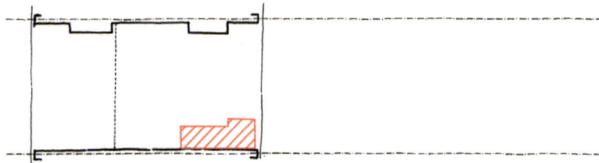

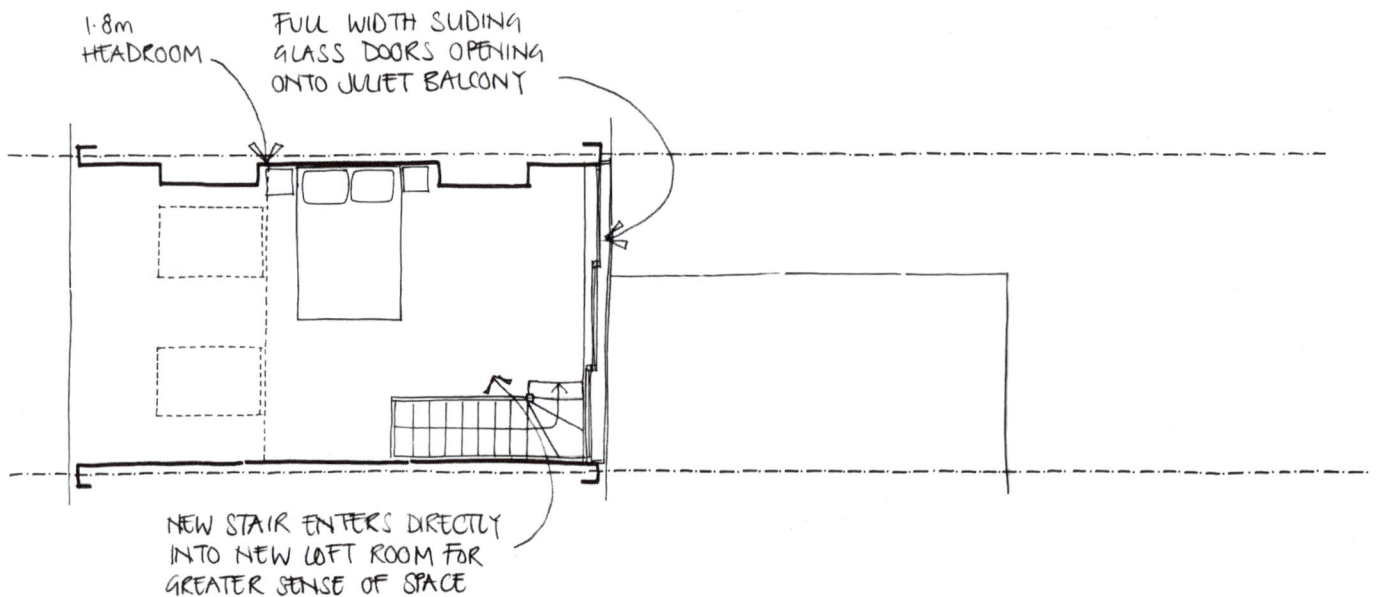

1·8m HEADROOM

FULL WIDTH SLIDING GLASS DOORS OPENING ONTO JULIET BALCONY

NEW STAIR ENTERS DIRECTLY INTO NEW LOFT ROOM FOR GREATER SENSE OF SPACE

OPTION 2

(Based on the Slim House project by Alma-nac)

This option also involves the construction of a full-width rear dormer, but in this instance there is a lobby at the top of the stairs and eaves storage at the front of the house. Skylights inserted into the front pitch of the roof and full-width glazing bring ample light into the room, and afford unobstructed views to the rear. As there is a door at the top of the stairs, no door is required at the bottom, as shown in First-floor Option 4.

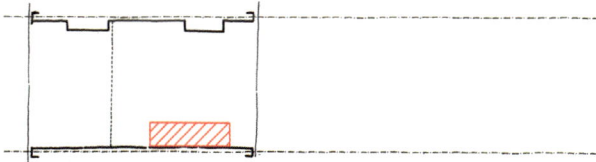

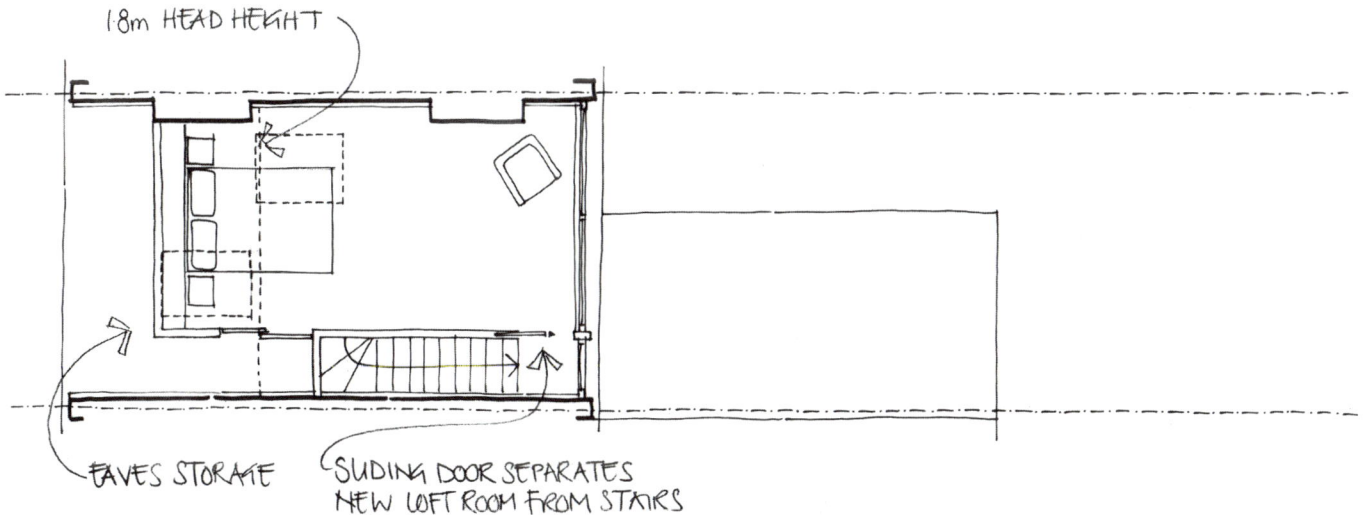

1.8m HEAD HEIGHT

EAVES STORAGE

SLIDING DOOR SEPARATES NEW LOFT ROOM FROM STAIRS

Slim House by Alma-nac, Clapham, London, 2012.
Carefully positioned skylights add interest.

OPTION 3

In this option, there is an en-suite positioned towards the front of the house with adjacent storage. The en-suite is relatively narrow, which gives more space for the bedroom. Again, as there is a door at the top of the stairs, this option should be read in conjunction with First-floor Option 4.

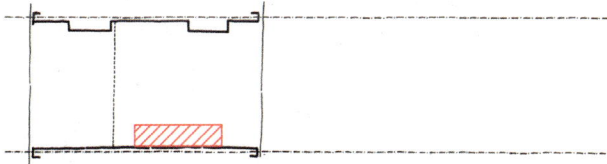

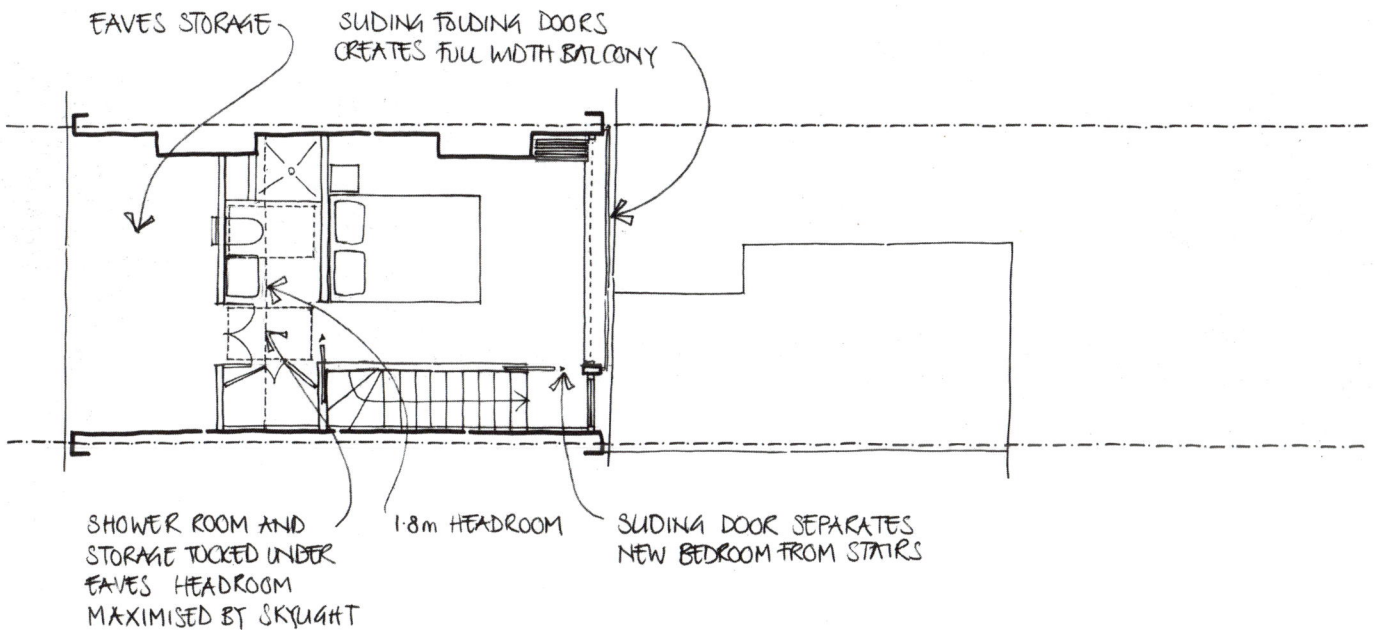

EAVES STORAGE

SLIDING FOLDING DOORS
CREATES FULL WIDTH BALCONY

SHOWER ROOM AND
STORAGE TUCKED UNDER
EAVES HEADROOM
MAXIMISED BY SKYLIGHT

1.8m HEADROOM

SLIDING DOOR SEPARATES
NEW BEDROOM FROM STAIRS

THE THREE UP THREE DOWN

This case study illustrates a typical two-storey, three-bedroomed terraced house. It is built on a 4.9m plot and is not split level, but has a garden that slopes up from the rear of the house.

GROUND FLOOR

In the existing plan, the front door opens into a hallway through which the front and rear reception rooms are accessed. It leads to the stairs serving the first floor and to the existing kitchen, which is located in the outrigger.

OPTION 1

*(Based on the Lacy Brick project
by Pamphilon Architects)*

This option retains much of the existing structure, which keeps costs down. The garden door has been blocked up to free up space for kitchen units. The chimneybreast has been removed and the kitchen sink has been slotted into the existing bay window, raising the sill level, to make the most of the available space.

A section of the rear wall has been removed and a corner window seat has been designed to match the depth of the existing outbuilding, providing space efficient seating for the dining area. The door to the outbuilding has been relocated to allow direct access from the kitchen diner. This can be used as storage or a small utility room. Locating the garden door between the kitchen and the dining areas minimizes circulation space, enabling the whole of the rear of the outrigger to be used as a dining area. As the garden steps up at the rear of the house, positioning a window seat, which will be at a similar height to the garden, in this location rather than a door eliminates the need to excavate to provide level access.

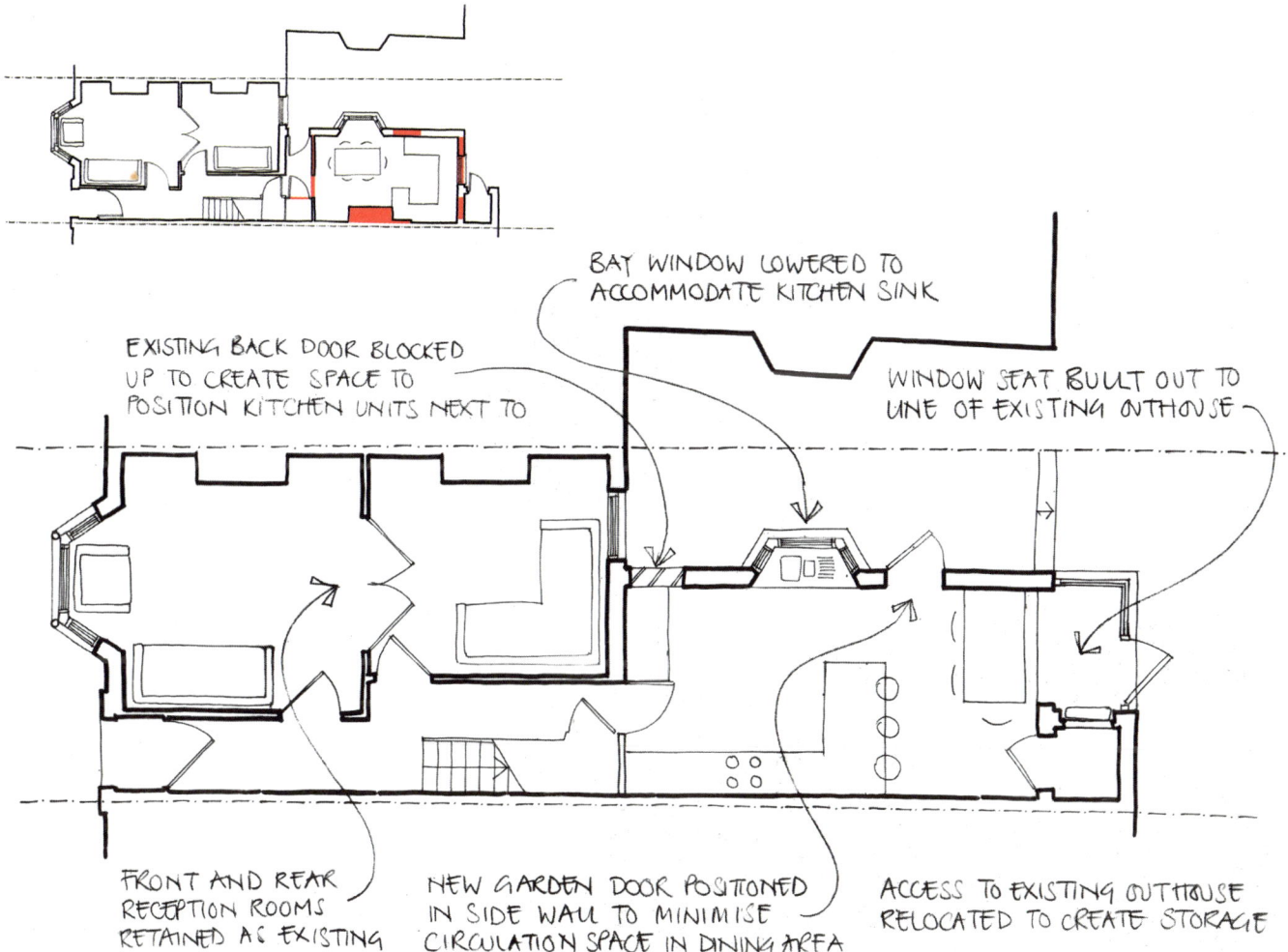

BAY WINDOW LOWERED TO ACCOMMODATE KITCHEN SINK

EXISTING BACK DOOR BLOCKED UP TO CREATE SPACE TO POSITION KITCHEN UNITS NEXT TO

WINDOW SEAT BUILT OUT TO LINE OF EXISTING OUTHOUSE

FRONT AND REAR RECEPTION ROOMS RETAINED AS EXISTING

NEW GARDEN DOOR POSITIONED IN SIDE WALL TO MINIMISE CIRCULATION SPACE IN DINING AREA

ACCESS TO EXISTING OUTHOUSE RELOCATED TO CREATE STORAGE

Lacy Brick by Pamphilon Architects, Harringay, London, 2016. Window seat makes the most of the view.

OPTION 2
(As depicted in section B)

This option, again, retains much of the existing structure and shows the existing garden door blocked up below work surface with a window above to maximize light. The central section of the chimneybreast has been removed, retaining the sides to reduce costs. A shelf positioned at sill level in the bay can be used to create a herb garden without replacing the window. A small WC has been slotted in under the stair.

The rear of the outrigger has been designed to accommodate the dining area. Removing the existing outhouse enlarges the space available for the dining area. The garden door is moved to between the kitchen and dining area and a window seat provides space efficient seating with a view to the garden. This window could be extended up vertically, as shown in First-floor Options 2 and 4.

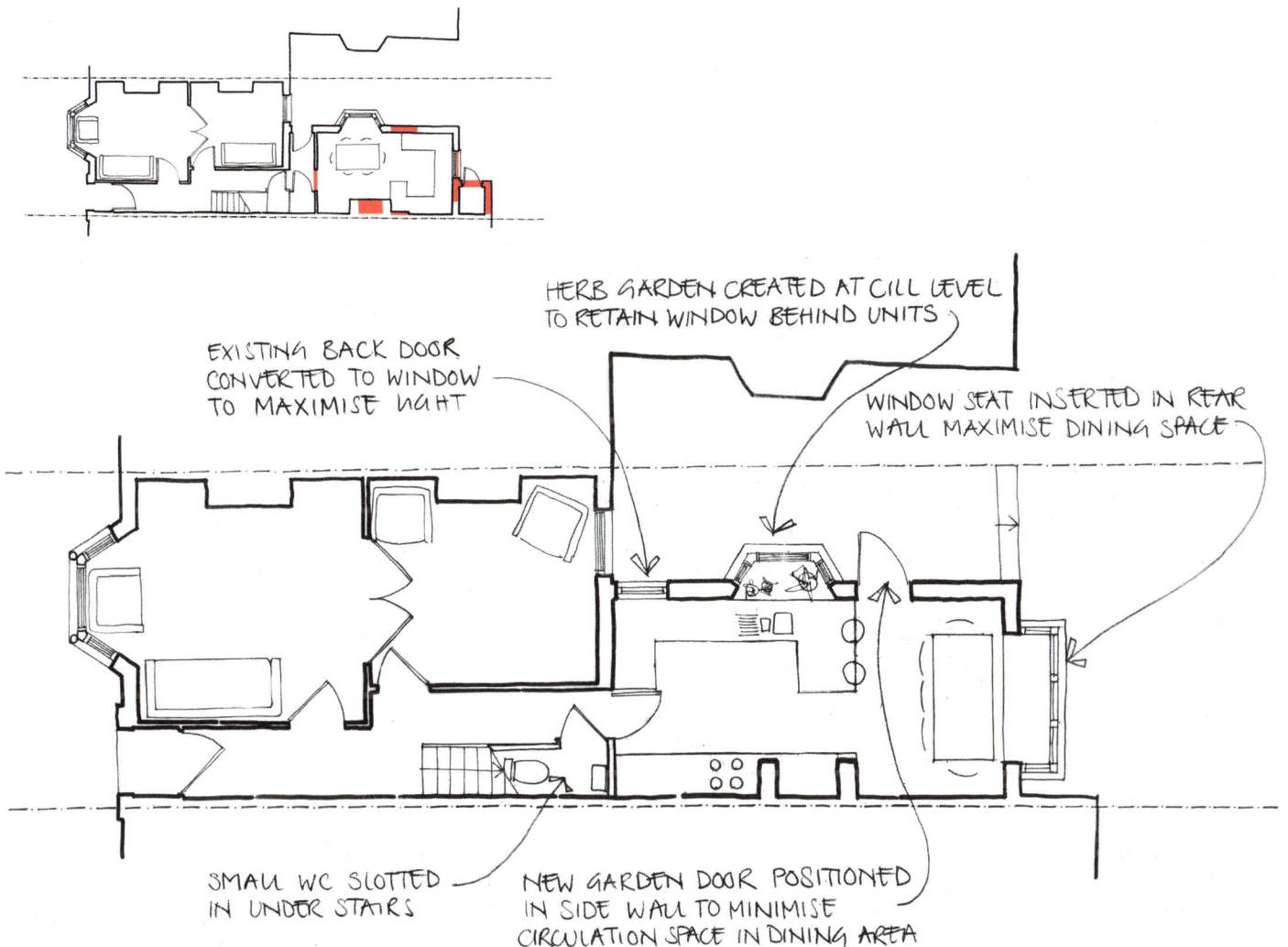

HERB GARDEN CREATED AT CILL LEVEL
TO RETAIN WINDOW BEHIND UNITS

EXISTING BACK DOOR
CONVERTED TO WINDOW
TO MAXIMISE LIGHT

WINDOW SEAT INSERTED IN REAR
WALL MAXIMISE DINING SPACE

SMALL WC SLOTTED
IN UNDER STAIRS

NEW GARDEN DOOR POSITIONED
IN SIDE WALL TO MINIMISE
CIRCULATION SPACE IN DINING AREA

OPTION 3
(As depicted in Section A)

The dividing wall between front and rear reception rooms has been removed to create a single, large reception room. A door replaces the window of the rear reception room, providing direct access to the side return. A small WC has been slotted in under the stairs.

As with the previous two options, most of the outrigger has been retained. Its rear wall, including the existing outhouse, has been removed to make way for a full-width window seat. Again, the dining area has been positioned at the far end of the outrigger and the garden door has been relocated to reduce circulation space.

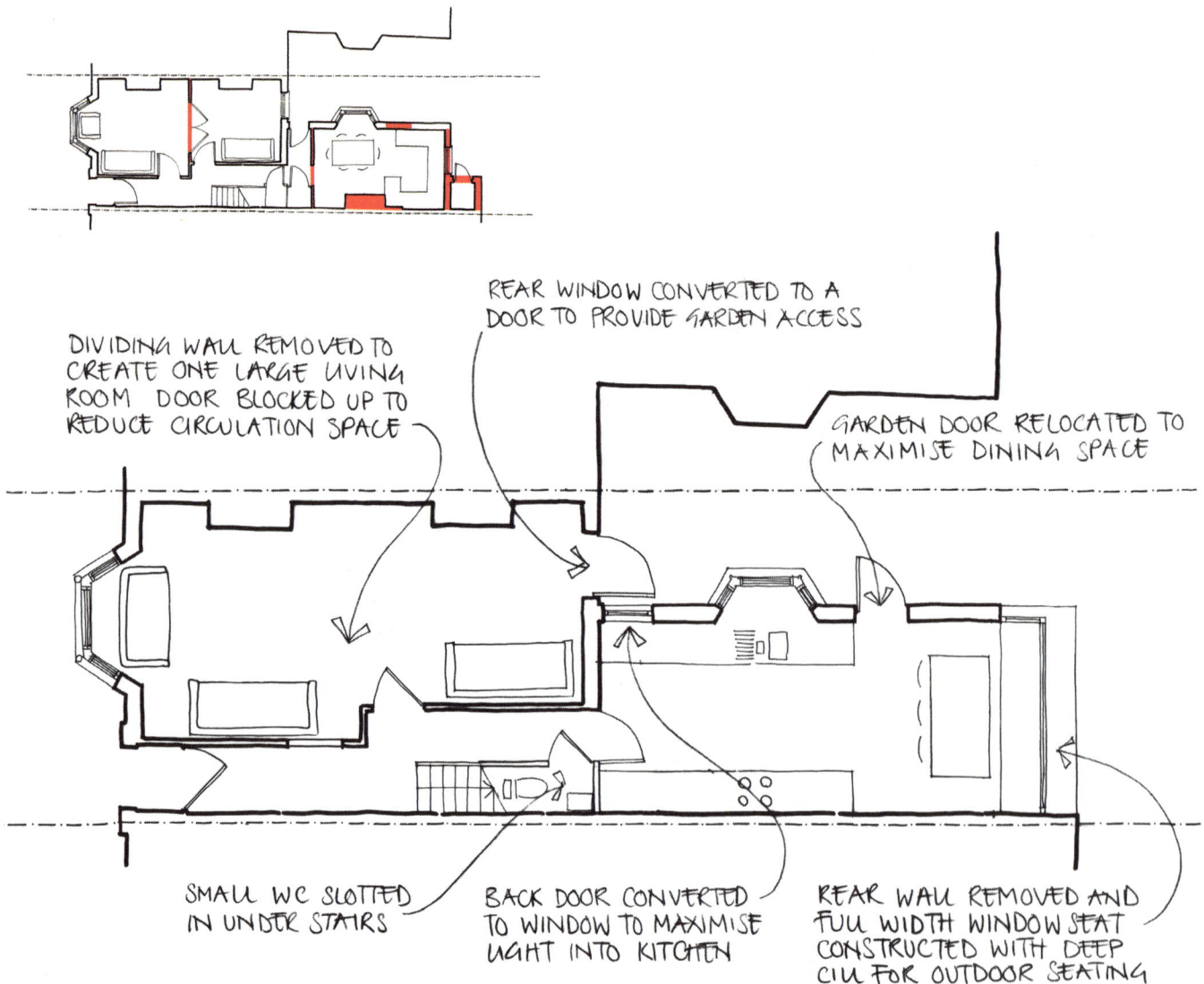

REAR WINDOW CONVERTED TO A DOOR TO PROVIDE GARDEN ACCESS

DIVIDING WALL REMOVED TO CREATE ONE LARGE LIVING ROOM DOOR BLOCKED UP TO REDUCE CIRCULATION SPACE

GARDEN DOOR RELOCATED TO MAXIMISE DINING SPACE

SMALL WC SLOTTED IN UNDER STAIRS

BACK DOOR CONVERTED TO WINDOW TO MAXIMISE LIGHT INTO KITCHEN

REAR WALL REMOVED AND FULL WIDTH WINDOW SEAT CONSTRUCTED WITH DEEP CILL FOR OUTDOOR SEATING

Sink sits on top of worktop, which is at cill height to retain existing window. Lowering the counter around the sink avoids the need to raise the cill.

A window has been inserted where the garden door was, and the kitchen work surface slots into the bay window. To achieve this, the cill must be raised or a Belfast–type sink placed on a lowered countertop in order to retain the original cill height, as shown in the photograph. The chimneybreast has been removed completely.

OPTION 4

(Based on the Hatcham Park Road project by Green & Teggin Architects)

The main part of the house remains unchanged, to retain separate uses for the two existing reception rooms.

This option removes the external side wall of the outrigger at ground-floor level and extends fully into the side return. However, it retains the rear-reception-room window, allowing separate use of that room without making it a 'corridor' through to the new extension. A glass roof over the extension provides light to the dining area and rear reception room. As the house is only 4.9m wide,

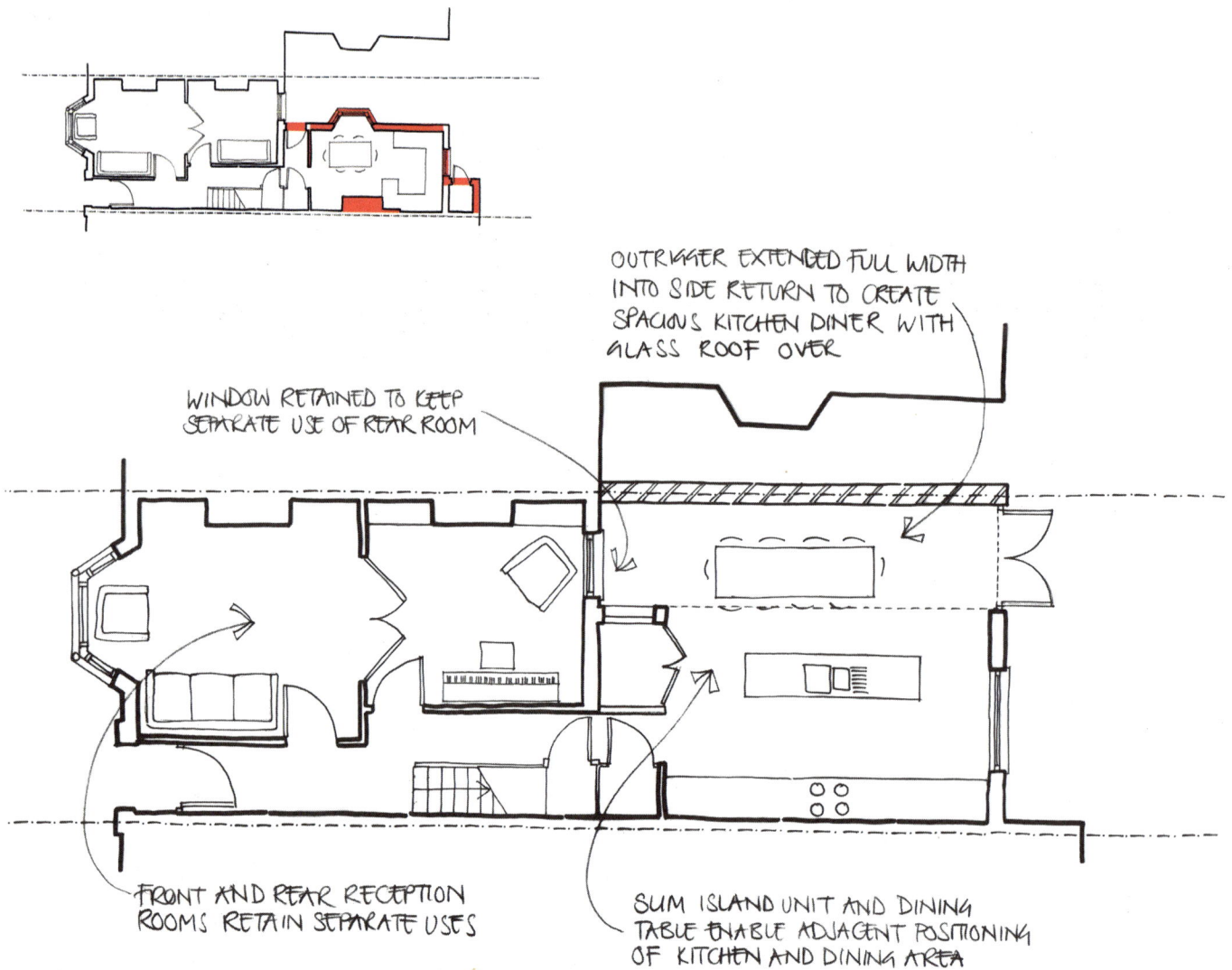

OUTRIGGER EXTENDED FULL WIDTH INTO SIDE RETURN TO CREATE SPACIOUS KITCHEN DINER WITH GLASS ROOF OVER

WINDOW RETAINED TO KEEP SEPARATE USE OF REAR ROOM

FRONT AND REAR RECEPTION ROOMS RETAIN SEPARATE USES

SLIM ISLAND UNIT AND DINING TABLE ENABLE ADJACENT POSITIONING OF KITCHEN AND DINING AREA

Hatcham Park Road by Green & Teggin Architects,
Lewisham, London, 2016. Slim island unit and dining
table facilitate this arrangement.

it is difficult to accommodate an island unit and dining-room table adjacent to each other. Although tight, this has been achieved with a narrow island unit and a narrow table, using the 1.2m minimum advisable distance between kitchen units. Another option would be to install a bench to the rear of the island unit, moving the dining table nearer the centre of the room to create more circulation space beside the new party wall.

Hatcham Park Road by Green & Teggin Architects, Lewisham, London, 2016. Existing window retained to reduce circulation space.

OPTION 5

In this option, the main section of the house remains mostly unchanged. A small WC is slotted underneath the stairs and the rear window has been removed to create a connection to the new side-return extension.

Much of the side wall of the outrigger has been removed at ground-floor level, but some sections have been retained to minimise structural work. A plot width of around 6m would be required to comfortably accommodate a kitchen island and a dining table in the side return. So, in this option the dining area is at the rear of the property, with a window seat providing space-efficient dining seating. Although this option does create a great sense of space, much of the space created is for circulation.

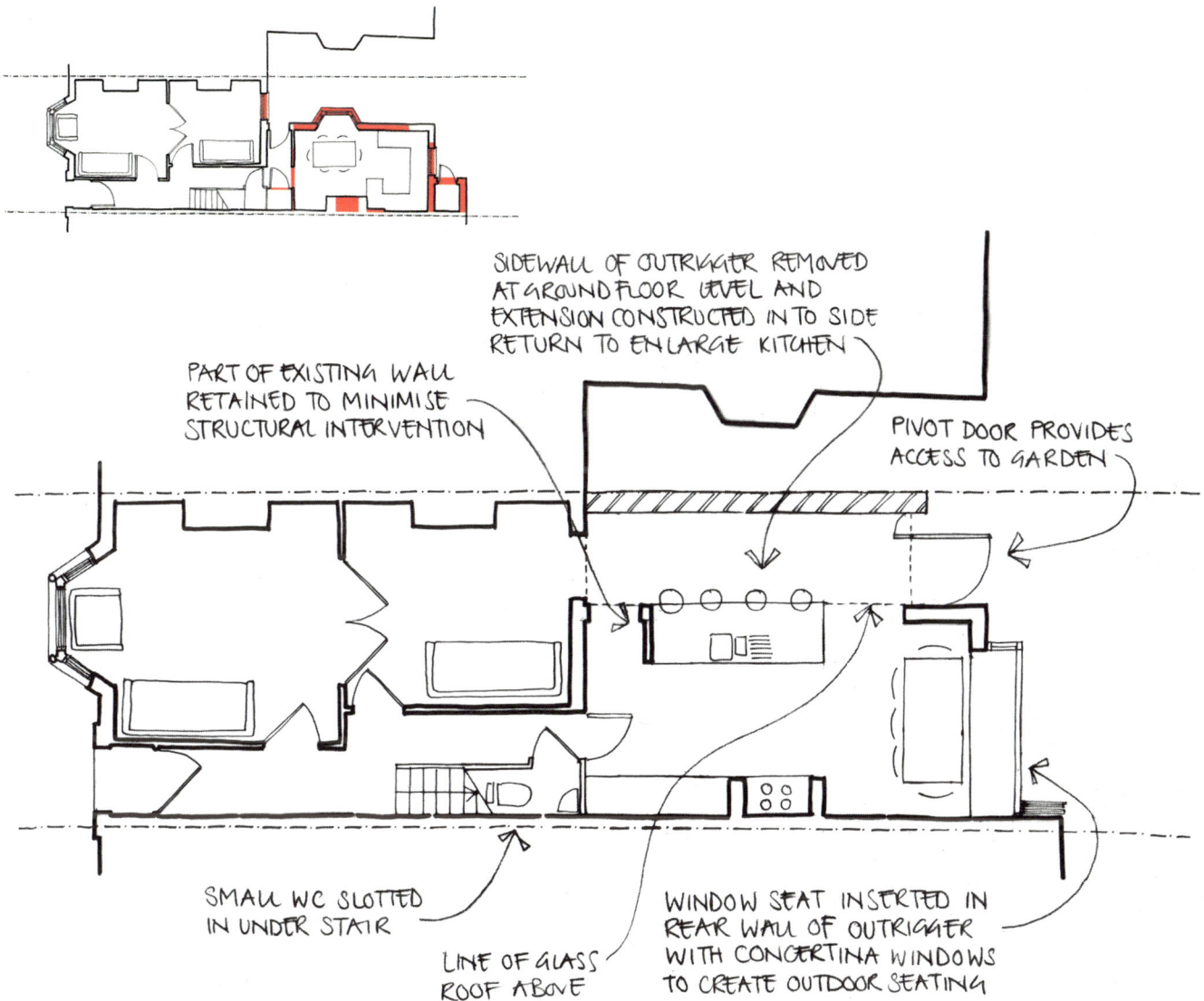

SIDEWALL OF OUTRIGGER REMOVED AT GROUND FLOOR LEVEL AND EXTENSION CONSTRUCTED INTO SIDE RETURN TO ENLARGE KITCHEN

PART OF EXISTING WALL RETAINED TO MINIMISE STRUCTURAL INTERVENTION

PIVOT DOOR PROVIDES ACCESS TO GARDEN

SMALL WC SLOTTED IN UNDER STAIR

LINE OF GLASS ROOF ABOVE

WINDOW SEAT INSERTED IN REAR WALL OF OUTRIGGER WITH CONCERTINA WINDOWS TO CREATE OUTDOOR SEATING

OPTION 6

(Based on the Hatcham Park
Conservation Area project
by Hartslane Studios)

This is a very open-plan option. Not only is the wall between the front and rear reception rooms removed but also much of the rear wall connecting the main section of the house to the outrigger, which has been extended into the side return with a glass roof over. To reduce circulation space, the existing route to the outrigger has been used to create a coat cupboard and WC/utility room. The kitchen is then accessed solely through the rear reception room. The rear wall of the outrigger remains intact to reduce structural alterations and retain some of the property's original charm. This enlarged outrigger accommodates a full-width kitchen/diner.

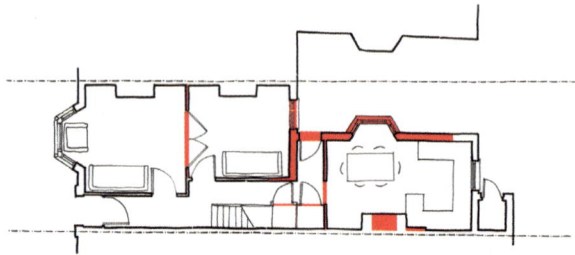

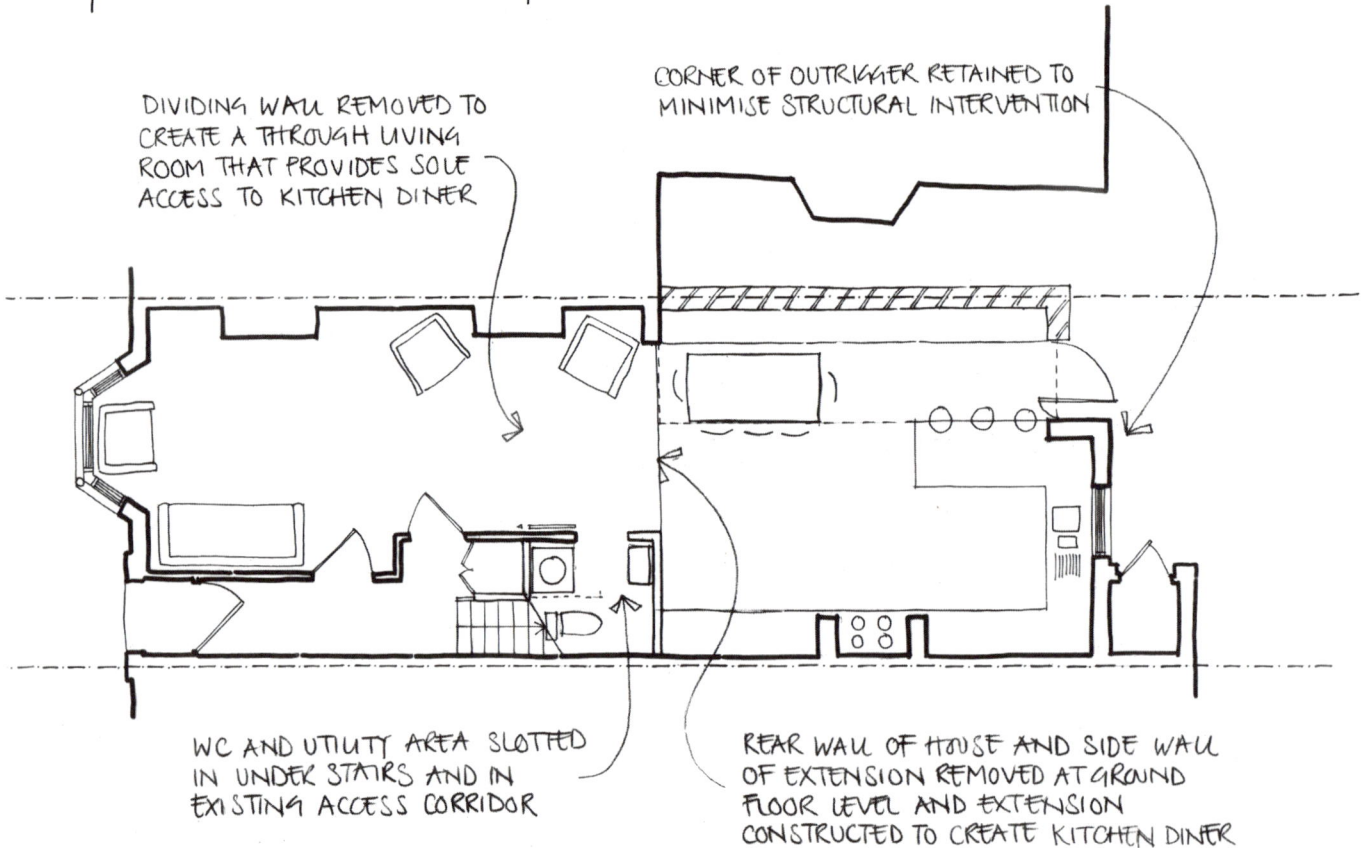

DIVIDING WALL REMOVED TO CREATE A THROUGH LIVING ROOM THAT PROVIDES SOLE ACCESS TO KITCHEN DINER

CORNER OF OUTRIGGER RETAINED TO MINIMISE STRUCTURAL INTERVENTION

WC AND UTILITY AREA SLOTTED IN UNDER STAIRS AND IN EXISTING ACCESS CORRIDOR

REAR WALL OF HOUSE AND SIDE WALL OF EXTENSION REMOVED AT GROUND FLOOR LEVEL AND EXTENSION CONSTRUCTED TO CREATE KITCHEN DINER

Hatcham Park Conservation Area project by
Hartslane Studios, Lewisham, London, 2011. Dining
area demarcated by glass roof. Image mirrored to
reflect plan.

Hatcham Park Conservation Area project by
Hartslane Studios, Lewisham, London, 2011. Rear
reception room extended into circulation space.
Image mirrored to reflect plan.

OPTION 7

In this option, the kitchen has been relocated to the rear reception room, and the front reception room now accommodates the dining room. A section of this room has been used to create storage for the dining room and a coat cupboard accessed from the entrance hall. A WC has been slotted under the stairs.

All walls of the outrigger have been removed at ground-floor level to create a full-width living room that extends fully into the side return. A small study area has been created overlooking the garden. The window serving this study area continues up to meet the new glass roof, the width of the original side return.

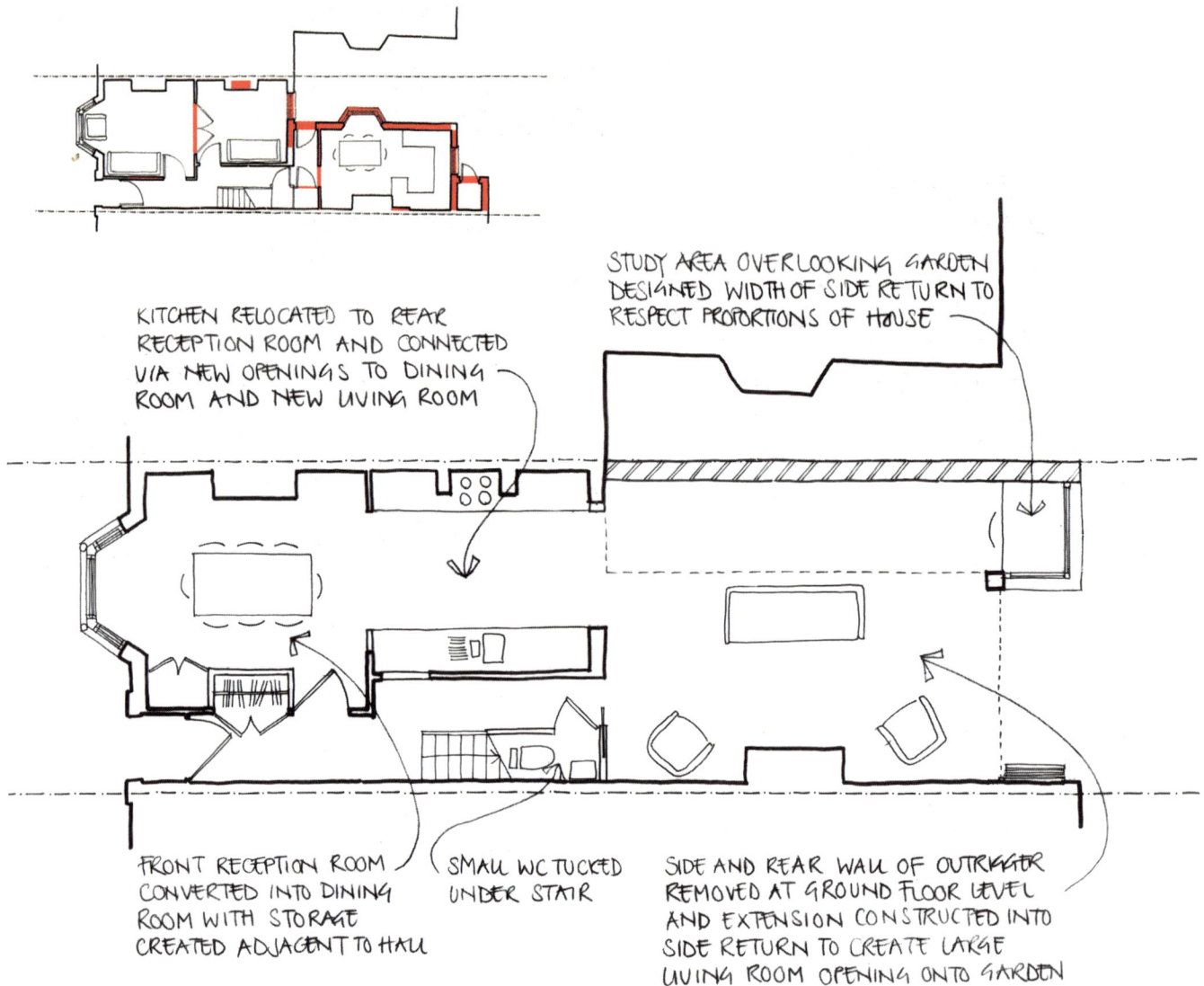

STUDY AREA OVERLOOKING GARDEN DESIGNED WIDTH OF SIDE RETURN TO RESPECT PROPORTIONS OF HOUSE

KITCHEN RELOCATED TO REAR RECEPTION ROOM AND CONNECTED VIA NEW OPENINGS TO DINING ROOM AND NEW LIVING ROOM

FRONT RECEPTION ROOM CONVERTED INTO DINING ROOM WITH STORAGE CREATED ADJACENT TO HALL

SMALL WC TUCKED UNDER STAIR

SIDE AND REAR WALL OF OUTRIGGER REMOVED AT GROUND FLOOR LEVEL AND EXTENSION CONSTRUCTED INTO SIDE RETURN TO CREATE LARGE LIVING ROOM OPENING ONTO GARDEN

Artist's impression of view from kitchen into new
rear extension.

OPTION 8

(Based on the Tooting Contemporaine project by Yard Architects)

This option is similar to that shown in Ground-floor Option 7, with the dining area at the front of the house and the kitchen relocated to the rear reception room. Some space has been carved out of this room to create storage space, accessed from the hall, and a WC has been slotted under the stairs.

The outrigger, which has been extended into the side return, has been used to accommodate a large reception room with direct access to the garden via slightly projecting, sliding glass doors. A glazed slot is shown at the junction of the outrigger and the main section of the house. This would not be possible if the outrigger extended up beyond ground-floor level.

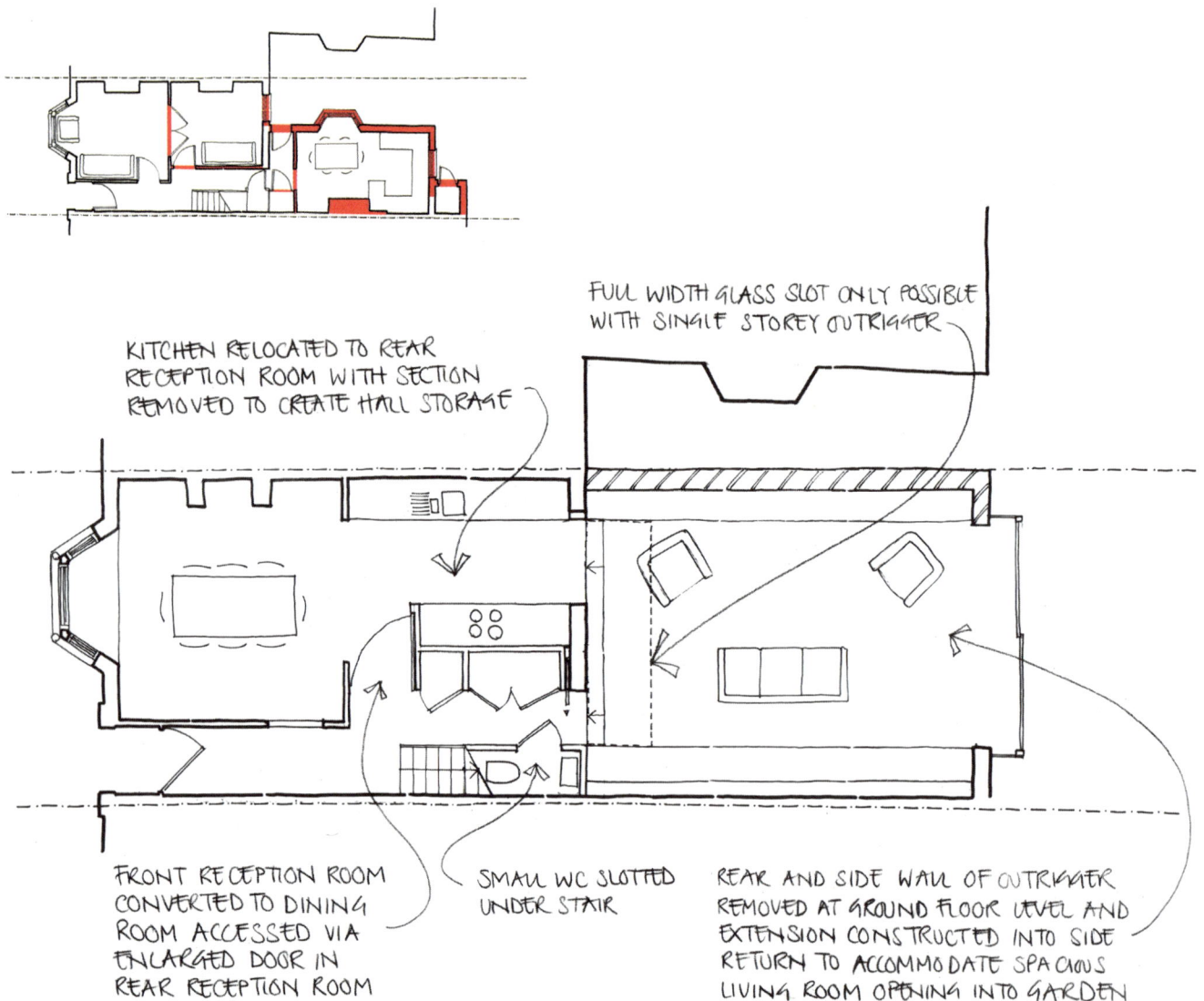

KITCHEN RELOCATED TO REAR
RECEPTION ROOM WITH SECTION
REMOVED TO CREATE HALL STORAGE

FULL WIDTH GLASS SLOT ONLY POSSIBLE
WITH SINGLE STOREY OUTRIGGER

FRONT RECEPTION ROOM
CONVERTED TO DINING
ROOM ACCESSED VIA
ENLARGED DOOR IN
REAR RECEPTION ROOM

SMALL WC SLOTTED
UNDER STAIR

REAR AND SIDE WALL OF OUTRIGGER
REMOVED AT GROUND FLOOR LEVEL AND
EXTENSION CONSTRUCTED INTO SIDE
RETURN TO ACCOMMODATE SPACIOUS
LIVING ROOM OPENING INTO GARDEN

Tooting Contemporaine by Yard Architects,
Wandsworth, London, 2018. View from galley
kitchen into living room.

Tooting Contemporaine by Yard Architects,
Wandsworth, London, 2018. Living room with view
through kitchen to dining room.

OPTION 9

(Based on the Burrard House project by Paul Archer Design)

The front reception room is extended part way into the rear reception room in this option. The remaining portion of the rear reception room accommodates a downstairs WC, utility cupboard and part of the kitchen.

Most of the rear walls have been removed at ground-floor level and the side return has been fully extended to accommodate a large family kitchen/ diner/living room. A glass roof over the extension maximises light levels into the rear room.

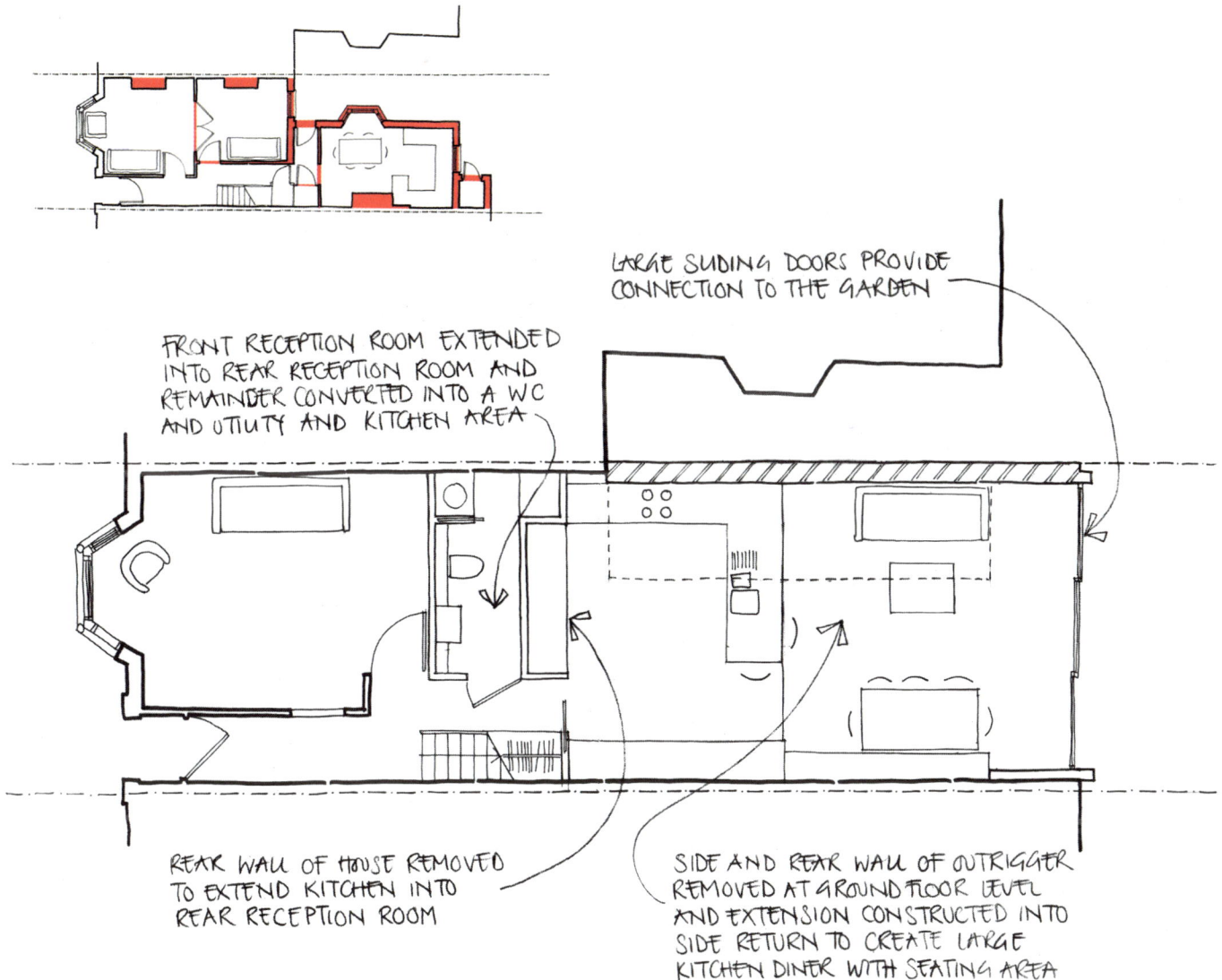

LARGE SLIDING DOORS PROVIDE CONNECTION TO THE GARDEN

FRONT RECEPTION ROOM EXTENDED INTO REAR RECEPTION ROOM AND REMAINDER CONVERTED INTO A WC AND UTILITY AND KITCHEN AREA

REAR WALL OF HOUSE REMOVED TO EXTEND KITCHEN INTO REAR RECEPTION ROOM

SIDE AND REAR WALL OF OUTRIGGER REMOVED AT GROUND FLOOR LEVEL AND EXTENSION CONSTRUCTED INTO SIDE RETURN TO CREATE LARGE KITCHEN DINER WITH SEATING AREA

Burrard House by Paul Archer Design, Camden,
London, 2017. Kitchen unit faces into dining room
and garden. Burrard House by Paul Archer Design,
Camden, London, 2017. Kitchen unit faces into
dining room and garden.

Burrard House by Paul Archer Design, Camden,
London, 2017. Glass roof over extension creates a
bright room.

OPTION 10

(Based on the Gellatly Road project by Delve Architects)

Most of the outrigger has been removed at ground-floor level in this option, including the chimneybreast. However, a column remains at the corner of the existing footprint to reduce the amount of new structure required. This space accommodates a spacious kitchen/diner with room for a small seating area.

The existing entrance to the outrigger has been blocked off to make space for a WC. Access to the kitchen/diner will be via the rear reception room. A section of the rear reception room has been used to create a cloak cupboard accessed from the original corridor. The remainder of this room is shown here as a study. The door to the front reception room has also been blocked off to make more space for furniture, meaning that this room must now also be accessed via the rear reception room.

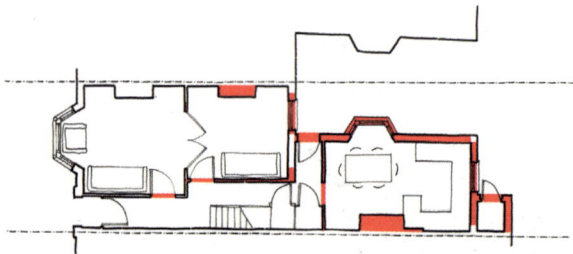

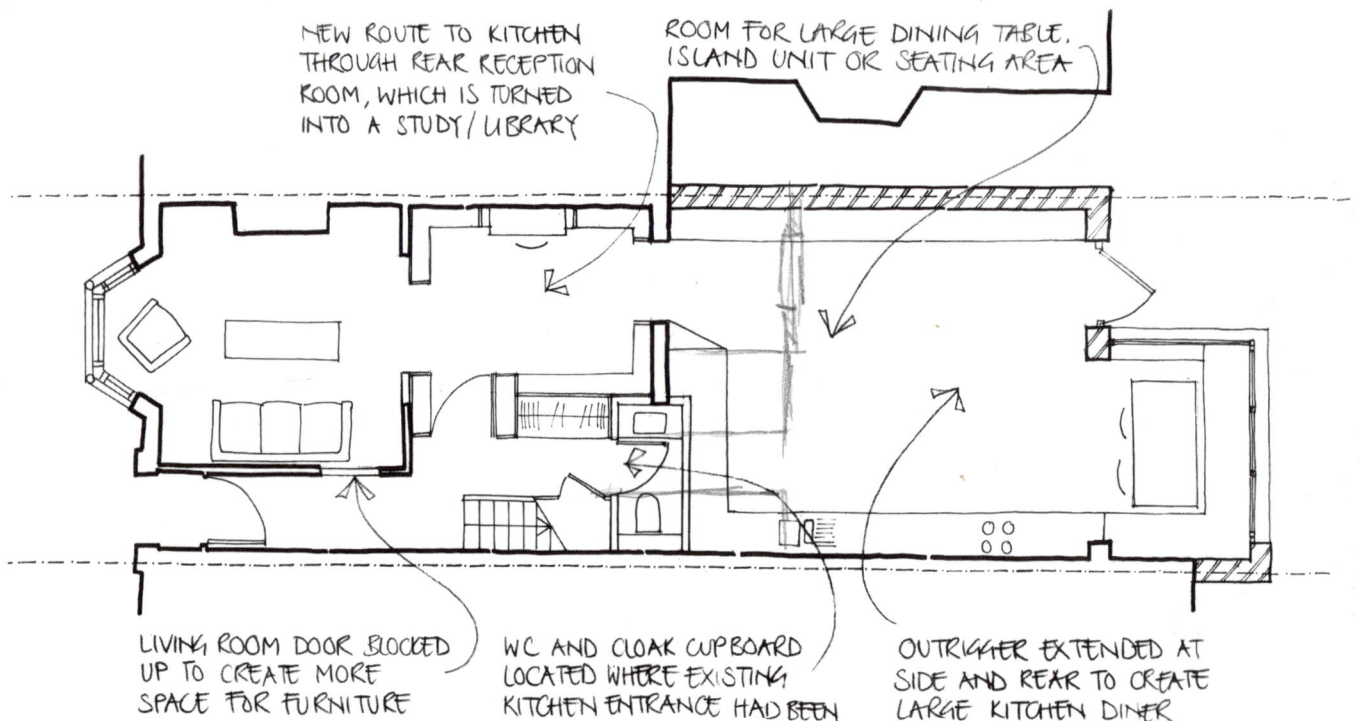

NEW ROUTE TO KITCHEN THROUGH REAR RECEPTION ROOM, WHICH IS TURNED INTO A STUDY/LIBRARY

ROOM FOR LARGE DINING TABLE, ISLAND UNIT OR SEATING AREA

LIVING ROOM DOOR BLOCKED UP TO CREATE MORE SPACE FOR FURNITURE

WC AND CLOAK CUPBOARD LOCATED WHERE EXISTING KITCHEN ENTRANCE HAD BEEN

OUTRIGGER EXTENDED AT SIDE AND REAR TO CREATE LARGE KITCHEN DINER

Gellatly Road by Delve Architects, Brockley, London, 2019. View out from kitchen into garden. Image mirrored to reflect plan.

Gellatly Road by Delve Architects, Brockley, 2019. View through doorway from study area. Image mirrored to reflect plan.

Gellatly Road by Delve Architects, Brockley, 2019.
Ply shelving add a modern layer to the traditional
Victorian style. Image mirrored to reflect plan.

FIRST FLOOR

There are three double bedrooms on the first floor, and a bathroom accessed via the rear bedroom within the outrigger.

OPTION 1

The front two rooms remain largely unchanged, except for a slight relocation of the front bedroom door to make space to insert a stair to access a loft room. This option shows the most common way of rearranging the rear of the first floor to avoid walking through a bedroom to reach the bathroom. A small bathroom is created off a corridor that accesses a double bedroom at the very back of the outrigger. The existing side window is blocked up, and a new one inserted to serve the bathroom.

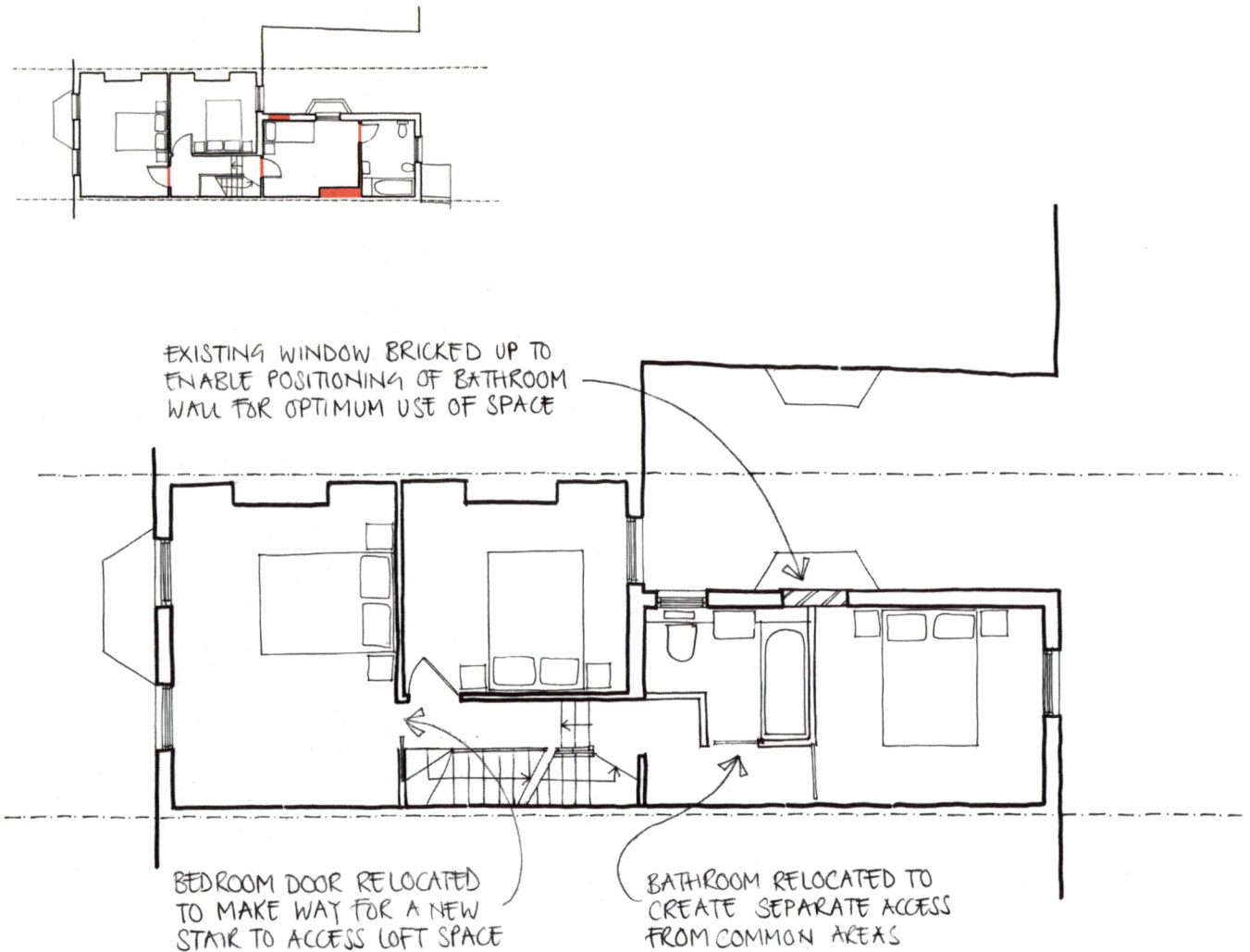

EXISTING WINDOW BRICKED UP TO ENABLE POSITIONING OF BATHROOM WALL FOR OPTIMUM USE OF SPACE

BEDROOM DOOR RELOCATED TO MAKE WAY FOR A NEW STAIR TO ACCESS LOFT SPACE

BATHROOM RELOCATED TO CREATE SEPARATE ACCESS FROM COMMON AREAS

OPTION 2
(As depicted in Section B)

As with First-floor Option 1, the front two bedrooms remain untouched, a new loft stair has been inserted and the bathroom has been relocated off the corridor that accesses a back bedroom within the outrigger.

However, the stairs have been rearranged to enable linear access to the outrigger. This reduces circulation space and creates enough room for a cupboard at the top of the stairs. The bathroom is also larger in this option, incorporating the existing window, which reduces the space available for the rear bedroom. However, a square bay is shown, which could be a continuation of the window seat shown in Ground-floor Option 2, to increase the space available to accommodate a double bed.

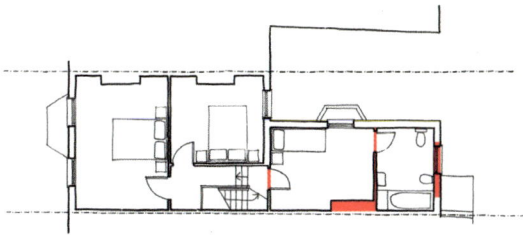

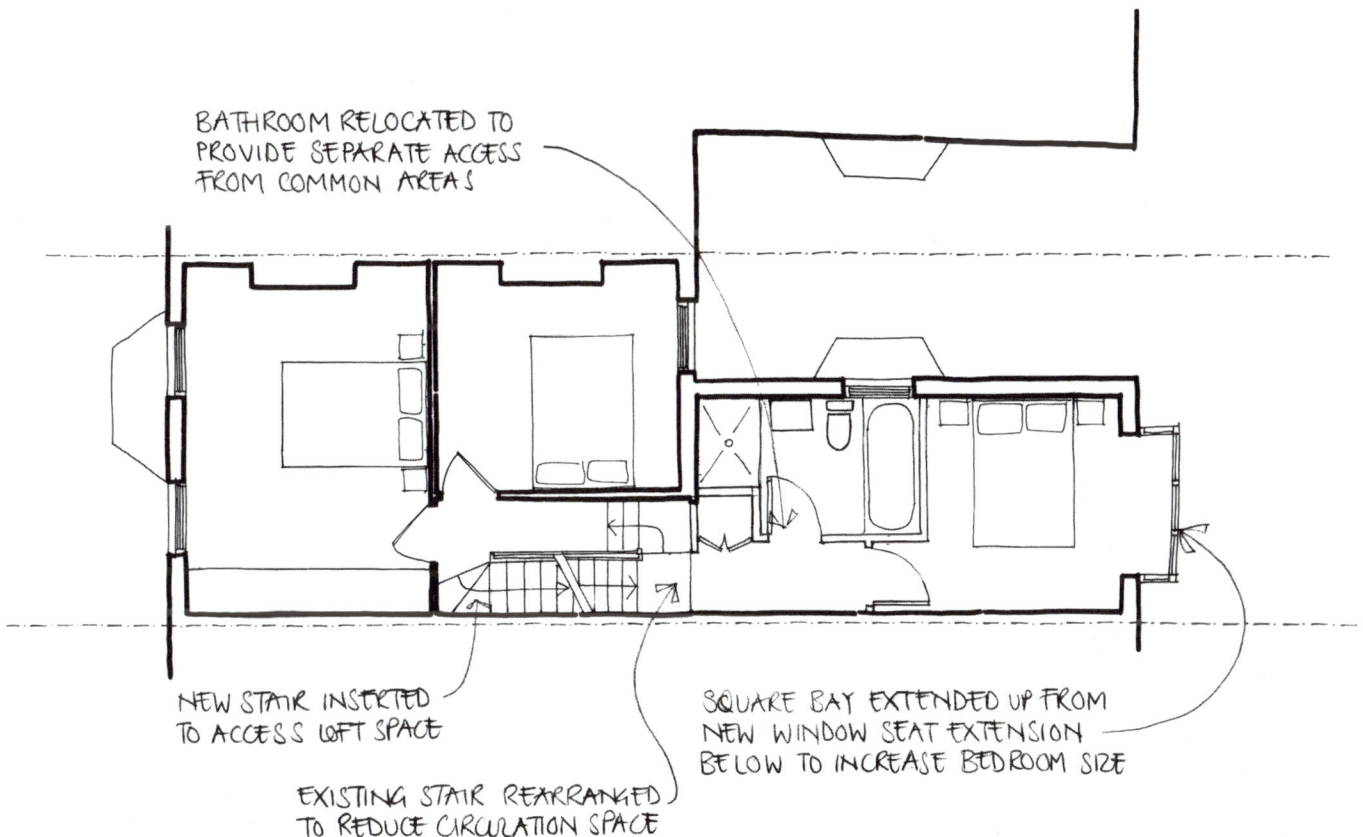

BATHROOM RELOCATED TO PROVIDE SEPARATE ACCESS FROM COMMON AREAS

NEW STAIR INSERTED TO ACCESS LOFT SPACE

EXISTING STAIR REARRANGED TO REDUCE CIRCULATION SPACE

SQUARE BAY EXTENDED UP FROM NEW WINDOW SEAT EXTENSION BELOW TO INCREASE BEDROOM SIZE

OPTION 3
(As depicted in Section A)

In this option, the front room is divided into two equally sized single bedrooms. This option, which should be read in conjunction with Loft Options 6 or 7, removes the ceiling in the front bedroom to create enough space for a mezzanine bed platform. Double sliding doors have been included so that it is possible to connect the two rooms (ideal for younger children, as this gives both a sense of privacy and shared space). The middle bedroom has been converted into a spacious bathroom and the outrigger accommodates a large double bedroom. Stairs have been shown accessing the loft.

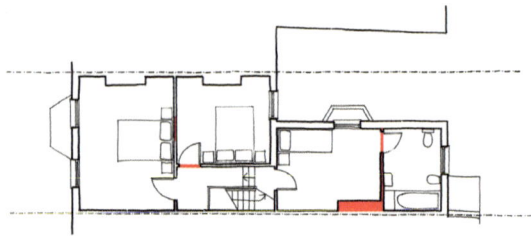

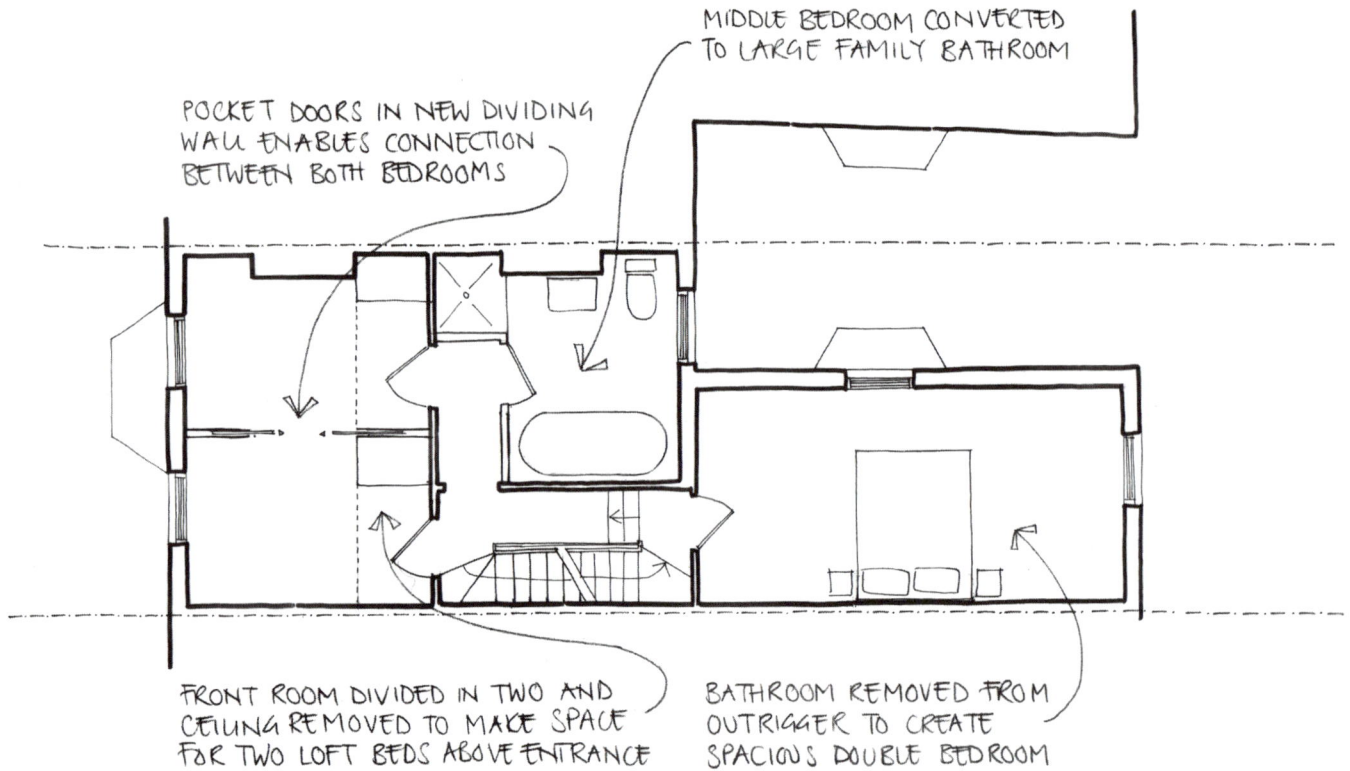

MIDDLE BEDROOM CONVERTED TO LARGE FAMILY BATHROOM

POCKET DOORS IN NEW DIVIDING WALL ENABLES CONNECTION BETWEEN BOTH BEDROOMS

FRONT ROOM DIVIDED IN TWO AND CEILING REMOVED TO MAKE SPACE FOR TWO LOFT BEDS ABOVE ENTRANCE

BATHROOM REMOVED FROM OUTRIGGER TO CREATE SPACIOUS DOUBLE BEDROOM

OPTION 4

This option reduces the number of bedrooms on this floor to two very generous ones. The middle bedroom has been converted into a family bathroom and an en-suite for the front bedroom. As in First-floor Option 3, the entire outrigger has been converted into a large, double bedroom. A window seat has been shown at the rear of the room that could be a continuation of that shown in Ground-floor Option 2.

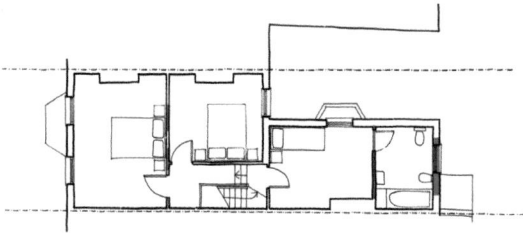

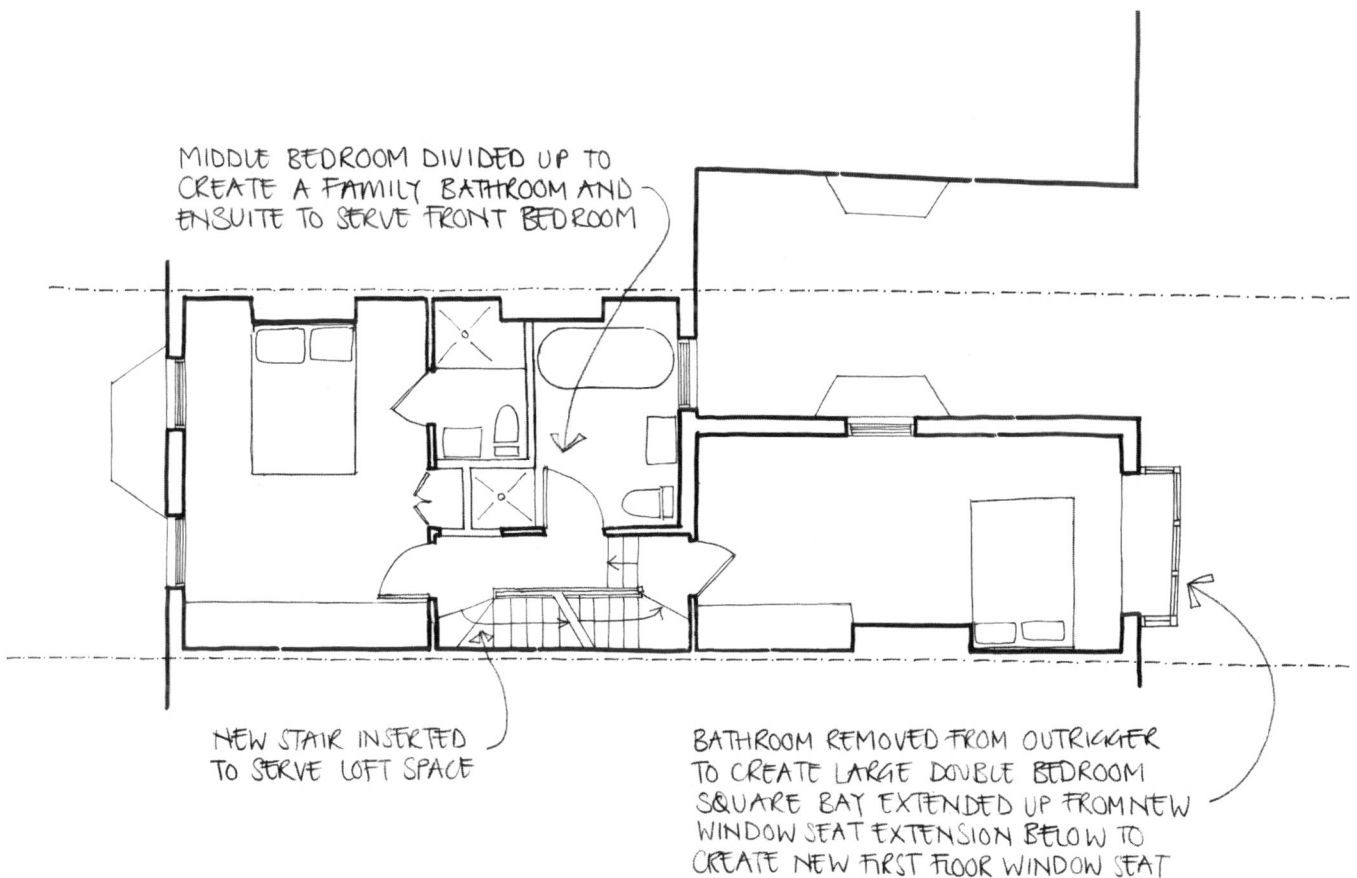

MIDDLE BEDROOM DIVIDED UP TO
CREATE A FAMILY BATHROOM AND
ENSUITE TO SERVE FRONT BEDROOM

NEW STAIR INSERTED
TO SERVE LOFT SPACE

BATHROOM REMOVED FROM OUTRIGGER
TO CREATE LARGE DOUBLE BEDROOM
SQUARE BAY EXTENDED UP FROM NEW
WINDOW SEAT EXTENSION BELOW TO
CREATE NEW FIRST FLOOR WINDOW SEAT

OPTION 5

The loft stair in this option has been shown taking up space in the front bedroom. The benefit of this arrangement is that it creates more useable space on the floor above by tucking the stairs in under the eaves, as shown in Loft Option 2, leaving three similarly sized rooms on the first floor. The existing stairs have been rearranged slightly to enable linear access to the outrigger, as in First-floor Options 2 and 6. This frees up enough space to create a family bathroom and a double bedroom at the rear. The bathroom window has been relocated to allow for a wall positioning that creates the most efficient use of space.

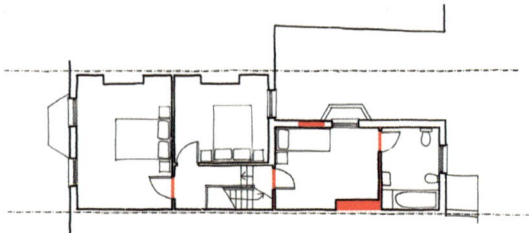

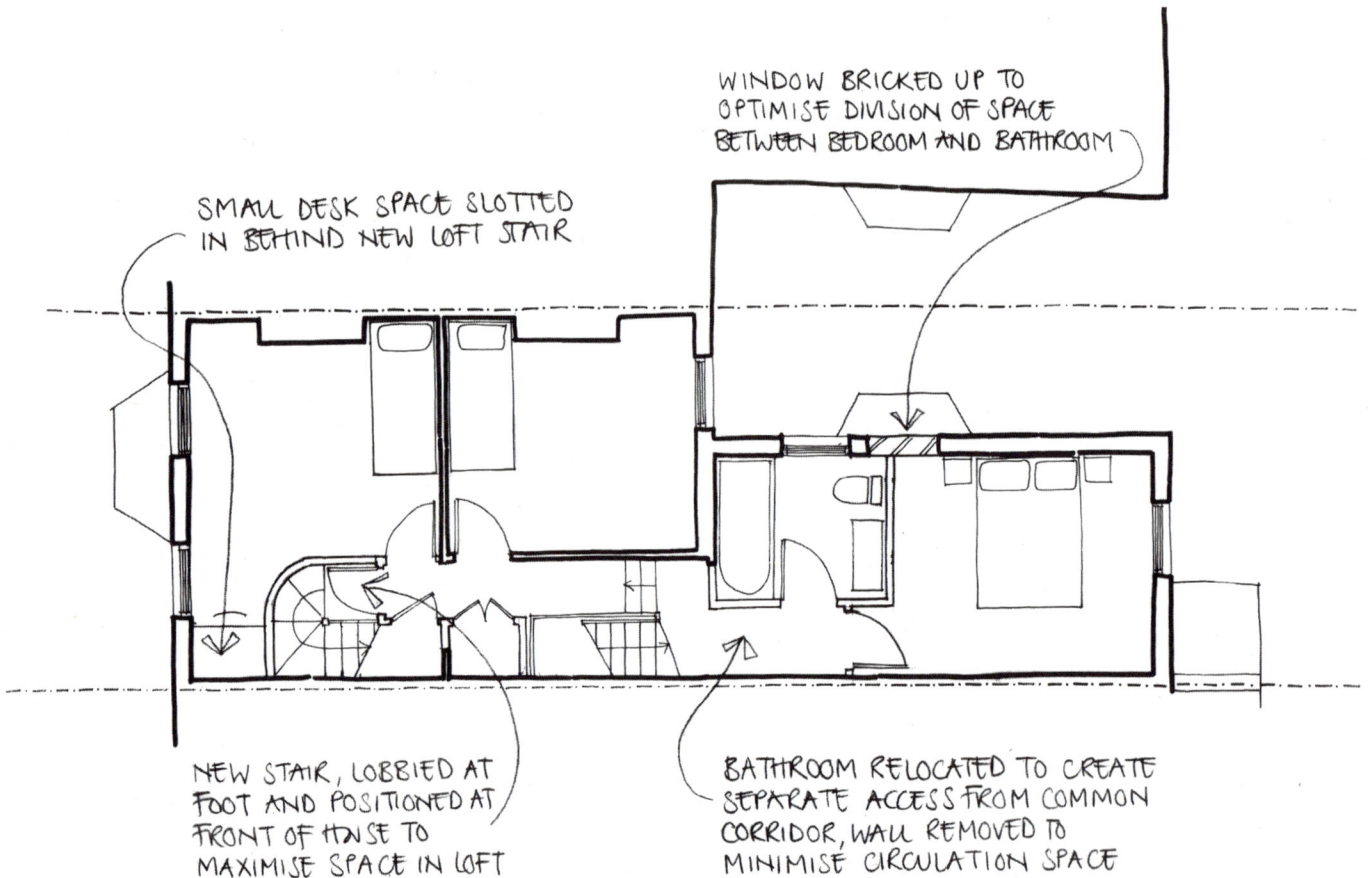

WINDOW BRICKED UP TO OPTIMISE DIVISION OF SPACE BETWEEN BEDROOM AND BATHROOM

SMALL DESK SPACE SLOTTED IN BEHIND NEW LOFT STAIR

NEW STAIR, LOBBIED AT FOOT AND POSITIONED AT FRONT OF HOUSE TO MAXIMISE SPACE IN LOFT

BATHROOM RELOCATED TO CREATE SEPARATE ACCESS FROM COMMON CORRIDOR, WALL REMOVED TO MINIMISE CIRCULATION SPACE

OPTION 6

The front bedroom has been divided to create a new bathroom while still retaining enough space to accommodate a double bed. Again, the existing stairs have been altered to allow linear access to the bedroom in the outrigger. The bathroom in the outrigger has been removed and the space converted into a double bedroom with an en-suite shower room. The side window has been relocated to serve this new en-suite. No stairs to access the loft have been shown in this option, but it would work with any option showing new stairs above the existing ones.

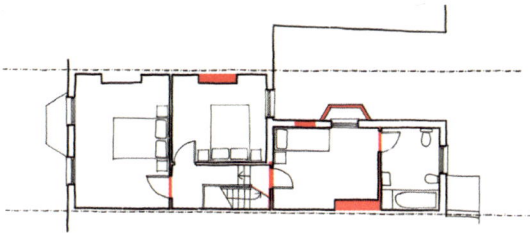

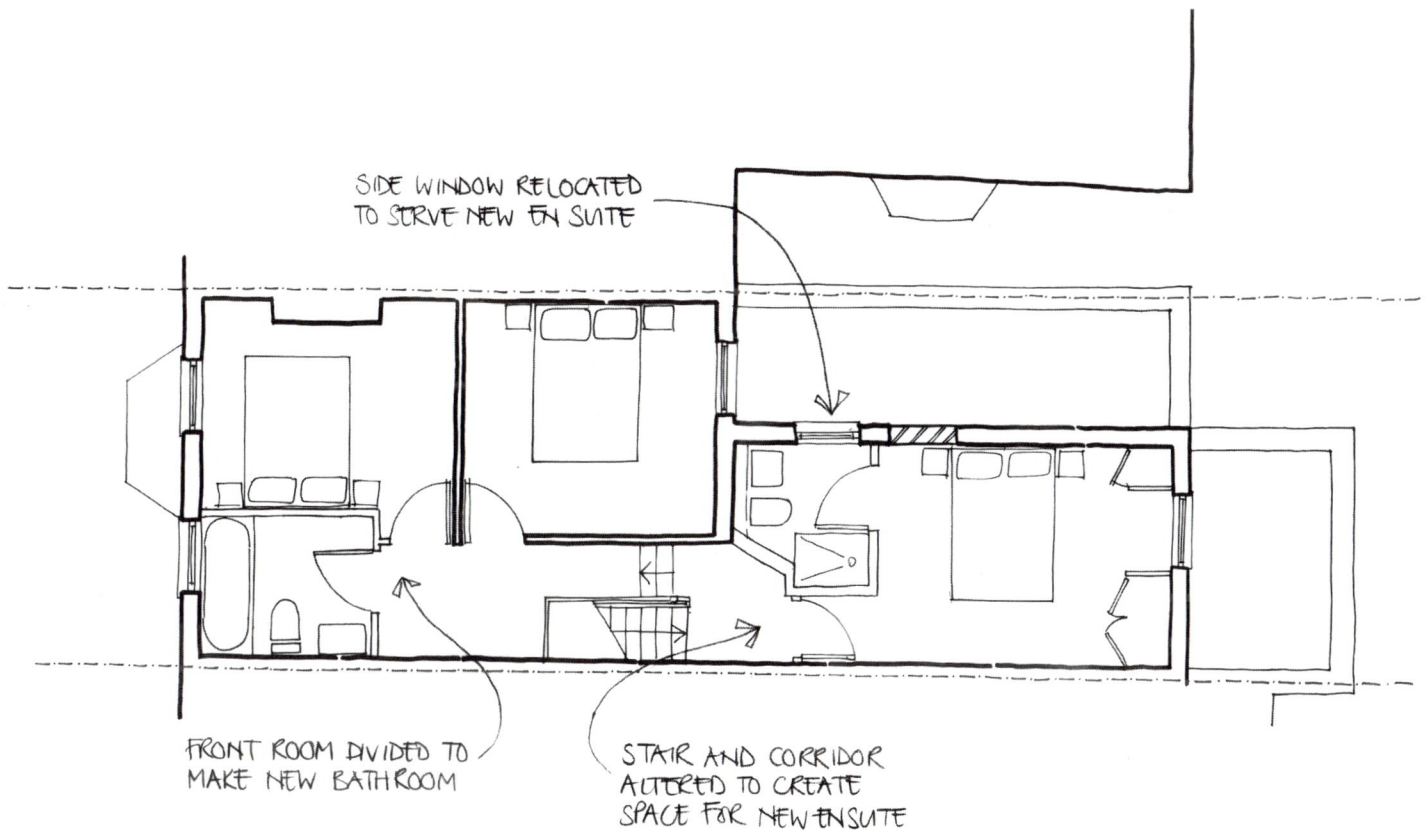

SIDE WINDOW RELOCATED
TO SERVE NEW EN SUITE

FRONT ROOM DIVIDED TO
MAKE NEW BATHROOM

STAIR AND CORRIDOR
ALTERED TO CREATE
SPACE FOR NEW ENSUITE

LOFT

The beam-to-ridge height in this loft is only 2.2m. This means that once insulation and additional structure have been installed, the floor-to-ceiling height will only be about 2m. (See the Rules of Thumb section of this book for more information.)

OPTION 1
(Based on the Shepherd's Bush House project by Studio 30 Architects)

This option works with First floor options 1, 2 and 4 or option 6 if a staircase up to the loft is added. A dressing room has been tucked into the eaves space behind the bed, and a small shower room has been tucked behind the stairs. Please note that this shower room may require a macerator and pump to take the waste to the soil pipe at the rear of the building. Sliding, folding doors create a full-width Juliet balcony for the bedroom.

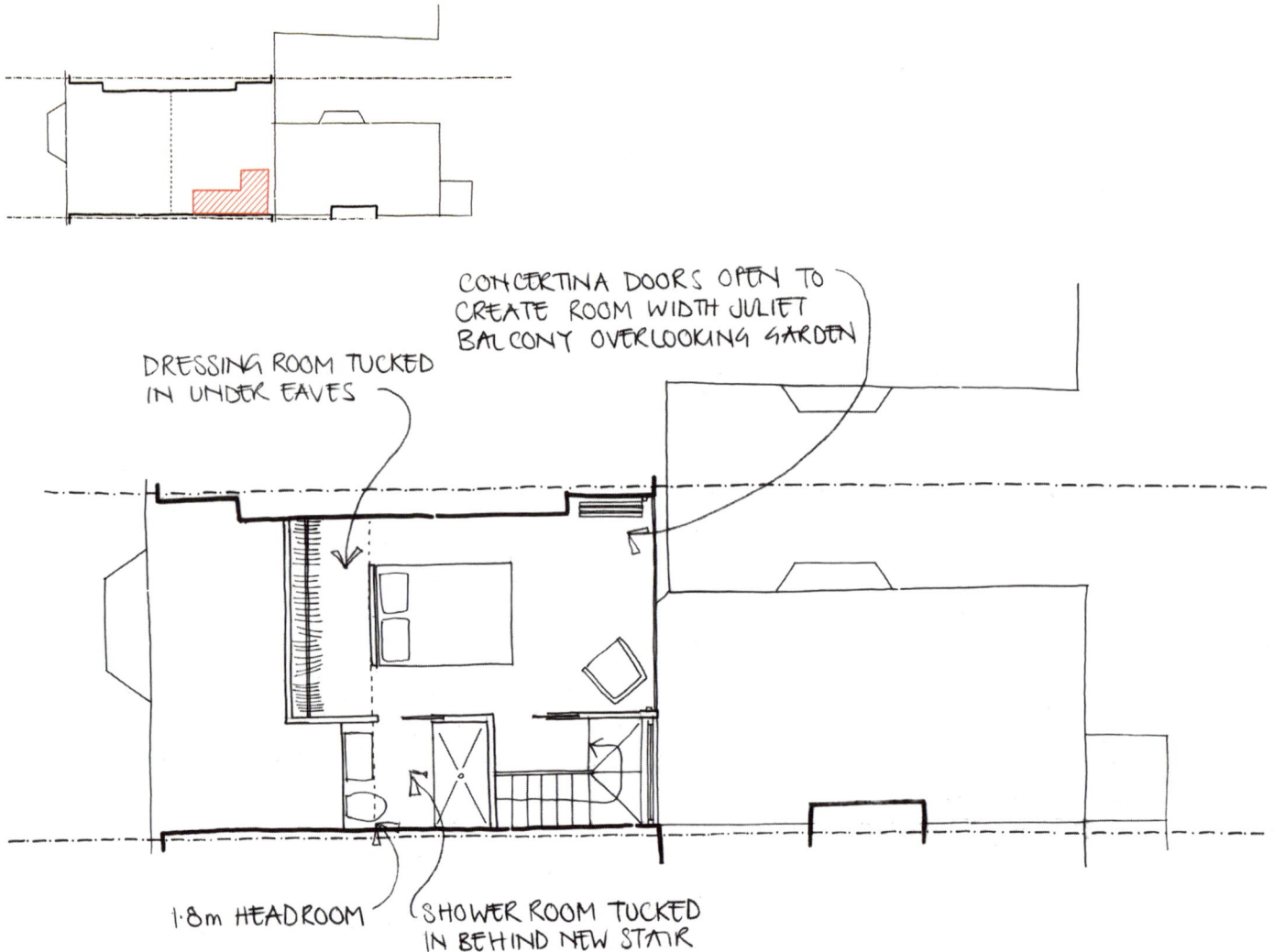

CONCERTINA DOORS OPEN TO CREATE ROOM WIDTH JULIET BALCONY OVERLOOKING GARDEN

DRESSING ROOM TUCKED IN UNDER EAVES

1·8m HEADROOM

SHOWER ROOM TUCKED IN BEHIND NEW STAIR

Shepherd's Bush House by Studio 30 Architects,
Shepherd's Bush, London, 2014. Full-width sliding,
folding doors create wide Juliet balcony.

Next page. Shepherd's Bush House by Studio 30
Architects, Shepherd's Bush, London, 2014. Dressing
room tucked into eaves behind bed.

OPTION 2

This option is to be read in conjunction with First-floor Option 5. The stairs arrive directly into the full-width bedroom, with large sliding doors creating a large Juliet balcony and a light-filled room. A small shower room tucked under the eaves behind the bed has carefully positioned roof lights that provide extra headroom beneath them.

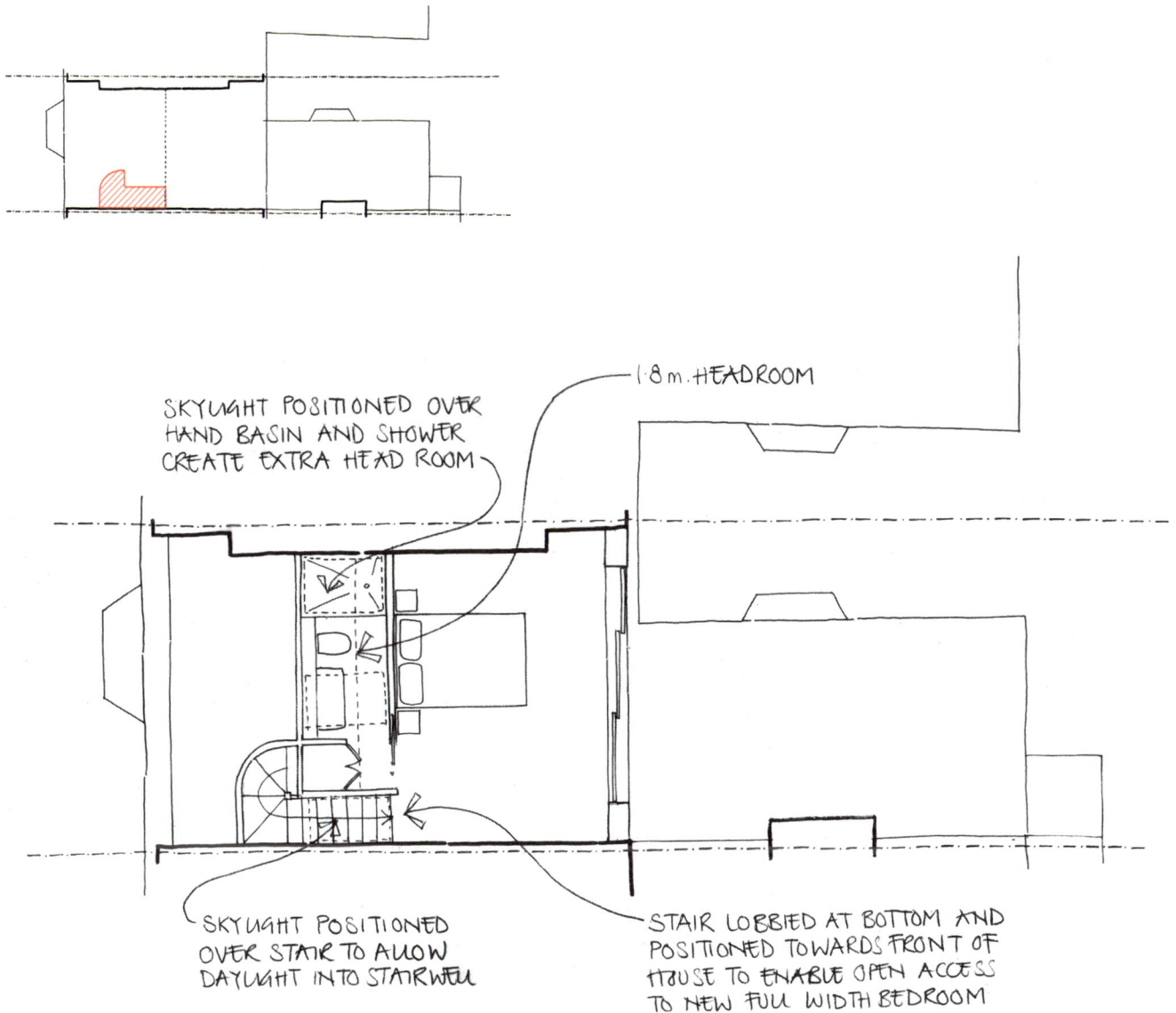

1·8 m. HEADROOM

SKYLIGHT POSITIONED OVER HAND BASIN AND SHOWER CREATE EXTRA HEAD ROOM

SKYLIGHT POSITIONED OVER STAIR TO ALLOW DAYLIGHT INTO STAIRWELL

STAIR LOBBIED AT BOTTOM AND POSITIONED TOWARDS FRONT OF HOUSE TO ENABLE OPEN ACCESS TO NEW FULL WIDTH BEDROOM

OPTION 3

The stair opens directly into the loft room without a lobby in this option, which means that a door will need to be located at the foot of the new stair. This frees up much more floor space in the loft to dedicate to the main bedroom area. Large, sliding doors span the width of the extension and open up to create a Juliet balcony. A shower room and dressing room have been tucked into the eaves, to make the most of the available space.

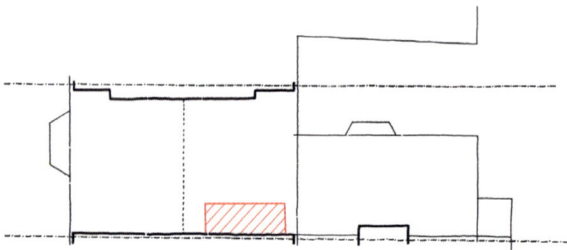

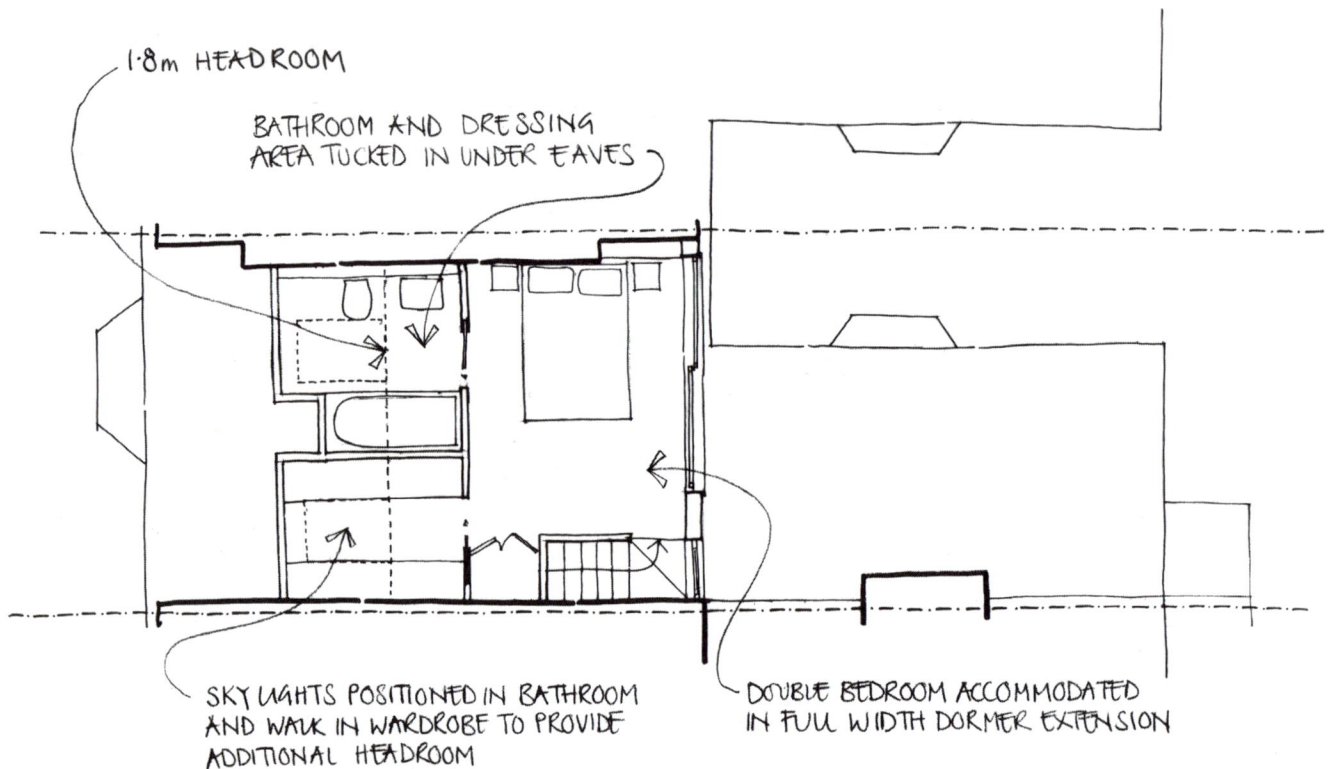

1·8m HEADROOM

BATHROOM AND DRESSING AREA TUCKED IN UNDER EAVES

SKY LIGHTS POSITIONED IN BATHROOM AND WALK IN WARDROBE TO PROVIDE ADDITIONAL HEADROOM

DOUBLE BEDROOM ACCOMMODATED IN FULL WIDTH DORMER EXTENSION

Kentish Town House by Yard Architects, Kentish Town,
London, 2016. Dressing area tucked into eaves.

Kentish Town House by Yard Architects, Kentish
Town, London, 2016. A carefully positioned skylight
in the front pitch increases the headroom in the
bathroom.

OPTION 4

This option includes a small extension over the outrigger that accommodates a shower room. The extension has been designed to be only the width of the existing stairwell to enable glazing to be installed almost the full width of the bedroom. The added benefit of this arrangement is that only the tallest section of the outrigger is developed at this level, creating less additional volume. This could be critical in a volume calculation for a permitted development application. There is a lobby at the top of the stairs, enabling this plan to be used in conjunction with First-floor Options 1, 2 and 4 or option 6 if a staircase accessing the loft was added. The new bedroom fills the entire loft conversion, which includes a full-width dormer extension.

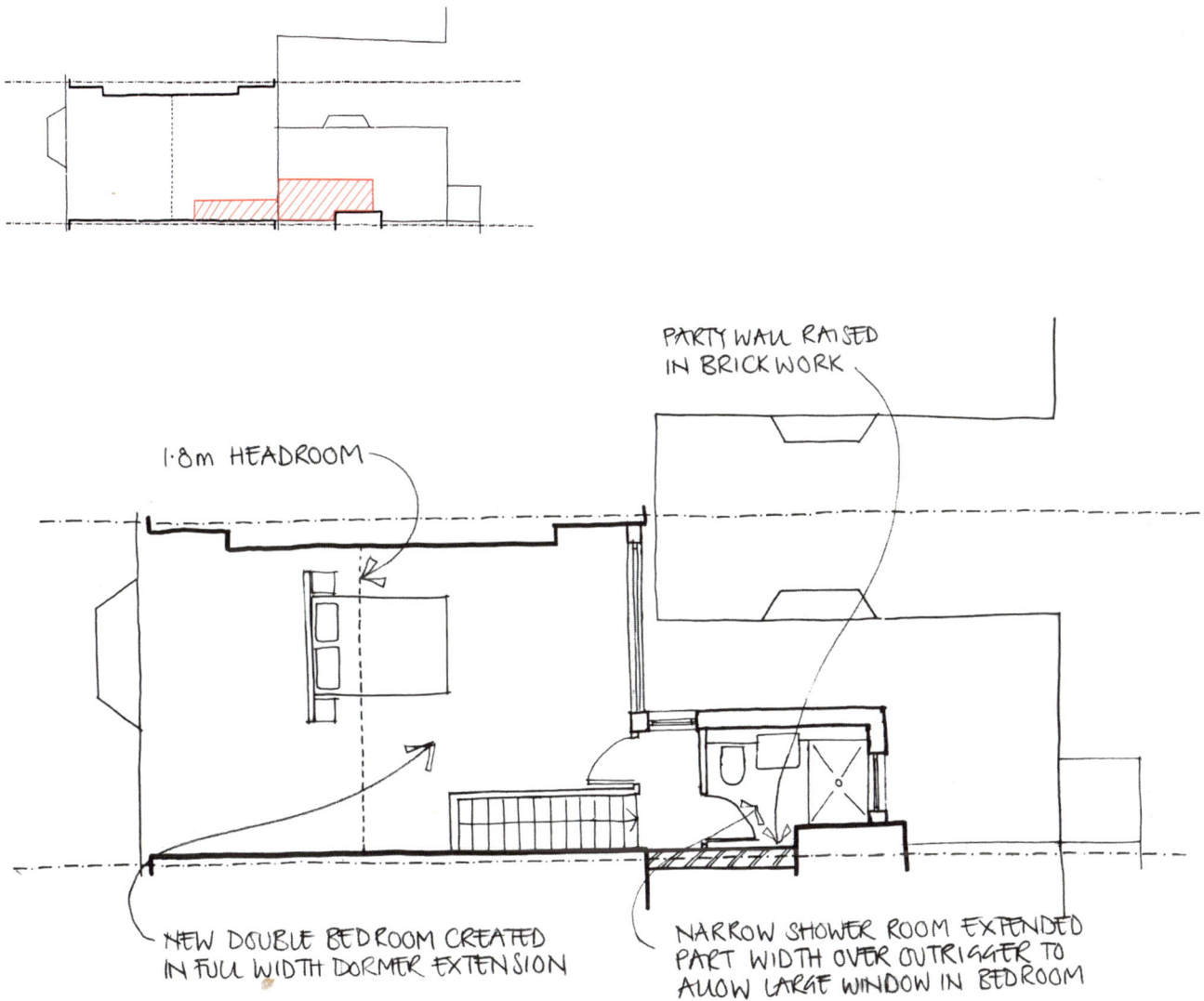

PARTY WALL RAISED IN BRICKWORK

1·8m HEADROOM

NEW DOUBLE BEDROOM CREATED IN FULL WIDTH DORMER EXTENSION

NARROW SHOWER ROOM EXTENDED PART WIDTH OVER OUTRIGGER TO ALLOW LARGE WINDOW IN BEDROOM

OPTION 5

In this option, the stairs have been designed to continue into the new outrigger extension, creating more room in the loft bedroom. A small shower room and storage room have also been positioned in the outrigger extension. Again, the size of this rear section depends on the overall external volume of the loft extension if applying through permitted development rights. The floor under the front section of roof has been removed to create a void down to the bedroom below. As this is under the sloping section of the roof, not much useable loft space is lost in doing this. This plan could be used in conjunction with First-floor Options 1 to 4.

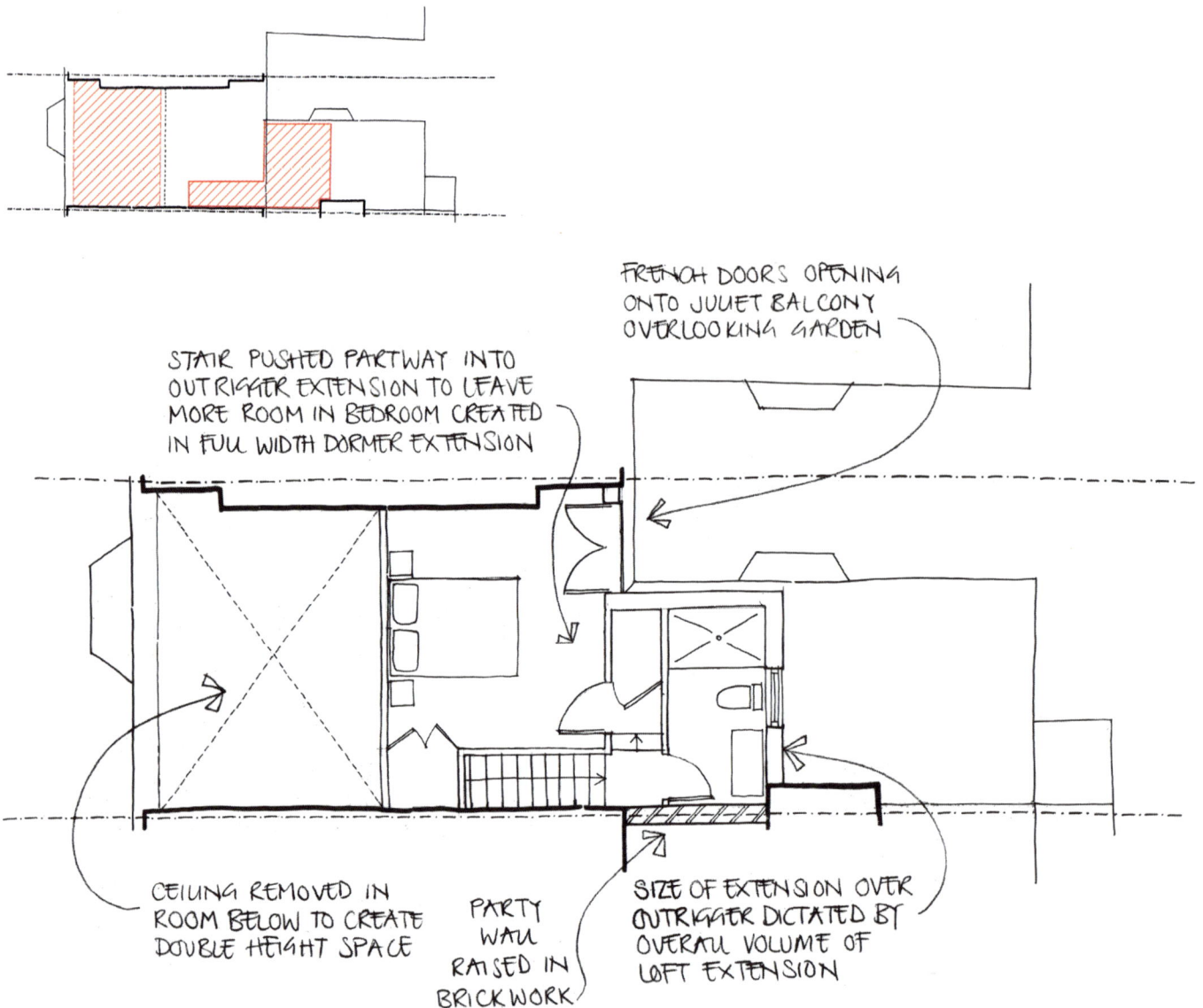

FRENCH DOORS OPENING ONTO JULIET BALCONY OVERLOOKING GARDEN

STAIR PUSHED PARTWAY INTO OUTRIGGER EXTENSION TO LEAVE MORE ROOM IN BEDROOM CREATED IN FULL WIDTH DORMER EXTENSION

CEILING REMOVED IN ROOM BELOW TO CREATE DOUBLE HEIGHT SPACE

PARTY WALL RAISED IN BRICKWORK

SIZE OF EXTENSION OVER OUTRIGGER DICTATED BY OVERALL VOLUME OF LOFT EXTENSION

OPTION 6

The new bathroom, shown above the existing outrigger, and the new bedroom accommodated in the full-width dormer extension are connected in this option. This creates a sense of space, and also makes the most of the views and light through large windows. A small toilet is shown separate from this main room.

The front half of the loft has been separated and used to create mezzanine bedrooms on the first floor, as shown in First-floor Option 3. It could equally be retained as part of the loft room.

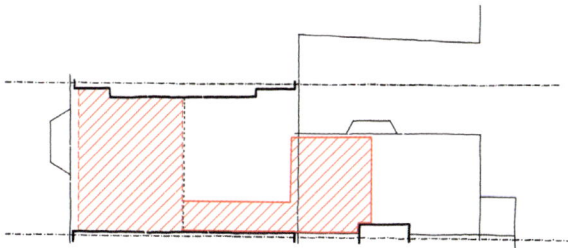

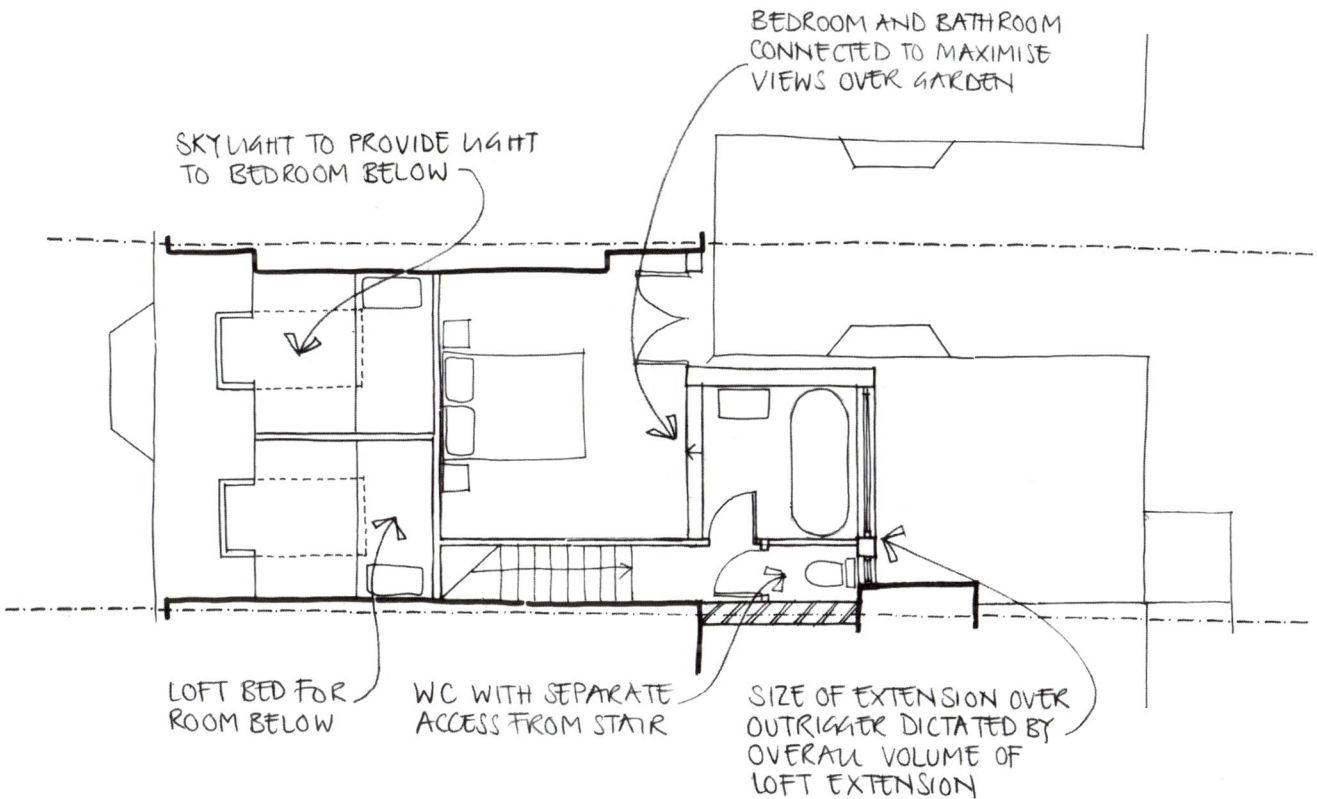

BEDROOM AND BATHROOM
CONNECTED TO MAXIMISE
VIEWS OVER GARDEN

SKYLIGHT TO PROVIDE LIGHT
TO BEDROOM BELOW

LOFT BED FOR
ROOM BELOW

WC WITH SEPARATE
ACCESS FROM STAIR

SIZE OF EXTENSION OVER
OUTRIGGER DICTATED BY
OVERALL VOLUME OF
LOFT EXTENSION

OPTION 7

By not extending the full width of the main house at loft level, the extension over the outrigger can be longer while not exceeding the 40m³ limit required under permitted development guidelines. (See the What to Consider When Designing an Extension section of this book for more information.) This option works very well where headroom in the loft space is limited, as the floor of the outrigger is usually at a lower level to that of the main house. Positioning the bedroom above the outrigger gives more scope for the location of windows – and some councils, but not all, will allow access on to a terrace at the very rear, provided adequate screening is proposed.

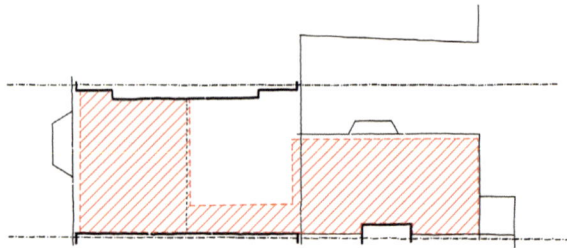

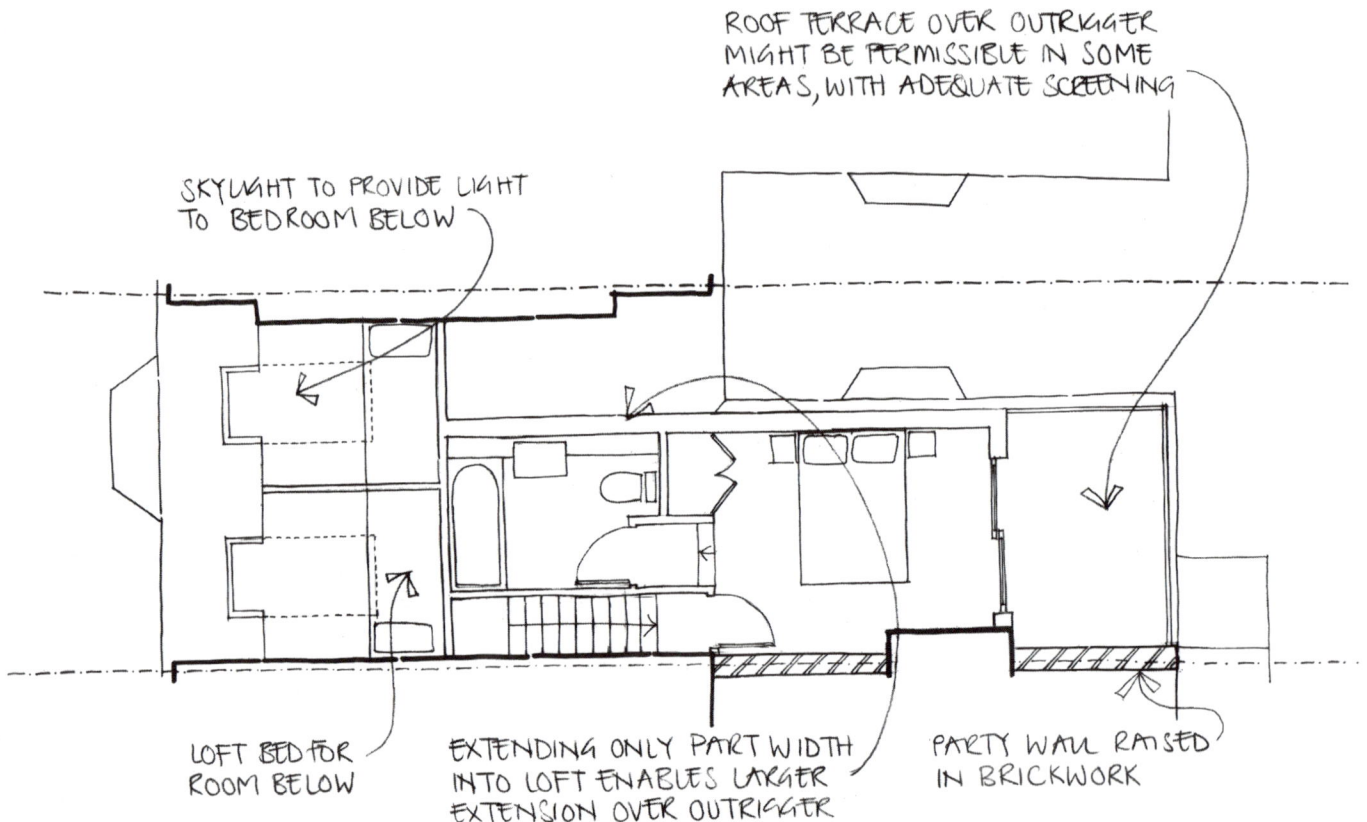

ROOF TERRACE OVER OUTRIGGER MIGHT BE PERMISSIBLE IN SOME AREAS, WITH ADEQUATE SCREENING

SKYLIGHT TO PROVIDE LIGHT TO BEDROOM BELOW

LOFT BED FOR ROOM BELOW

EXTENDING ONLY PART WIDTH INTO LOFT ENABLES LARGER EXTENSION OVER OUTRIGGER

PARTY WALL RAISED IN BRICKWORK

CEILING REMOVED IN FRONT ROOM, WHICH IS DIVIDED IN TWO TO CREATE TWO BEDROOMS WITH LOFT BEDS

LINE OF ENSUITE SERVING NEW BEDROOM

ROOF TERRACE CREATED ABOVE OUTRIGGER WITH GREEN ROOF AND 1.8m OPAQUE GLASS SCREEN

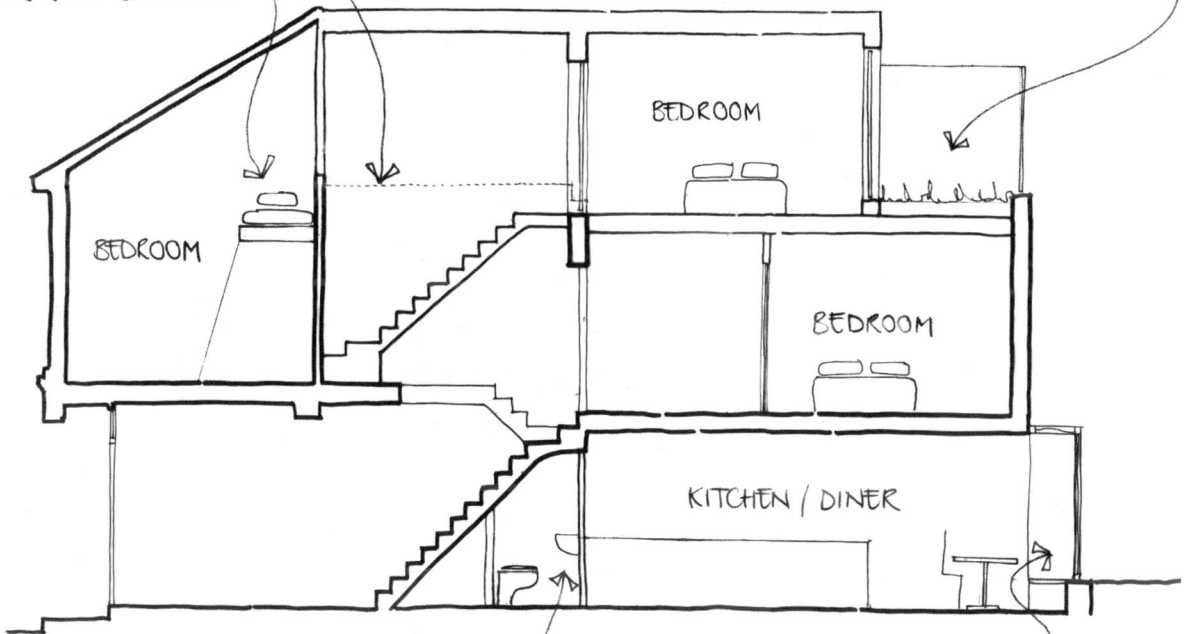

BEDROOM

BEDROOM

BEDROOM

KITCHEN / DINER

WC TUCKED UNDER EXISTING STAIR

WINDOW SEAT CREATED TO OPTIMISE SPACE FOR DINING AREA

OPTION 8

This option is something of a 'wild card' that has not yet been tested, but it seems to adhere to all the permitted development guidelines. It is also a good solution if headroom is an issue, as most of the upwards extension is over the lower outrigger.

A small section of the main roof is extended upwards to make space for a stair that serves a full-width, full-length extension over the existing outrigger. The remaining portion of the rear half of the roof is removed and converted into a terrace. This looks down into the garden to the rear, and into the front room at first-floor level via clerestory glazing towards the front. The outrigger extension accommodates a bedroom and small shower room. It is shown here with a new projecting bay that extends the entire height of the newly extended outrigger, as shown in Ground-floor Option 2 and First-floor Options 2 and 4.

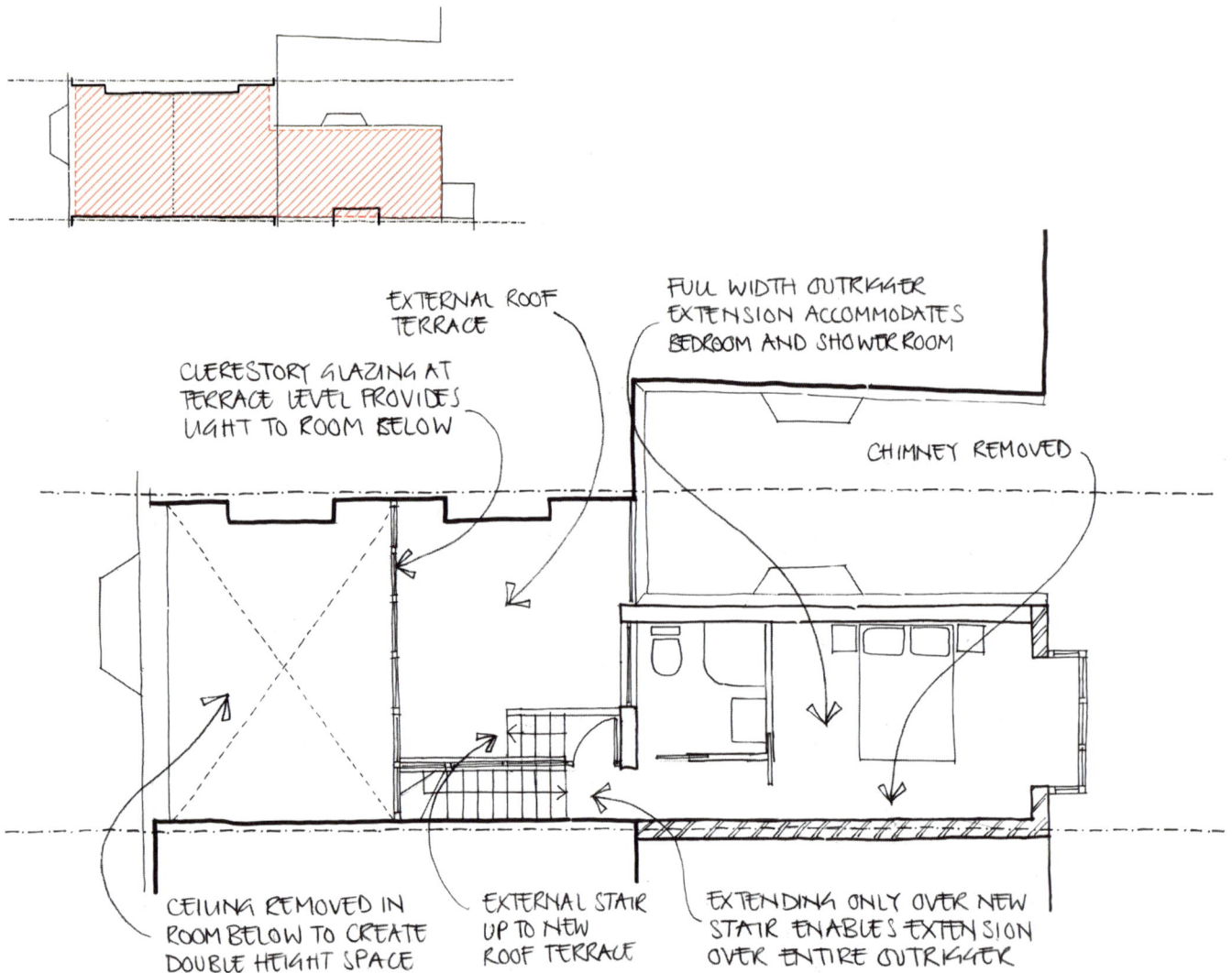

EXTERNAL ROOF TERRACE

CLERESTORY GLAZING AT TERRACE LEVEL PROVIDES LIGHT TO ROOM BELOW

FULL WIDTH OUTRIGGER EXTENSION ACCOMMODATES BEDROOM AND SHOWER ROOM

CHIMNEY REMOVED

CEILING REMOVED IN ROOM BELOW TO CREATE DOUBLE HEIGHT SPACE

EXTERNAL STAIR UP TO NEW ROOF TERRACE

EXTENDING ONLY OVER NEW STAIR ENABLES EXTENSION OVER ENTIRE OUTRIGGER

CEILING ABOVE FIRST FLOOR
BEDROOM REMOVED AND GLAZING
INSTALLED AT HIGH LEVEL

NEW SECOND FLOOR EXTENSION
OVER ENTIRE OUTRIGGER CREATES
NEW BEDROOM AND SHOWER ROOM

NEW SQUARE BAY
EXTENDS UP
THREE STOREYS

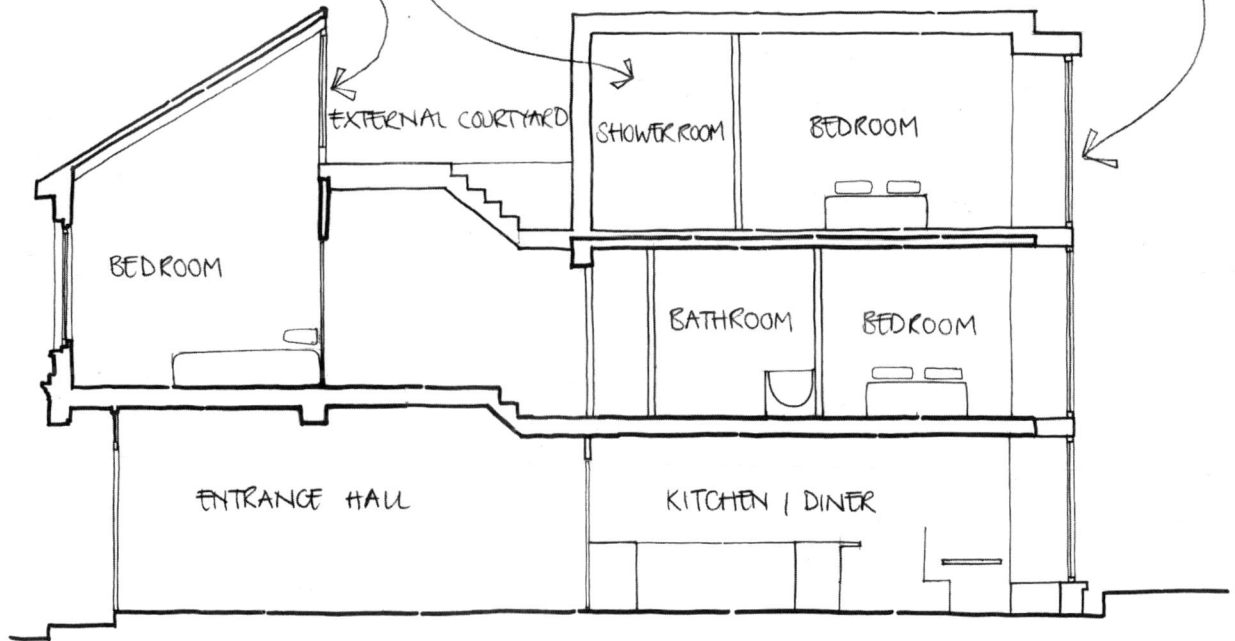

EXTERNAL COURTYARD

SHOWER ROOM

BEDROOM

BEDROOM

BATHROOM

BEDROOM

ENTRANCE HALL

KITCHEN / DINER

CASE STUDY 5
THE TALL TERRACE

The Tall Terrace, constructed on a 5.4m plot, is a three-storey terraced house. It is situated on a busy road, but has a long, green rear garden. It also has a two-storey outrigger that, being 2m shorter than that of the adjoining house, creates additional opportunities to extend. The outrigger is at a slightly lower level than the main section of the house, but is level with the garden. Headspace in the loft is very limited, at only 2m. There is also a narrow cellar that isn't featured in this case study. Please see the basement options from the Split Level case study for an idea of what could be possible if the cellar were to be excavated.

GROUND FLOOR

As with the previous case study, in the existing plan the front door opens into a hall that leads to the two reception rooms and the kitchen in the outrigger. Here, there is also a small utility room at the rear, accessed via the kitchen. The door to the rear reception room is, unusually, located via the outrigger.

OPTION 1

*(Based on the Timber Frame Extension
project by Yard Architects)*

In this option the dining area and small WC have been slotted within the existing width of the side return, retaining the outrigger's existing external walls.

A section of existing external wall has been removed to connect the rear reception room with the new dining area, as has the wall between the front and rear reception rooms. Since the floor level at the front is higher than that at the back, a glass balustrade divides the two spaces. Steps are possible, but would restrict space and furniture positioning. Central double doors have been introduced, giving a grander entrance to the front reception room. The chimneybreast and inner wall of the outrigger have been removed to enlarge the kitchen and connect it to the garden. As well as double doors from the kitchen, the garden is also accessed via a large, pivot door at the end of the new dining room.

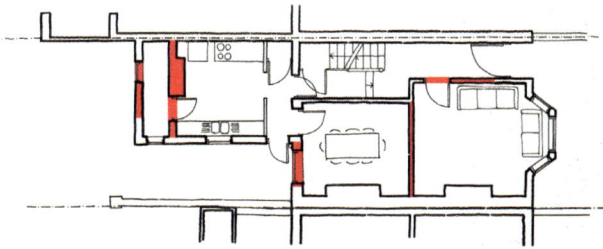

DOUBLE DOORS INSERTED REAR WALL OF OUTRIGGER TO CONNECT WITH GARDEN

DIVIDING WALL REMOVED AND GLASS BALUSTRADE INSTALLED TO CONNECT FRONT RECEPTION ROOM WITH LOWER REAR ROOM

DOUBLE DOORS POSITIONED CENTRALLY IN WALL TO CREATE GRAND ENTRANCE

USING A PIVOT DOOR MAXIMISES DOOR SIZE

SIDEWALL OF OUTRIGGER RETAINED TO MINIMISE STRUCTURAL ALTERATIONS

TIMBER FRAMED EXTENSION CONSTRUCTED IN SIDE RETURN TO CREATE DINING AREA AND WC

SECTION OF REAR WALL REMOVED TO CONNECT WITH SIDE RETURN EXTENSION

Timber Frame Extension by Yard Architects,
Camden, London, 2014. Slim dining room slotted
into side return. Image mirrored to reflect plan.

Mapledene Road by Platform 5 Architects, Hackney,
London, 2008. Use of glass enhances view of garden.
Image mirrored to reflect plan.

OPTION 2

*(Based on the Mapledene Road project
by Platform 5 Architects)*

Access to the rear reception room has been relocated in this option, and
its floor has been raised to match that of the front reception room. Double
concertina doors have been inserted in the wall between the two reception
rooms to enable connection.

The side wall of the outrigger and the chimneybreast have been removed
to enable full extension into the side return. Part of the rear wall has been
retained, which has had a window seat inserted into it. The garden is accessed
via a large pivot door in the new extension, which accommodates a dining
area. The existing outrigger has been opened up to accommodate a spacious
kitchen with island unit.

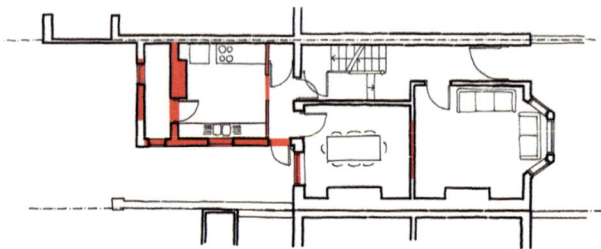

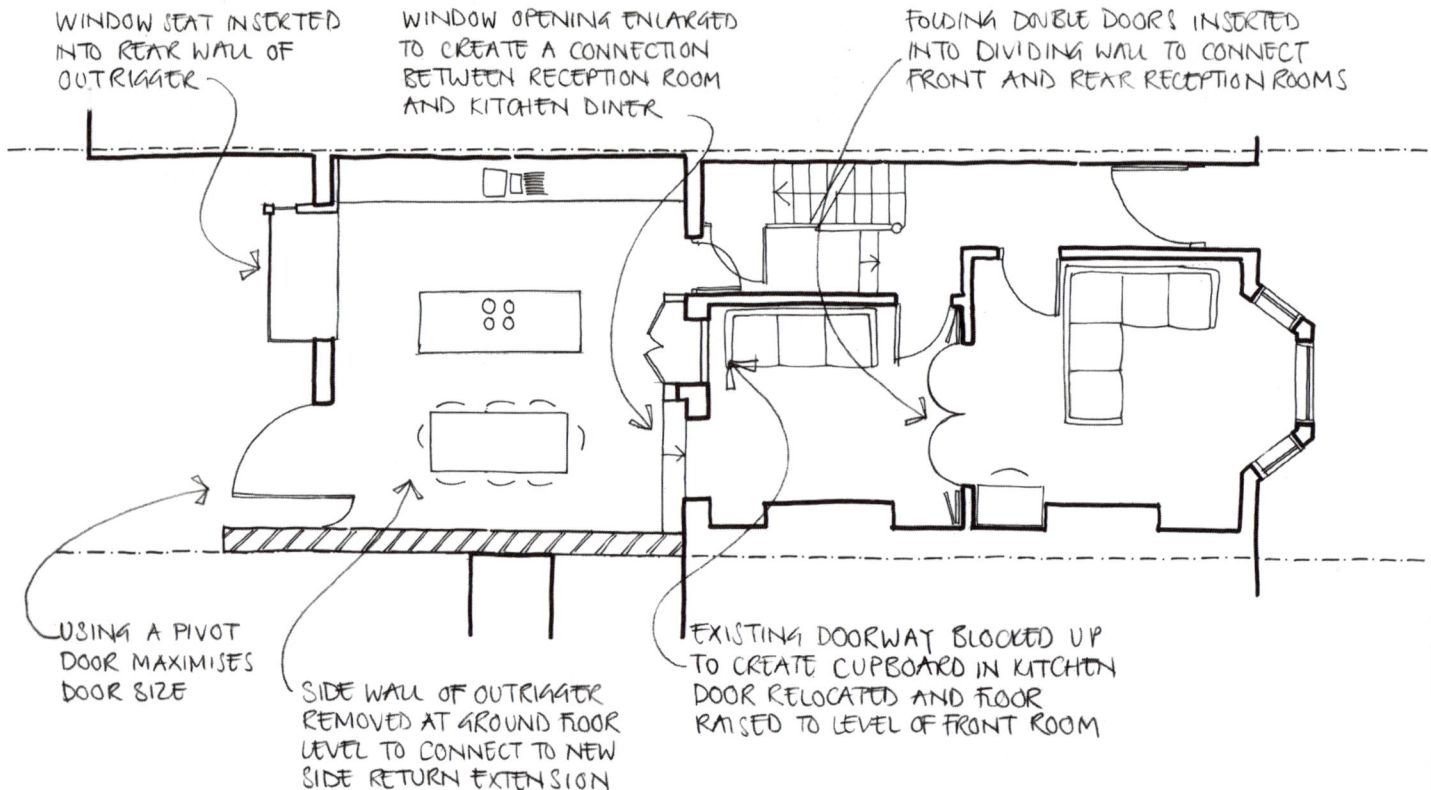

WINDOW SEAT INSERTED
INTO REAR WALL OF
OUTRIGGER

WINDOW OPENING ENLARGED
TO CREATE A CONNECTION
BETWEEN RECEPTION ROOM
AND KITCHEN DINER

FOLDING DOUBLE DOORS INSERTED
INTO DIVIDING WALL TO CONNECT
FRONT AND REAR RECEPTION ROOMS

USING A PIVOT
DOOR MAXIMISES
DOOR SIZE

SIDE WALL OF OUTRIGGER
REMOVED AT GROUND FLOOR
LEVEL TO CONNECT TO NEW
SIDE RETURN EXTENSION

EXISTING DOORWAY BLOCKED UP
TO CREATE CUPBOARD IN KITCHEN
DOOR RELOCATED AND FLOOR
RAISED TO LEVEL OF FRONT ROOM

Mapledene Road by Platform 5 Architects, Hackney,
London, 2008. Oriel window creates additional
seating. Image mirrored to reflect plan.

OPTION 3

(Based on the 'Timber Box' project by Green & Teggin Architects)

This proposal shows minimal structural changes. The front reception room remains untouched, while the rear reception room becomes the kitchen. The rear wall and chimneybreast of the outrigger have been removed to create a new living room. This extends to the rear and part way into the side return to create additional space while retaining access to the garden from the existing back door. The existing outrigger, where the kitchen was originally located, accommodates a new dining area that flows into the new extension to create a large, flexible, open-plan space.

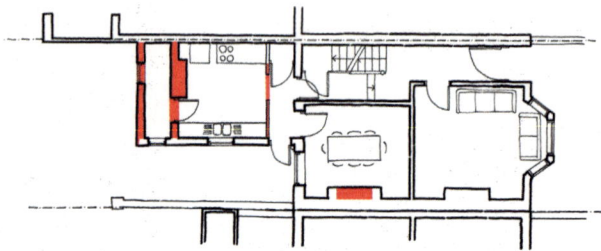

CORNER OF NEW EXTENSION OPEN AND SLIDING FOLDING DOORS INSTALLED TO ENABLE NEW ROOM TO BE OPENED UP TO THE GARDEN

LOCATING THE KITCHEN IN THE REAR RECEPTION ROOM CREATES A LARGE, FLEXIBLE OPEN PLAN ROOM AT THE REAR

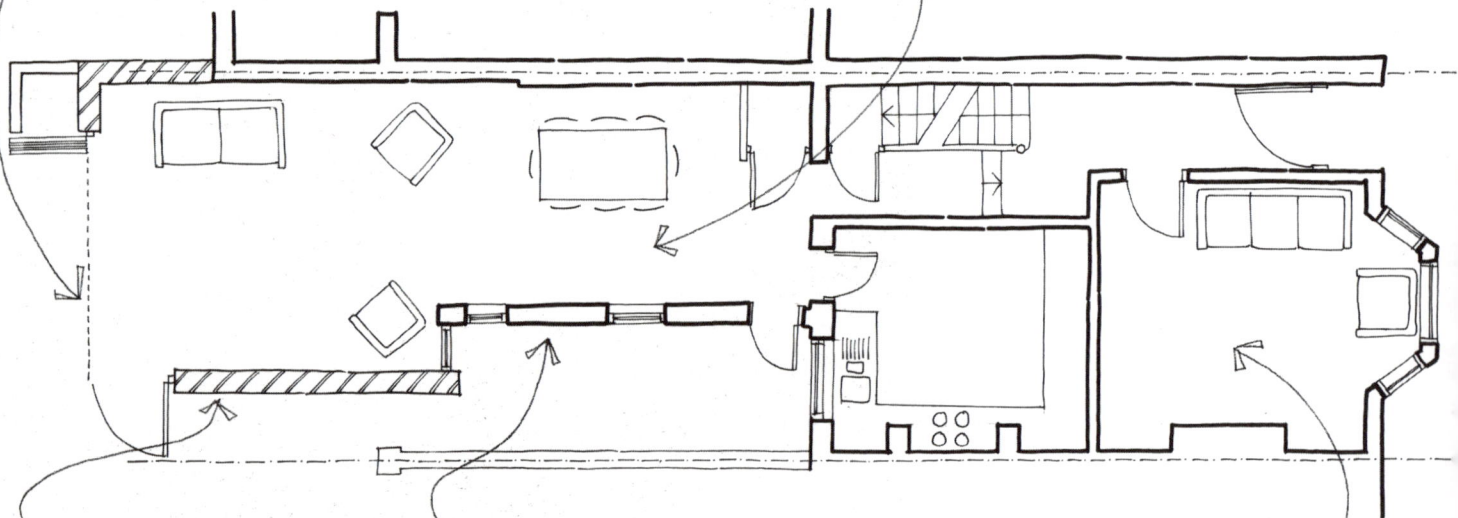

NEW EXTENSION COMES PART WAY INTO SIDE RETURN TO MAXIMISE SPACE WHILST RETAINING SIDE ACCESS

SIDE WALL OF EXISTING OUTRIGGER RETAINED TO MINIMISE STRUCTURAL ALTERATIONS

FRONT RECEPTION ROOM RETAINED AS EXISTING

'Timber Box', Lausanne Road by Green & Teggin Architects, Peckham, London, 2011. Sliding, folding doors tuck in under overhanging eaves. Image mirrored to reflect plan.

'Our House', Lausanne Road (Phase One) by Green & Teggin Architects, Peckham, London, 2009. View from kitchen through dining room to garden.

'Timber Box', Lausanne Road by Green & Teggin Architects, Peckham, London, 2011. Continuation of inside to outside. Image mirrored to reflect plan.

OPTION 4

(Based on Phase One of the 'Our House', Lausanne Road project by Green & Teggin Architects, as depicted in Section A)

The ground floor remains largely untouched in this option. The only structural change is the removal of the chimneybreast and rear wall in the outrigger to connect to the new, full-width rear extension. An efficient galley kitchen occupies the original outrigger, with a dining and seating area in the new extension.

The side return becomes a courtyard – retaining light and ventilation in the rear reception room and kitchen, and preserving the depth of view from

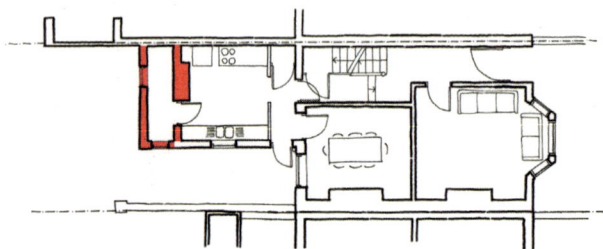

EXTENDING PARTWAY INTO SIDE RETURN CREATES ROOM TO ACCOMMODATE A SEATING AREA WITHIN DINING ROOM

POSITIONING OF GALLEY KITCHEN IN THIS LOCATION CONSOLIDATES CIRCULATION SPACE, MAKING MOST OF AVAILABLE SPACE

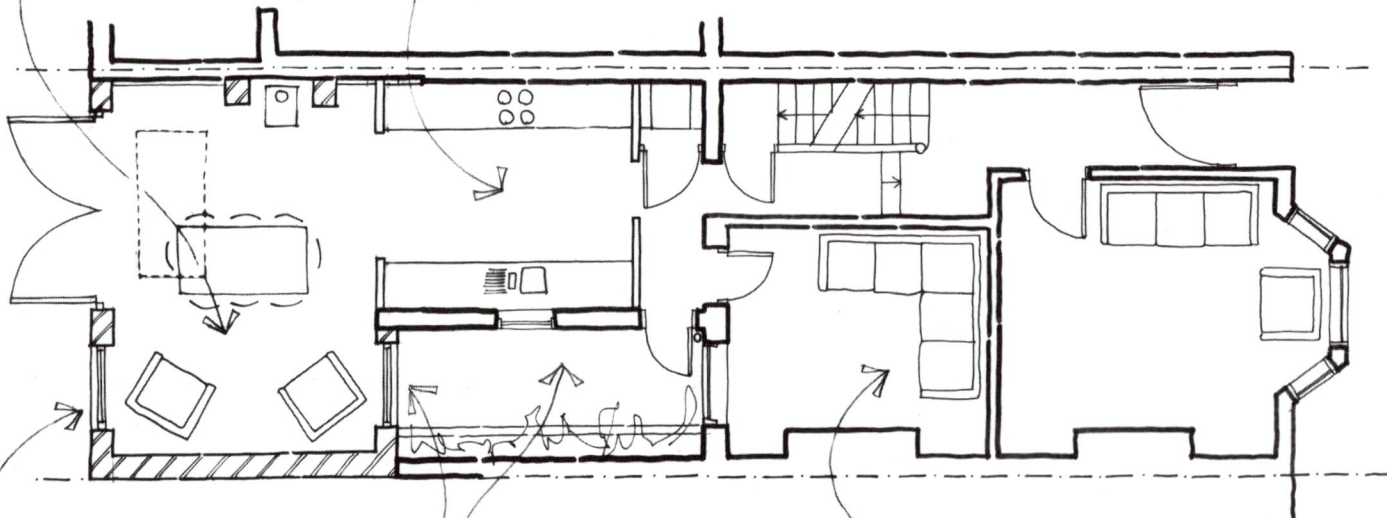

FULL HEIGHT WINDOWS LINE UP WITH EXISTING REAR RECEPTION ROOM WINDOW TO RETAIN VIEW INTO GARDEN

COURTYARD CREATED TO RETAIN LIGHT, AIR AND DEPTH OF VIEW TO EXISTING KITCHEN AND RECEPTION ROOM

FRONT AND REAR RECEPTION ROOMS RETAINED AS EXISTING

'Our House', Lausanne Road (Phase One) by Green & Teggin Architects, Peckham, London, 2009. Retaining side return to create a courtyard. Ceiling hatch creates double-height space.

them. The extension's full-length windows line up with that of the rear reception room, framing garden views. By not extending into the side return, the drainage can remain untouched – thus saving money. (This is also true of Ground-floor Option 3.) The rear reception room can remain separate for maximum flexibility of use.

A skylight with mirrored sides maximises light and visual interest. There is also a ceiling hatch (shown in the photographs) that, when open, creates a double-height space and vertical connection to the room above.

OPTION 5

(Based on the Kelross House project by Paul Archer Design as depicted in Section B)

Much of the structure at the rear of the house has been removed in this option. A side extension has been designed to create a large kitchen/diner that extends into the rear reception room and links via steps to the front reception room. The long run of kitchen units becomes a bench that continues along the same line out into the garden, which is accessed via large sliding doors. The stairs have also been reconfigured and show a link to a basement level (not shown in this case study). The roof over the side return extension is glazed to bring light into the kitchen.

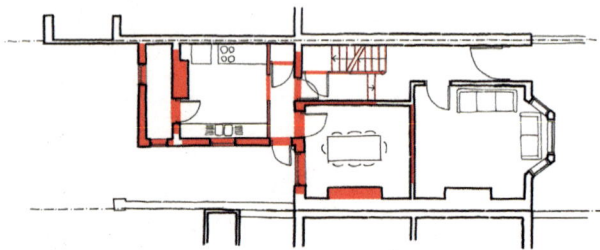

SECTION OF GARDEN EXCAVATED TO CREATE LEVEL ACCESS FROM KITCHEN DINER

CORNER OF NEW FIRST FLOOR EXTENSION CARRIED DOWN TO MINIMISE STRUCTURE

SECTION OF SIDE WALL AND REAR WALL OF REAR RECEPTION ROOM REMOVED TO AMALGAMATE WITH EXTENDED OUTRIGGER

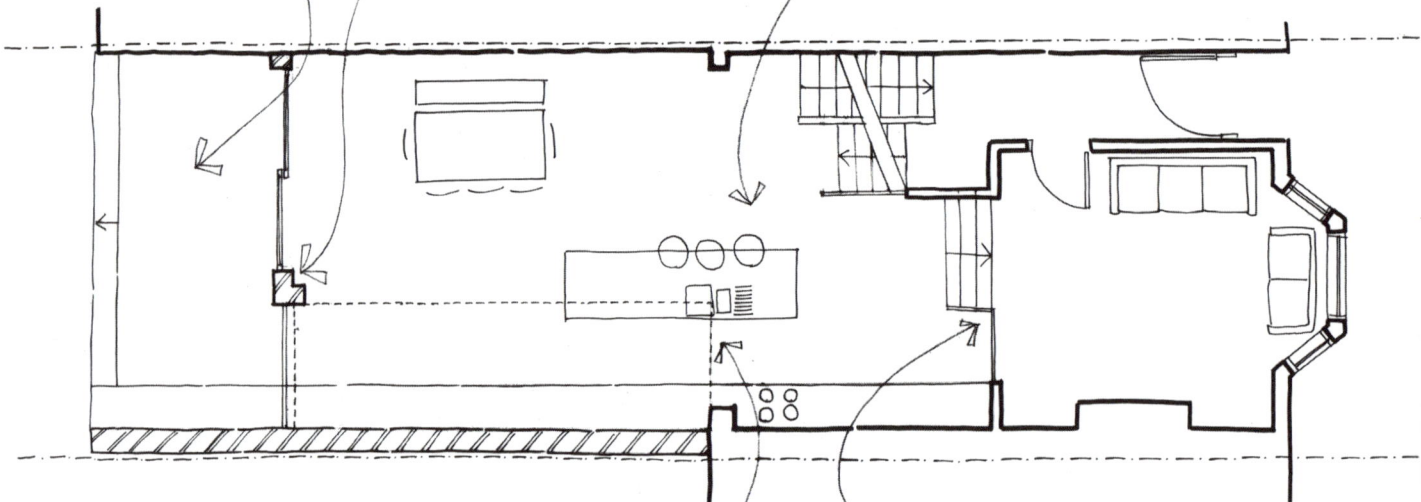

SPACIOUS KITCHEN ACCOMMODATED WITHIN REAR RECEPTION ROOM AND NEW SIDE RETURN EXTENSION

DIVIDING WALL REMOVED TO CREATE OPEN PLAN GROUND FLOOR FAMILY SPACE

Kelross House by Paul Archer Design, Islington,
London, 2014. Walls of rear reception room removed
to amalgamate it with kitchen diner at rear of house.
Image mirrored to reflect plan.

Kelross House by Paul Archer Design, Islington,
London, 2014. Large dining area created at rear.
Image reflected to match plan.

Kelross House by Paul Archer Design, Islington,
London, 2014. Existing level change demarks differing
room uses whilst creating full width connection
between them. Image mirrored to reflect plan.

OPTION 6

This option is a little more sensitive to the existing structure than the plan in Option 5. The front reception room remains untouched and the chimneybreast at the rear of the outrigger has been retained. It now accommodates a new, double-sided woodburning stove that serves both the seating area in the existing outrigger and the new, glass-sided rear extension. The walls of this extension are formed of sliding glass doors that open up to connect it fully with the garden. The existing outrigger has been extended into the side return to create a dining area. The rear wall of the rear reception room, which accommodates the kitchen in this option, has been removed to afford greater connection to the new extension.

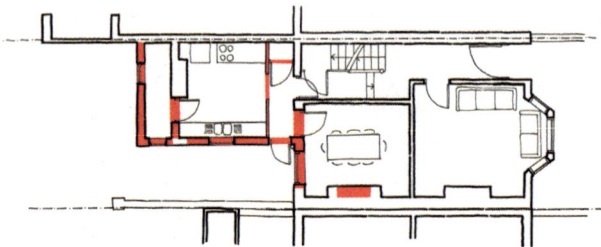

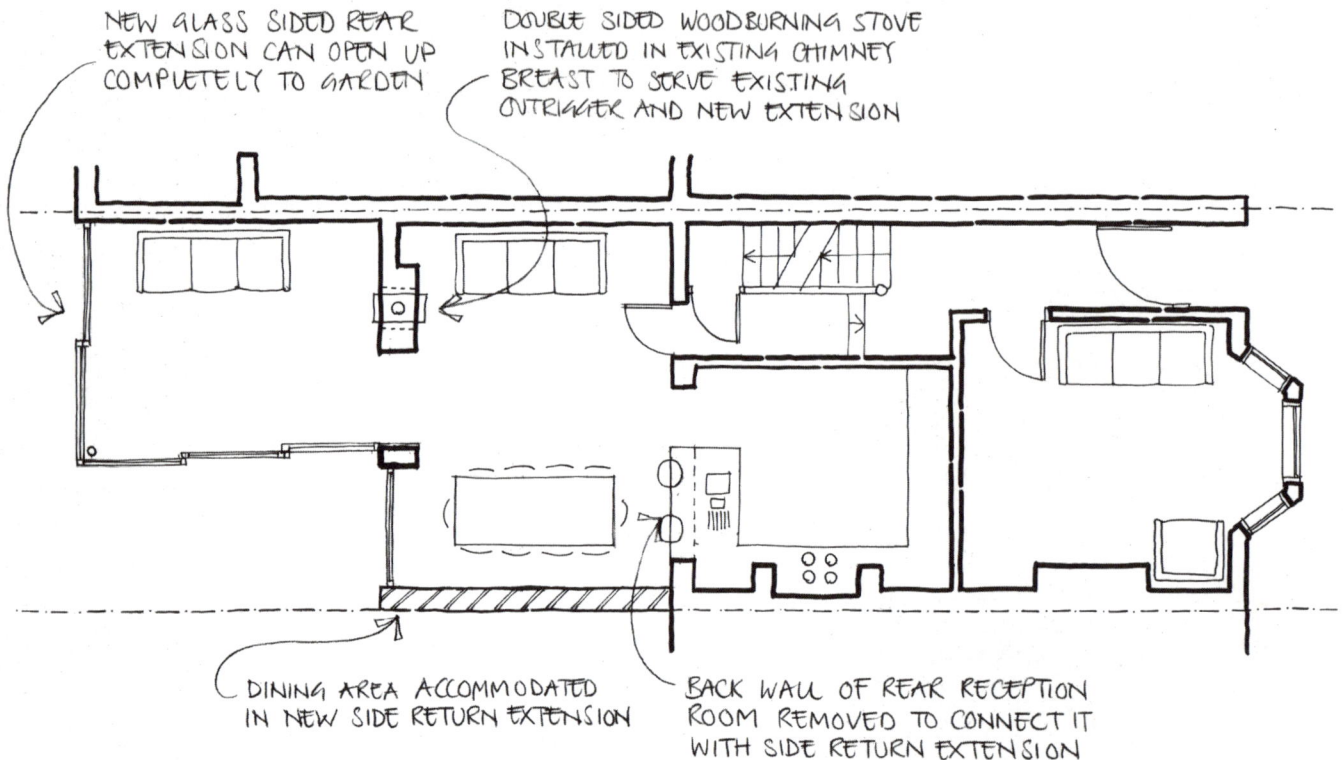

NEW GLASS SIDED REAR EXTENSION CAN OPEN UP COMPLETELY TO GARDEN

DOUBLE SIDED WOODBURNING STOVE INSTALLED IN EXISTING CHIMNEY BREAST TO SERVE EXISTING OUTRIGGER AND NEW EXTENSION

DINING AREA ACCOMMODATED IN NEW SIDE RETURN EXTENSION

BACK WALL OF REAR RECEPTION ROOM REMOVED TO CONNECT IT WITH SIDE RETURN EXTENSION

Artist's impression of rear view of new extension.

Artist's impression of internal view of new extension.

OPTION 7

(Based on the Hennessy House project by Paul Archer Design)

Room uses have been flipped in this option. The dining room now occupies the front reception room, with part of its hall wall replaced with glass. The living room has moved to the back of the house, opening out to the garden via sliding, folding doors. The existing corridor has been used to construct a large cupboard. Access to the rear of the house is now through the new kitchen/diner, with the kitchen situated in the heart of the ground floor.

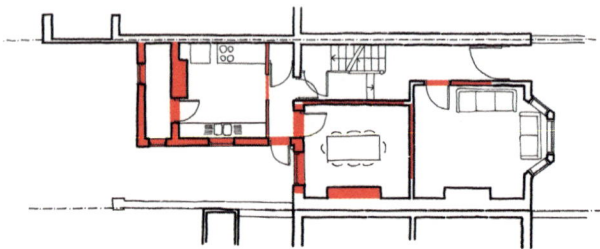

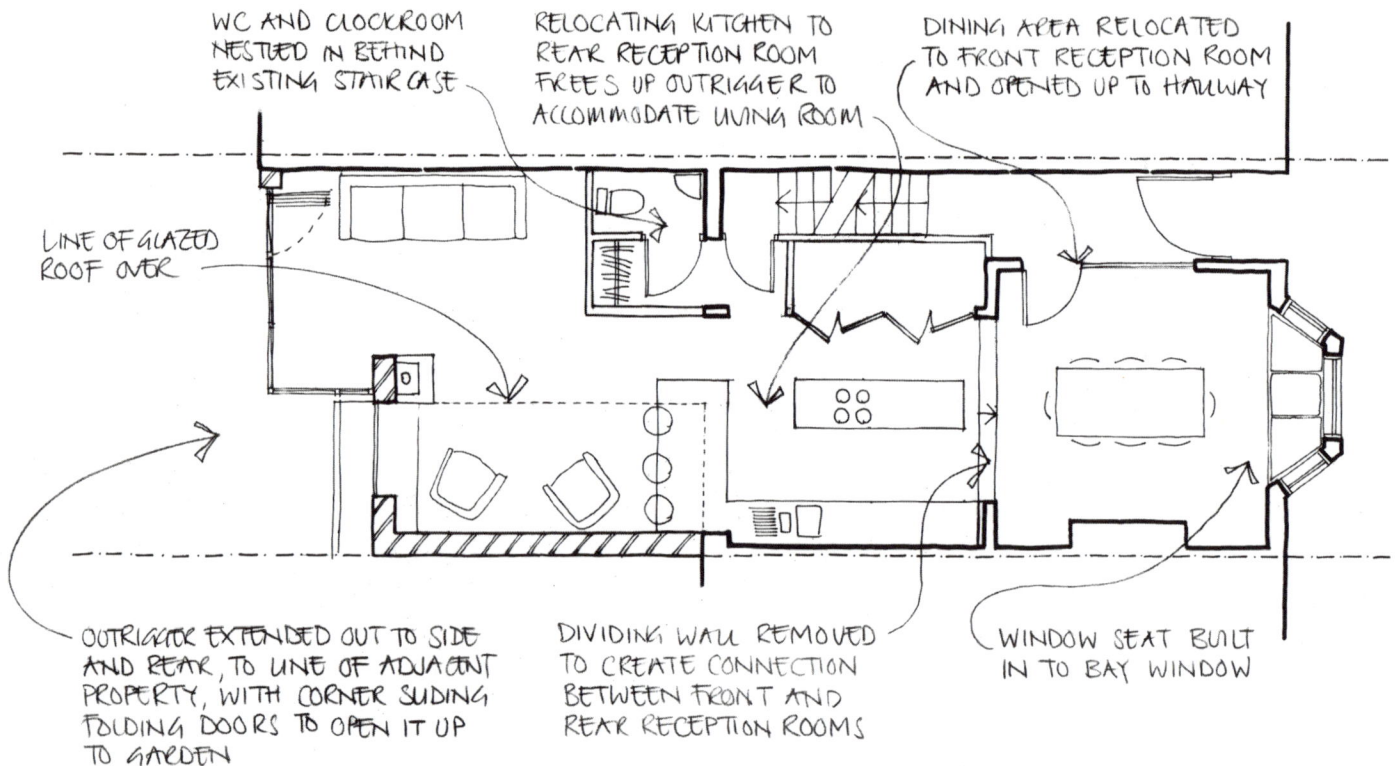

WC AND CLOCKROOM NESTLED IN BEHIND EXISTING STAIRCASE

RELOCATING KITCHEN TO REAR RECEPTION ROOM FREES UP OUTRIGGER TO ACCOMMODATE LIVING ROOM

DINING AREA RELOCATED TO FRONT RECEPTION ROOM AND OPENED UP TO HALLWAY

LINE OF GLAZED ROOF OVER

OUTRIGGER EXTENDED OUT TO SIDE AND REAR, TO LINE OF ADJACENT PROPERTY, WITH CORNER SLIDING FOLDING DOORS TO OPEN IT UP TO GARDEN

DIVIDING WALL REMOVED TO CREATE CONNECTION BETWEEN FRONT AND REAR RECEPTION ROOMS

WINDOW SEAT BUILT IN TO BAY WINDOW

Hennessy House by Paul Archer Design, Chiswick,
London, 2016. Spaces flow from one to another.

The rear wall of the rear reception room and the side and rear walls of
the outrigger have been removed. A side-and-rear extension has been
designed, creating an open, flowing ground floor – as in Ground-floor
Option 5. A cloakroom and WC have been tucked in behind the stairs. A
new chimneybreast, which is close enough to the outrigger's existing one to
consider connecting it to the chimneybreast above, has been designed as a
focal point to serve the new garden room.

Hennessy House by Paul Archer Design, Chiswick, London, 2016. View from dining room at front through kitchen to garden.

Hennessy House by Paul Archer Design, Chiswick,
London, 2016. Corner of existing outrigger removed
to open it up to garden.

OPTION 8

(Based on the Jimi House project by Paul Archer Design)

An opening in the wall between the front and rear reception rooms has been created, and the floor raised in the rear room to connect the two spaces. The side wall of the rear reception room has been removed to amalgamate the corridor space with the living room.

The outrigger has been extended out to the side and rear in this option to create a kitchen/diner that connects directly to the garden via large, sliding glass doors. The kitchen has been slotted into the side extension, with the side wall of the outrigger being retained or rebuilt to minimise structural alterations. A glazed roof above this extension brings light into the new kitchen.

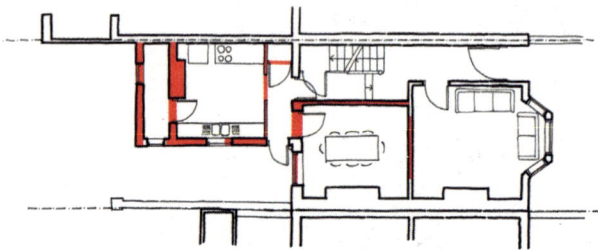

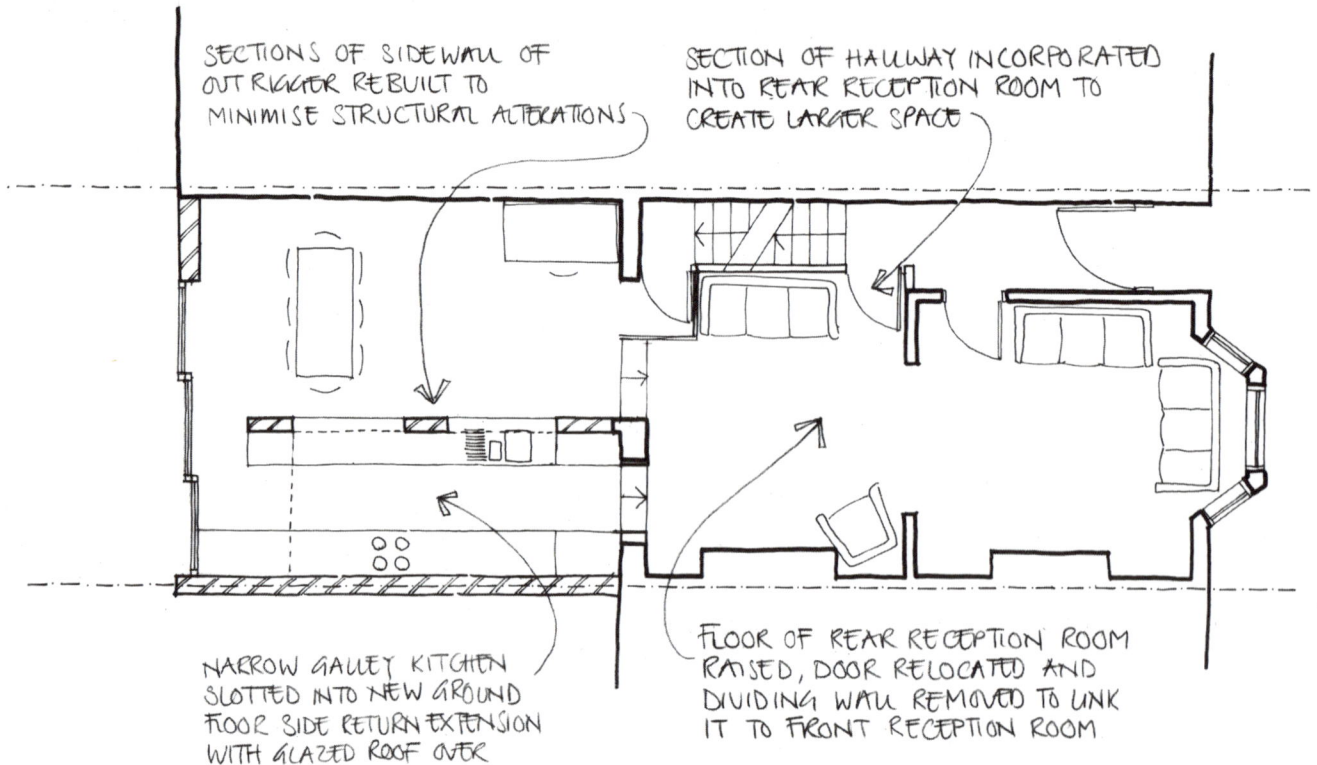

SECTIONS OF SIDE WALL OF OUTRIGGER REBUILT TO MINIMISE STRUCTURAL ALTERATIONS

SECTION OF HALLWAY INCORPORATED INTO REAR RECEPTION ROOM TO CREATE LARGER SPACE

NARROW GALLEY KITCHEN SLOTTED INTO NEW GROUND FLOOR SIDE RETURN EXTENSION WITH GLAZED ROOF OVER

FLOOR OF REAR RECEPTION ROOM RAISED, DOOR RELOCATED AND DIVIDING WALL REMOVED TO LINK IT TO FRONT RECEPTION ROOM

Jimi House by Paul Archer Design, Hackney, London, 2013. Dining area created in existing outrigger.

Lined Extension by Yard Architects, Kensington,
London, 2016. Kitchen accommodated in existing
outrigger.

Jimi House by Paul Archer Design, Hackney, London,
2013. Galley kitchen accommodated in new side-
return extension.

OPTION 9

(Based on the Lined Extension project by Yard Architects)

The floor of the rear reception room has been raised in this option to match the level of the floor in the front reception room. An opening has been made in the dividing wall to connect the two rooms. The door into the rear reception room has been blocked off, and a new entrance has been created at the top of the stairs that lead down to the outrigger.

The side and rear walls of the outrigger have been removed at ground-floor level. It has been extended to the side and to the rear to create a large, open-plan kitchen/diner with a window seat and access to the garden via sliding, folding doors. The window in the rear reception room has been removed to provide access to the dining room extension.

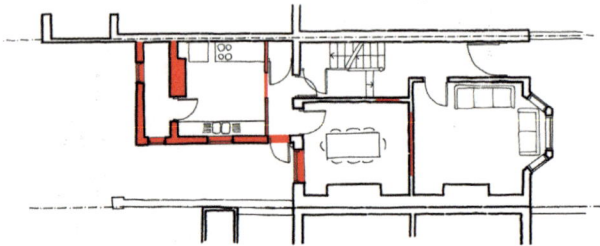

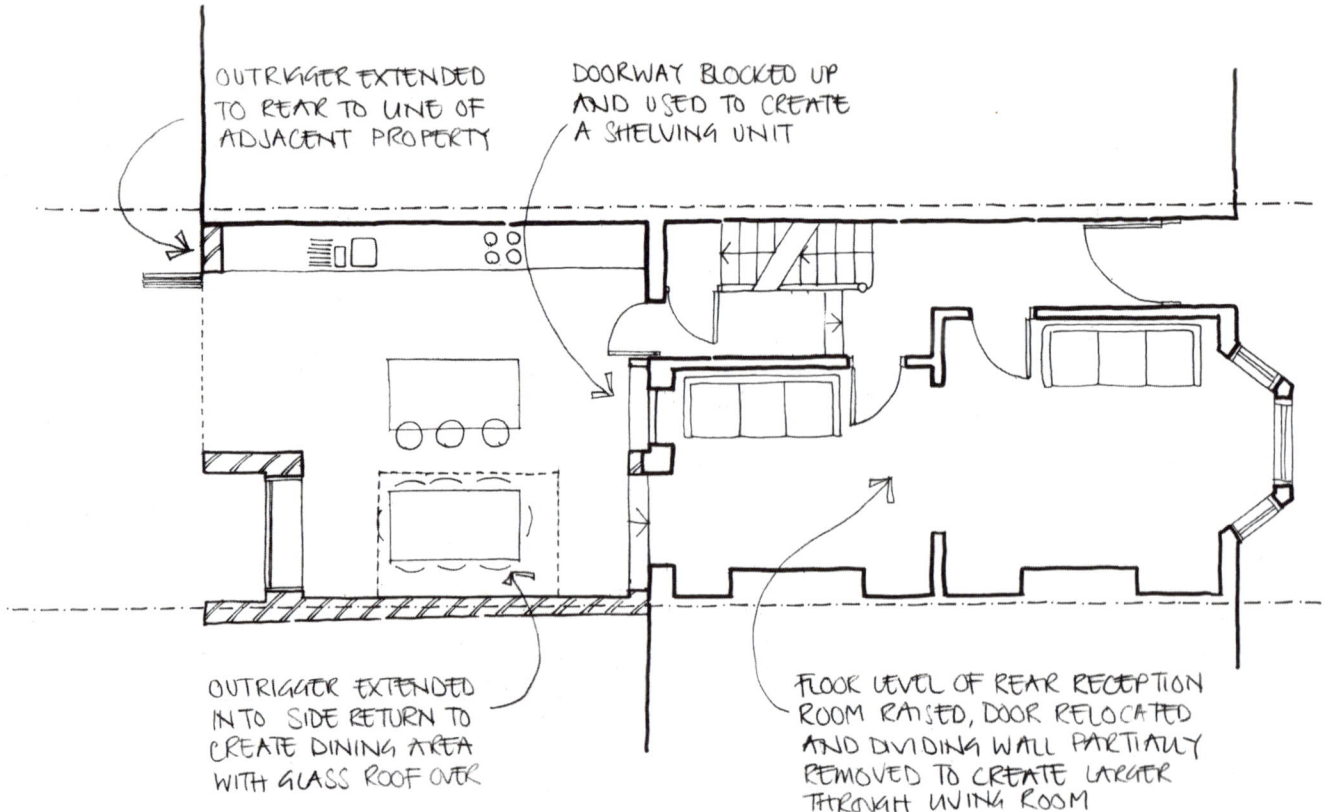

OUTRIGGER EXTENDED TO REAR TO LINE OF ADJACENT PROPERTY

DOORWAY BLOCKED UP AND USED TO CREATE A SHELVING UNIT

OUTRIGGER EXTENDED INTO SIDE RETURN TO CREATE DINING AREA WITH GLASS ROOF OVER

FLOOR LEVEL OF REAR RECEPTION ROOM RAISED, DOOR RELOCATED AND DIVIDING WALL PARTIALLY REMOVED TO CREATE LARGER THROUGH LIVING ROOM

Lined Extension by Yard Architects, Kensington,
London, 2016. Dining area and window seat created
in new extension.

FIRST FLOOR

The fact that the adjacent property has a longer outrigger makes the chance of gaining planning permission for a first-floor extension to the same line much more likely. So, making the most of this opportunity, the rear room has been extended to match that of its neighbour in all of the first-floor options.

OPTION 1

*Based on the Rug Room project
by Nic Howlett*

This option retains the front two rooms as bedrooms, but extends the outrigger to the rear. This creates sufficient space to accommodate a family bathroom and small study that overlooks the garden.

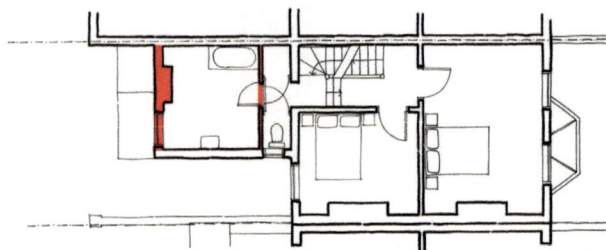

FAMILY BATHROOM AND SMALL STUDY ROOM ACCOMMODATED IN EXTENDED OUTRIGGER

SHELVING INSTALLED THE LENGTH OF THE CORRIDOR

OUTRIGGER EXTENDED AT FIRST FLOOR LEVEL TO MATCH LENGTH OF NEIGHBOURING PROPERTY

Rug Room by Nic Howlett, Oval, London, 2016. Rear wall removed to accommodate full-width window overlooking garden.

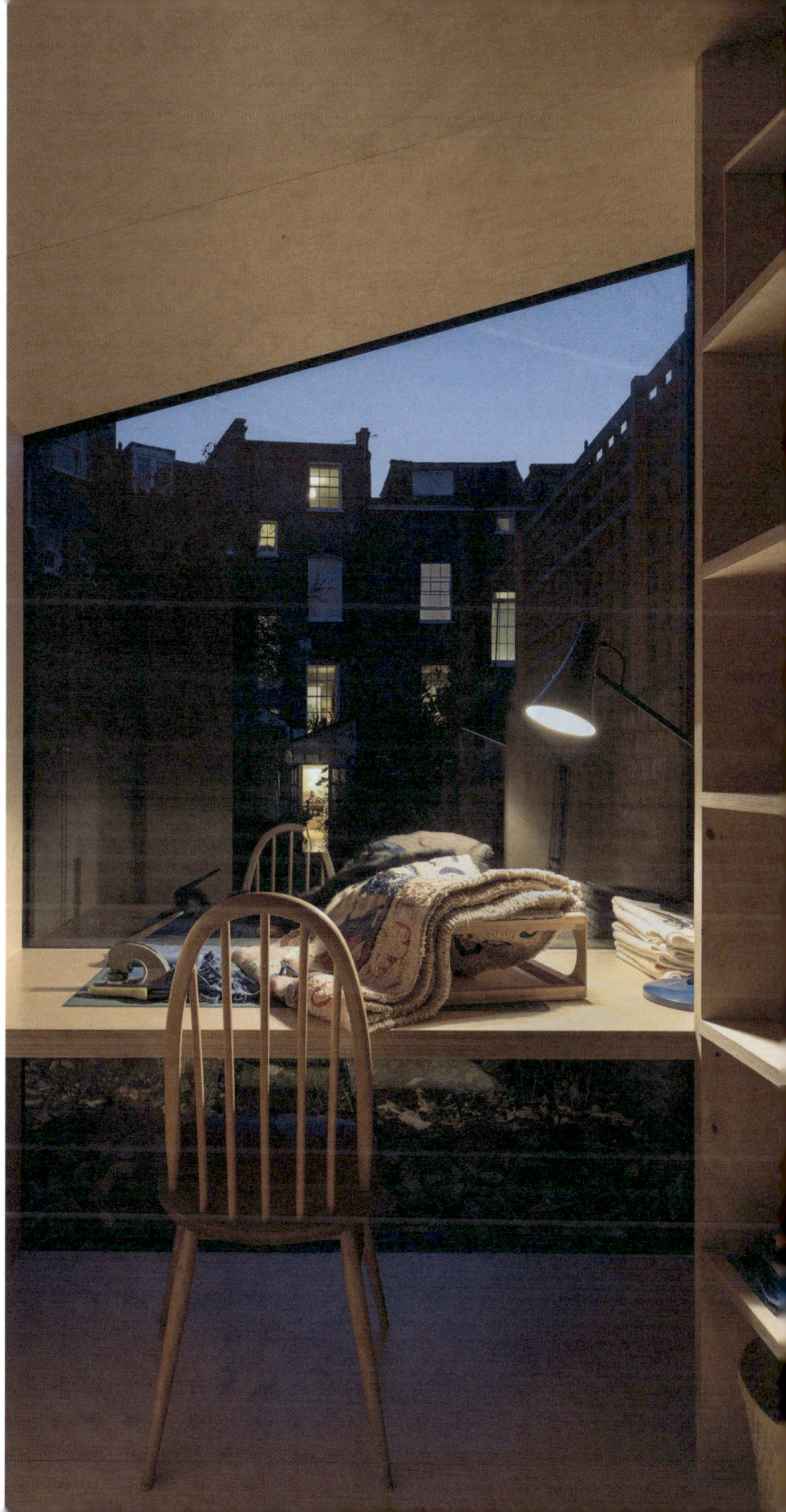

OPTION 2

The front bedroom has been divided up to accommodate an en-suite shower room. Careful planning of this shower room and integral wardrobe allows the door to avoid clashing with the existing window. Another shower room has been shown in the outrigger, which has been extended backwards to the line of the neighbouring house to create an additional double bedroom.

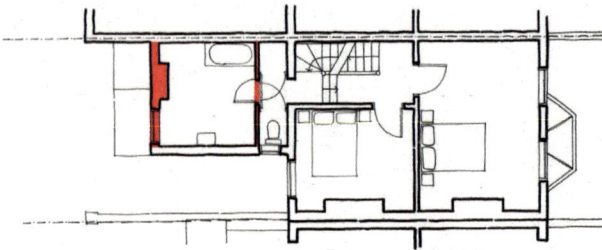

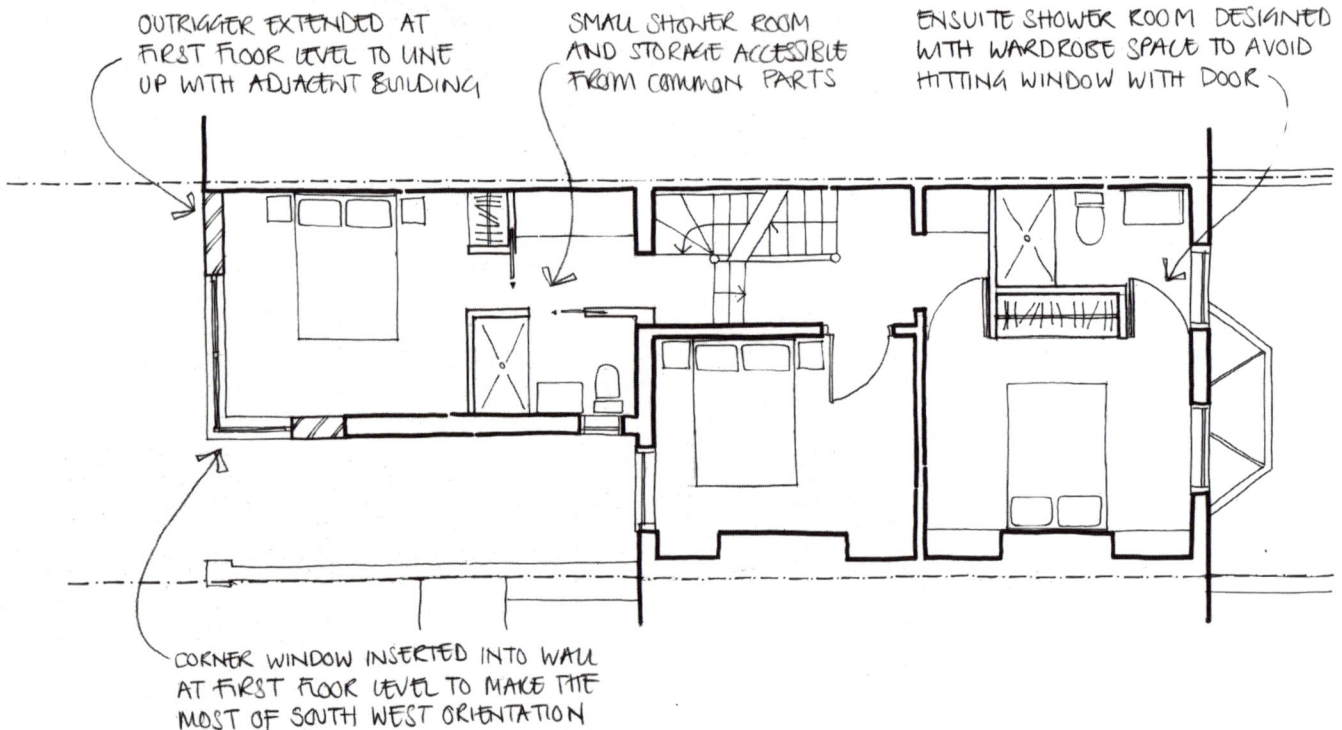

OUTRIGGER EXTENDED AT FIRST FLOOR LEVEL TO LINE UP WITH ADJACENT BUILDING

SMALL SHOWER ROOM AND STORAGE ACCESSIBLE FROM COMMON PARTS

ENSUITE SHOWER ROOM DESIGNED WITH WARDROBE SPACE TO AVOID HITTING WINDOW WITH DOOR

CORNER WINDOW INSERTED INTO WALL AT FIRST FLOOR LEVEL TO MAKE THE MOST OF SOUTH WEST ORIENTATION

Artist's impression of window seat in outrigger
bedroom. Based on option 3.

OPTION 3

(Based on Phase One of the 'Our House', Lausanne Road project by Green & Teggin Architects as depicted in Section A)

The front bedroom remains untouched in this option, while the middle bedroom has been converted into a spacious family bathroom. The extended outrigger accommodates a double bedroom with a window seat overlooking the garden, and a dressing area at the entrance to the room. As shown in the sketch, the ceiling of the rear reception room has been sloped to give a grander feel to the room – also depicted in image of First-floor Option 5.

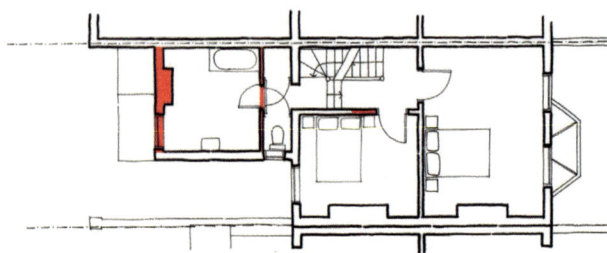

WINDOW SEAT AND STORE CREATED IN NEW FIRST FLOOR EXTENSION, DESIGNED TO LINE UP WITH REAR WALL OF ADJACENT BUILDING

CEILING IN BEDROOM AREA REMOVED AND SKYLIGHT INSTALLED TO CREATE LIGHT AND AIRY ROOM

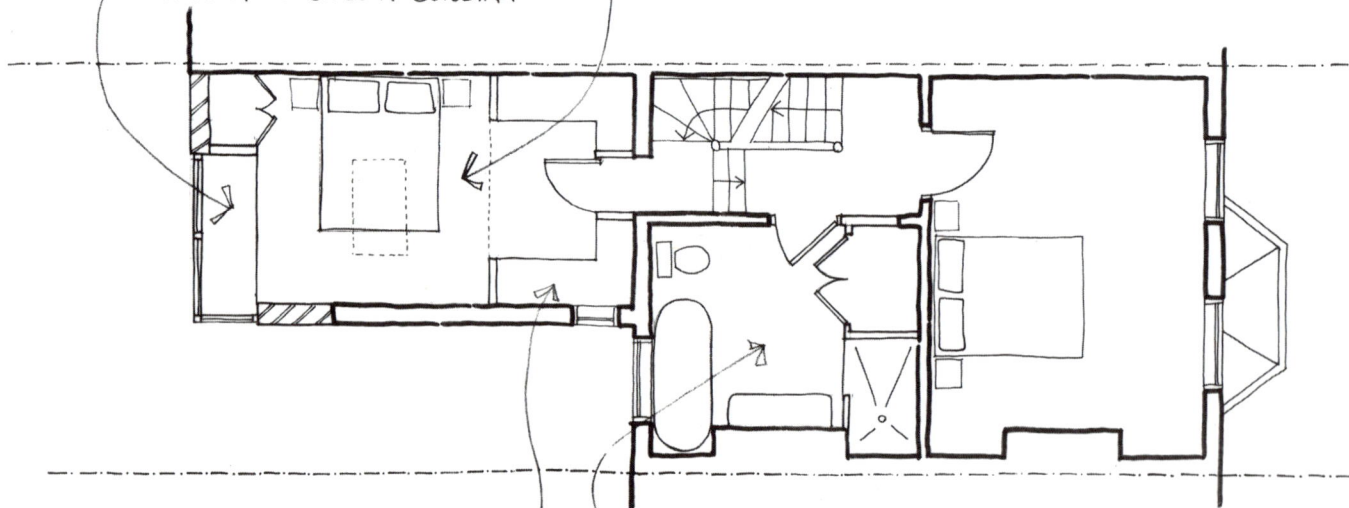

WC AND STORE REMOVED TO CREATE ROOM FOR A DRESSING AREA.

CENTRAL BEDROOM CONVERTED INTO LARGE FAMILY BATHROOM

'Our House', Lausanne Road (Phase One) by Green & Teggin Architects, Peckham, London, 2009. A mix of old and new.

OPTION 4

(As depicted in Section B)

The front bedroom has been divided into a bedroom and study in this option, with the middle bedroom accommodating a bathroom and dressing room to serve this bedroom. A small shower room and dressing area has been slotted into the outrigger, still leaving enough room for a rear double bedroom.

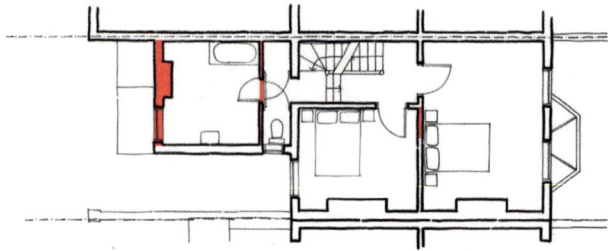

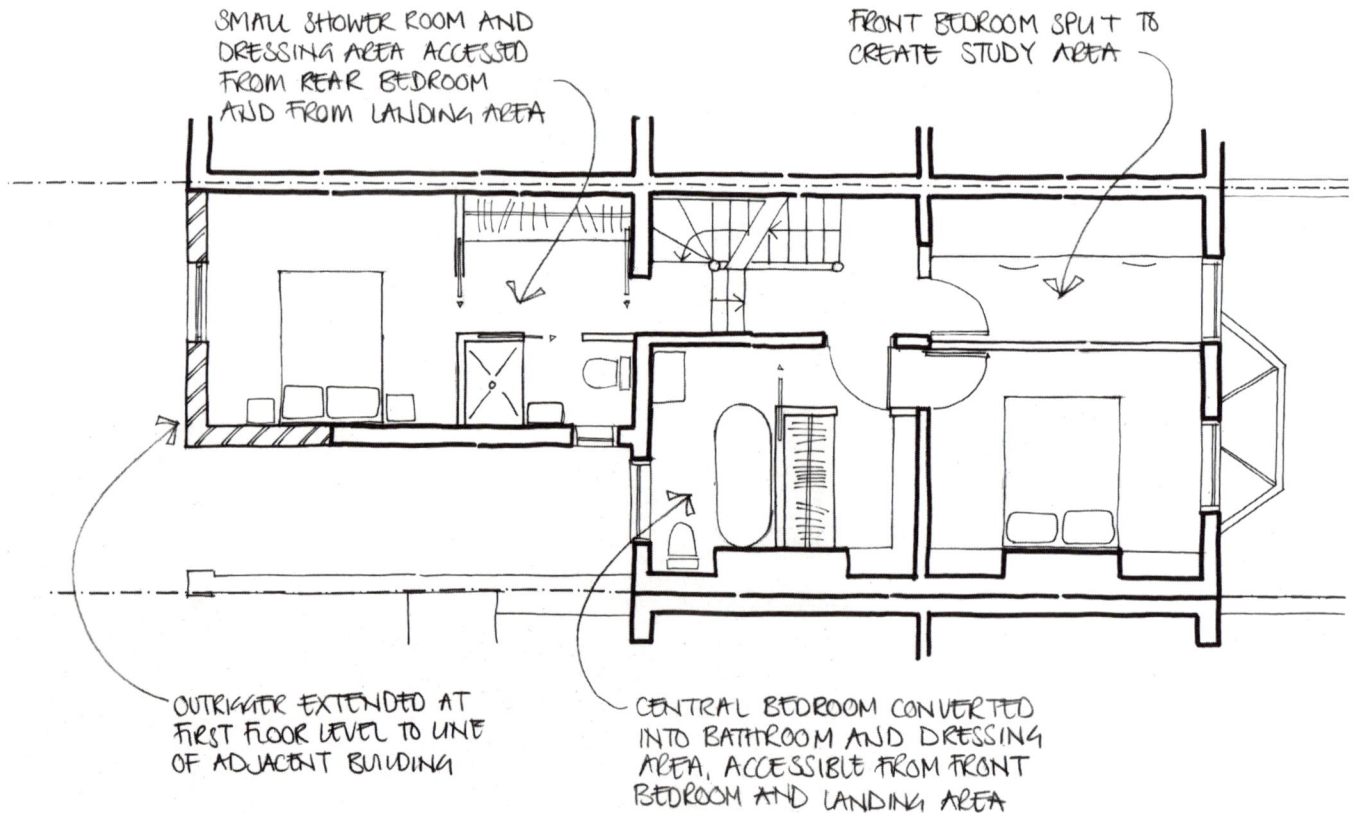

SMALL SHOWER ROOM AND DRESSING AREA ACCESSED FROM REAR BEDROOM AND FROM LANDING AREA

FRONT BEDROOM SPLIT TO CREATE STUDY AREA

OUTRIGGER EXTENDED AT FIRST FLOOR LEVEL TO LINE OF ADJACENT BUILDING

CENTRAL BEDROOM CONVERTED INTO BATHROOM AND DRESSING AREA, ACCESSIBLE FROM FRONT BEDROOM AND LANDING AREA

Hennessy House by Paul Archer Design, Chiswick,
London, 2016. Master bedroom with entrance to
en-suite and dressing area.

OPTION 5

(Based on the Hennessy House project by Paul Archer Design)

The door of the front bedroom has been relocated and a study area created in one half of the room, behind the bed. The middle bedroom has been employed as an en-suite shower room and dressing area to serve the front bedroom. A small utility cupboard has been shown and an en-suite shower room created in the extended outrigger, with the remainder of the space accommodating a double bedroom. Sloping the ceiling makes an essentially small room appear more spacious.

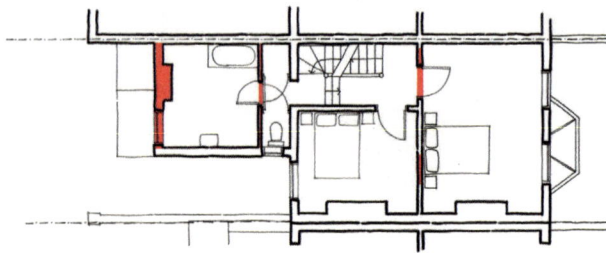

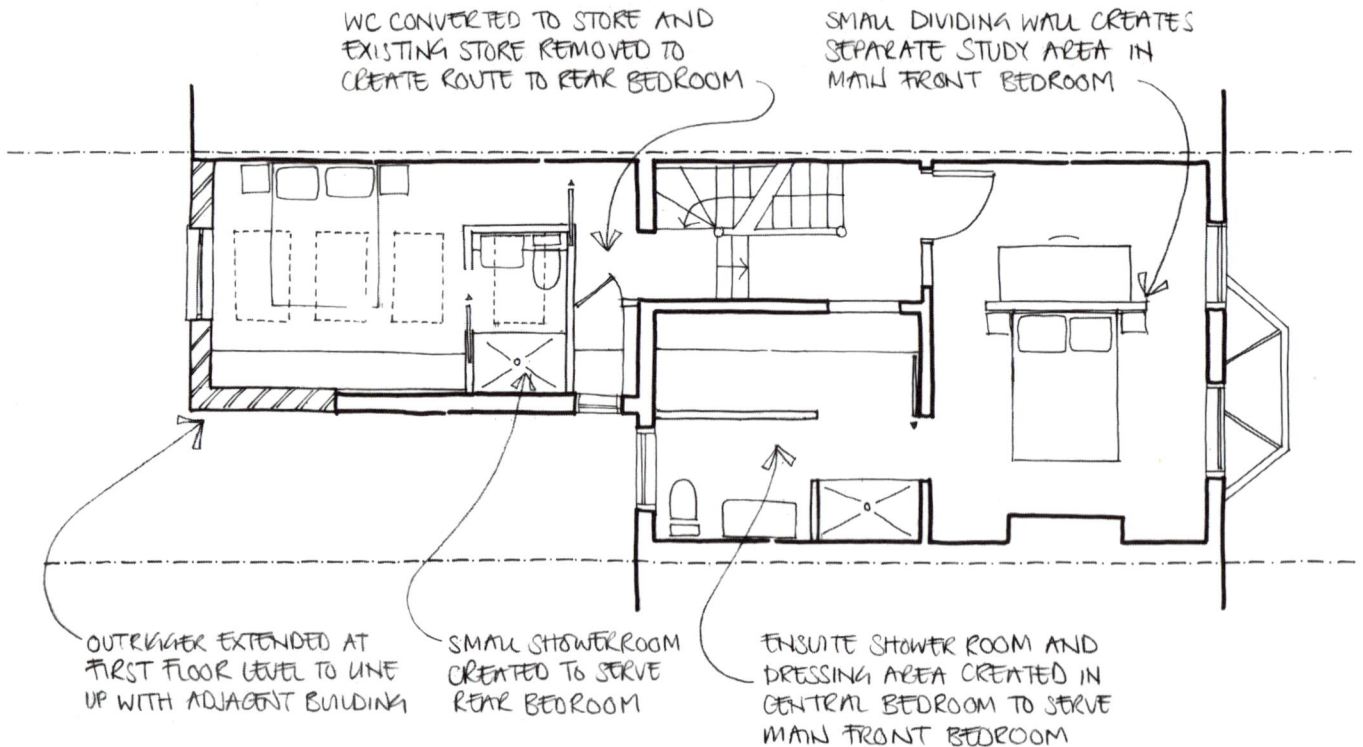

WC CONVERTED TO STORE AND EXISTING STORE REMOVED TO CREATE ROUTE TO REAR BEDROOM

SMALL DIVIDING WALL CREATES SEPARATE STUDY AREA IN MAIN FRONT BEDROOM

OUTRIGGER EXTENDED AT FIRST FLOOR LEVEL TO LINE UP WITH ADJACENT BUILDING

SMALL SHOWER ROOM CREATED TO SERVE REAR BEDROOM

ENSUITE SHOWER ROOM AND DRESSING AREA CREATED IN CENTRAL BEDROOM TO SERVE MAIN FRONT BEDROOM

Hennessy House by Paul Archer Design, Chiswick, London, 2016. Ceiling removed to create more spacious feel.

SECOND FLOOR

The second floor accommodates two bedrooms. It does not extend over the outrigger. Much of the success of the loft extension depends on the positioning of the stairs that serve it – especially where headroom is tight. Therefore, most of these options show varying stair arrangements.

OPTION 1

The front bedroom has been divided to accommodate a new loft stair, positioned to make the most of the space above, and a shower room. This still leaves enough room for a double bedroom at the front. The rear bedroom remains untouched. This should be read in conjunction with Loft Option 1.

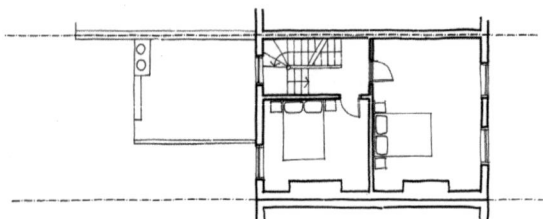

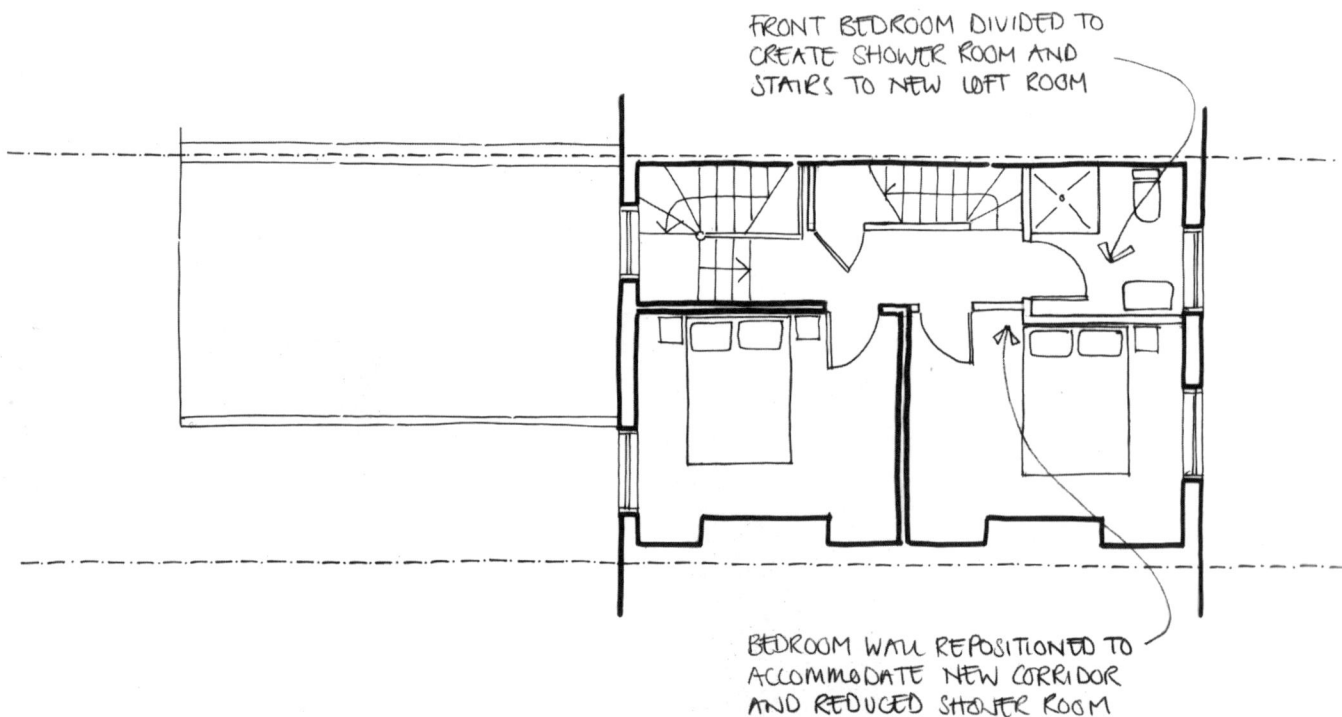

FRONT BEDROOM DIVIDED TO
CREATE SHOWER ROOM AND
STAIRS TO NEW LOFT ROOM

BEDROOM WALL REPOSITIONED TO
ACCOMMODATE NEW CORRIDOR
AND REDUCED SHOWER ROOM

OPTION 2

A section has been taken from both the front and the rear bedrooms to create a small shower room between the two, with a new stair opposite the entrance to this room. A sloping ceiling with skylights is shown in the front bedroom. This plan is to be read in conjunction with Loft Option 2.

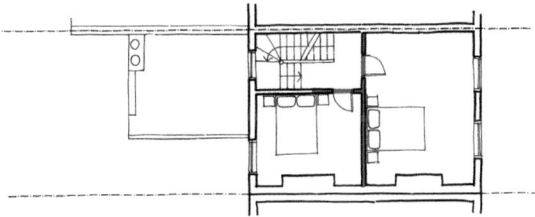

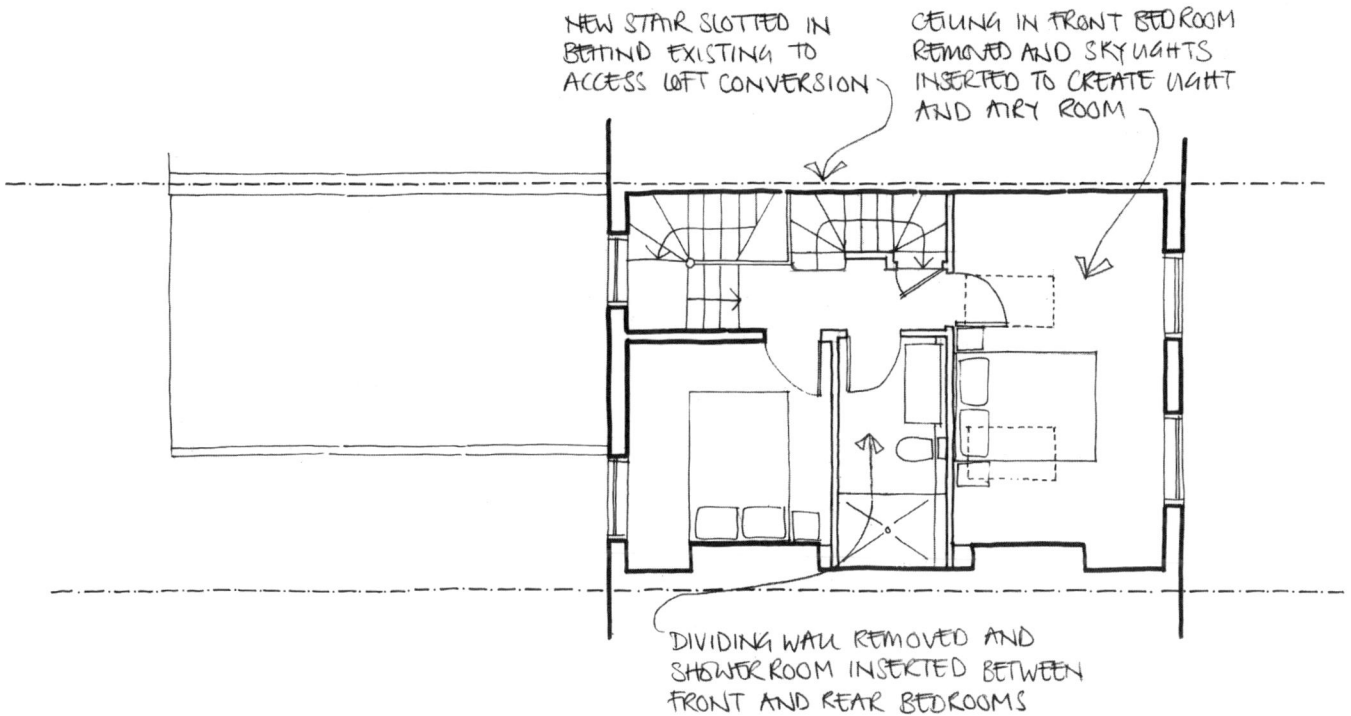

NEW STAIR SLOTTED IN
BEHIND EXISTING TO
ACCESS LOFT CONVERSION

CEILING IN FRONT BEDROOM
REMOVED AND SKYLIGHTS
INSERTED TO CREATE LIGHT
AND AIRY ROOM

DIVIDING WALL REMOVED AND
SHOWER ROOM INSERTED BETWEEN
FRONT AND REAR BEDROOMS

OPTION 3

(Based on Phase Two of the 'Our House', Lausanne Road project by Green & Teggin Architects as depicted in Section A)

If your house is situated on a busy main road, you may want to move all the bedrooms to the rear of the property. In this option, the ceiling of the front room has been removed to create a double-height space, which has been divided in two to accommodate two equally sized study areas. The ceiling above the original rear bedroom, which has been converted into a shower room and toilet, has been lowered to create more headroom above. Alternate-tread stairs from the study areas access the loft extension above. This plan is to be read in conjunction with Loft Option 3.

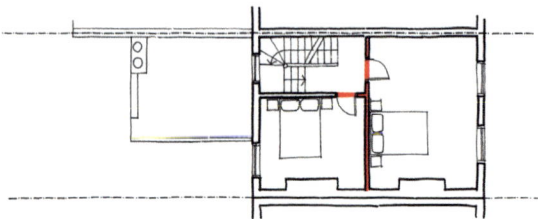

FRONT ROOM DIVIDED IN TWO TO ACCOMMODATE TWO STUDY AREAS OVERLOOKING BUSY ROAD

CEILING IN STUDY AREAS REMOVED TO CREATE DOUBLE HEIGHT SPACE AND ENABLE CONNECTION TO MEZZANINE ABOVE

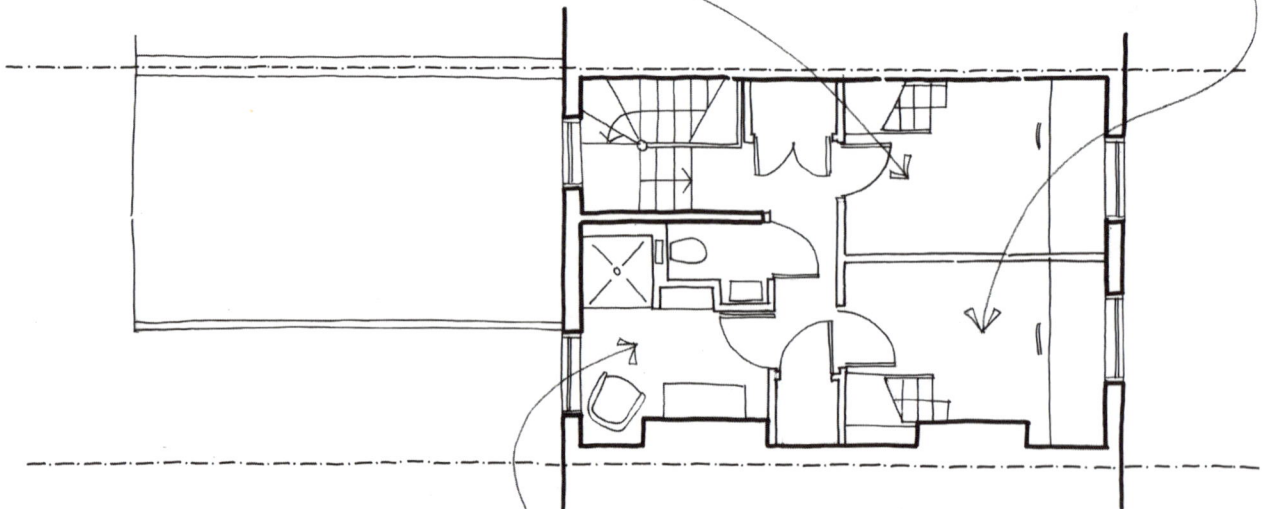

REAR BEDROOM CONVERTED INTO SHOWER ROOM AND SEPARATE WC

'Our House', Lausanne Road (Phase Two) by Green & Teggin Architects, Peckham, London, 2017. View from mezzanine down to study area.

Next page. 'Our House', Lausanne Road (Phase Two) by Green & Teggin Architects, Peckham, London, 2017. Double-height study bedroom.

OPTION 4

Similarly to Second-floor Option 2, a small shower room has been slotted in between the front and rear bedrooms and the ceiling above the front room has been opened up. Storage is shown under the new set of stairs. This plan is to be read in conjunction with Loft Option 4.

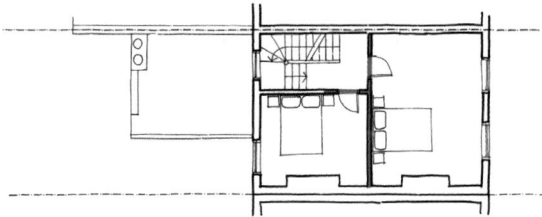

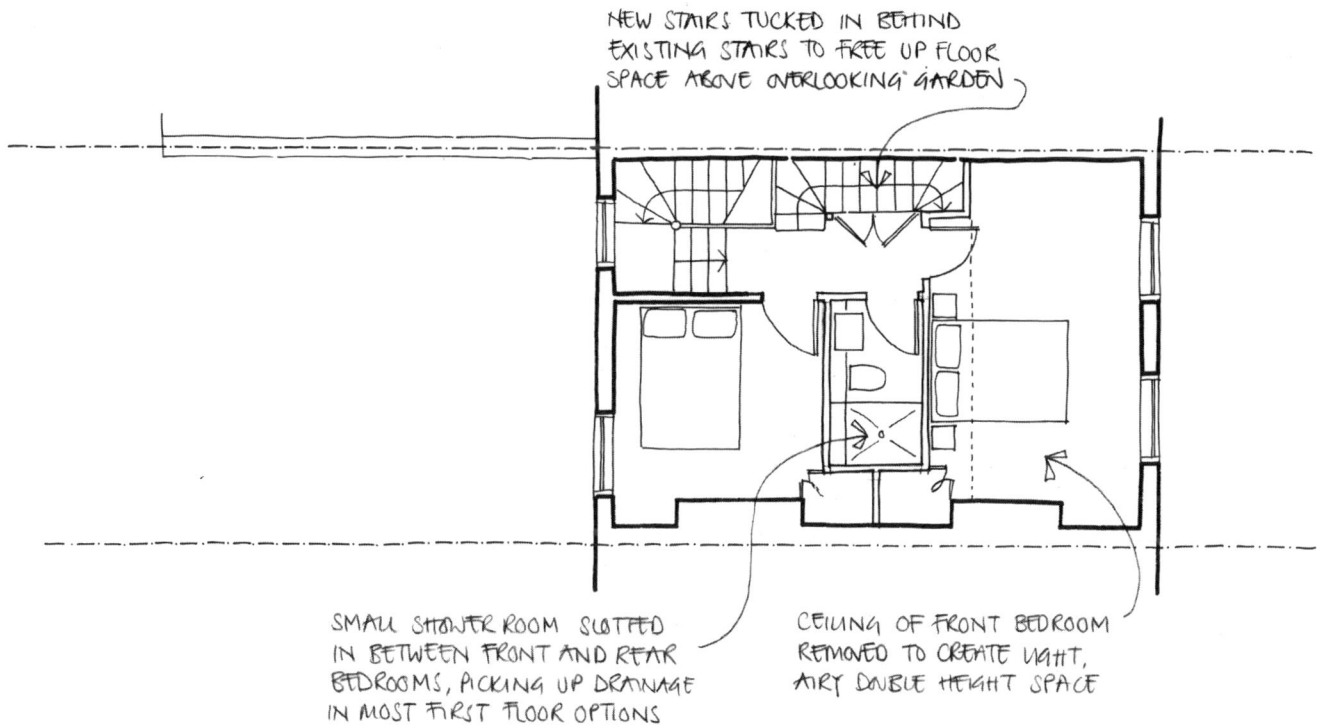

NEW STAIRS TUCKED IN BEHIND EXISTING STAIRS TO FREE UP FLOOR SPACE ABOVE OVERLOOKING GARDEN

SMALL SHOWER ROOM SLOTTED IN BETWEEN FRONT AND REAR BEDROOMS, PICKING UP DRAINAGE IN MOST FIRST FLOOR OPTIONS

CEILING OF FRONT BEDROOM REMOVED TO CREATE LIGHT, AIRY DOUBLE HEIGHT SPACE

OPTION 5

This option cuts a section out of the large front bedroom to create a good-sized bathroom, while still leaving enough room for a double bed. The rear bedroom remains unchanged. A new stair serving the loft room has been placed above the existing. This option is to be read in conjunction with Loft Option 5.

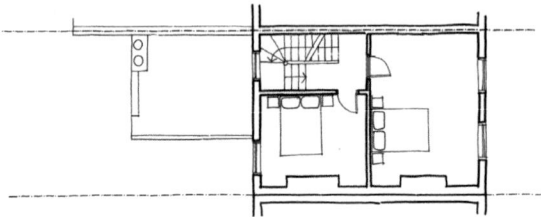

NEW STAIR POSITIONED ABOVE EXISTING TO SERVE LOFT EXTENSION

LARGE FRONT ROOM DIVIDED IN TWO TO ACCOMMODATE A BATHROOM AND SMALLER DOUBLE BEDROOM

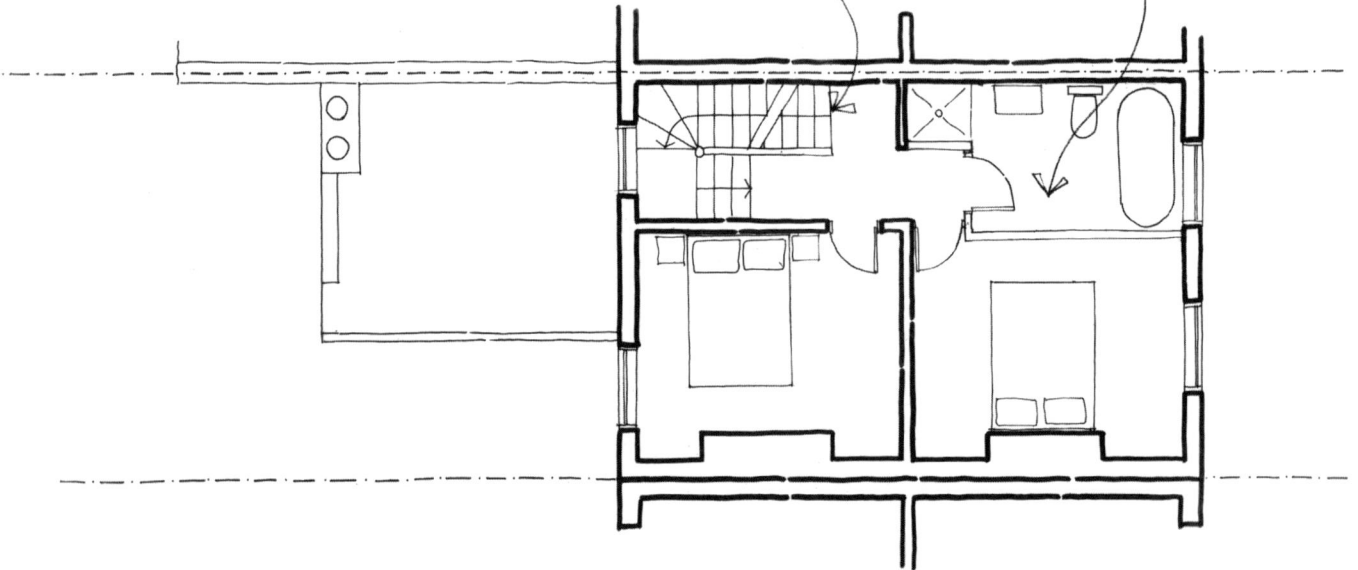

OPTION 6

(As depicted in Section B)

A small outrigger extension, which would accommodate a family bathroom, is shown in this option. The plan of the two existing bedrooms has not been changed, but their ceilings have been removed. A new lower ceiling has been designed in the central part of the plan (as shown dotted on the plan), the rest of which is left open, sloping up with the line of the roof. This plan is to be read in conjunction with Loft Option 6, which has not yet been tested at Planning.

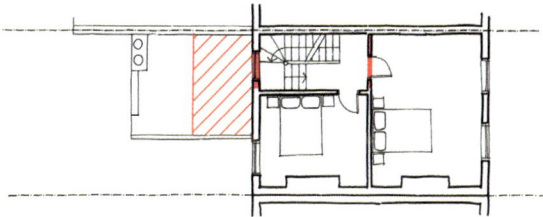

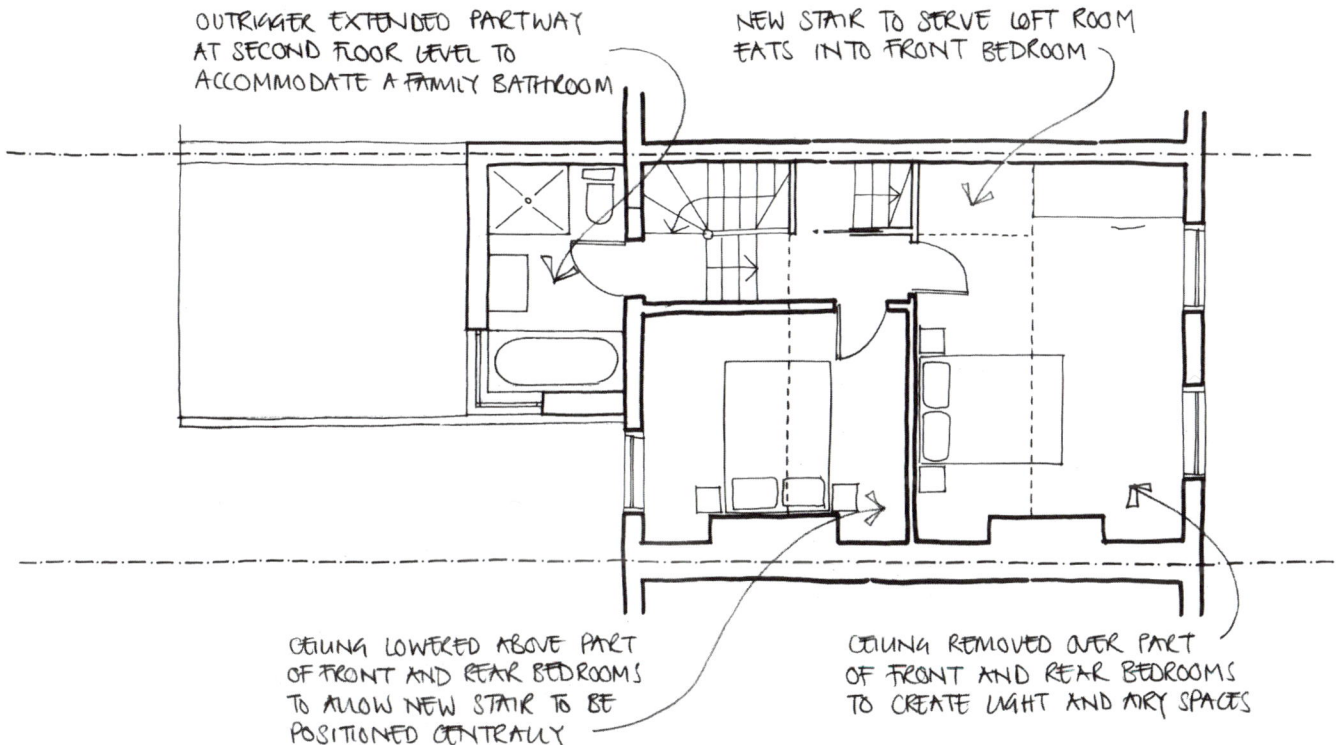

OUTRIGGER EXTENDED PARTWAY AT SECOND FLOOR LEVEL TO ACCOMMODATE A FAMILY BATHROOM

NEW STAIR TO SERVE LOFT ROOM EATS INTO FRONT BEDROOM

CEILING LOWERED ABOVE PART OF FRONT AND REAR BEDROOMS TO ALLOW NEW STAIR TO BE POSITIONED CENTRALLY

CEILING REMOVED OVER PART OF FRONT AND REAR BEDROOMS TO CREATE LIGHT AND AIRY SPACES

LOFT

In the existing arrangement, the floor-to-underside-of-ridge-beam height was only 2m. Accordingly, taking additional structure and insulation into account, the ceiling in the floor below needed to be lowered, or inventive solutions needed to be found to make this room habitable. There are no proposals to extend over the outrigger at loft level, as that would mean increasing the height of the outrigger by two storeys, which would not usually be permitted at planning stage.

OPTION 1

In this option, the loft door is at the top of the stairs, where a small shower room has also been designed. The wall of the eaves storage area has been positioned to create as much space as possible in the bedroom. Note that even with the ceiling of the floor below being lowered, the ceiling height at the head of the bed will still only be about 1.2m in this case. This option is to be read in conjunction with Second-floor Option 1.

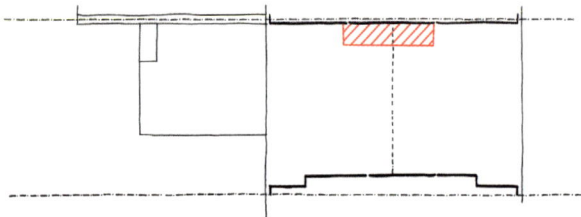

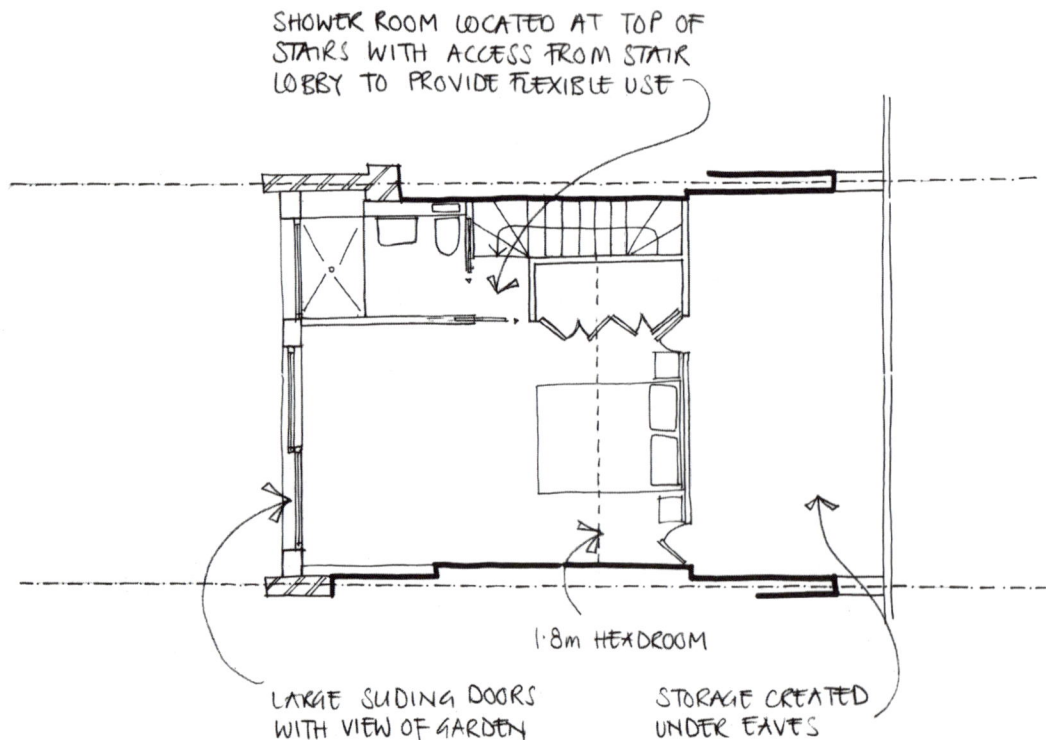

SHOWER ROOM LOCATED AT TOP OF STAIRS WITH ACCESS FROM STAIR LOBBY TO PROVIDE FLEXIBLE USE

1.8m HEADROOM

LARGE SLIDING DOORS WITH VIEW OF GARDEN

STORAGE CREATED UNDER EAVES

OPTION 2

This option follows on from Second-floor Option 2. A shower room is positioned above the one proposed for the floor below, which simplifies the plumbing. The floor under the eaves at the front has been removed to create a double-height space in the bedroom below. The ceiling height on the second floor has been lowered to create a more standard ceiling height in the loft.

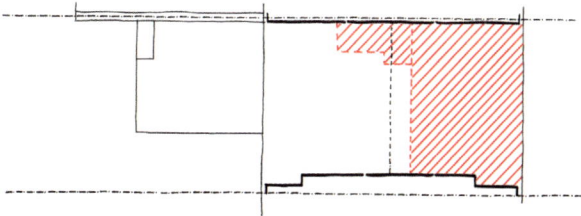

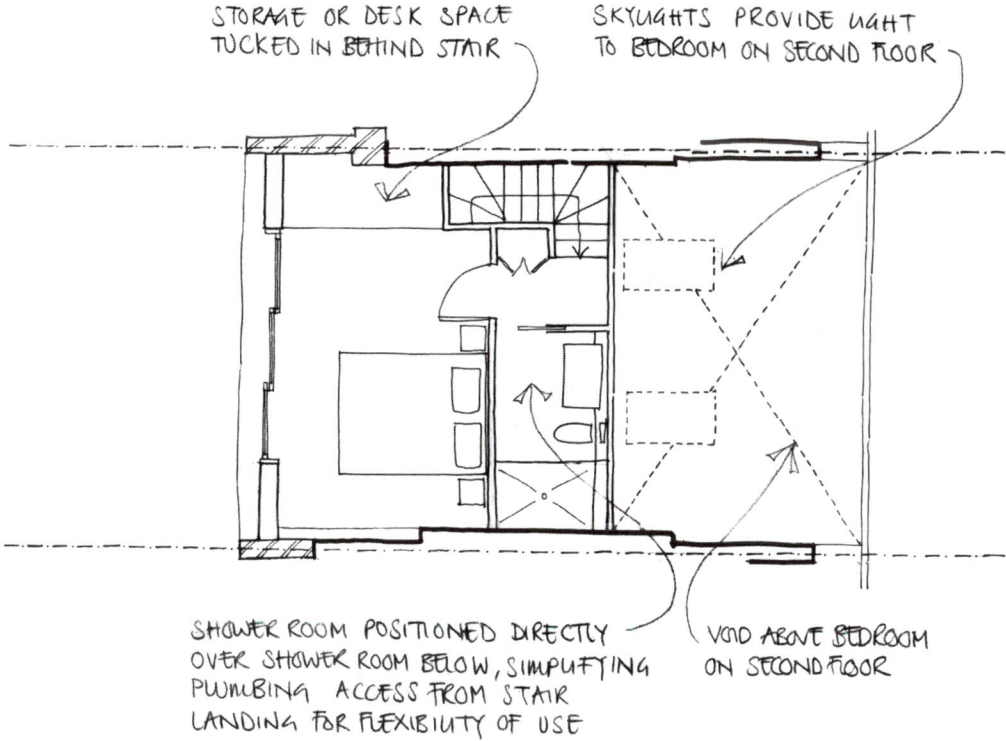

STORAGE OR DESK SPACE TUCKED IN BEHIND STAIR

SKYLIGHTS PROVIDE LIGHT TO BEDROOM ON SECOND FLOOR

SHOWER ROOM POSITIONED DIRECTLY OVER SHOWER ROOM BELOW, SIMPLIFYING PLUMBING ACCESS FROM STAIR LANDING FOR FLEXIBILITY OF USE

VOID ABOVE BEDROOM ON SECOND FLOOR

OPTION 3

(Based on Phase Two of the 'Our House', Lausanne Road project by Green & Teggin Architects)

In this option the new, full-width dormer extension is split in half to create two equally sized bedrooms that connect via alternate tread stairs to the study areas shown in Second-floor Option 3. These bedrooms have views over the rear garden through large double doors with Juliet balconies, and are shielded from the noise of the road at the front.

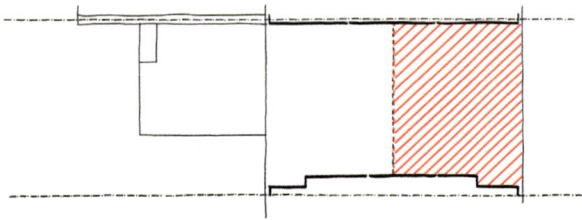

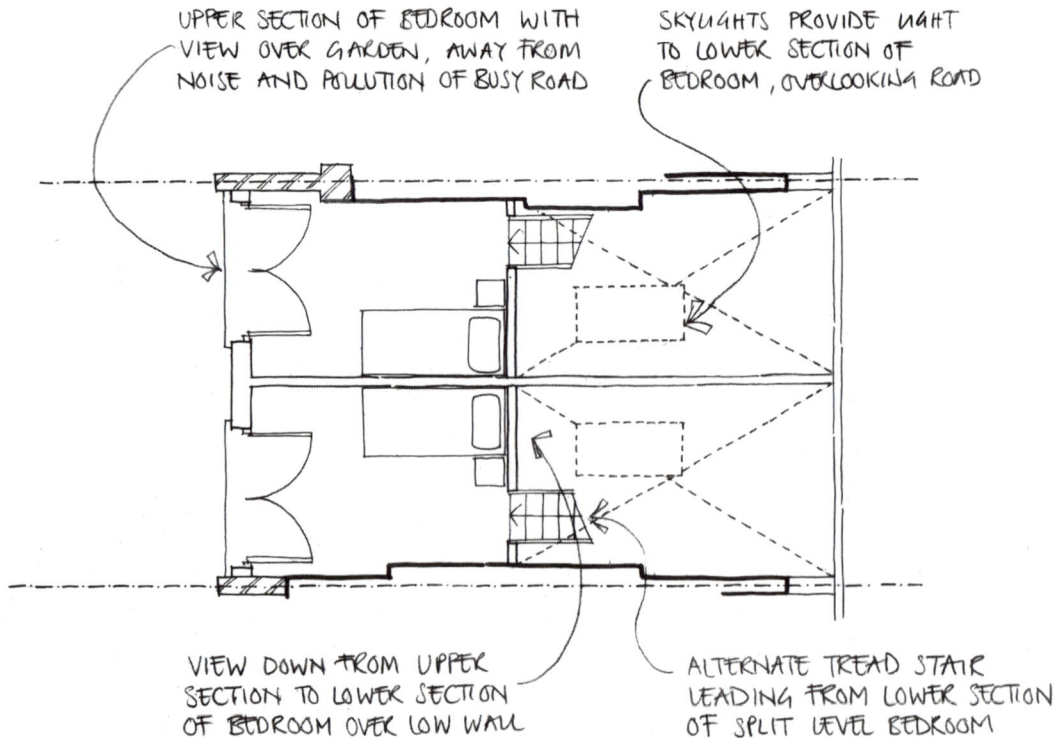

UPPER SECTION OF BEDROOM WITH VIEW OVER GARDEN, AWAY FROM NOISE AND POLLUTION OF BUSY ROAD

SKYLIGHTS PROVIDE LIGHT TO LOWER SECTION OF BEDROOM, OVERLOOKING ROAD

VIEW DOWN FROM UPPER SECTION TO LOWER SECTION OF BEDROOM OVER LOW WALL

ALTERNATE TREAD STAIR LEADING FROM LOWER SECTION OF SPLIT LEVEL BEDROOM

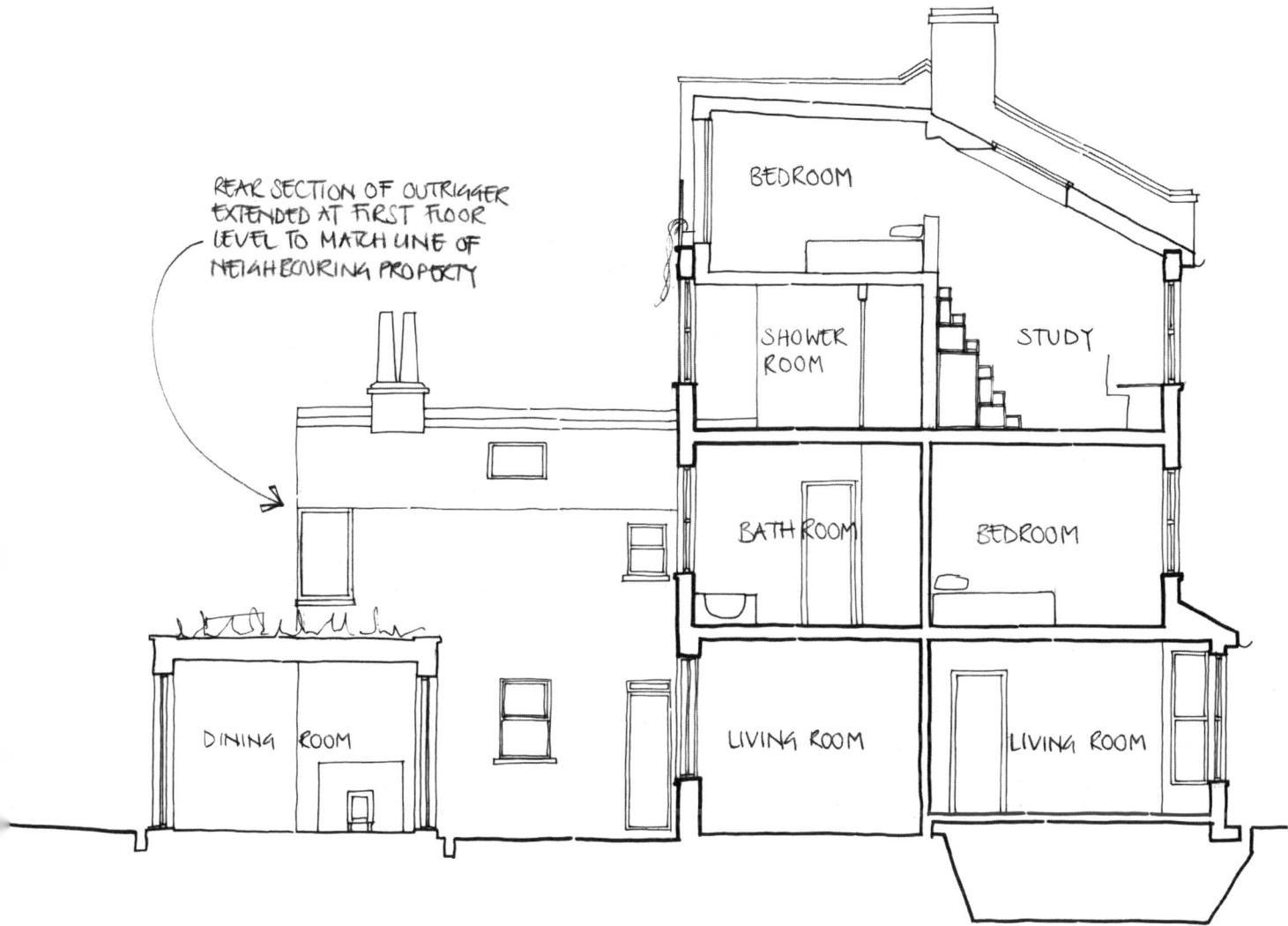

REAR SECTION OF OUTRIGGER
EXTENDED AT FIRST FLOOR
LEVEL TO MATCH LINE OF
NEIGHBOURING PROPERTY

BEDROOM

SHOWER
ROOM

STUDY

BATH ROOM

BEDROOM

DINING ROOM

LIVING ROOM

LIVING ROOM

'Our House', Lausanne Road (Phase Two) by Green
& Teggin Architects, Peckham, London, 2017.
Mezzanine bedroom.

OPTION 4

This option is to be read in conjunction with Second-floor Option 4. It omits the shower room seen in other loft examples here to create a grand loft room – although there is space for a narrow shower room tucked in alongside the stairs, if desired. The floor under the front of the roof has been removed to create a double-height space in the bedroom below, but could be retained and used as storage or incorporated into the new loft room. The ceiling over the rear of the second floor has been lowered to give greater ceiling height in the loft room.

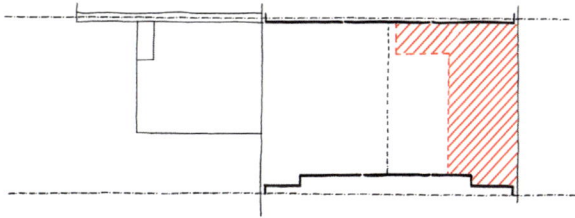

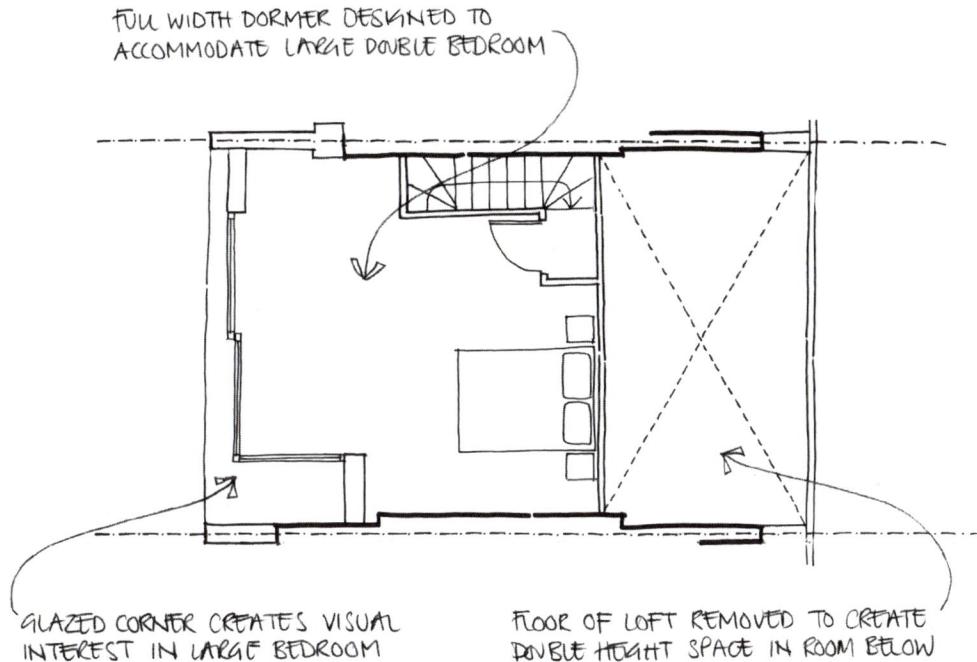

FULL WIDTH DORMER DESIGNED TO ACCOMMODATE LARGE DOUBLE BEDROOM

GLAZED CORNER CREATES VISUAL INTEREST IN LARGE BEDROOM

FLOOR OF LOFT REMOVED TO CREATE DOUBLE HEIGHT SPACE IN ROOM BELOW

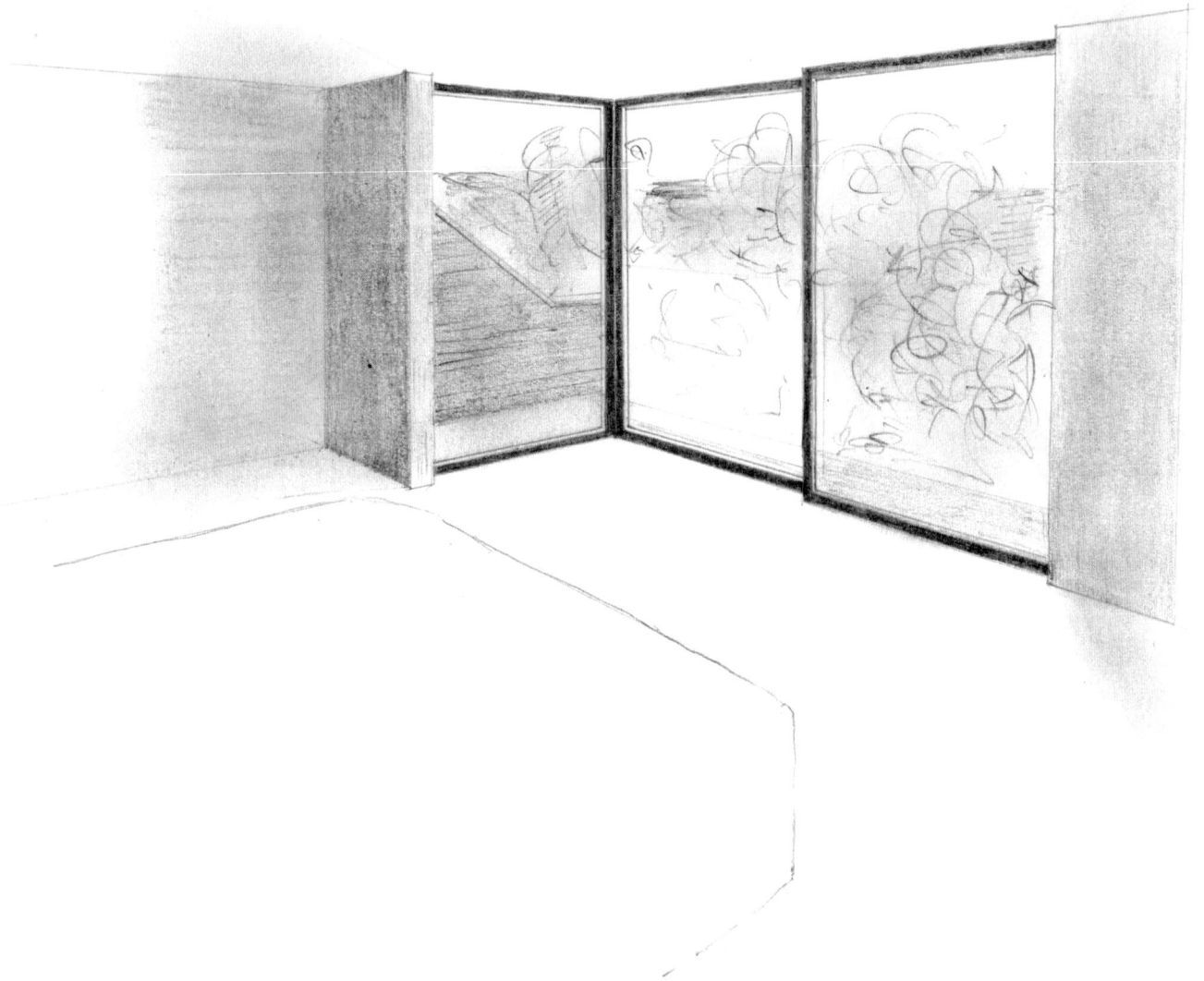

Artist's impression of dormer extension viewed from
bedroom door. Based on option 4.

OPTION 5

A new stair is positioned directly above the existing stair below and a small WC is designed along side this stair to create a landing at the top. An open bathroom has been tucked in behind the stair, with the bath located under the eaves to make the most of the reduced headroom. The ceiling on the floor below must be lowered to create a decent room height in this new extension.

This option should be read in conjunction with Second-floor Option 5.

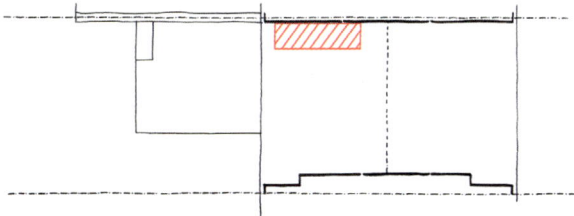

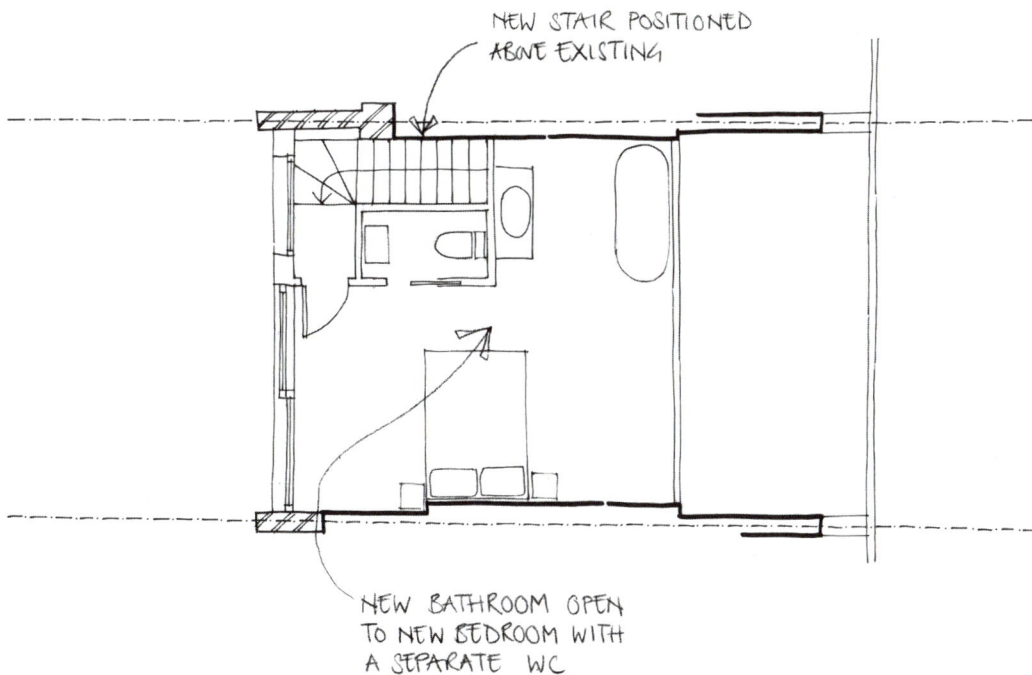

NEW STAIR POSITIONED
ABOVE EXISTING

NEW BATHROOM OPEN
TO NEW BEDROOM WITH
A SEPARATE WC

OPTION 6

This option is to be read in conjunction with Second-floor Option 6. It retains the ceilings in the floor below by raising the ridge height and introducing clerestory glazing into the existing roof. This creates a light, airy loft room with a double aspect. This idea has not yet been tested at Planning.

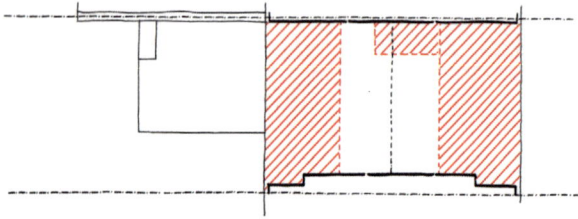

CLERESTORY GLAZING INSERTED ABOVE ROOFLINE, RAISING THE RIDGE OF THE EXISTING ROOF

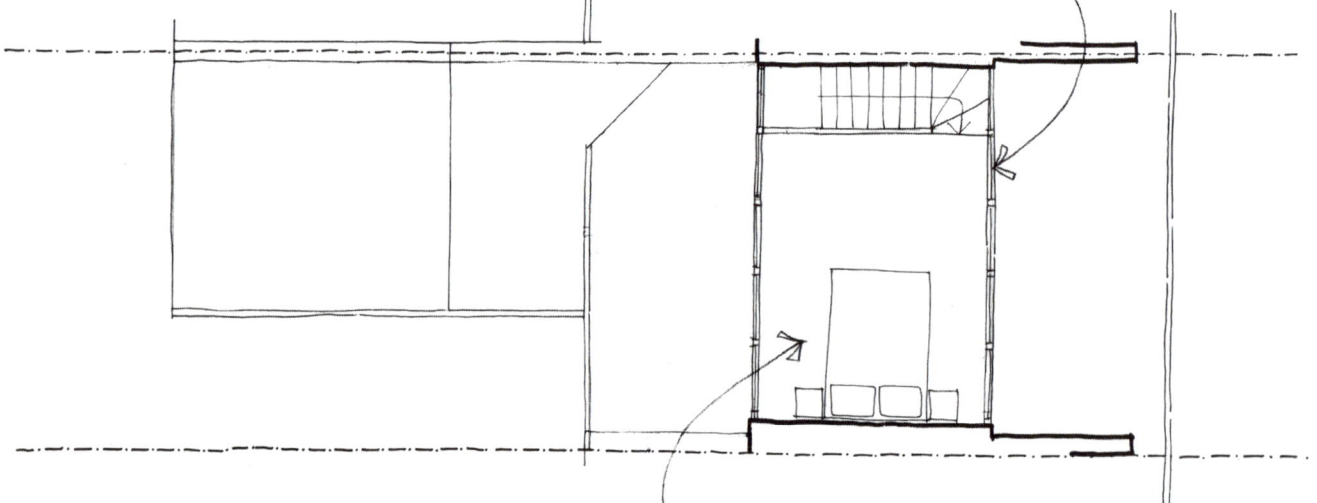

DOUBLE ASPECT BEDROOM CREATED UNDER NEW RAISED SECTION OF ROOF

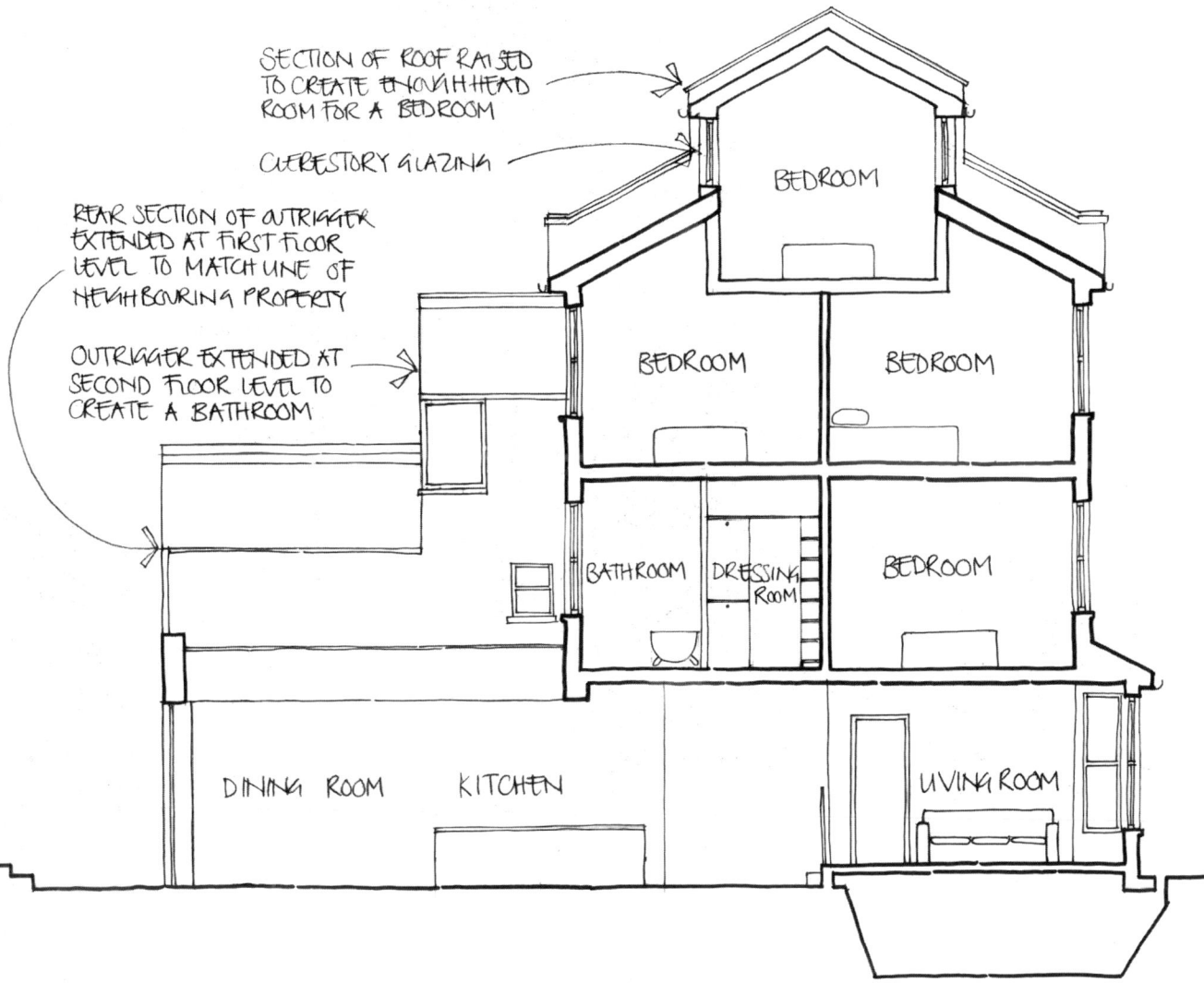

SECTION OF ROOF RAISED
TO CREATE ENOUGH HEAD
ROOM FOR A BEDROOM

CLERESTORY GLAZING

REAR SECTION OF OUTRIGGER
EXTENDED AT FIRST FLOOR
LEVEL TO MATCH LINE OF
NEIGHBOURING PROPERTY

OUTRIGGER EXTENDED AT
SECOND FLOOR LEVEL TO
CREATE A BATHROOM

BEDROOM

BEDROOM

BEDROOM

BEDROOM

BATHROOM

DRESSING
ROOM

DINING ROOM

KITCHEN

LIVING ROOM

THE SPLIT LEVEL

This case study is based on a three-storey, split-level house constructed on a 5.3m-wide plot. The main front door is located on the raised ground floor, with a secondary entrance located at basement level. There is also already a room in the main loft space, which is open to the stairs. The split-level nature of this property affords opportunities to link the floors vertically as well as horizontally.

BASEMENT

The ground floor of the outrigger is only four steps higher than the basement at the front of the house, so it has been included on these plans. There is access to the basement level via a door in the bay window at the front, and to the garden via a door into the side return. As it is such a large house, it makes sense to create a separate flat in this area. However, there are also options for a guest bedroom, kitchen/diner or separate living area connected to the main house. The ground floor of the outrigger has a large bay window and an external door into the side return. It may have been two separate rooms at one time, as it has two fireplaces.

OPTION 1

As this is a relatively large house, there is ample space to accommodate all the living space on the basement level without the need to extend. The wall between the front and rear reception rooms has been removed to create a large kitchen/diner with access to a utility room under the stairs. A section of wall has also been removed and steps installed to create a connection between the kitchen/diner and the living area, accommodated on the ground floor of the outrigger. Part of the outrigger is shown here as a study, with a desk inserted into the bay window and shelves along the opposite wall. This still leaves plenty of room for a living area with direct access to the garden via large sliding doors. The outbuilding has been removed to maximise this connection. This option can be read in conjunction with Ground-floor Option 2, where the ceiling above the dining room has been removed.

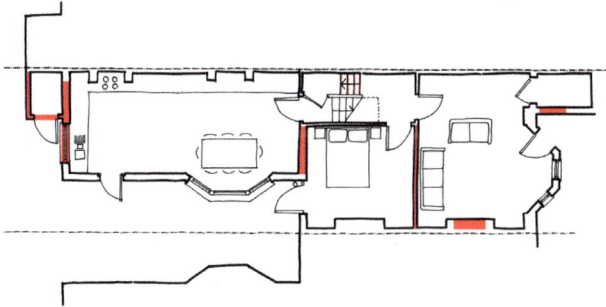

OUTHOUSE REMOVED AND SLIDING DOORS INSTALLED TO ACCESS GARDEN

STAIRS TO LOWER GROUND FLOOR REMOVED TO CREATE WC AND UTILITY ROOM

DOOR UNDER STAIR RELOCATED TO FREE UP SPACE TO INSTALL KITCHEN CABINETS

SIDE DOOR BLOCKED AND WINDOW INSERTED

DESK BUILT IN TO BAY WINDOW

WALL REMOVED AND STAIRS INSTALLED TO CREATE LINK BETWEEN DINING AND LIVING

OPTION 2

The entrance door has been relocated in this option to move the circulation space to the side, creating an enclosed living area for this self-contained one-bedroomed flat. A bay window seat provides storage below. Removing the existing stairs frees up space to accommodate a small shower room. A WC is slotted in adjacent to this at garden level. A double bedroom fits neatly into the back room of this floor, retaining direct access to the side return, which becomes a private courtyard.

The rear section of the outrigger has been extended into the side return to create a dining area whilst retaining the bay window, the access from the basement and the window of the rear reception room above. This minimises structural intervention.

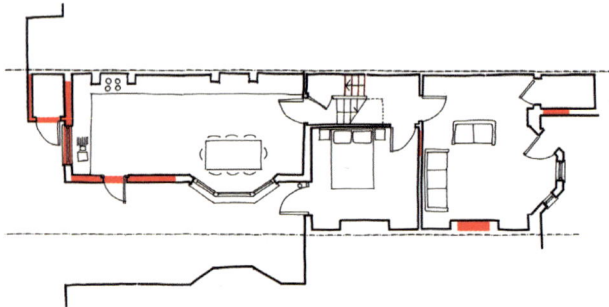

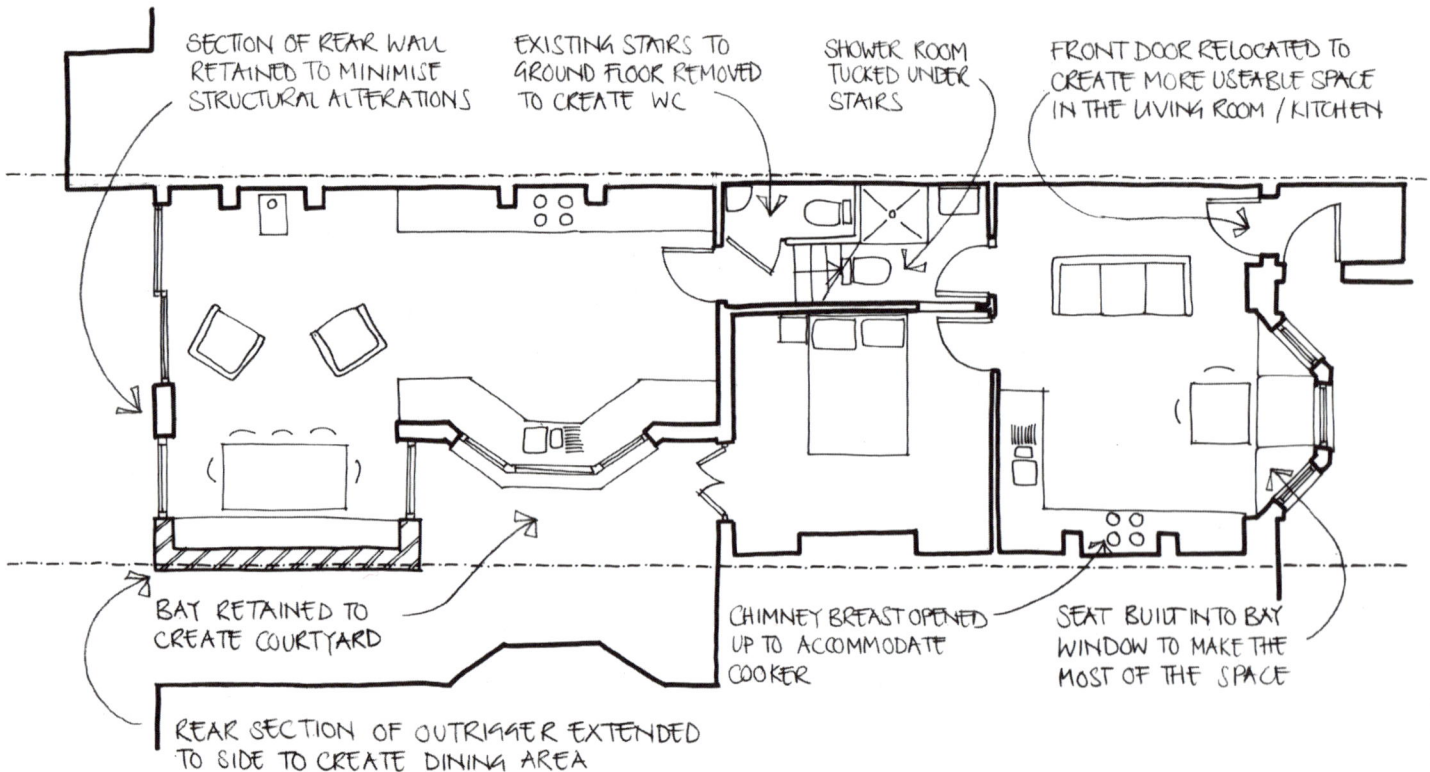

SECTION OF REAR WALL RETAINED TO MINIMISE STRUCTURAL ALTERATIONS

EXISTING STAIRS TO GROUND FLOOR REMOVED TO CREATE WC

SHOWER ROOM TUCKED UNDER STAIRS

FRONT DOOR RELOCATED TO CREATE MORE USEABLE SPACE IN THE LIVING ROOM / KITCHEN

BAY RETAINED TO CREATE COURTYARD

REAR SECTION OF OUTRIGGER EXTENDED TO SIDE TO CREATE DINING AREA

CHIMNEY BREAST OPENED UP TO ACCOMMODATE COOKER

SEAT BUILT INTO BAY WINDOW TO MAKE THE MOST OF THE SPACE

OPTION 3

(As depicted in section A)

As with the previous layout, the door is relocated beneath the external steps in this option. However the existing stairs are retained to connect the guest bedroom and en-suite at the front of the house with the rest of the dwelling. The ceiling of the rear room has been removed, as shown in ground floor option 2, to create a grand, double height dining room that connects to the ground floor of the outrigger via a set of wide stairs. It can be looked down upon from the front reception room above. Access to the garden is retained.

The outrigger bay window is retained, as with Basement Options 1 and 2. The rear corner has been removed to create a corner window seat that extends out to the line of the existing outhouse to the rear and part way into the side return. The outhouse can be used as a pantry or utility cupboard by relocating access via the kitchen.

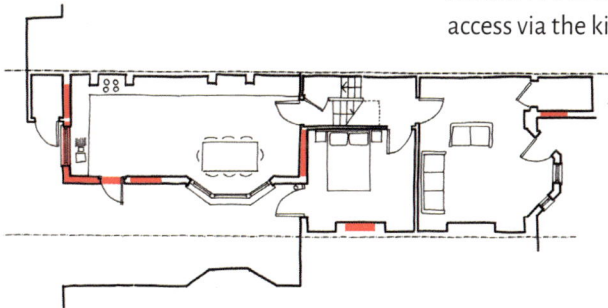

CORNER OF GROUND FLOOR OF OUTRIGGER REMOVED AND WINDOW SEAT CONSTRUCTED TO LINE OF EXISTING OUTHOUSE

SMALL SHOWER ROOM LOCATED OPPOSITE, AND THE SAME WIDTH AS, THE EXISTING STAIRWELL

FRONT DOOR RELOCATED TO CREATE MORE USEABLE SPACE IN THE FRONT ROOM

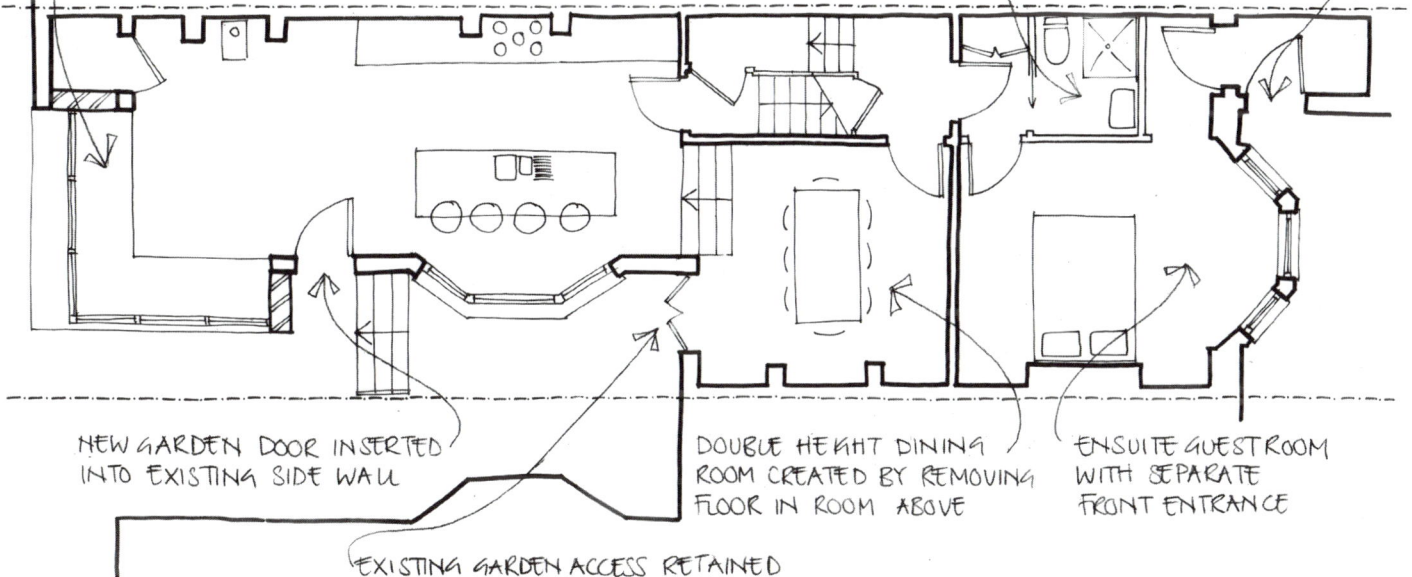

NEW GARDEN DOOR INSERTED INTO EXISTING SIDE WALL

DOUBLE HEIGHT DINING ROOM CREATED BY REMOVING FLOOR IN ROOM ABOVE

ENSUITE GUEST ROOM WITH SEPARATE FRONT ENTRANCE

EXISTING GARDEN ACCESS RETAINED

OPTION 4

The stairs have been retained in this option to connect the basement-level living room with the rest of the house. The ground floor of the outrigger has been extended full width into the side return to connect it with the rear of the basement floor. The kitchen has been relocated to the rear room of the main house. The height of the glazed roof over the extension is set above the head of the window of the rear reception room on the ground floor and the window has been removed, to create a vertical connection between the two spaces. To be read in conjunction with Ground-floor Option 1.

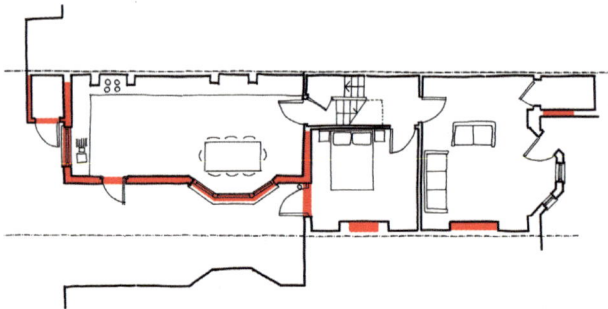

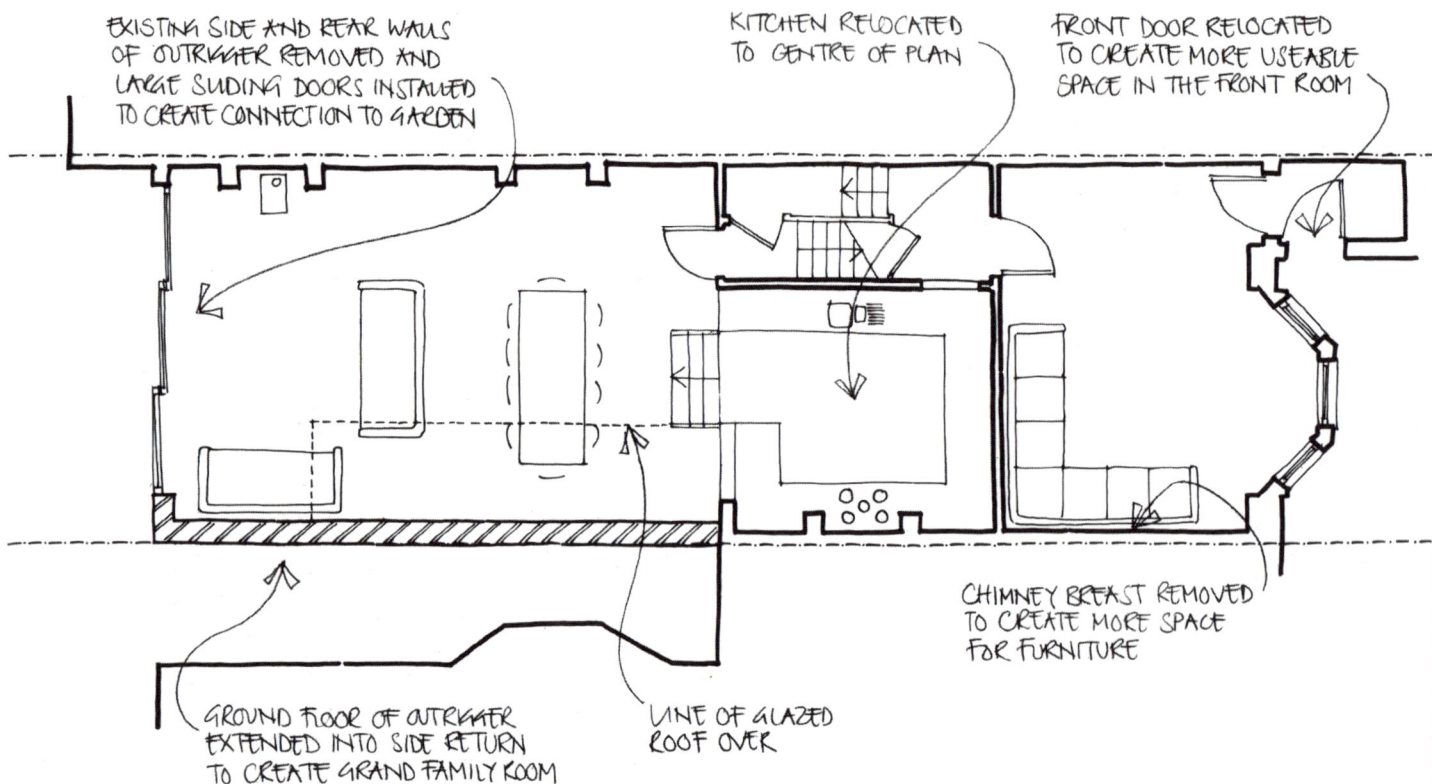

EXISTING SIDE AND REAR WALLS
OF OUTRIGGER REMOVED AND
LARGE SLIDING DOORS INSTALLED
TO CREATE CONNECTION TO GARDEN

KITCHEN RELOCATED
TO CENTRE OF PLAN

FRONT DOOR RELOCATED
TO CREATE MORE USEABLE
SPACE IN THE FRONT ROOM

CHIMNEY BREAST REMOVED
TO CREATE MORE SPACE
FOR FURNITURE

GROUND FLOOR OF OUTRIGGER
EXTENDED INTO SIDE RETURN
TO CREATE GRAND FAMILY ROOM

LINE OF GLAZED
ROOF OVER

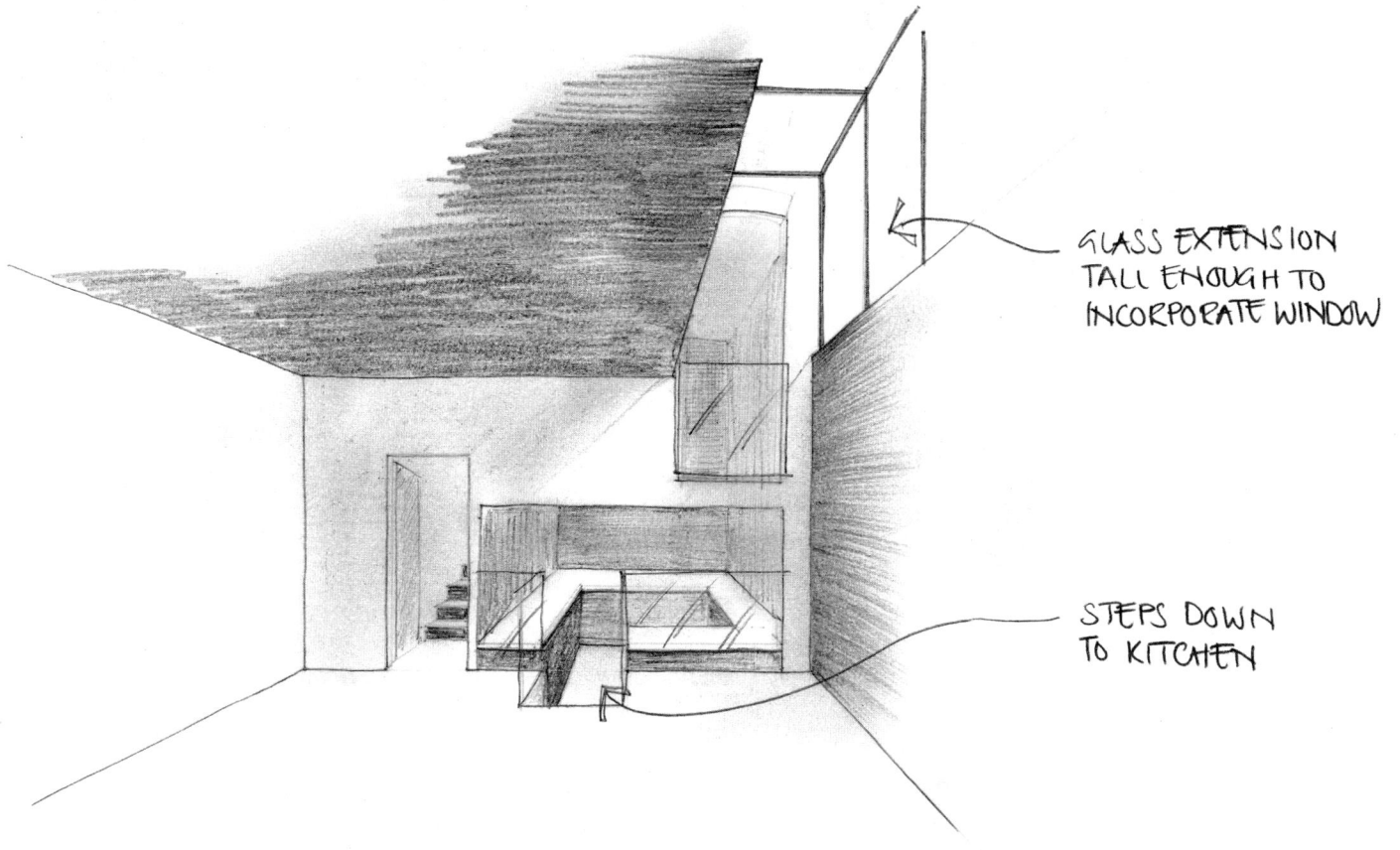

GLASS EXTENSION
TALL ENOUGH TO
INCORPORATE WINDOW

STEPS DOWN
TO KITCHEN

Artist's impression of basement kitchen and up to
living room above viewed from new double height
side return extension. Based on Basement Option 4

Mackeson Road by MW Architects, Hampstead,
London, 2015. View through galley kitchen out
to the garden.

OPTION 5

*(Based on the Mackeson Road project
by MW Architects)*

This option makes the most of the split-level nature of this property by cutting out sections of floor to create vertical connections between levels. It should be read in conjunction with Ground-floor Option 3. The dividing wall between the front and rear reception rooms has been removed to create a large, open-plan living room in the main section of the house. This can be subdivided using the sliding, folding wall shown where the existing dividing wall was. This room connects via wide steps to the ground floor of the outrigger, which has been extended fully into the side return to create a spacious kitchen/diner. The stairs connecting this space to the rest of the house have been relocated. The leftover space has been used to accommodate a WC and utility room, and additional kitchen units.

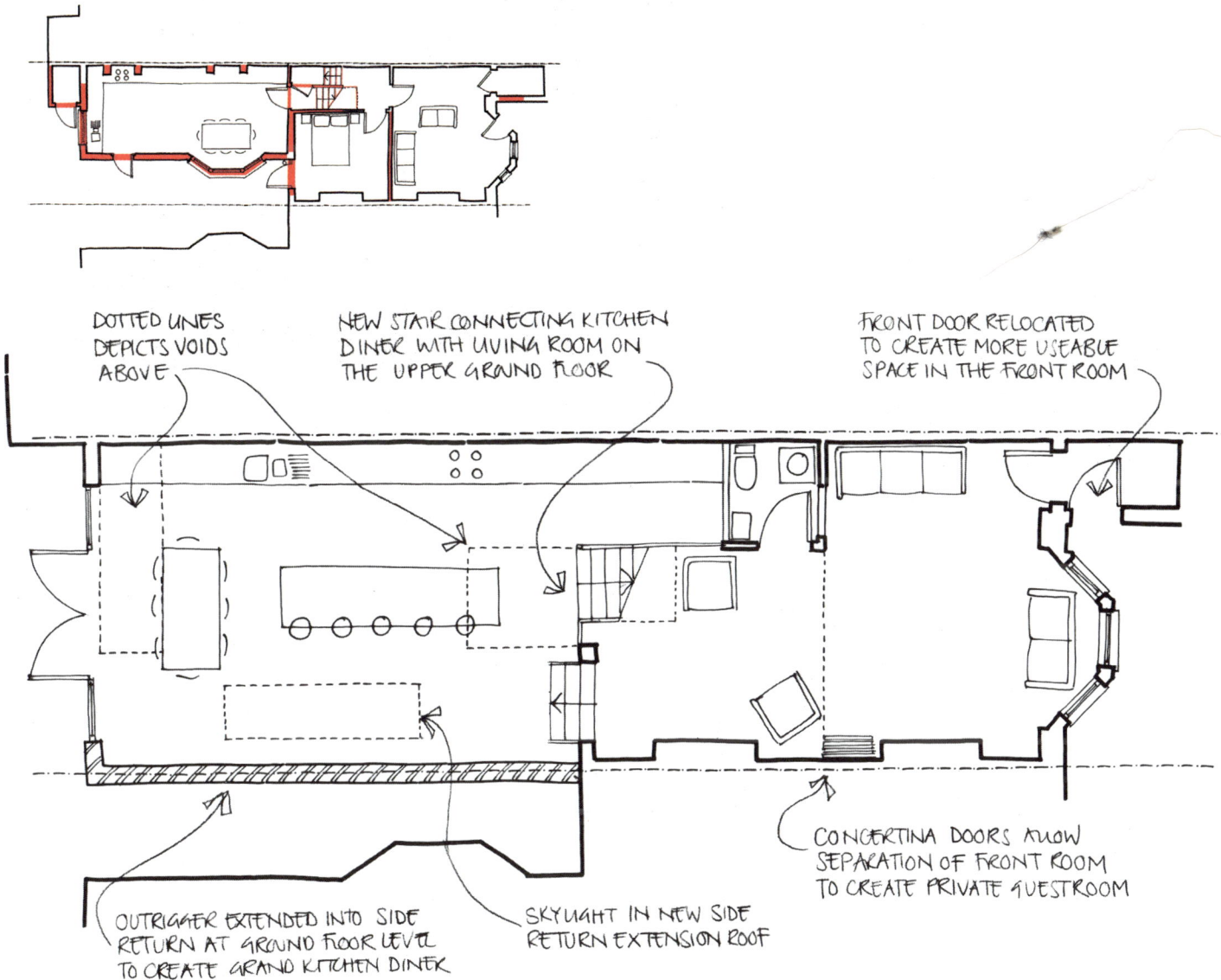

DOTTED LINES DEPICTS VOIDS ABOVE

NEW STAIR CONNECTING KITCHEN DINER WITH LIVING ROOM ON THE UPPER GROUND FLOOR

FRONT DOOR RELOCATED TO CREATE MORE USEABLE SPACE IN THE FRONT ROOM

OUTRIGGER EXTENDED INTO SIDE RETURN AT GROUND FLOOR LEVEL TO CREATE GRAND KITCHEN DINER

SKYLIGHT IN NEW SIDE RETURN EXTENSION ROOF

CONCERTINA DOORS ALLOW SEPARATION OF FRONT ROOM TO CREATE PRIVATE GUESTROOM

Mackeson Road by MW Architects, Hampstead, London, 2015. View from kitchen/diner into living room at front of house, and up to study above.

Mackeson Road by MW Architects, Hampstead, London, 2015. Axonometric of rear of house, showing vertical connection of spaces.

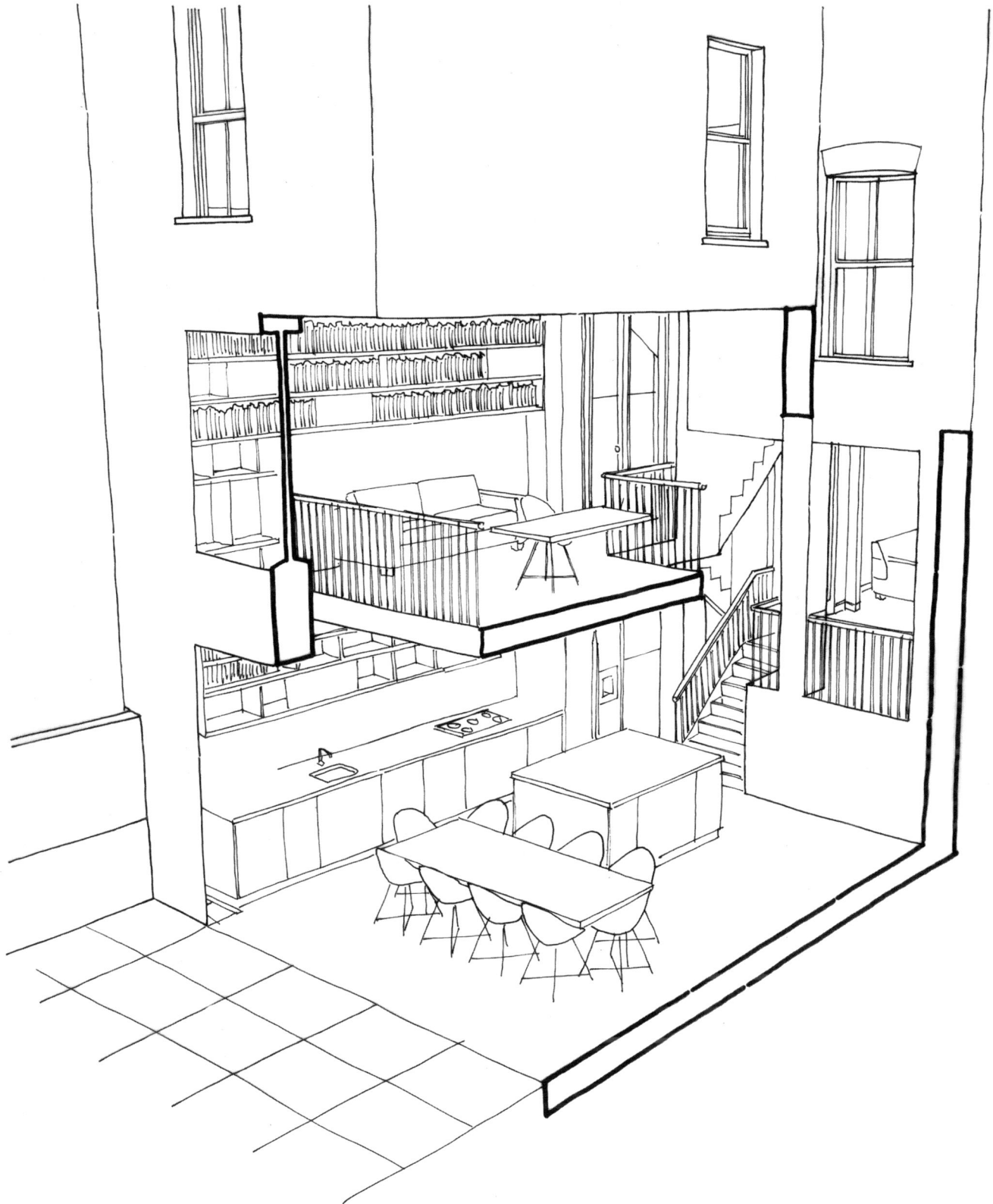

OPTION 6

(Based on the Scenario House project by Scenario Architecture)

In this option, to be read in conjunction with Ground-floor Option 4, the front reception room becomes a bedroom with its own separate entrance. It has an en-suite shower room and a separate guest WC accommodated in part of the rear reception room. The remaining part of the rear reception room becomes a study that connects to the large kitchen/diner in the outrigger, which has been extended fully into the side return.

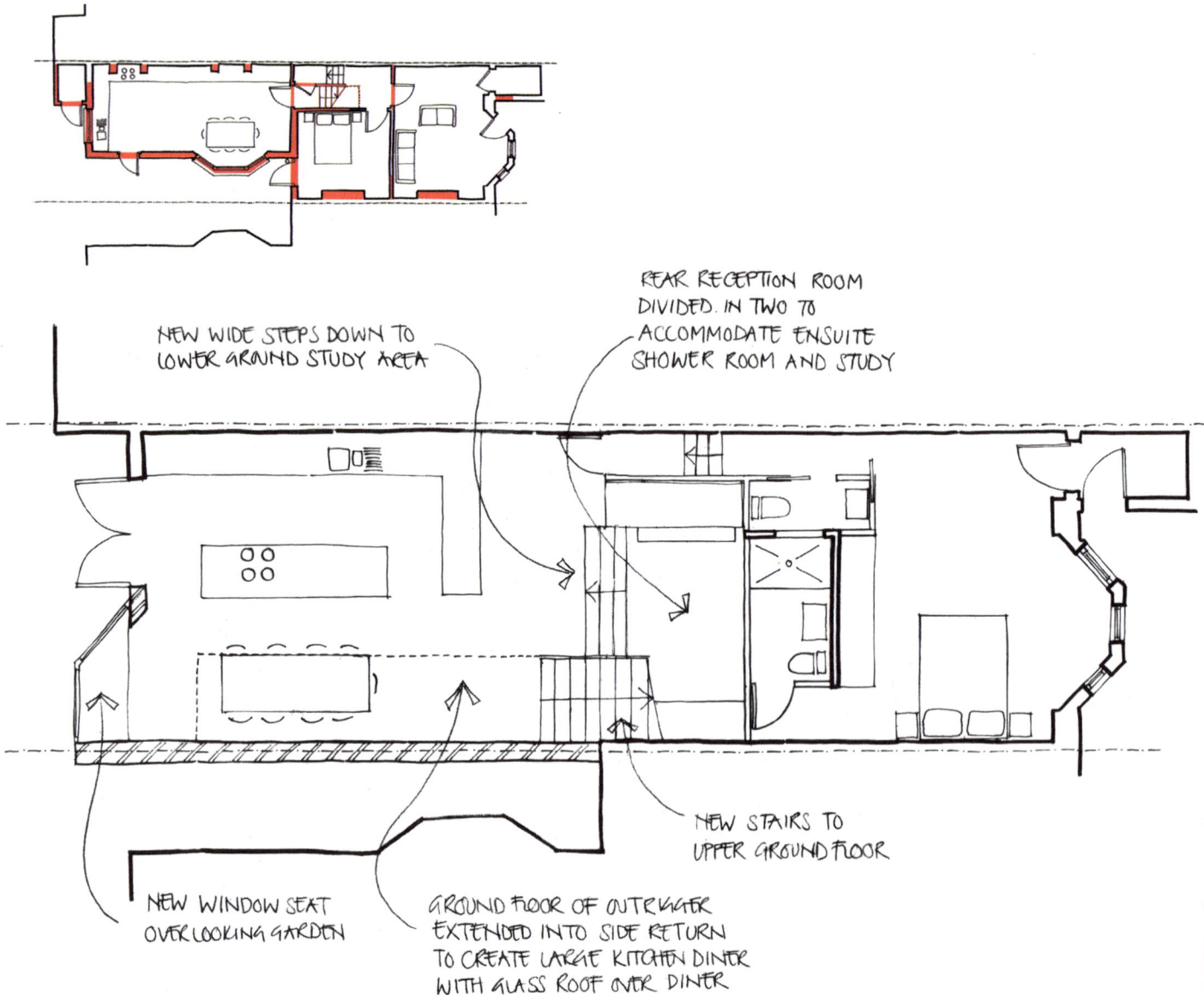

REAR RECEPTION ROOM
DIVIDED IN TWO TO
ACCOMMODATE ENSUITE
SHOWER ROOM AND STUDY

NEW WIDE STEPS DOWN TO
LOWER GROUND STUDY AREA

NEW STAIRS TO
UPPER GROUND FLOOR

NEW WINDOW SEAT
OVERLOOKING GARDEN

GROUND FLOOR OF OUTRIGGER
EXTENDED INTO SIDE RETURN
TO CREATE LARGE KITCHEN DINER
WITH GLASS ROOF OVER DINER

Scenario House by Scenario Architecture, Clapham,
London, 2016. View from kitchen/diner down to
study area and up to living room.

Scenario House by Scenario Architects, Clapham,
London, 2016. View down to study area.

GROUND FLOOR

The main entrance to the house is on the raised ground floor, via steps leading up from street level. The front and rear reception rooms are connected by double doors. One set of stairs leads down to the ground floor of the outrigger, which has been included in the basement plans above. Another leads up to the first floor of the outrigger, included in this section. All the following options show the front rooms as reception rooms, but if the living, dining and kitchen areas are accommodated in the basement — as in Basement Option 4 — these rooms could be used as bedrooms.

OPTION 1

Very little has been altered in this option. The double doors connecting the front and rear reception rooms have been replaced with sliding doors, and a cupboard has been inserted adjacent to the bathroom. The window of the rear reception room has been removed to create a balcony that overlooks the kitchen below, as shown in Basement Option 4.

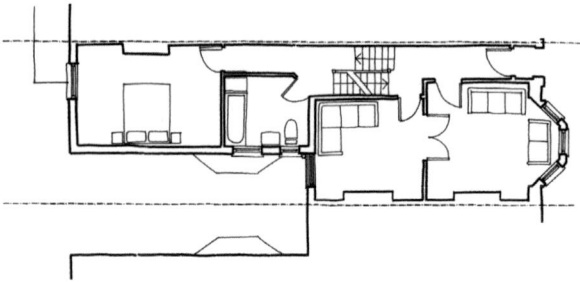

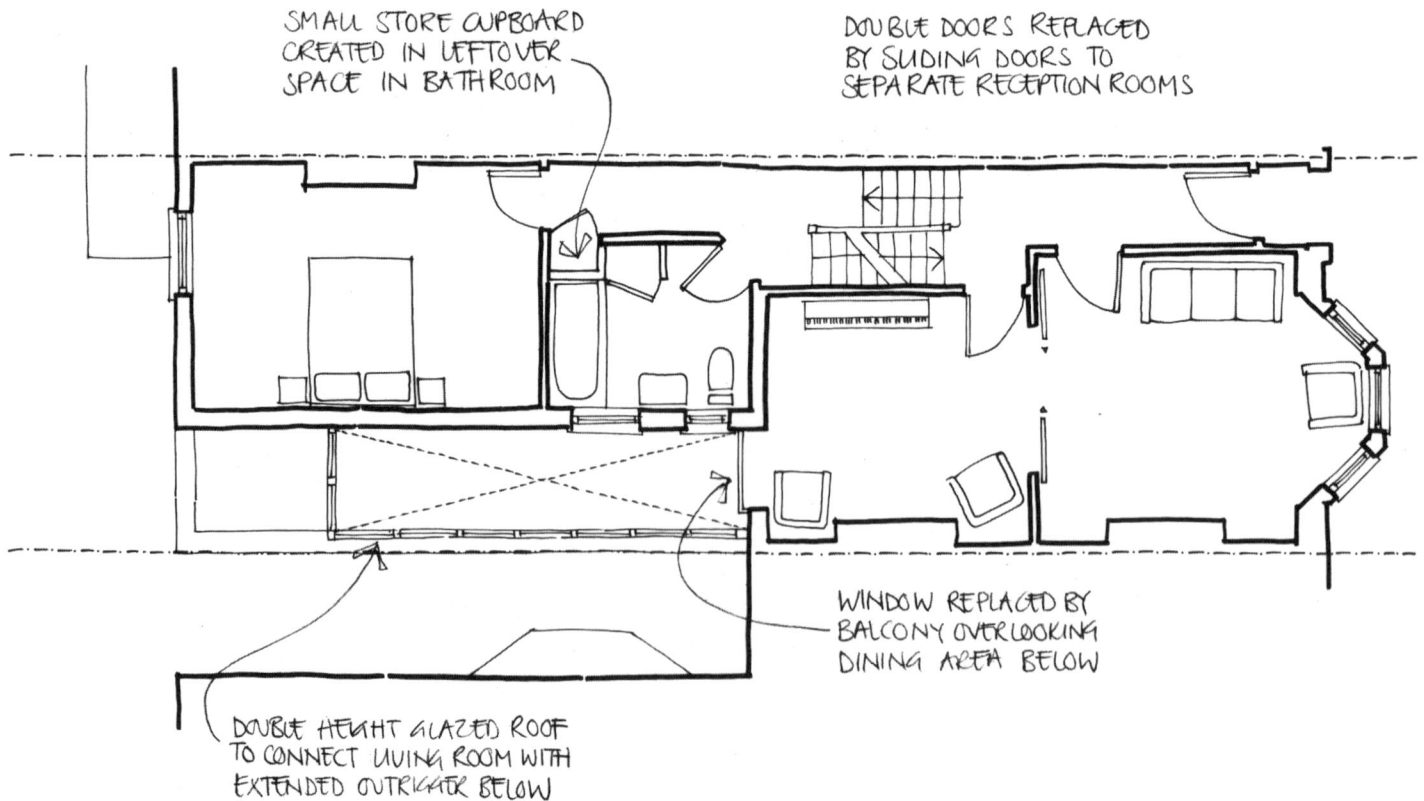

SMALL STORE CUPBOARD
CREATED IN LEFTOVER
SPACE IN BATHROOM

DOUBLE DOORS REPLACED
BY SLIDING DOORS TO
SEPARATE RECEPTION ROOMS

WINDOW REPLACED BY
BALCONY OVERLOOKING
DINING AREA BELOW

DOUBLE HEIGHT GLAZED ROOF
TO CONNECT LIVING ROOM WITH
EXTENDED OUTRIGGER BELOW

OPTION 2

The floor of the rear reception room has been removed in this option to create a double-height dining room in the basement, as shown in Basement Options 1 or 3. A balustrade has been shown behind the reception-room double doors to create a balcony looking down from the front reception room. The bathroom has been divided to create a separate WC for flexibility of use.

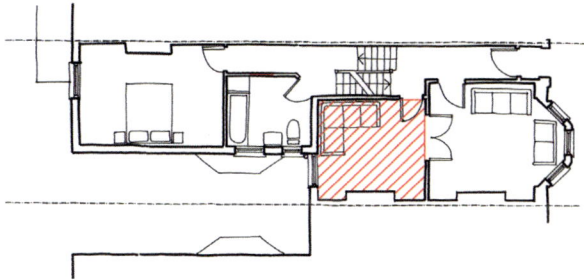

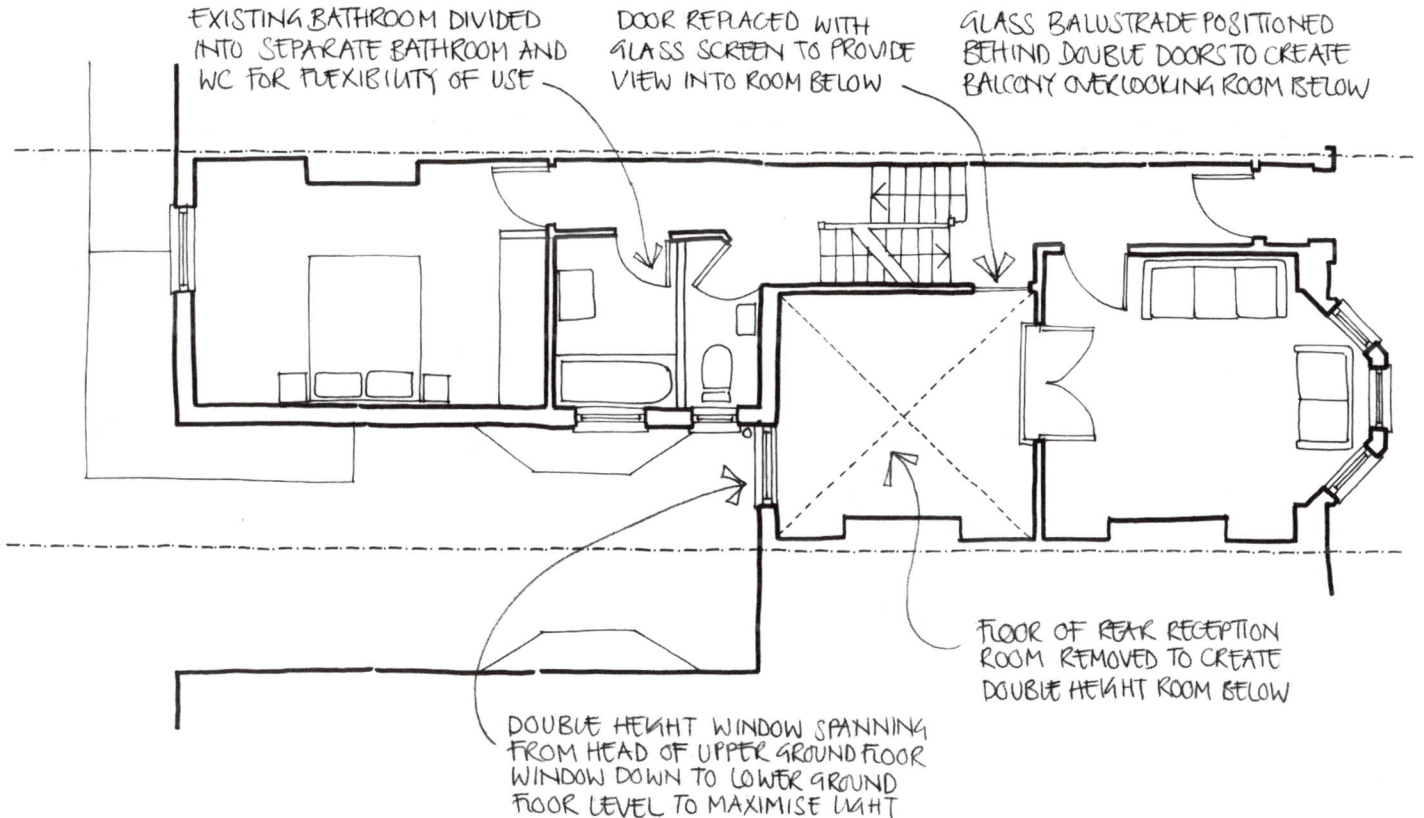

EXISTING BATHROOM DIVIDED INTO SEPARATE BATHROOM AND WC FOR FLEXIBILITY OF USE

DOOR REPLACED WITH GLASS SCREEN TO PROVIDE VIEW INTO ROOM BELOW

GLASS BALUSTRADE POSITIONED BEHIND DOUBLE DOORS TO CREATE BALCONY OVERLOOKING ROOM BELOW

DOUBLE HEIGHT WINDOW SPANNING FROM HEAD OF UPPER GROUND FLOOR WINDOW DOWN TO LOWER GROUND FLOOR LEVEL TO MAXIMISE LIGHT

FLOOR OF REAR RECEPTION ROOM REMOVED TO CREATE DOUBLE HEIGHT ROOM BELOW

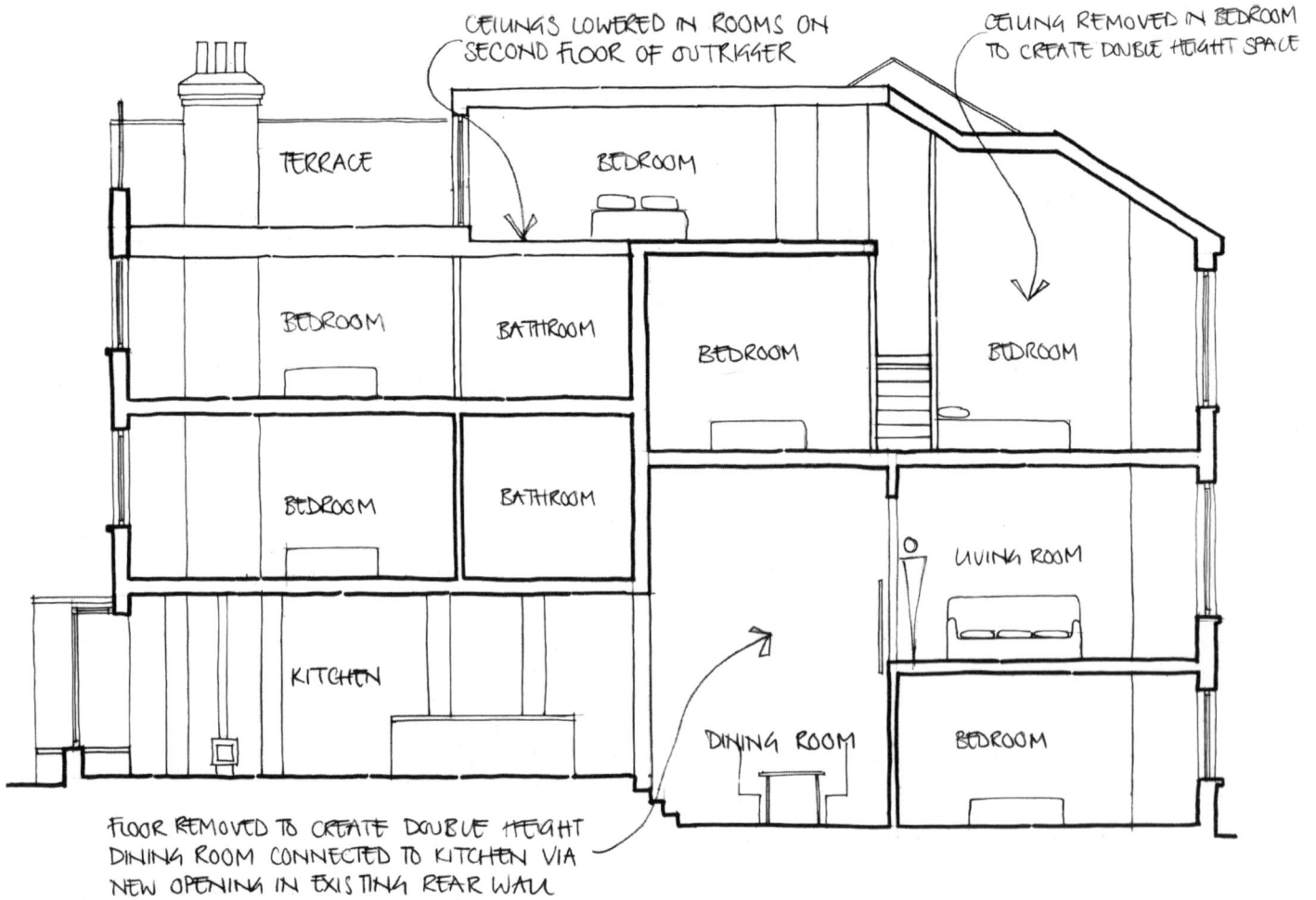

Section A

CEILINGS LOWERED IN ROOMS ON
SECOND FLOOR OF OUTRIGGER

CEILING REMOVED IN BEDROOM
TO CREATE DOUBLE HEIGHT SPACE

TERRACE

BEDROOM

BEDROOM

BEDROOM

BEDROOM

BATHROOM

BEDROOM

BEDROOM

BEDROOM

BATHROOM

LIVING ROOM

KITCHEN

DINING ROOM

BEDROOM

FLOOR REMOVED TO CREATE DOUBLE HEIGHT
DINING ROOM CONNECTED TO KITCHEN VIA
NEW OPENING IN EXISTING REAR WALL

Mackeson Road by MW Architects, Hampstead, London, 2015. View of study on first floor of outrigger, with balconies over kitchen/diner.

OPTION 3

(Based on the Mackeson Road project by MW Architects)

The front and rear reception rooms have been amalgamated in this option. New stairs lead down to the ground floor of the outrigger, shown in Basement Option 5. Sections of the floor have been removed at the front and rear of the first floor of the outrigger to create a visual connection vertically between the floors. This room is shown here as a study.

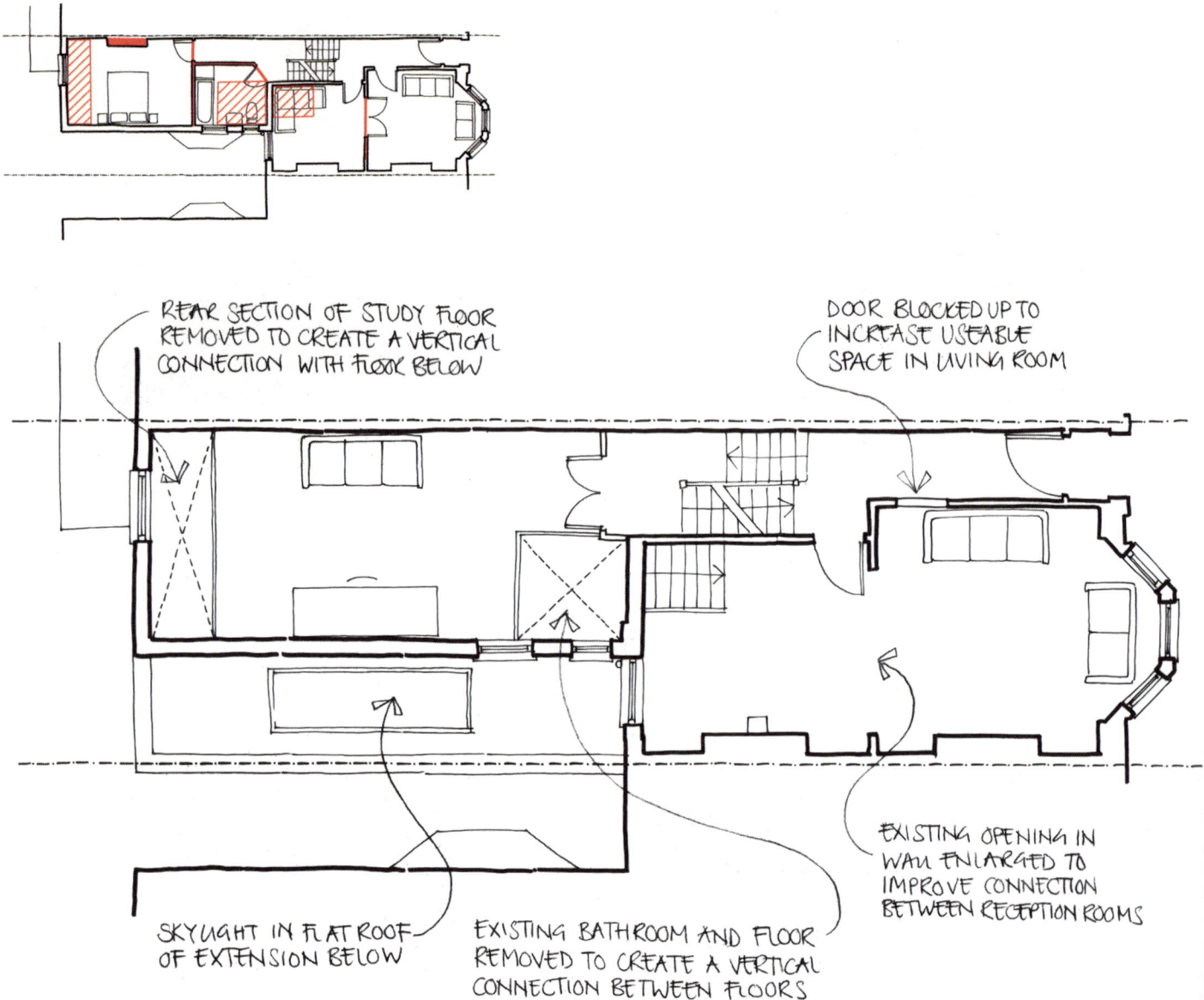

REAR SECTION OF STUDY FLOOR REMOVED TO CREATE A VERTICAL CONNECTION WITH FLOOR BELOW

DOOR BLOCKED UP TO INCREASE USEABLE SPACE IN LIVING ROOM

SKYLIGHT IN FLAT ROOF OF EXTENSION BELOW

EXISTING BATHROOM AND FLOOR REMOVED TO CREATE A VERTICAL CONNECTION BETWEEN FLOORS

EXISTING OPENING IN WALL ENLARGED TO IMPROVE CONNECTION BETWEEN RECEPTION ROOMS

Mackeson Road by MW Architects, Hampstead, London, 2015. View from living room down to kitchen/diner and up to study.

OPTION 4

(Based on the Scenario House project by Scenario Architects)

This option, to be read in conjunction with Basement Option 6 and First-floor Option 4, again amalgamates the front and rear reception rooms to create one large living room. However, it steps the rear section down to distinguish the two spaces but also to reduce the number of steps required to connect it to the outrigger below. Part of the floor has been removed to create a vertical connection down to the study area in the basement. Glazing has also been inserted into the wall above this void to create a visual connection between the reception rooms and the first floor of the outrigger – a section of which has been converted into a small library.

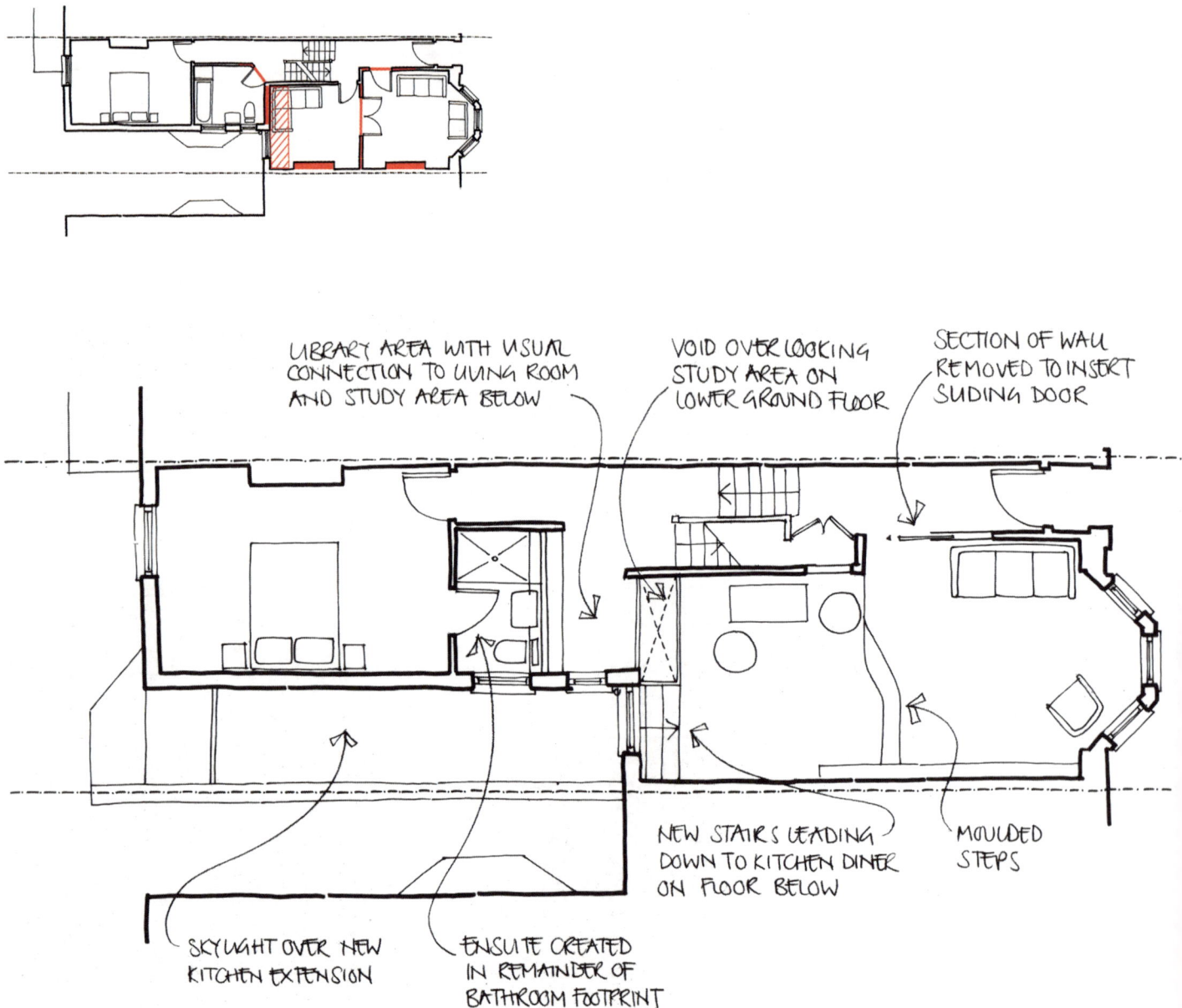

LIBRARY AREA WITH VISUAL CONNECTION TO LIVING ROOM AND STUDY AREA BELOW

VOID OVERLOOKING STUDY AREA ON LOWER GROUND FLOOR

SECTION OF WALL REMOVED TO INSERT SLIDING DOOR

NEW STAIRS LEADING DOWN TO KITCHEN DINER ON FLOOR BELOW

MOULDED STEPS

SKYLIGHT OVER NEW KITCHEN EXTENSION

ENSUITE CREATED IN REMAINDER OF BATHROOM FOOTPRINT

Scenario House by Scenario Architecture, Clapham,
London, 2016. View from living room down to
kitchen/diner and up to landing library.

Next page. Scenario House by Scenario Architecture,
Clapham, London, 2016. View from stair into rear
bedroom past library area.

FIRST FLOOR

This is a typical first-floor plan, with three good-sized double bedrooms and a separate bathroom. There is also a stair leading up to the loft, which is already in use.

OPTION 1

By replacing the existing loft stair with a new set of stairs, located in a walled-off section of the front bedroom, it is possible to create a large, open-plan loft room (shown in Loft Option 1) while still retaining three good-sized double bedrooms on the first floor. The space left by the removal of the existing stair has been used to create a cupboard. The cupboard in the bathroom has been removed to make room for a large, double-ended bath and separate shower. The bedroom in the outrigger remains untouched.

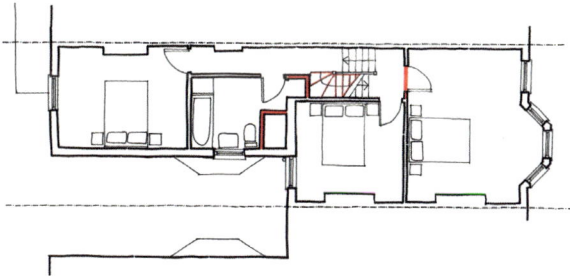

REAR BEDROOM
REMAINS UNALTERED

EXISTING LOFT STAIR
REMOVED AND
REPLACED BY STORAGE

STAIR UP TO LOFT CONSTRUCTED
IN SECTION OF FRONT BEDROOM
TO CREATE MORE ROOM IN LOFT

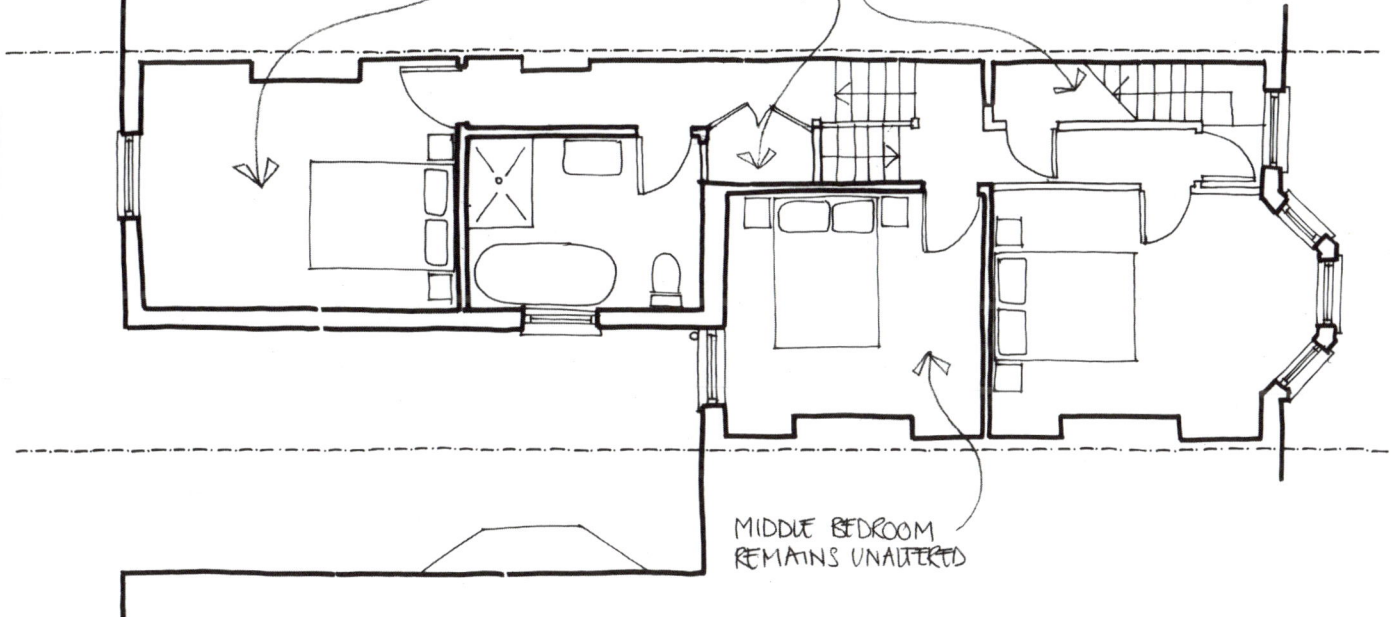

MIDDLE BEDROOM
REMAINS UNALTERED

OPTION 2

(As depicted in Section A)

This option, to be read in conjunction with Loft Option 2, shows a stair cutting through a section of the front bedroom perpendicular to the existing stair. This still leaves ample room in the front bedroom, where the ceiling has been removed to create a double-height space with skylights inserted in the roof to bring in additional light. The space created by the removal of the existing loft stair has again been used to insert a cupboard. The existing bathroom has been reduced in size to free up space to slot in an en-suite shower room to serve the rear bedroom, which is still large enough to accommodate a double bed.

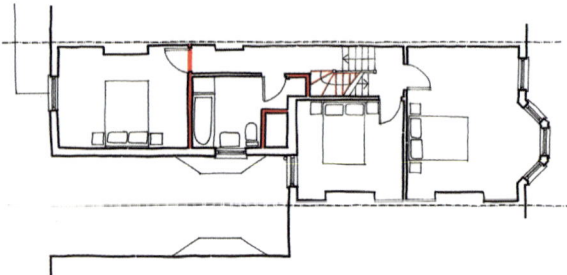

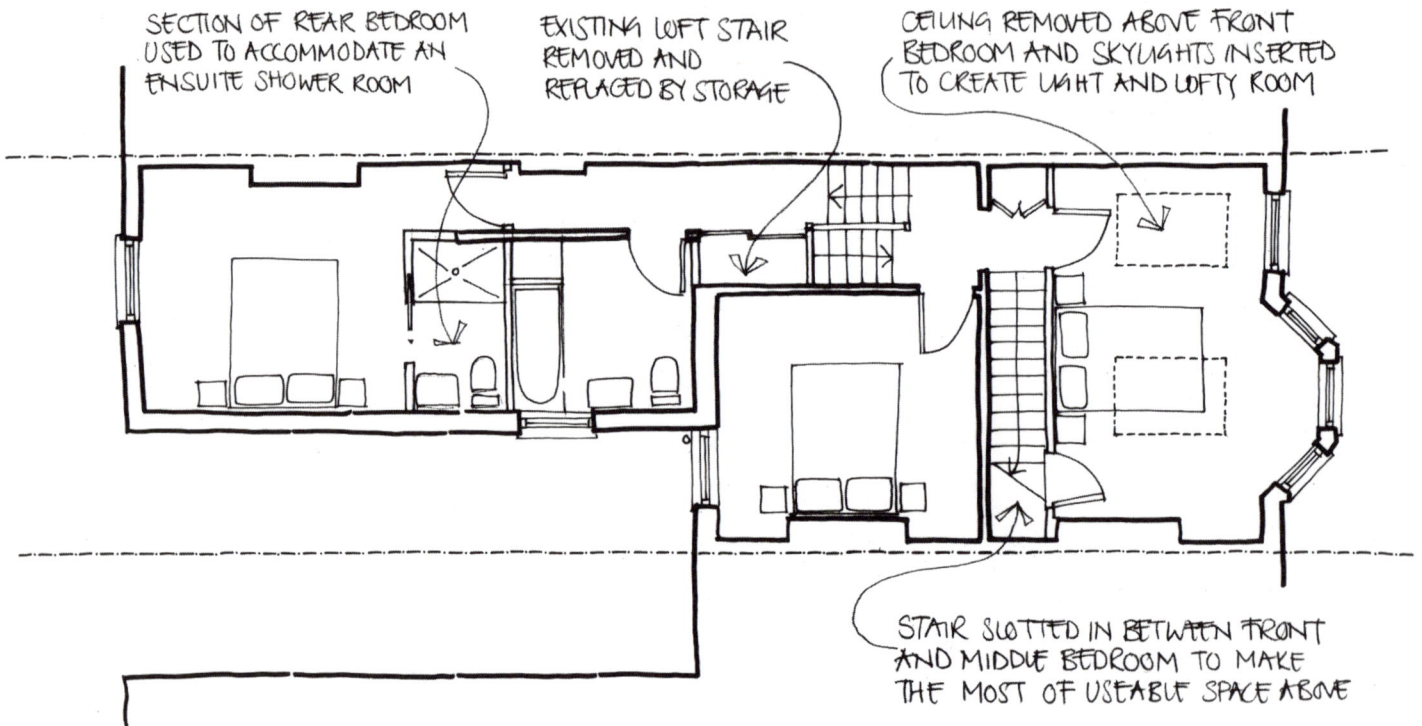

SECTION OF REAR BEDROOM USED TO ACCOMMODATE AN ENSUITE SHOWER ROOM

EXISTING LOFT STAIR REMOVED AND REPLACED BY STORAGE

CEILING REMOVED ABOVE FRONT BEDROOM AND SKYLIGHTS INSERTED TO CREATE LIGHT AND LOFTY ROOM

STAIR SLOTTED IN BETWEEN FRONT AND MIDDLE BEDROOM TO MAKE THE MOST OF USEABLE SPACE ABOVE

OPTION 3

(Based on the Mackeson Road project by MW Architects)

This is a very decadent use of the available space, but given that there is another bedroom at the rear and yet another in the loft the property still has sufficient bedrooms for a family house. This design uses the middle bedroom to accommodate an en-suite bathroom and dressing area to serve the main, front bedroom. The entrance to the existing bathroom, which has been reduced in size to make room for a further dressing area, has been relocated to provide access from the rear bedroom. This option works with Loft Options 3, 4 and 5.

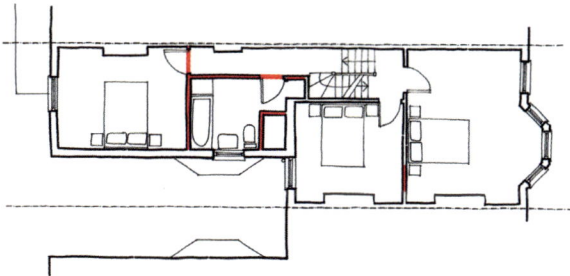

EXISTING BATHROOM REPLACED BY NEW SMALLER ENSUITE BATHROOM AND WARDROBE TO SERVE BEDROOM

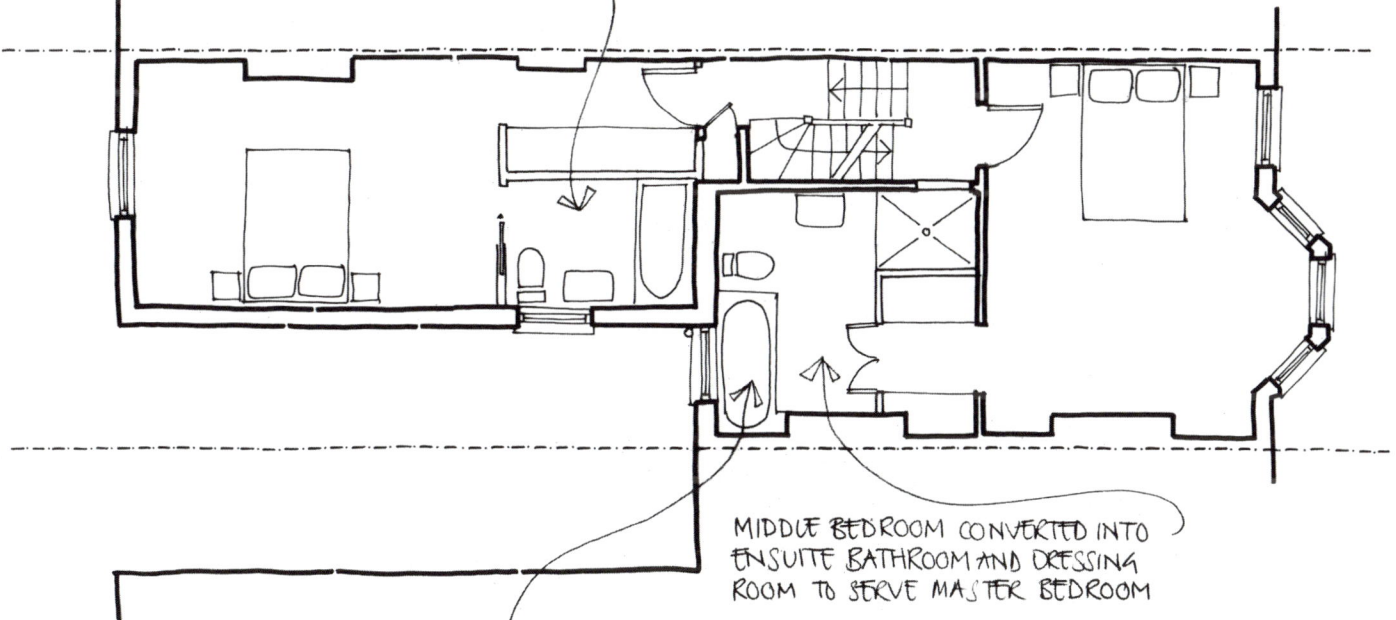

MIDDLE BEDROOM CONVERTED INTO ENSUITE BATHROOM AND DRESSING ROOM TO SERVE MASTER BEDROOM

BATH POSITIONED NEAR WINDOW TO GIVE VIEW OUT OVER GARDEN

Mackeson Road by MW Architects, Hampstead,
London, 2015. Master bedroom connecting to
en-suite.

OPTION 4

(Based on the Scenario House project by Scenario)

This option, to be read in conjunction with Ground-floor Option 4, amalgamates the two bedrooms in the main part of the house to create a master suite, including an en-suite bathroom at the front of the house and a large dressing room at the rear. The store in the existing bathroom has been removed to make room for a large bath and separate shower. A section of the ceiling in the rear bedroom has been removed to create a mezzanine level within the existing roof space. This extends over the bathroom, as shown in Loft Option 4, but can also be read in conjunction with Loft Options 3 and 5, in which the mezzanine level is just underneath the existing roofline.

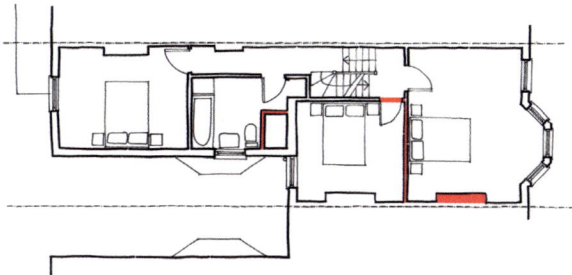

MEZZANINE OVER REAR BEDROOM ALSO EXTENDED OVER CORRIDOR AND BATHROOM

FRONT BEDROOM DIVIDED TO CREATE AN ENSUITE

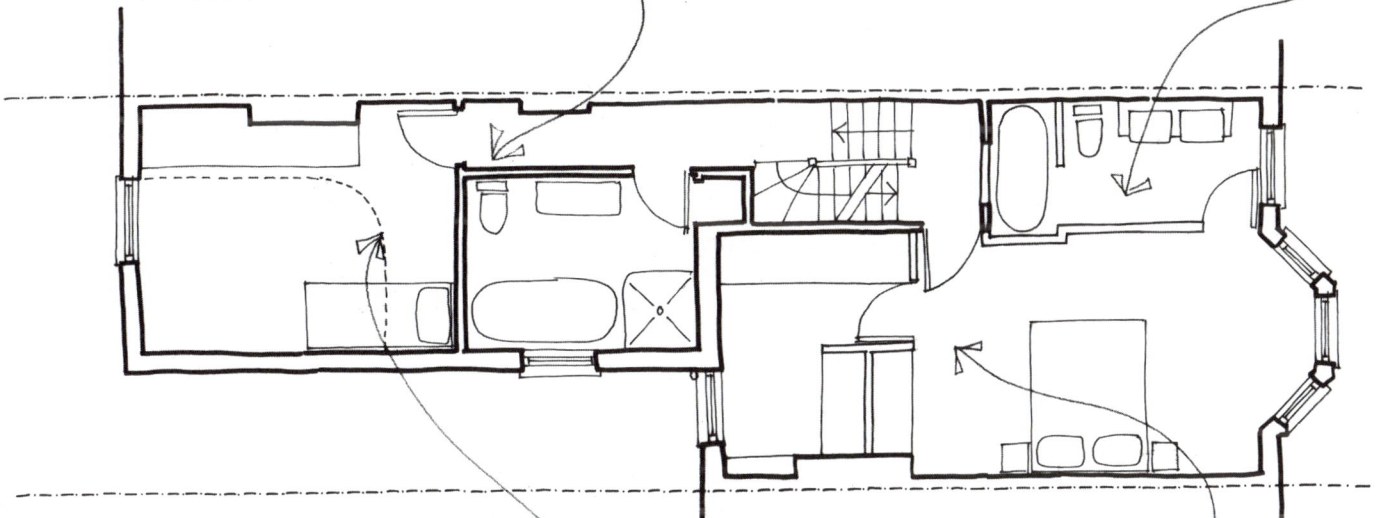

SECTION CUT OUT OF CEILING TO CREATE A MEZZANINE ACCESSED VIA LADDER

DIVIDING WALL BETWEEN FRONT AND MIDDLE BEDROOM REMOVED TO ENLARGE MASTER BEDROOM AND CREATE A DRESSING ROOM

Scenario House by Scenario Architecture, Clapham, London, 2016. Loft space above bedroom opened up to create a play mezzanine.

LOFT

The house has an existing loft room, which sits under the pitched roof of the main section of the house and is accessed via an open stair. It is advisable to assess the level of insulation in the roof if not intending to extend, in order to ensure that the room will be warm enough in winter and cool enough in summer. This could reduce your heating bills substantially.

OPTION 1

This option, to be read in conjunction with First-floor Option 1, shows a new stair entering the loft space from the front of the house, under the eaves. A door at the bottom of the stair enables direct access at the top. A full-width, rear dormer extension creates a spacious double bedroom with large, glazed sliding doors providing light and a panoramic view. A higher window is positioned where the roof of the outrigger rises above the floor level of the loft room. There is plenty of room for a bathroom in this option if desired, either in front of the stair or or tucked into the eaves.

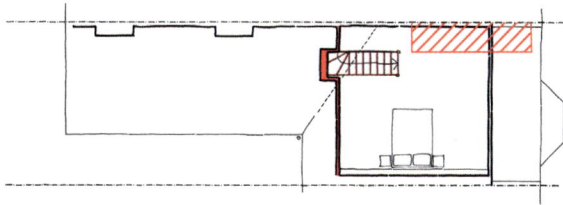

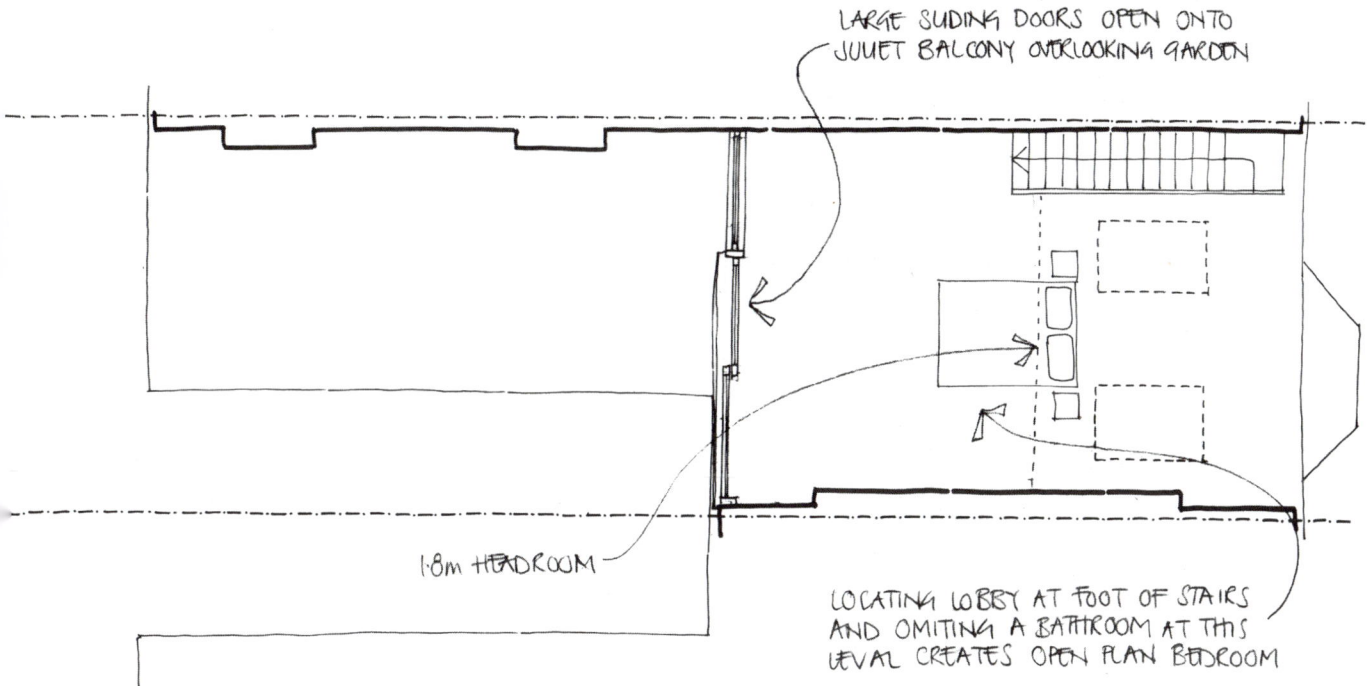

LARGE SLIDING DOORS OPEN ONTO
JULIET BALCONY OVERLOOKING GARDEN

1·8m HEADROOM

LOCATING LOBBY AT FOOT OF STAIRS
AND OMITING A BATHROOM AT THIS
LEVEL CREATES OPEN PLAN BEDROOM

OPTION 2

(As depicted in Section A)

This option, to be read in conjunction with First-floor Option 2, shows a full-width rear dormer and an extension over part of the outrigger above the bathroom. It accommodates a large double bedroom, a dressing area and a small, separate bathroom. A terrace has been shown over the remaining part of the outrigger. Although this is not usually permitted, some councils have allowed this type of development in certain circumstances – so it's always worth investigating. Stairs come up centrally in the plan. The ceiling above the front bedroom on the first floor has been removed to create a double-height space with skylights inserted for additional light.

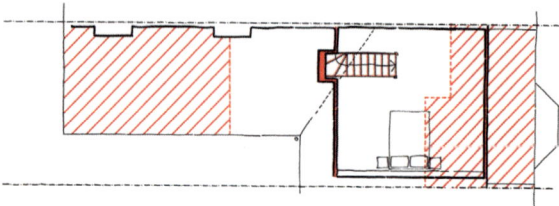

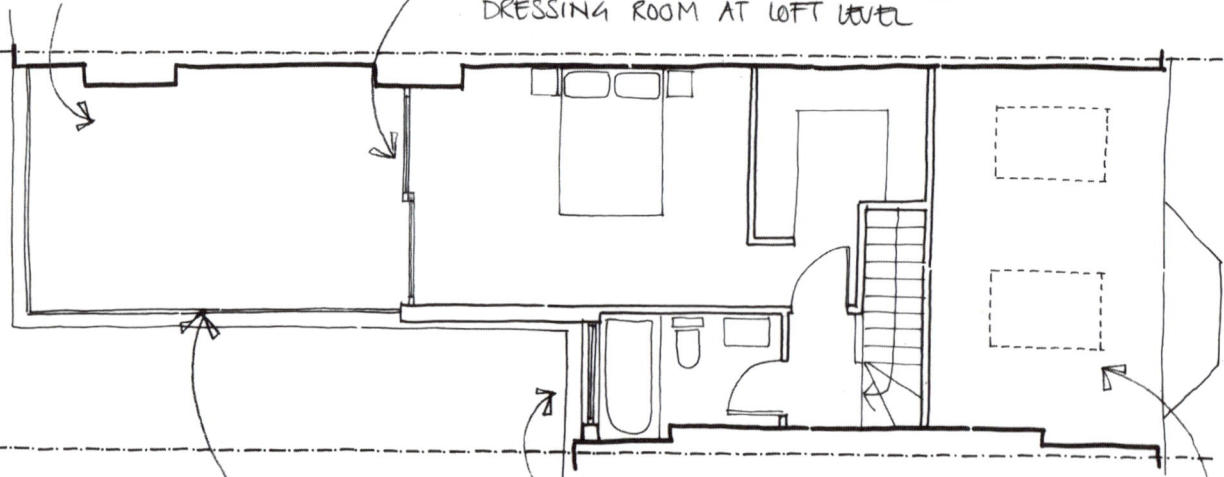

REMAINDER OF OUTRIGGER ROOF REMOVED TO CREATE A ROOF TERRACE ACCESSED VIA SLIDING DOORS

EXTENDING PARTWAY OVER OUTRIGGER CREATES ENOUGH ROOM TO ACCOMMODATE A DOUBLE BEDROOM, BATHROOM AND DRESSING ROOM AT LOFT LEVEL

OPAQUE GLAZING TO OBSCURE VIEW OUT

BATH POSITIONED WITH VIEW OVER GARDEN

REMOVING CEILING OF ROOM BELOW AND INSERTING ROOF LIGHTS CREATES BRIGHT DOUBLE HEIGHT BEDROOM

Wandsworth Loft Conversion by Martin Swatton Design, Wandsworth, London, 2011. Full-width doors create large Juliet balcony. Image mirrored to reflect plan.

OPTION 3

(Based on the Wandsworth Loft Conversion project by Martin Swatton Design)

This option uses the existing loft stair but encloses it at the top to give privacy and to satisfy fire regulations. A double bedroom has been created in a full-width dormer extension, and a small shower room has been slotted in under the front eaves at the top of the stairs. The ceiling of the floor below must be lowered to create sufficient headroom, and additional headroom is gained in the shower room by the introduction of a skylight over the WC and basin. As this option uses the existing stair, it can be carried out as a stand-alone project or read in conjunction with First-floor Options 3 or 4.

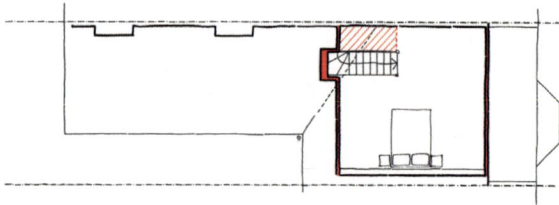

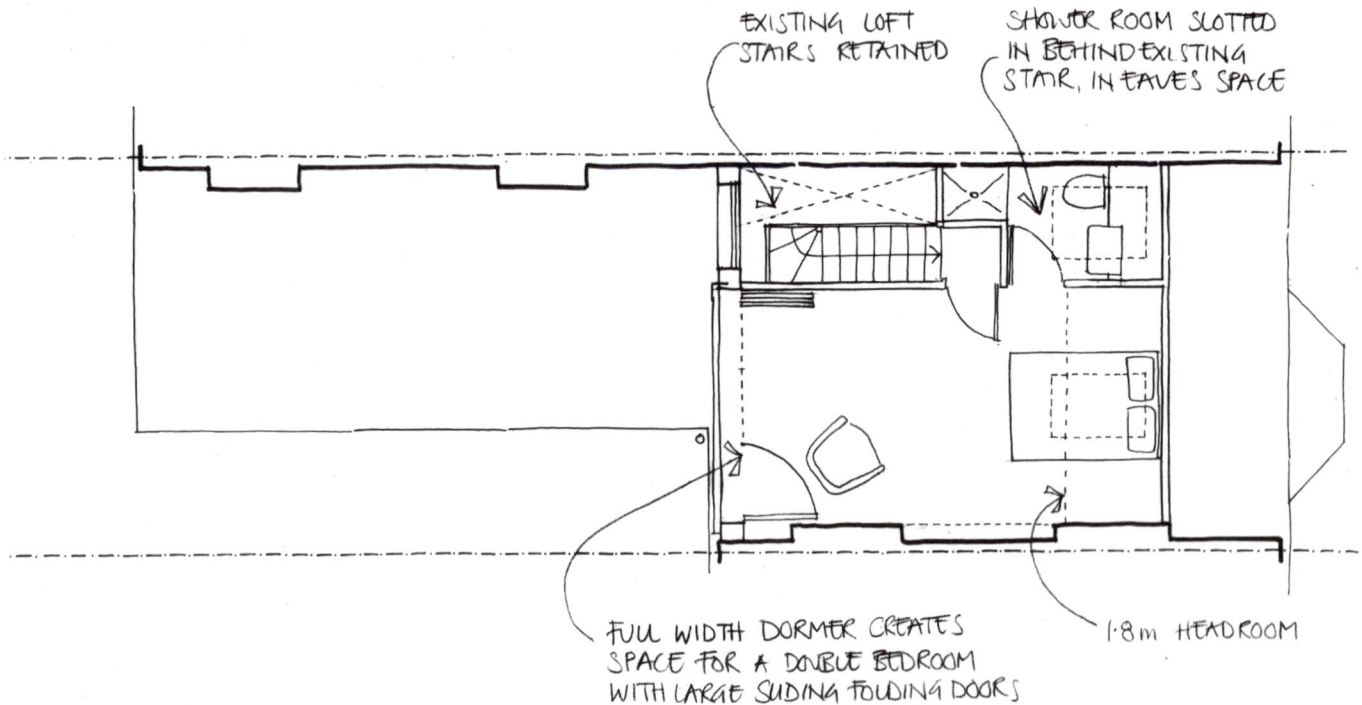

EXISTING LOFT STAIRS RETAINED

SHOWER ROOM SLOTTED IN BEHIND EXISTING STAIR, IN EAVES SPACE

FULL WIDTH DORMER CREATES SPACE FOR A DOUBLE BEDROOM WITH LARGE SLIDING FOLDING DOORS

1·8m HEADROOM

Wandsworth Loft Conversion by Martin Swatton Design, Wandsworth, London, 2011. Bed tucked into eaves to make the most of the useable space. Image mirrored to reflect plan.

OPTION 4

(Based on the Scenario House project by Scenario Architecture)

When your house lies within a Conservation Area, it might not be possible to gain planning permission for a full-width rear dormer. This option, shows a small, rear dormer window positioned in line with the window serving the room below. This helps to let light in and provides some additional standing room. A small en-suite shower room has been tucked into the front eaves space, as has the bed, optimising headroom with the use of carefully positioned skylights. The existing loft space of the outrigger has been used to create a mezzanine play area connected to the bedroom on the floor below. Again, as the existing stair is retained, this option can be carried out as a stand-alone project or read in conjunction with First-floor Options 3 or 4.

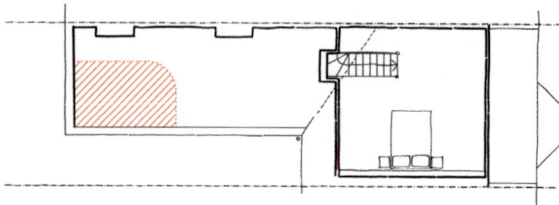

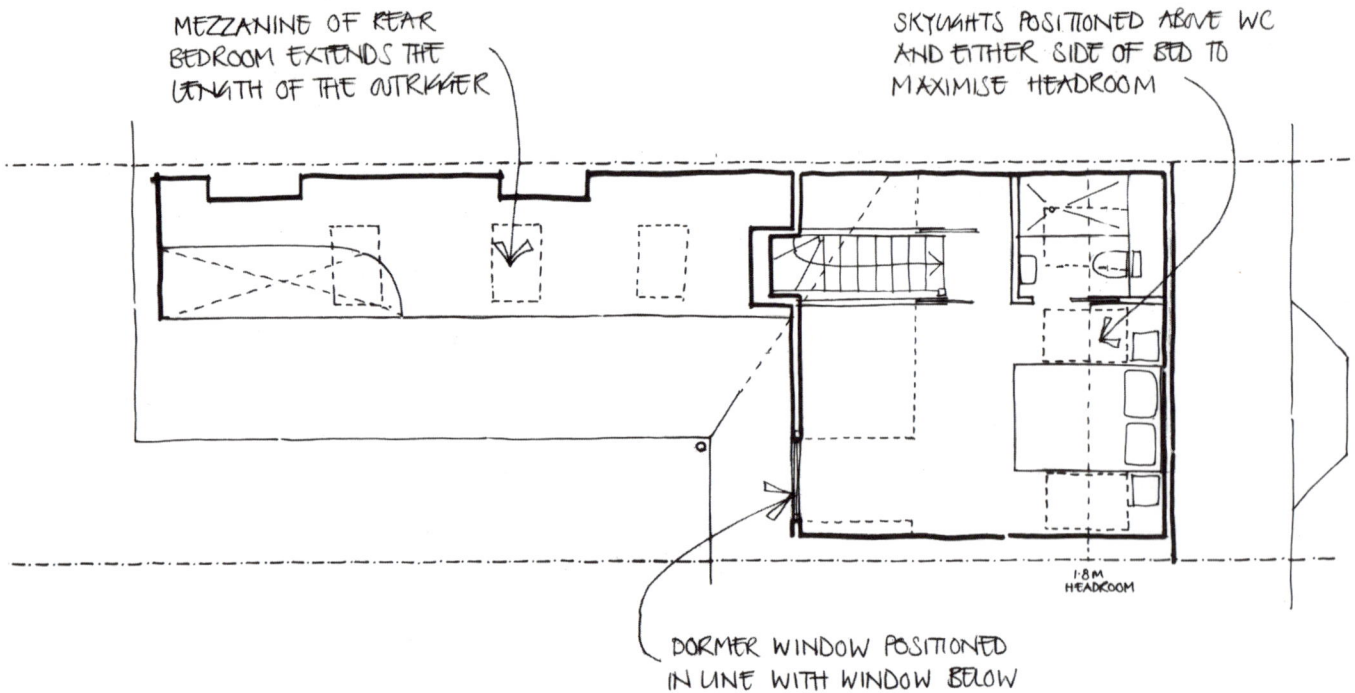

MEZZANINE OF REAR BEDROOM EXTENDS THE LENGTH OF THE OUTRIGGER

SKYLIGHTS POSITIONED ABOVE WC AND EITHER SIDE OF BED TO MAXIMISE HEADROOM

1·8 M HEADROOM

DORMER WINDOW POSITIONED IN LINE WITH WINDOW BELOW

Kelross House by Paul Archer Design, Islington, London, 2014. Open-plan bathroom tucked into eaves. Image mirrored to reflect plan.

OPTION 5

*(Based on the Kelross House project
by Paul Archer Design)*

As with Loft Options 3 and 4, this option retains the existing stairs — and again encloses them at the top to give privacy and satisfy fire regulations. It also retains the existing roof line, as in Loft Option 4, so it will work well in a Conservation Area. Tucking the bath and the bed under the front and rear eaves respectively makes the most of the limited headroom in these areas. This can be carried out as a stand-alone project or read in conjunction with First-floor Options 3 or 4.

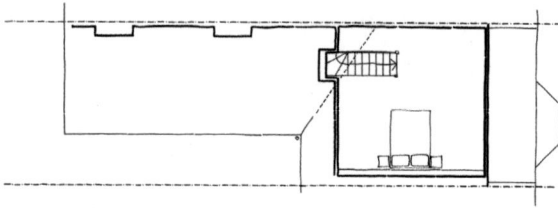

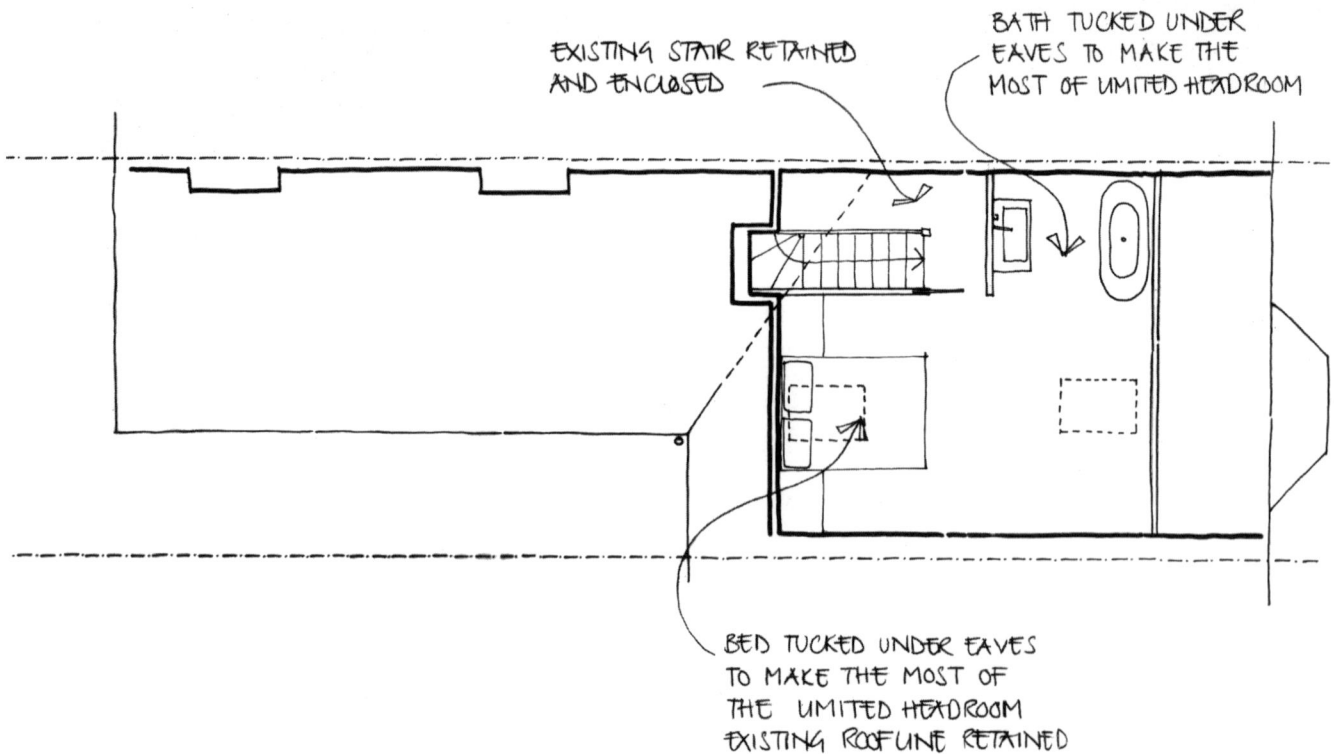

EXISTING STAIR RETAINED AND ENCLOSED

BATH TUCKED UNDER EAVES TO MAKE THE MOST OF LIMITED HEADROOM

BED TUCKED UNDER EAVES TO MAKE THE MOST OF THE LIMITED HEADROOM EXISTING ROOFLINE RETAINED

Kelross House by Paul Archer Design, Islington, London, 2014. Built-in cupboards behind the bed make the most of the eaves space. Image mirrored to reflect plan.

THE LARGE SEMI

This house is a 5m-wide semi-detached dwelling, built on a 6.4m-wide plot. It is a three-storey, split-level property with a basement and has limited headroom in the loft space, making it impossible to create a new loft extension.

BASEMENT

The basement, which is situated under the main section of the house, has limited headroom – so all options shown assume excavation to lower the floor in this area. (It should be noted that excavation work is often relatively costly.) It is at a slightly lower level than the garden but has direct access to it via French doors to the rear. In the existing plan, these doors are the only source of natural light into this level. It is also connected to the ground floor of the outrigger via two steps. As with many Victorian terraced houses, there is a utility room located to the rear of a small kitchen, both accommodated in the ground floor of the outrigger, providing very little connection to the garden.

In most plans, the ground floor of the outrigger has been shown together with the basement. However, if the two are not connected, as in Basement Option 4, it has been shown on the ground-floor plan.

OPTION 1

This option can be read in conjunction with Ground-floor Option 1. A section of the front garden has been excavated to continue the bay window down another level. This allows light into the new kitchen at the front of the house. A narrow utility room and a WC have been tucked in under the entrance hall above.

A dining room is located adjacent to this kitchen, and in this option the ceiling has been removed to make this dining space double height. However, this arrangement also works without any ceiling removal. The dining area is connected via three steps to the ground floor of the outrigger, which accommodates a large living area. A corner section of it has been removed to insert sliding, folding doors that open the new living room up to the garden.

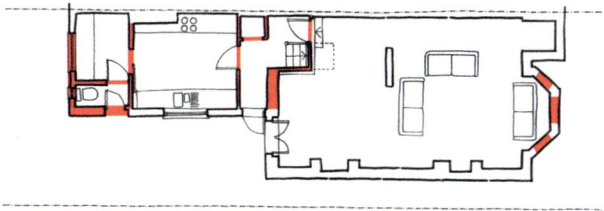

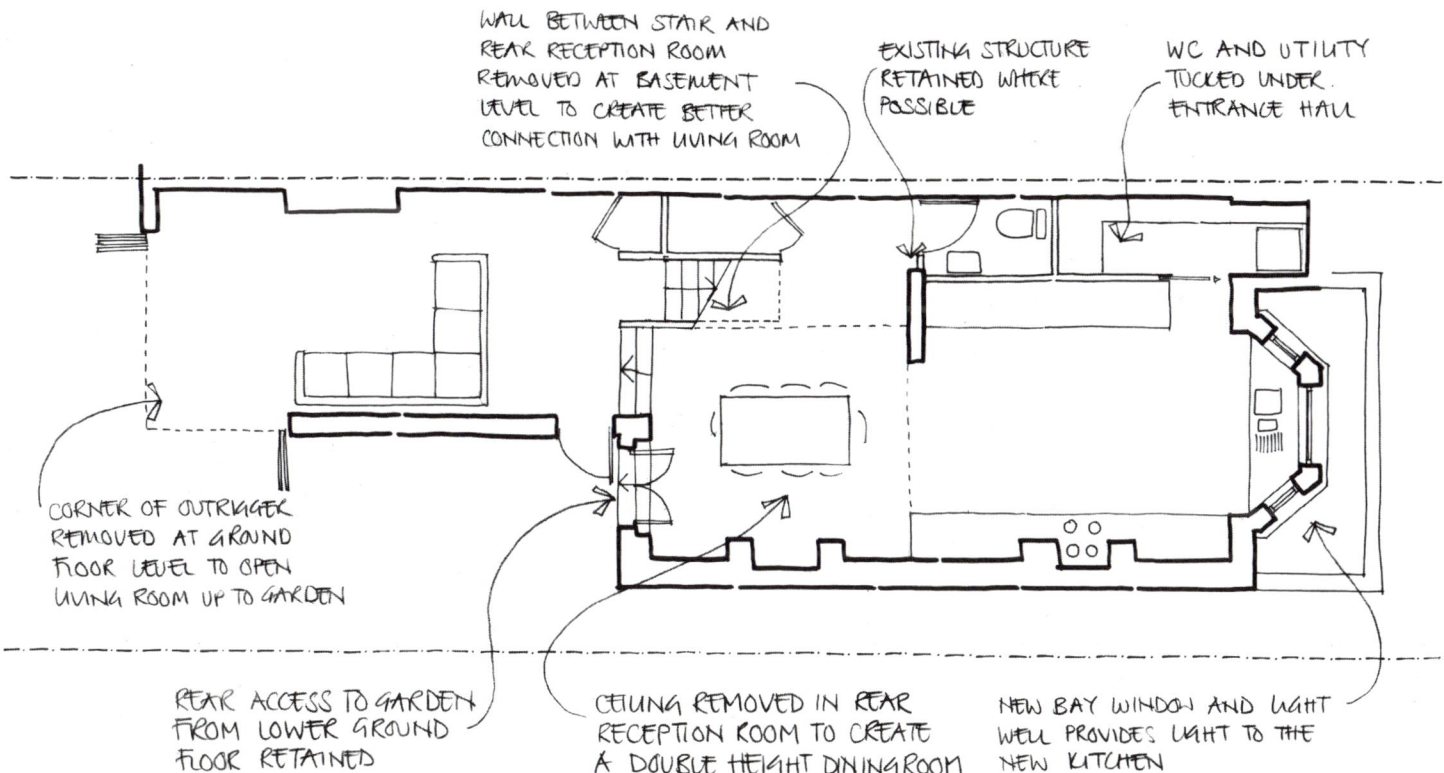

WALL BETWEEN STAIR AND REAR RECEPTION ROOM REMOVED AT BASEMENT LEVEL TO CREATE BETTER CONNECTION WITH LIVING ROOM

EXISTING STRUCTURE RETAINED WHERE POSSIBLE

WC AND UTILITY TUCKED UNDER ENTRANCE HALL

CORNER OF OUTRIGGER REMOVED AT GROUND FLOOR LEVEL TO OPEN LIVING ROOM UP TO GARDEN

REAR ACCESS TO GARDEN FROM LOWER GROUND FLOOR RETAINED

CEILING REMOVED IN REAR RECEPTION ROOM TO CREATE A DOUBLE HEIGHT DINING ROOM

NEW BAY WINDOW AND LIGHT WELL PROVIDES LIGHT TO THE NEW KITCHEN

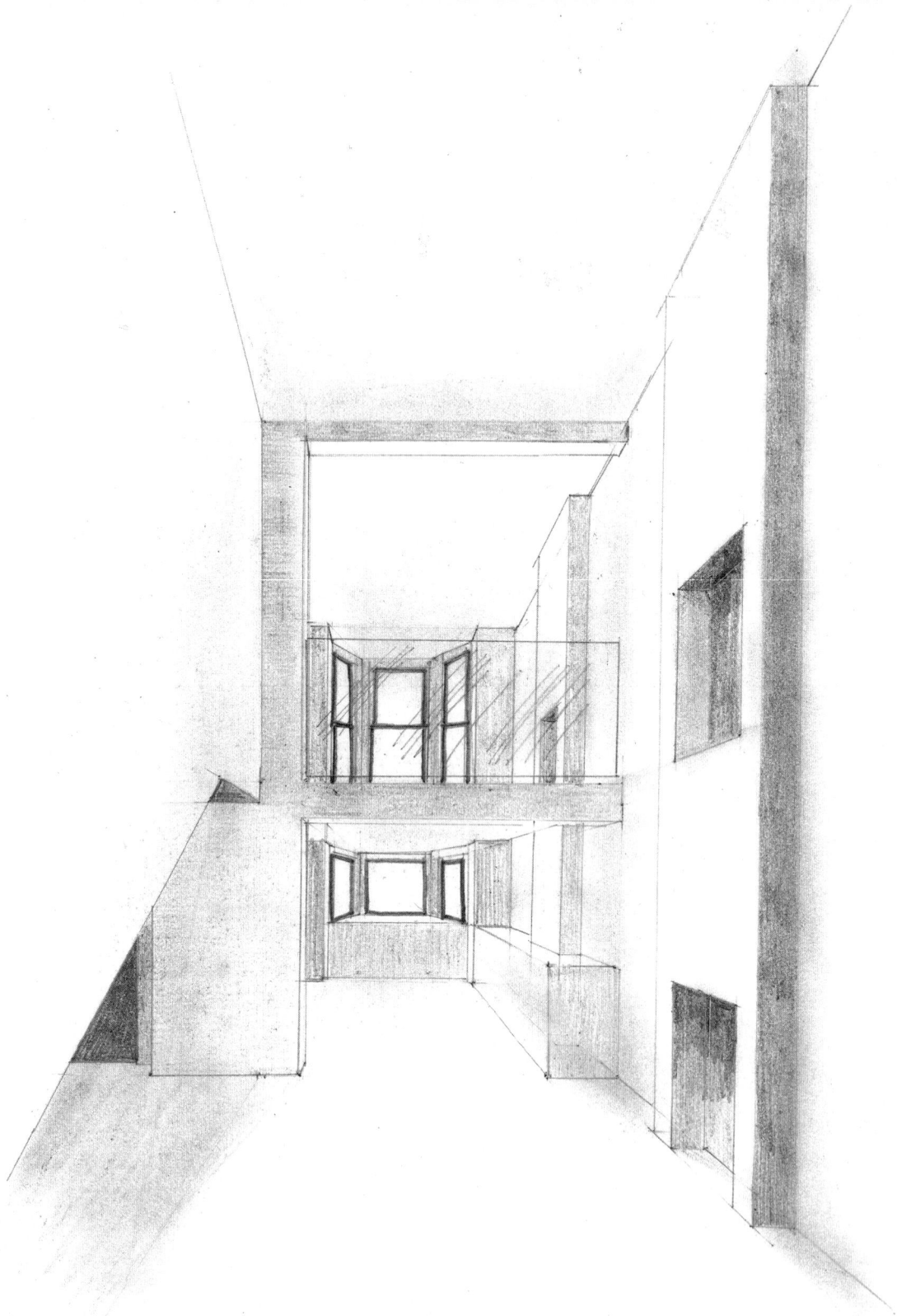

Artist's impression of view from double-storey
dining area to front of house. Based on option 1.

OPTION 2

This option can be read in conjunction with Ground-floor Option 3. It uses the existing basement and the ground floor of the outrigger to create a spacious, self-contained two-bedroomed flat with direct access to the garden. Again, a section of the front garden has been excavated to allow light into the front of the basement, which is being used as a bedroom in this option.

The entrance door to the flat is accessed via the side passage. If there is no side access, it may be possible to switch the front door and hall with the shower room. The outrigger has been extended part way into the side return at garden level. This creates a seating area adjoining a kitchen/diner that is accommodated within the footprint of the existing outrigger.

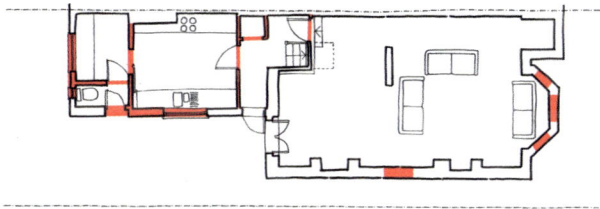

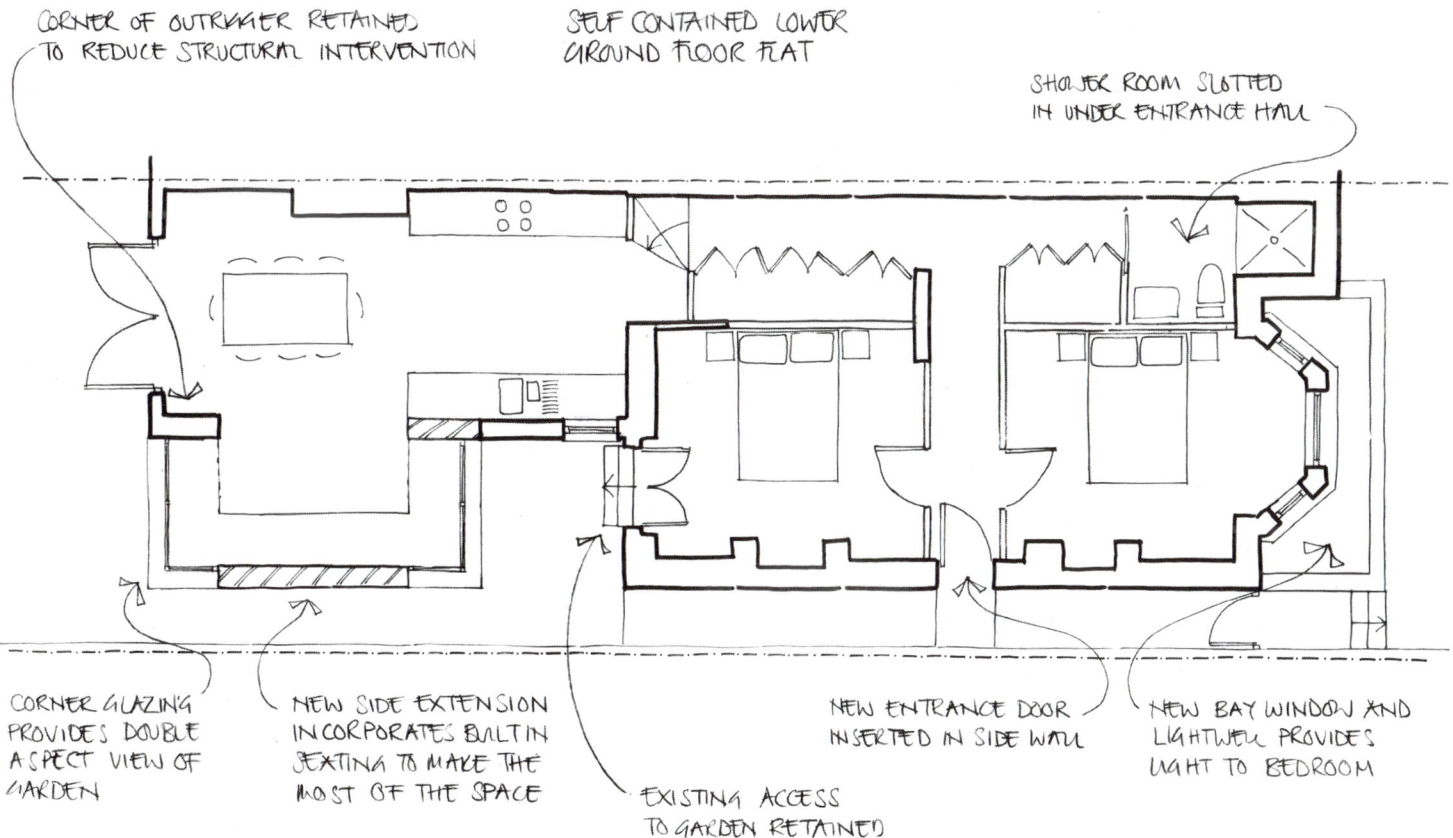

CORNER OF OUTRIGGER RETAINED TO REDUCE STRUCTURAL INTERVENTION

SELF CONTAINED LOWER GROUND FLOOR FLAT

SHOWER ROOM SLOTTED IN UNDER ENTRANCE HALL

CORNER GLAZING PROVIDES DOUBLE ASPECT VIEW OF GARDEN

NEW SIDE EXTENSION INCORPORATES BUILT IN SEATING TO MAKE THE MOST OF THE SPACE

EXISTING ACCESS TO GARDEN RETAINED

NEW ENTRANCE DOOR INSERTED IN SIDE WALL

NEW BAY WINDOW AND LIGHTWELL PROVIDES LIGHT TO BEDROOM

OPTION 3

The front half of the basement has been converted into a cinema room in this option – making the most of this dark area, with no additional windows required, although adequated ventilation must still be provided. The outrigger has been extended into the side return, in line with the existing house, and connected to the rear of the basement, which has been turned into a living area, via three wide steps. This extended outrigger accommodates a large kitchen/diner with a corner window seat and a skylight, allowing it to be read in conjunction with Ground-floor Option 7.

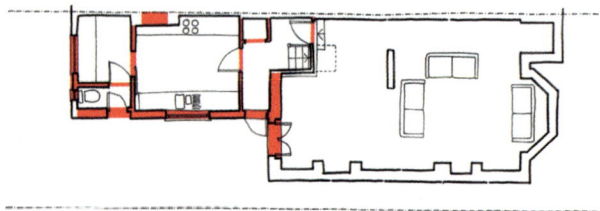

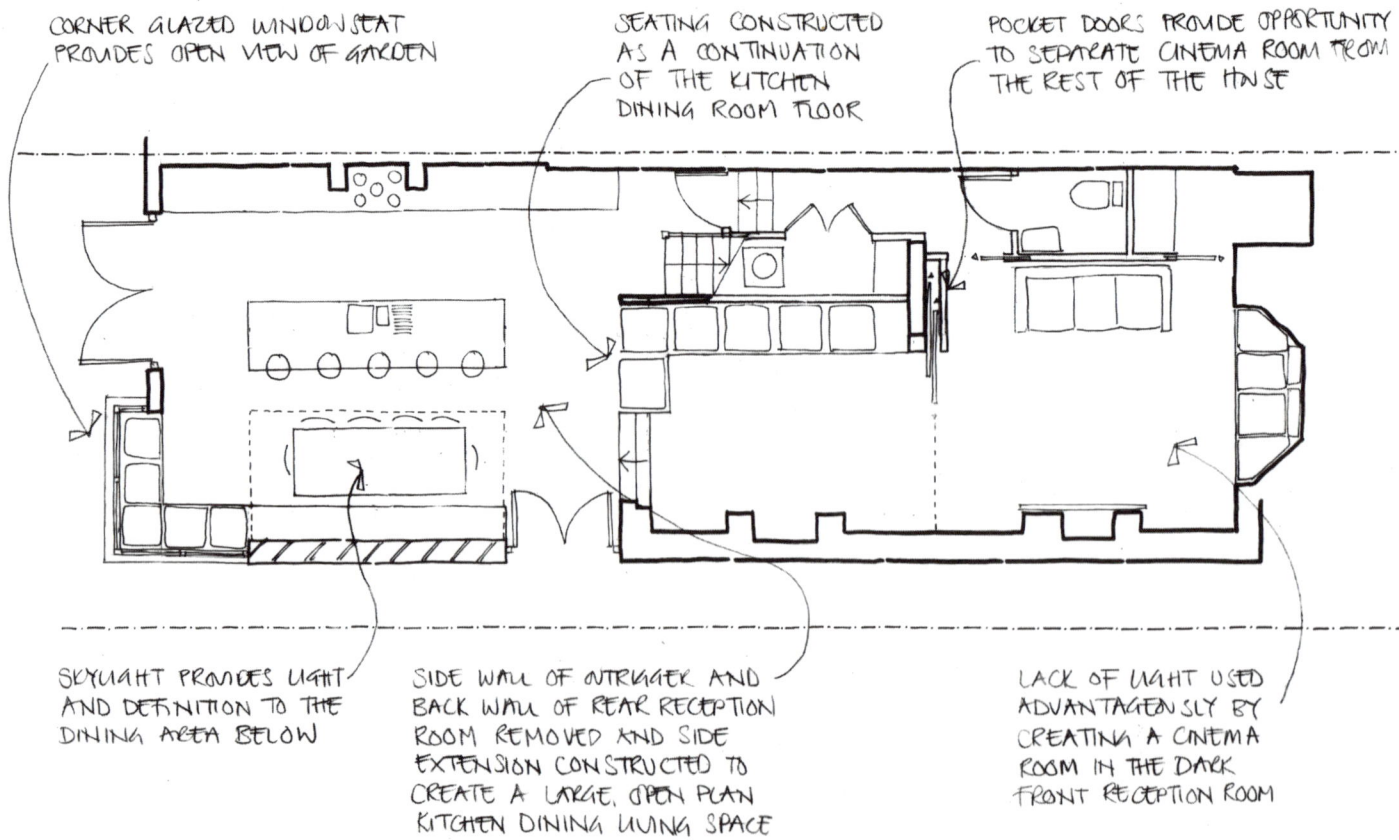

CORNER GLAZED WINDOW SEAT PROVIDES OPEN VIEW OF GARDEN

SEATING CONSTRUCTED AS A CONTINUATION OF THE KITCHEN DINING ROOM FLOOR

POCKET DOORS PROVIDE OPPORTUNITY TO SEPARATE CINEMA ROOM FROM THE REST OF THE HOUSE

SKYLIGHT PROVIDES LIGHT AND DEFINITION TO THE DINING AREA BELOW

SIDE WALL OF OUTRIGGER AND BACK WALL OF REAR RECEPTION ROOM REMOVED AND SIDE EXTENSION CONSTRUCTED TO CREATE A LARGE, OPEN PLAN KITCHEN DINING LIVING SPACE

LACK OF LIGHT USED ADVANTAGEOUSLY BY CREATING A CINEMA ROOM IN THE DARK FRONT RECEPTION ROOM

OPTION 4

This option can be read in conjunction with Ground-floor Options 2, 4, 5, 6 or 8 (although could be done as a stand-alone project). It converts the basement into a separate, self-contained, one-bedroomed flat. This involves digging down to create a light well in the front garden and inserting windows into the bay to allow light into the front half of the basement. A new entrance door, accessed via the side passage, has been inserted in the side wall between the two chimneybreasts. However, if there is no side access, the front door could be inserted into this bay.

If the level of the side return was lowered, direct access from the bedroom could be retained. The now redundant stairs leading up to the ground floor have been removed, creating space for a small shower room. The space under the entrance stair has been converted into a store accessed via the kitchen.

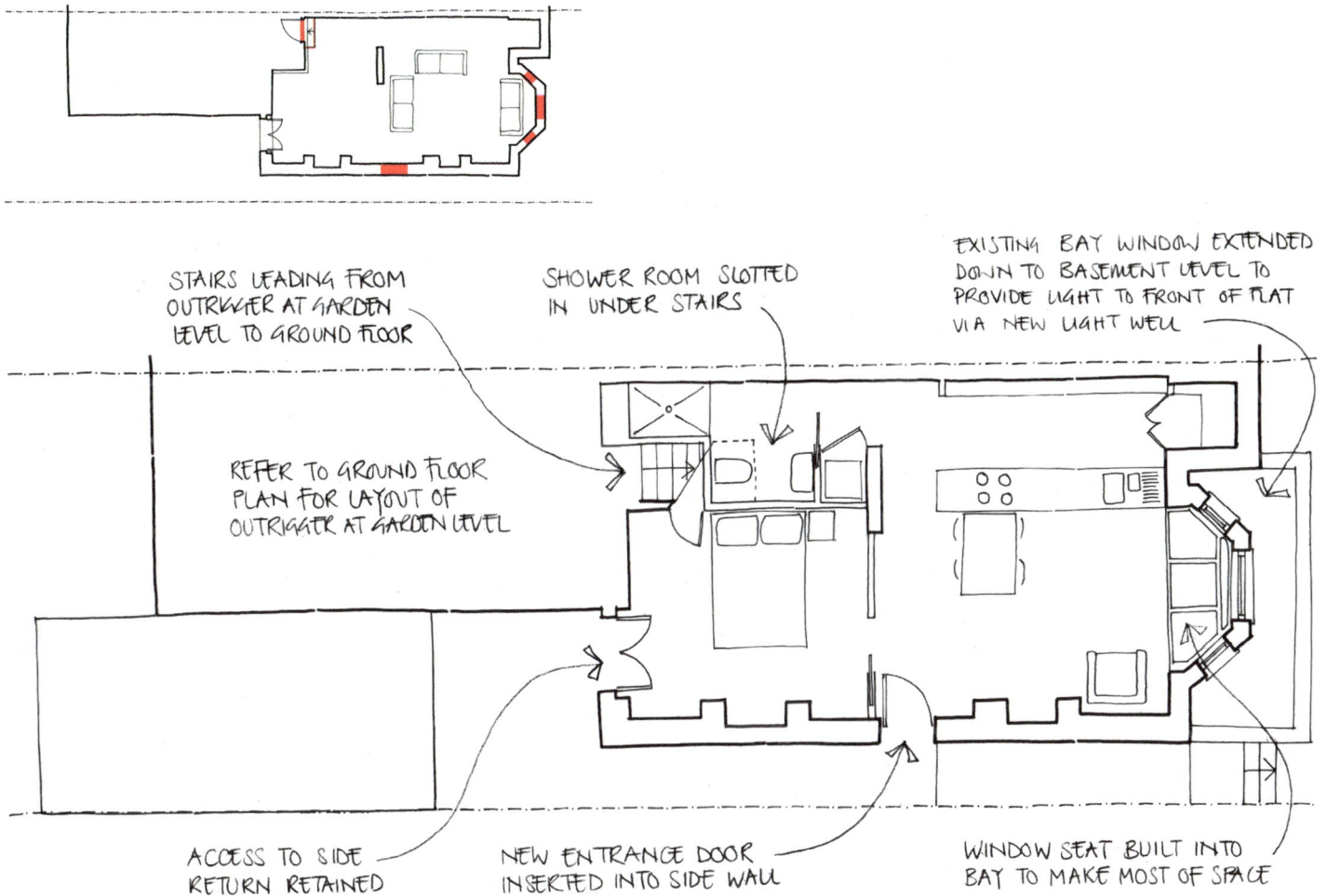

STAIRS LEADING FROM OUTRIGGER AT GARDEN LEVEL TO GROUND FLOOR

SHOWER ROOM SLOTTED IN UNDER STAIRS

EXISTING BAY WINDOW EXTENDED DOWN TO BASEMENT LEVEL TO PROVIDE LIGHT TO FRONT OF FLAT VIA NEW LIGHT WELL

REFER TO GROUND FLOOR PLAN FOR LAYOUT OF OUTRIGGER AT GARDEN LEVEL

ACCESS TO SIDE RETURN RETAINED

NEW ENTRANCE DOOR INSERTED INTO SIDE WALL

WINDOW SEAT BUILT INTO BAY TO MAKE MOST OF SPACE

OPTION 5

This option, to be read in conjunction with Ground-floor Option 9, converts the front of the basement into a bedroom suite with a shower room, digging down at the front to create a light well. The ground floor of the outrigger has been extended full length into the side return, in line with the side wall of the existing house, to connect with the rear of the basement via three steps, where the kitchen is shown. This large, rear room accommodates a dining area, living room and small study area overlooking the garden. The corner of the outrigger is retained to reduce structural intervention and respect the original proportions of the house. A glazed roof covers the extension, and is positioned above the level of the ground-floor window heads to create a connection between the basement and ground-floor levels.

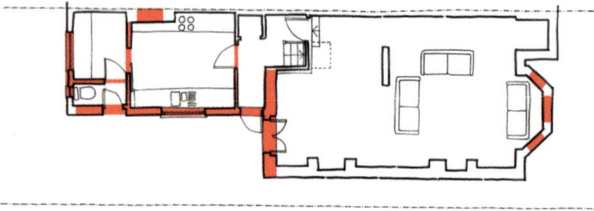

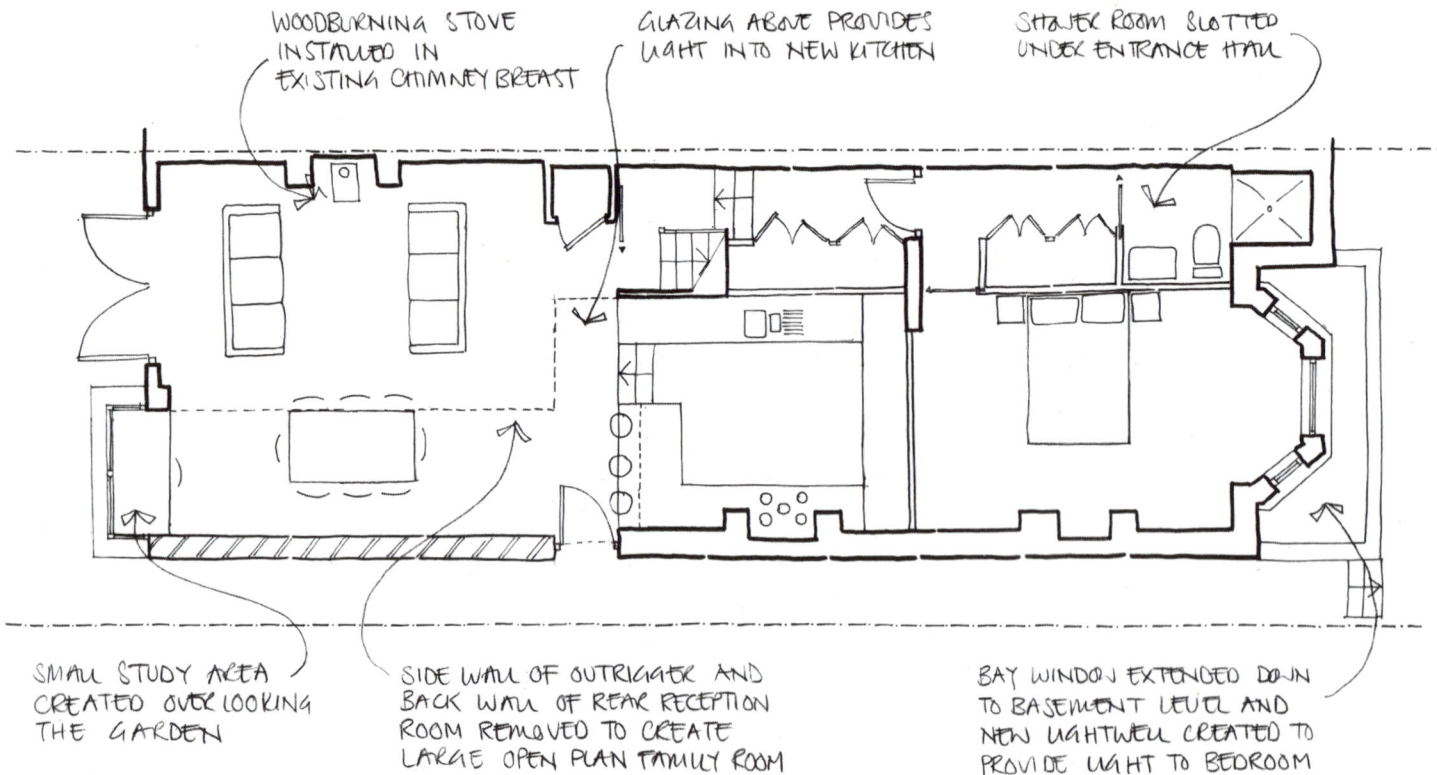

WOODBURNING STOVE INSTALLED IN EXISTING CHIMNEY BREAST

GLAZING ABOVE PROVIDES LIGHT INTO NEW KITCHEN

SHOWER ROOM SLOTTED UNDER ENTRANCE HALL

SMALL STUDY AREA CREATED OVERLOOKING THE GARDEN

SIDE WALL OF OUTRIGGER AND BACK WALL OF REAR RECEPTION ROOM REMOVED TO CREATE LARGE OPEN PLAN FAMILY ROOM

BAY WINDOW EXTENDED DOWN TO BASEMENT LEVEL AND NEW LIGHTWELL CREATED TO PROVIDE LIGHT TO BEDROOM

Power House by Paul Archer Design, Islington, London, 2012. High ceiling created by dropping the floor level.

OPTION 6

*(Based on the Power House project
by Paul Archer Design)*

This option involves lowering the floor not only in the basement but also in the outrigger. The latter has been extended into the side return, the full width of the plot, to create an expansive kitchen/diner with space for seating or a study area. Lowering the floor gives a generous floor-to-ceiling height. The double-height, glazed section over part of the side return also enables visual connection between this floor and the one above (see Ground-floor Option 10). A light well has been excavated at the front of the property to allow light into the basement, which is used here to accommodate a living room with storage and a WC. Proposed access via a side door and sliding pocket doors separating it from the kitchen allow this room to be used independently of the rest of the house.

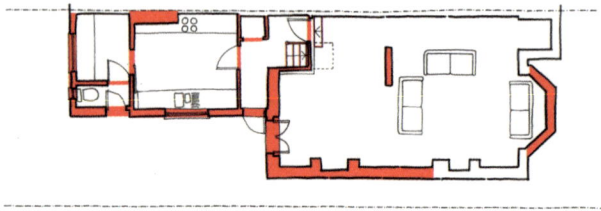

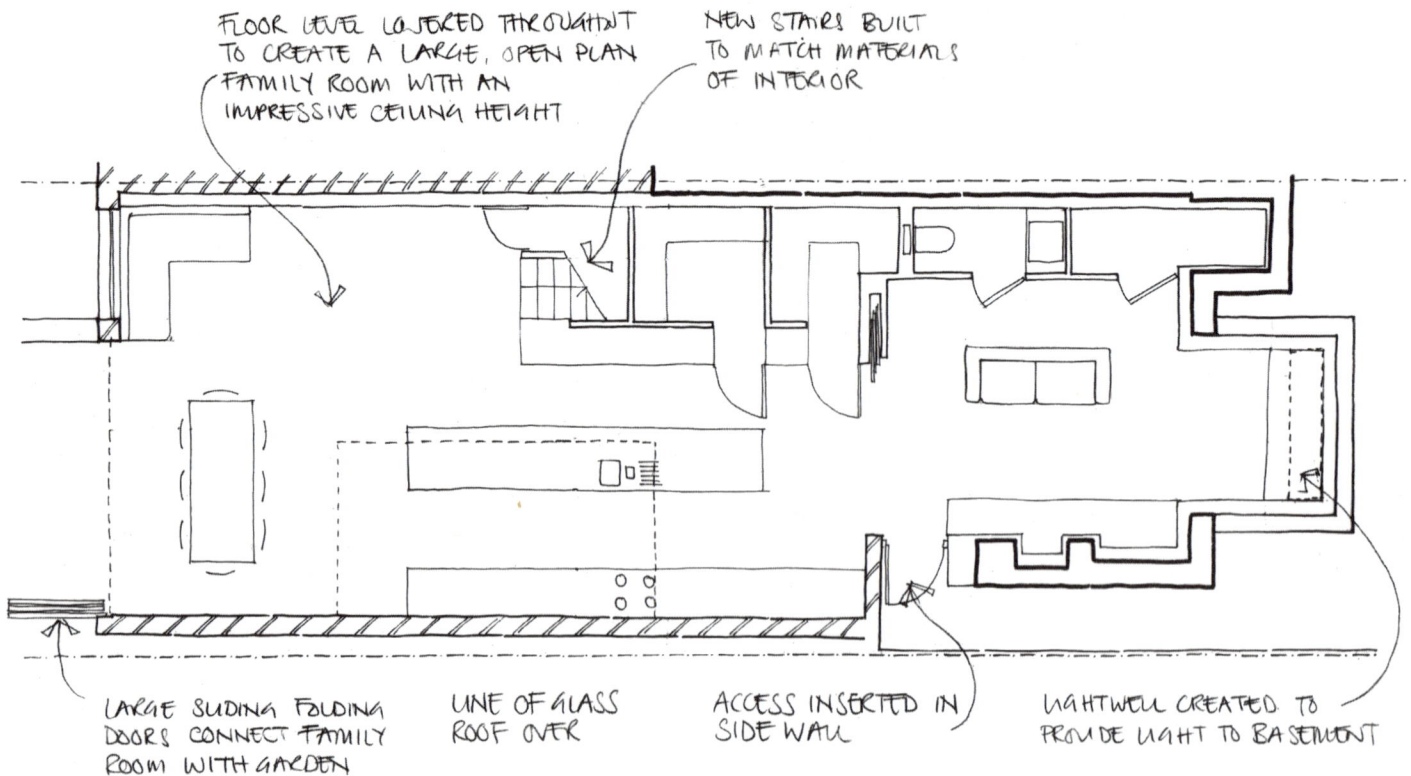

FLOOR LEVEL LOWERED THROUGHOUT TO CREATE A LARGE, OPEN PLAN FAMILY ROOM WITH AN IMPRESSIVE CEILING HEIGHT

NEW STAIRS BUILT TO MATCH MATERIALS OF INTERIOR

LARGE SLIDING FOLDING DOORS CONNECT FAMILY ROOM WITH GARDEN

LINE OF GLASS ROOF OVER

ACCESS INSERTED IN SIDE WALL

LIGHTWELL CREATED TO PROVIDE LIGHT TO BASEMENT

Power House by Paul Archer Design, Islington, London, 2012. Use of different ceiling height to demarcate different use zones.

Power House by Paul Archer Design, Islington, London, 2012. View from garden into newly excavated and extended based kitchen diner.

BEDROOM

BEDROOM

BEDROOM

BEDROOM

LIVING ROOM

LIVING ROOM

KITCHEN DINER

GROUND FLOOR

The ground floor, located in the main section of the house, is more than half a storey higher than the ground floor of the outrigger and is accessed via steps from the street. As is typical with many Victorian terraced houses, it accommodates two good sized reception rooms..

The ground level of the outrigger has been shown on the ground-floor plan if it does not connect to the basement – as in Basement Option 4, which depicts a self-contained flat.

OPTION 1

This option, to be read in conjunction with Basement Option 1, removes the floor from the rear reception room to create a double-height space in the room below. The wall between the two reception rooms has been removed and replaced with folding doors that tuck neatly into one corner when open. A glass balustrade has been positioned between these two spaces to create a balcony overlooking the room below when the folding doors are open.

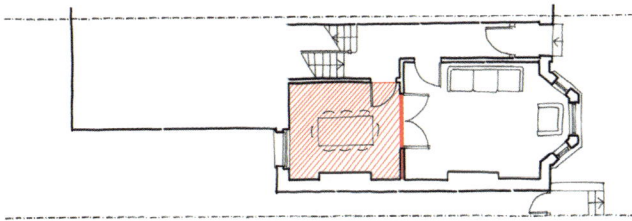

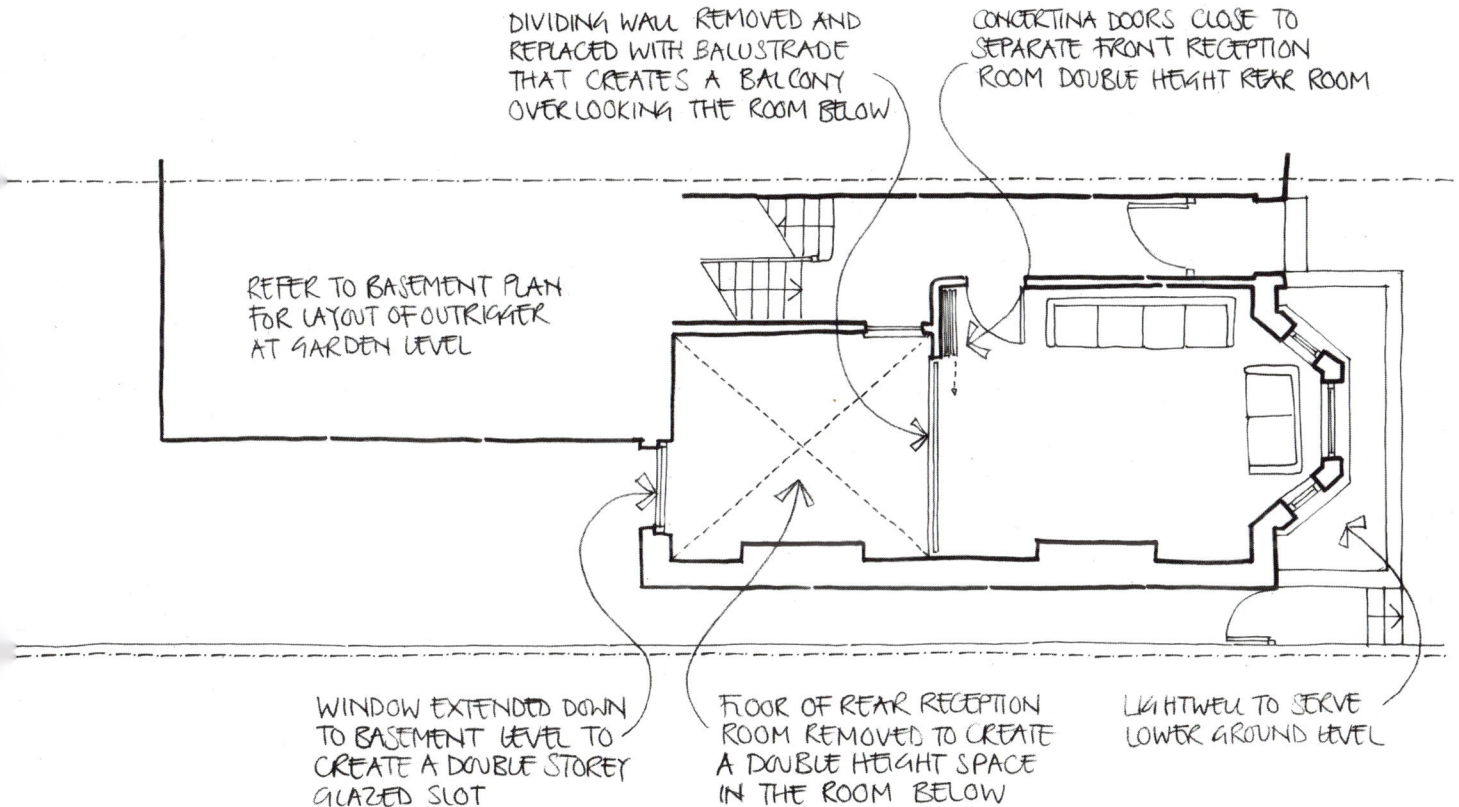

DIVIDING WALL REMOVED AND REPLACED WITH BALUSTRADE THAT CREATES A BALCONY OVERLOOKING THE ROOM BELOW

CONCERTINA DOORS CLOSE TO SEPARATE FRONT RECEPTION ROOM DOUBLE HEIGHT REAR ROOM

REFER TO BASEMENT PLAN FOR LAYOUT OF OUTRIGGER AT GARDEN LEVEL

WINDOW EXTENDED DOWN TO BASEMENT LEVEL TO CREATE A DOUBLE STOREY GLAZED SLOT

FLOOR OF REAR RECEPTION ROOM REMOVED TO CREATE A DOUBLE HEIGHT SPACE IN THE ROOM BELOW

LIGHTWELL TO SERVE LOWER GROUND LEVEL

OPTION 2

(Based on the Hennessy House project by Paul Archer Design)

This option relocates the kitchen/diner to the front of the house, with the living room being accommodated in the ground floor of the outrigger with direct access to the garden. Large glazed doors have been inserted into the wall between the front reception room and the hall to let more light into the hall and give a greater sense of space in the dining room. A small WC has been slotted in where the external side door was.

This option works well where the basement has been converted into a separate flat, as in Basement Option 4.

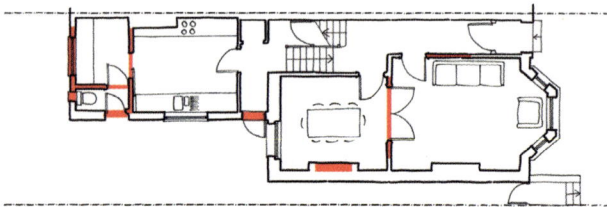

NEW LIVINGROOM IS ACCOMMODATED WITHIN THE EXISTING FOOTPRINT OF THE OUTRIGGER WITHOUT THE NEED TO EXTEND. INTERNAL WALLS REMOVED

KITCHEN DINER RELOCATED TO FRONT AND REAR RECEPTION ROOMS TO MAKE SPACE FOR A LIVING ROOM AT THE BACK OF THE HOUSE

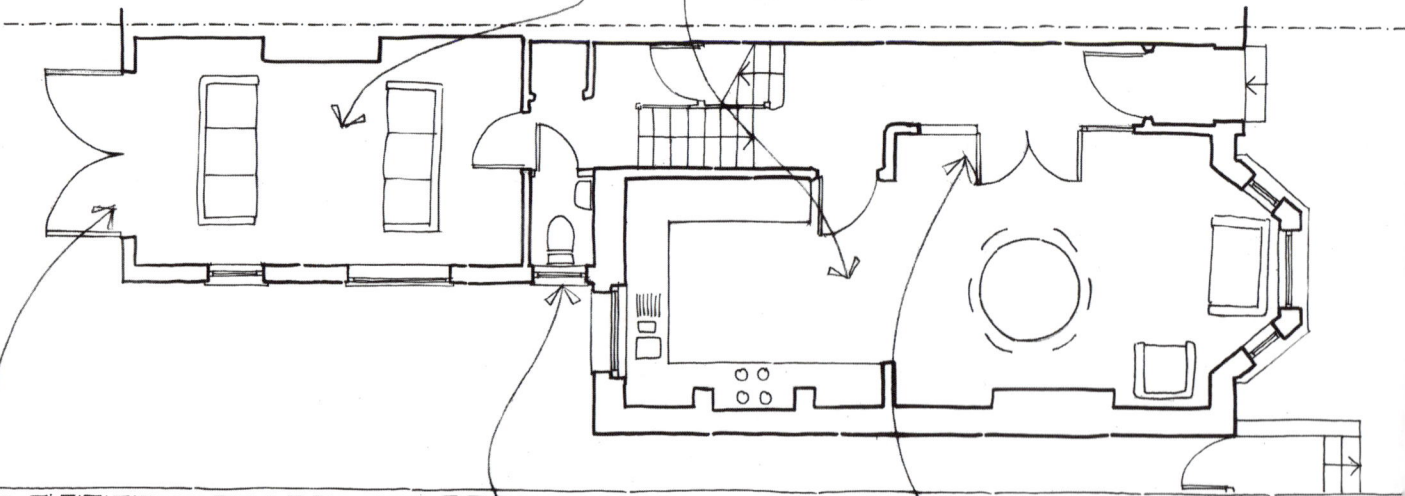

DOUBLE DOORS INSERTED IN REAR WALL OF OUTRIGGER TO CONNECT LIVING ROOM WITH GARDEN

WC SLOTTED IN TO LOBBY OF EXISTING GARDEN DOOR

LARGE GLASS DOORS INSERTED INTO WALL TO PROVIDE LIGHT TO ENTRANCE CORRIDOR

Hennessy House by Paul Archer Design, Chiswick, London, 2016. Glass doors inserted in corridor wall to give a sense of space and light.

OPTION 3

The front reception room has been converted into a bedroom in this option and the rear reception room has been divided into a bathroom and dressing area to serve the adjacent bedroom. The stairs down to the basement have been removed and the resultant space used to create a good sized store. This can be read in conjunction with Basement Option 2, a self contained two bedroomed flat, and Second-floor Option 4, which accommodates the living, dining and kitchen areas, creating an upside down house. It also works with any plan where the kitchen, dining and living areas are all accommodated in the basement.

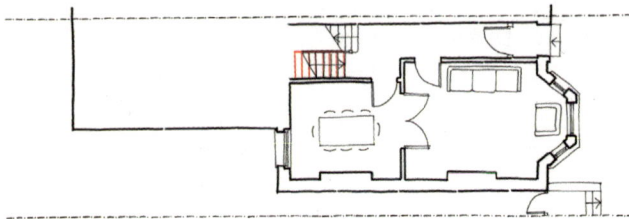

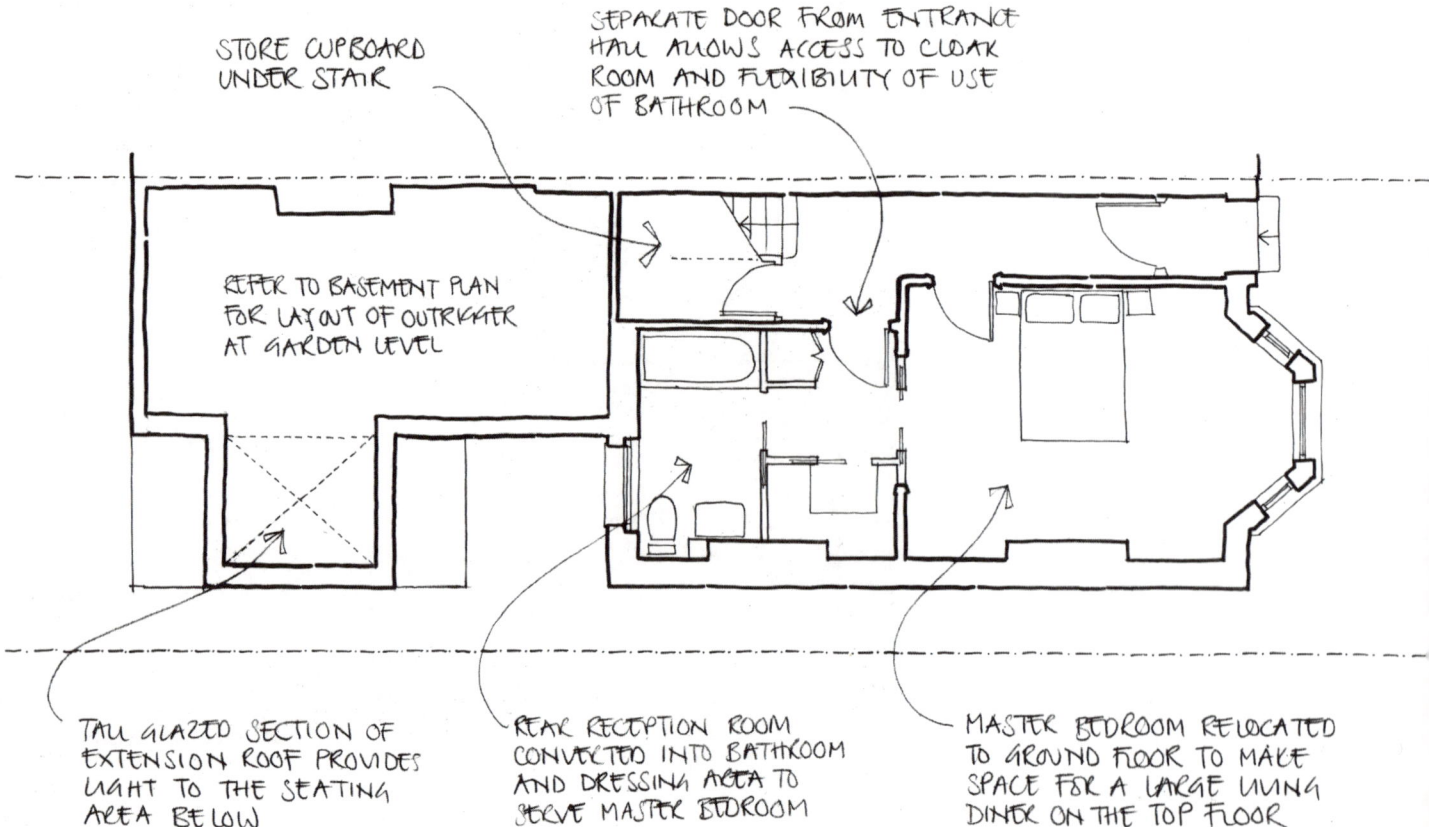

STORE CUPBOARD
UNDER STAIR

SEPARATE DOOR FROM ENTRANCE
HALL ALLOWS ACCESS TO CLOAK
ROOM AND FLEXIBILITY OF USE
OF BATHROOM

REFER TO BASEMENT PLAN
FOR LAYOUT OF OUTRIGGER
AT GARDEN LEVEL

TALL GLAZED SECTION OF
EXTENSION ROOF PROVIDES
LIGHT TO THE SEATING
AREA BELOW

REAR RECEPTION ROOM
CONVERTED INTO BATHROOM
AND DRESSING AREA TO
SERVE MASTER BEDROOM

MASTER BEDROOM RELOCATED
TO GROUND FLOOR TO MAKE
SPACE FOR A LARGE LIVING
DINER ON THE TOP FLOOR

Lantern Lean-To by Blee Halligan Architects,
Islington, London, 2019. Wide extension provides
ample room for a large dining table.

OPTION 4

(Based on the Lantern Lean-To project by Blee Halligan Architects)

By removing the central wall, the front and rear reception rooms have been amalgamated in this option. Blocking the door to the front reception room reduces circulation space, thus creating more useable space. A section of the outrigger has been removed at this level to connect to a new room that extends into the side return, the full width of the plot, and to the rear, leaving a section of courtyard that serves this new room. This extended outrigger accommodates a spacious kitchen/diner with a large window seat that juts out into the garden. This plan can be read in conjunction with Basement Option 4 or as a stand-alone scheme.

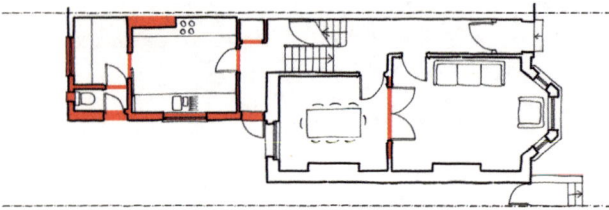

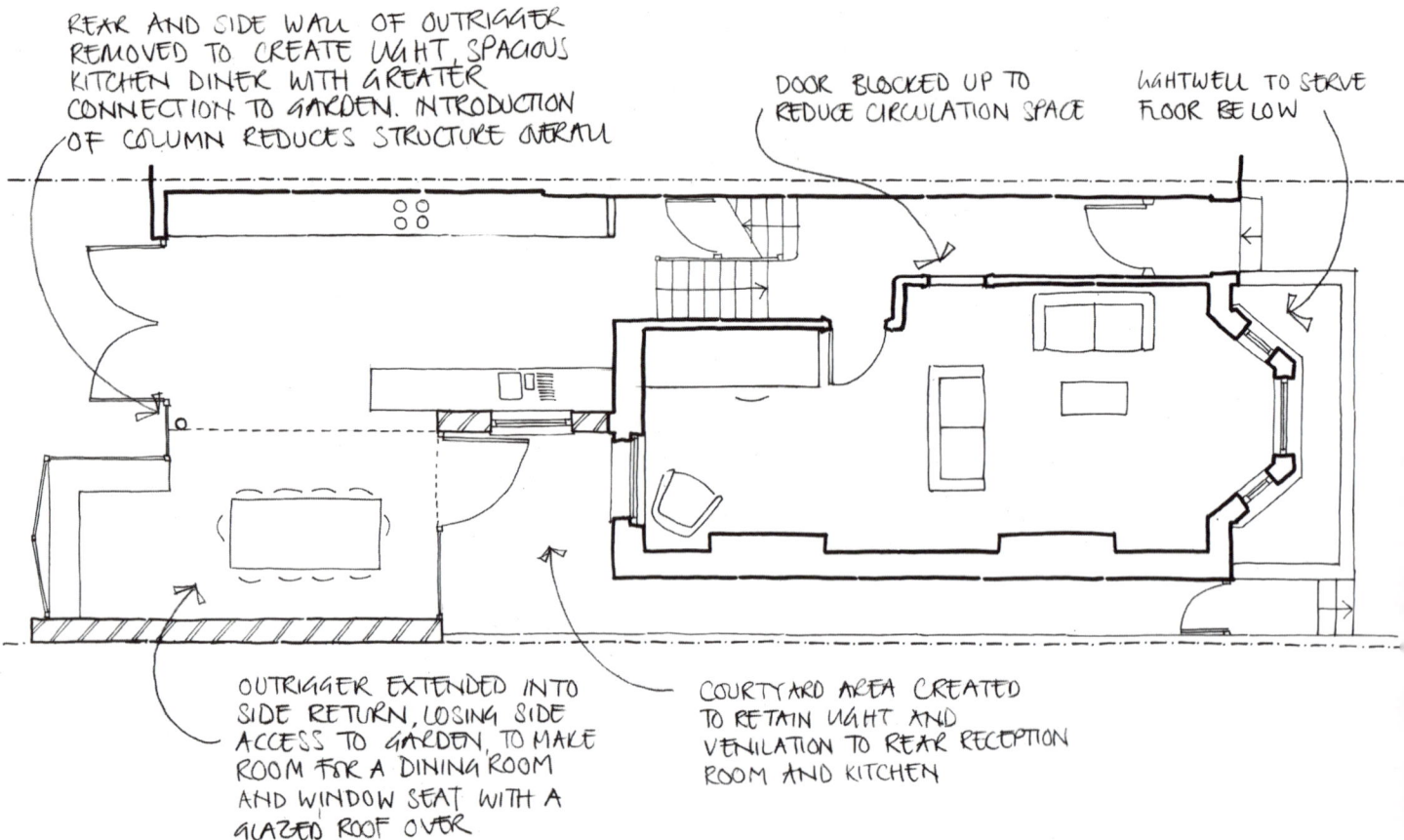

REAR AND SIDE WALL OF OUTRIGGER REMOVED TO CREATE LIGHT, SPACIOUS KITCHEN DINER WITH GREATER CONNECTION TO GARDEN. INTRODUCTION OF COLUMN REDUCES STRUCTURE OVERALL

DOOR BLOCKED UP TO REDUCE CIRCULATION SPACE

LIGHTWELL TO SERVE FLOOR BELOW

OUTRIGGER EXTENDED INTO SIDE RETURN, LOSING SIDE ACCESS TO GARDEN, TO MAKE ROOM FOR A DINING ROOM AND WINDOW SEAT WITH A GLAZED ROOF OVER

COURTYARD AREA CREATED TO RETAIN LIGHT AND VENTILATION TO REAR RECEPTION ROOM AND KITCHEN

Lantern Lean-To by Blee Halligan Architects,
Islington, London, 2019. View from courtyard
through new extension to garden.

OPTION 5

(Based on the Stack House project by Nimtim)

The central wall has been removed in this option to create one large sitting room. The plan, which also works well with Basement Option 4, extends the outrigger into the side return and to the rear. It retains the side access to the garden and creates a small courtyard adjacent to the rear reception room to preserve the light in the existing space, as in the previous option. Positioning the kitchen across the room, rather than front to back, leaves more room for the dining area.

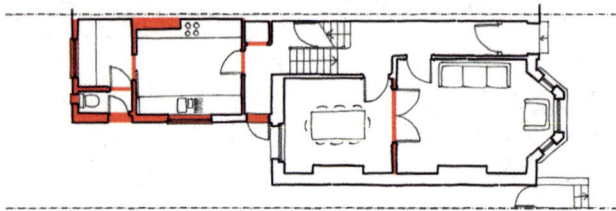

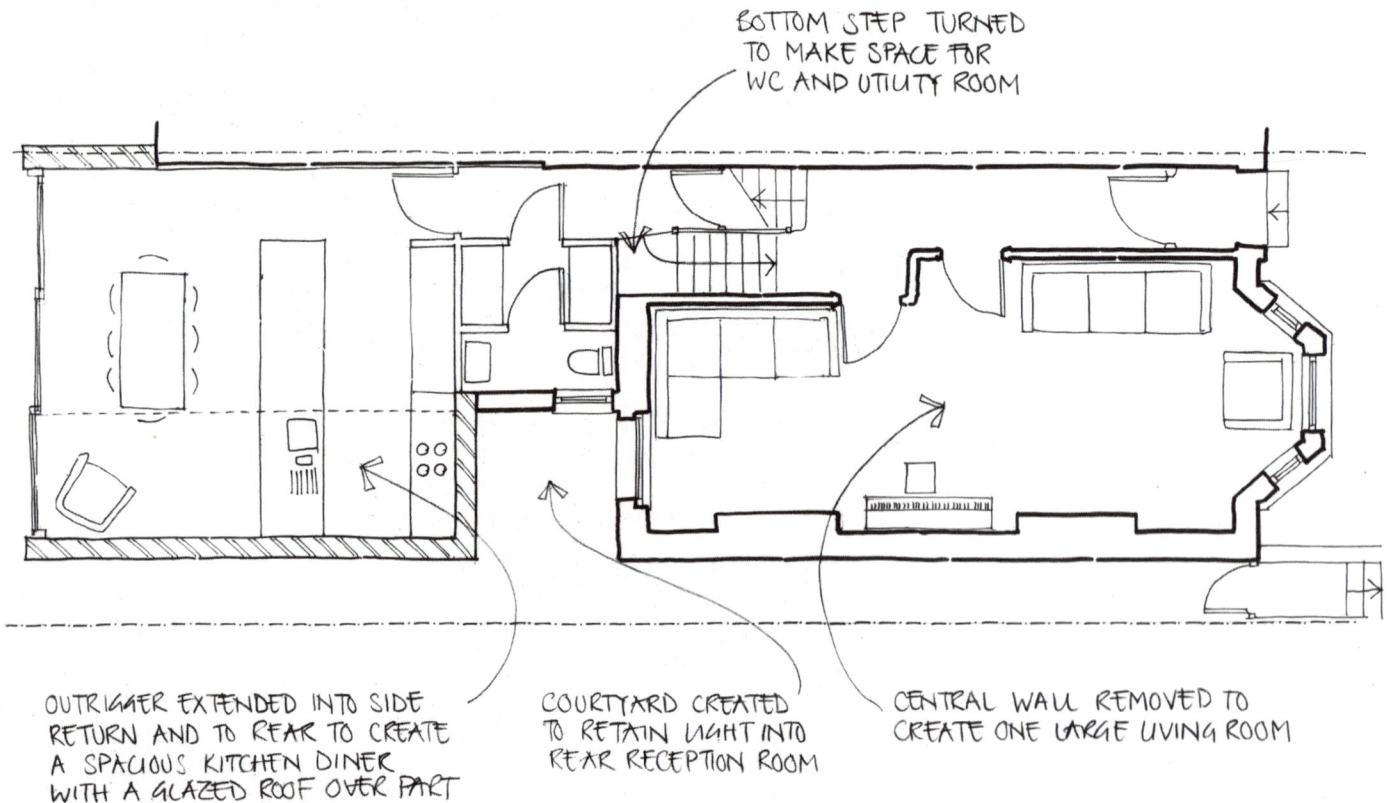

BOTTOM STEP TURNED TO MAKE SPACE FOR WC AND UTILITY ROOM

OUTRIGGER EXTENDED INTO SIDE RETURN AND TO REAR TO CREATE A SPACIOUS KITCHEN DINER WITH A GLAZED ROOF OVER PART

COURTYARD CREATED TO RETAIN LIGHT INTO REAR RECEPTION ROOM

CENTRAL WALL REMOVED TO CREATE ONE LARGE LIVING ROOM

Stack House by Nimtim, Dulwich, London, 2018.
Kitchen positioned full width across plan, leaving
rear to accommodate dining area.

OPTION 6

(Based on the Pages Lane project by Kirkwood McCarthy)

The front of the house has been left untouched in this option. Much of the side wall of the outrigger has also been retained, to keep the character of the property as well as minimising structural intervention. A single-storey extension has been shown, extending to the side the full width of the plot and the rear to accommodate a dining area and sitting room. A long kitchen is shown within the original footprint of the outrigger and a small WC has been slotted into the existing lobby that led to the original back door. Pulling back the extension from the existing rear window and creating a courtyard at this level has retained the integrity of the rear reception room by still allowing light to permeate. Again, this option works well with Basement Option 4 or as a stand alone project.

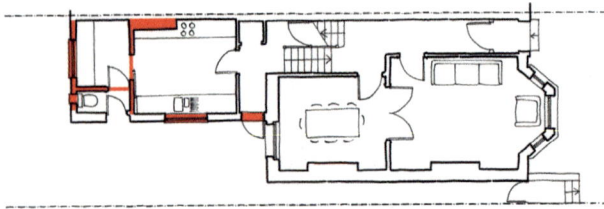

MUCH OF EXISTING SIDEWALL RETAINED TO MINIMISE STRUCTURAL ALTERATIONS

WC SLOTTED IN TO LOBBY OF EXISTING GARDEN DOOR

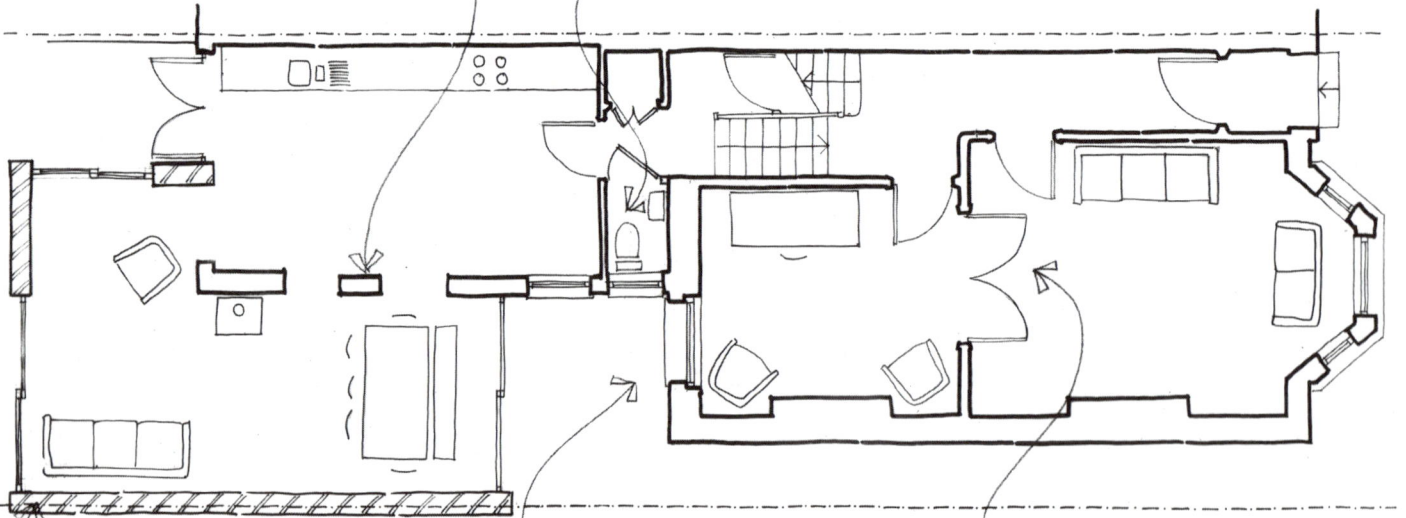

NEW LIVING DINING ROOM EXTENDS TO THE BOUNDARY AT THE SIDE AND INTO THE GARDEN TO THE REAR

EXTENSION SET BACK FROM REAR WALL OF HOUSE TO RETAIN INTEGRITY OF REAR RECEPTION ROOM

FRONT AND REAR RECEPTION ROOMS RETAINED FOR SEPARATE USE

Pages Lane by Kirkwood McCarthy, Muswell Hill,
London, 2016. Side wall of extension offset to create
connection between kitchen and living room. Image
mirrored to reflect plan.

Next page. Pages Lane by Kirkwood McCarthy,
Muswell Hill, London, 2016. Parts of existing side
wall retained to minimise structural alterations.

OPTION 7

The front section of the house has been retained as per the existing plan in this option, turning the rear reception room into a library. The outrigger has been extended into the side return at garden level and connected with the basement, which can be seen in Basement Option 3. A section of the side-return extension is taller, to give a double-height space above the dining table below. It reduces in height to avoid clashing with the window of the rear reception room.

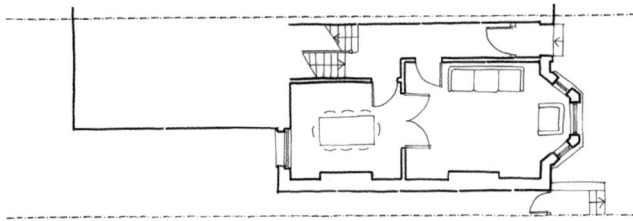

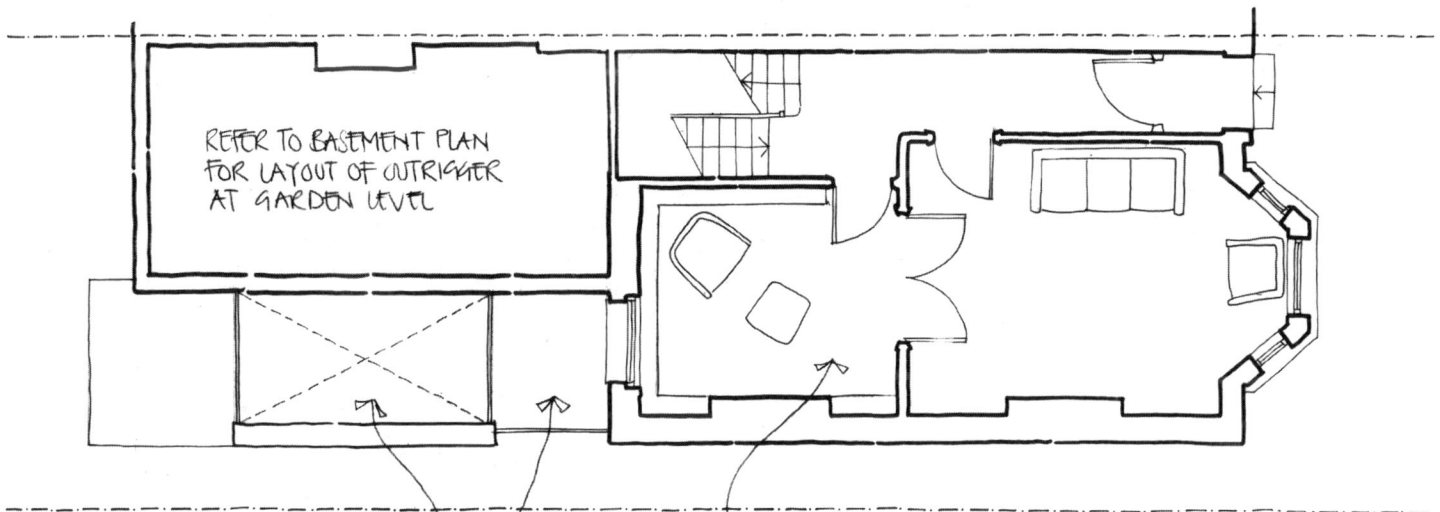

REFER TO BASEMENT PLAN
FOR LAYOUT OF OUTRIGGER
AT GARDEN LEVEL

TALL GLAZED SECTION OF
EXTENSION ROOF PROVIDES
LIGHT TO THE DINING
AREA BELOW

LOWER SECTION OF FLAT
ROOF RETAINS EXISTING
WINDOW SERVING REAR
RECEPTION ROOM

EXISTING RECEPTION ROOMS
RETAINED AS SEPARATE ROOMS,
THE REAR OF WHICH IS SHOWN
HERE AS A LIBRARY

OPTION 8

(Based on the Tibur House project by Paul Archer Design)

A section of the wall between the hall and the front reception room has been replaced with glass in this option, to create a sense of openness. The back wall of the rear reception room has been almost entirely removed to connect it, via a set of steps (more in the plan than in the corresponding images), to the proposed side-return extension at garden level. This option can be read in conjunction with Basement Option 4.

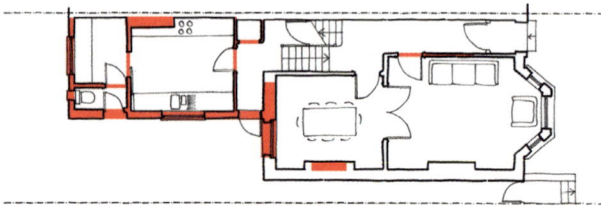

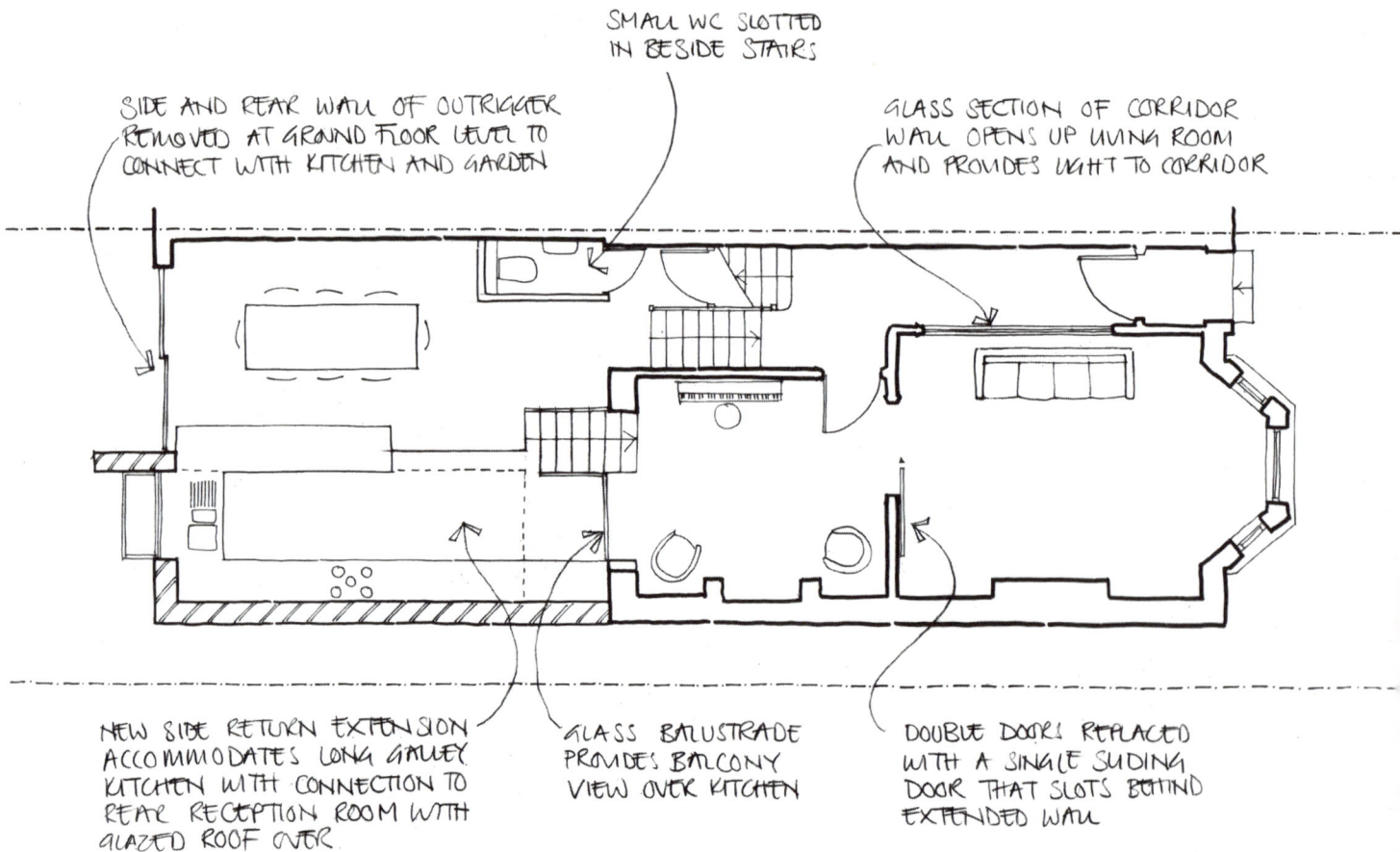

SMALL WC SLOTTED IN BESIDE STAIRS

SIDE AND REAR WALL OF OUTRIGGER REMOVED AT GROUND FLOOR LEVEL TO CONNECT WITH KITCHEN AND GARDEN

GLASS SECTION OF CORRIDOR WALL OPENS UP LIVING ROOM AND PROVIDES LIGHT TO CORRIDOR

NEW SIDE RETURN EXTENSION ACCOMMODATES LONG GALLEY KITCHEN WITH CONNECTION TO REAR RECEPTION ROOM WITH GLAZED ROOF OVER

GLASS BALUSTRADE PROVIDES BALCONY VIEW OVER KITCHEN

DOUBLE DOORS REPLACED WITH A SINGLE SLIDING DOOR THAT SLOTS BEHIND EXTENDED WALL

Tibur House by Paul Archer Design, Crouch End, London, 2016. Change in floor level demarcates different uses.

The extension accommodates a long kitchen, with a dining room located within the original footprint of the outrigger. A small WC has also been positioned near to the existing staircase. The French doors at the rear of the basement have been removed in this option, and no courtyard created. So, natural light would need to be provided with the addition of a light well and windows at the front of the property – as shown in the majority of the basement options. As the kitchen diner is open to the stairwell, an appropriate sprinkler system would need to be installed.

Tibur House by Paul Archer Design, Crouch End,
London, 2016. Concrete fin supports corner of
outrigger and concrete beams within.

OPTION 9

The front reception room remains as existing in this option, apart from replacing the double doors between the two reception rooms with sliding doors. The back wall of the rear reception room has been removed to create a vertical link with the double-height extension at the rear (see Basement Option 5). This turns the rear reception room into a mezzanine level that would work perfectly as a performance space. To be read in conjunction with first floor option 2.

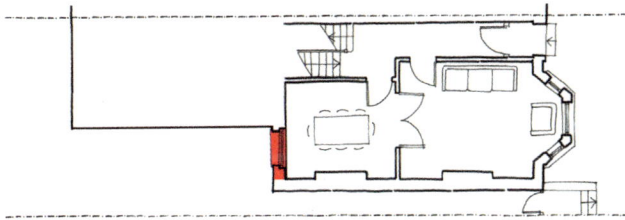

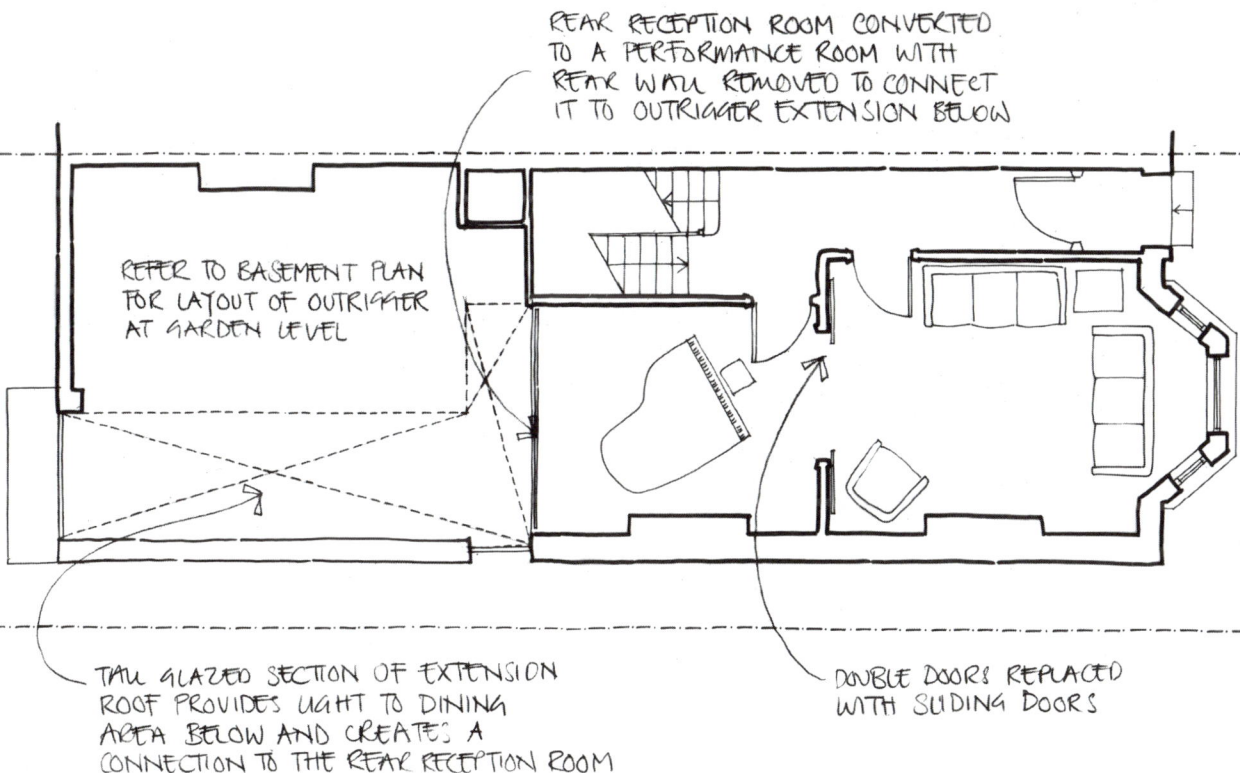

REAR RECEPTION ROOM CONVERTED
TO A PERFORMANCE ROOM WITH
REAR WALL REMOVED TO CONNECT
IT TO OUTRIGGER EXTENSION BELOW

REFER TO BASEMENT PLAN
FOR LAYOUT OF OUTRIGGER
AT GARDEN LEVEL

TALL GLAZED SECTION OF EXTENSION
ROOF PROVIDES LIGHT TO DINING
AREA BELOW AND CREATES A
CONNECTION TO THE REAR RECEPTION ROOM

DOUBLE DOORS REPLACED
WITH SLIDING DOORS

OPTION 10

(Based on the Power House project by Paul Archer Design)

The front and rear reception rooms have been amalgamated in this option. A section of the rear wall has been opened up to create a vertical connection with the double-height portion of the rear extension shown in Basement Option 6. A large, sliding door can close off this connection if desired. The stairs down to the garden level of the outrigger have been upgraded to give the rear of the house a more modern feel.

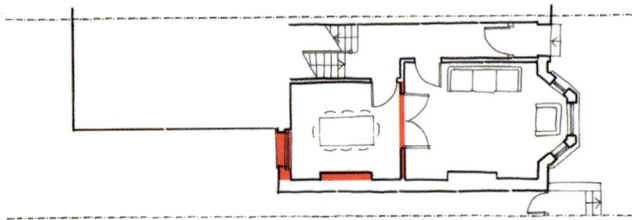

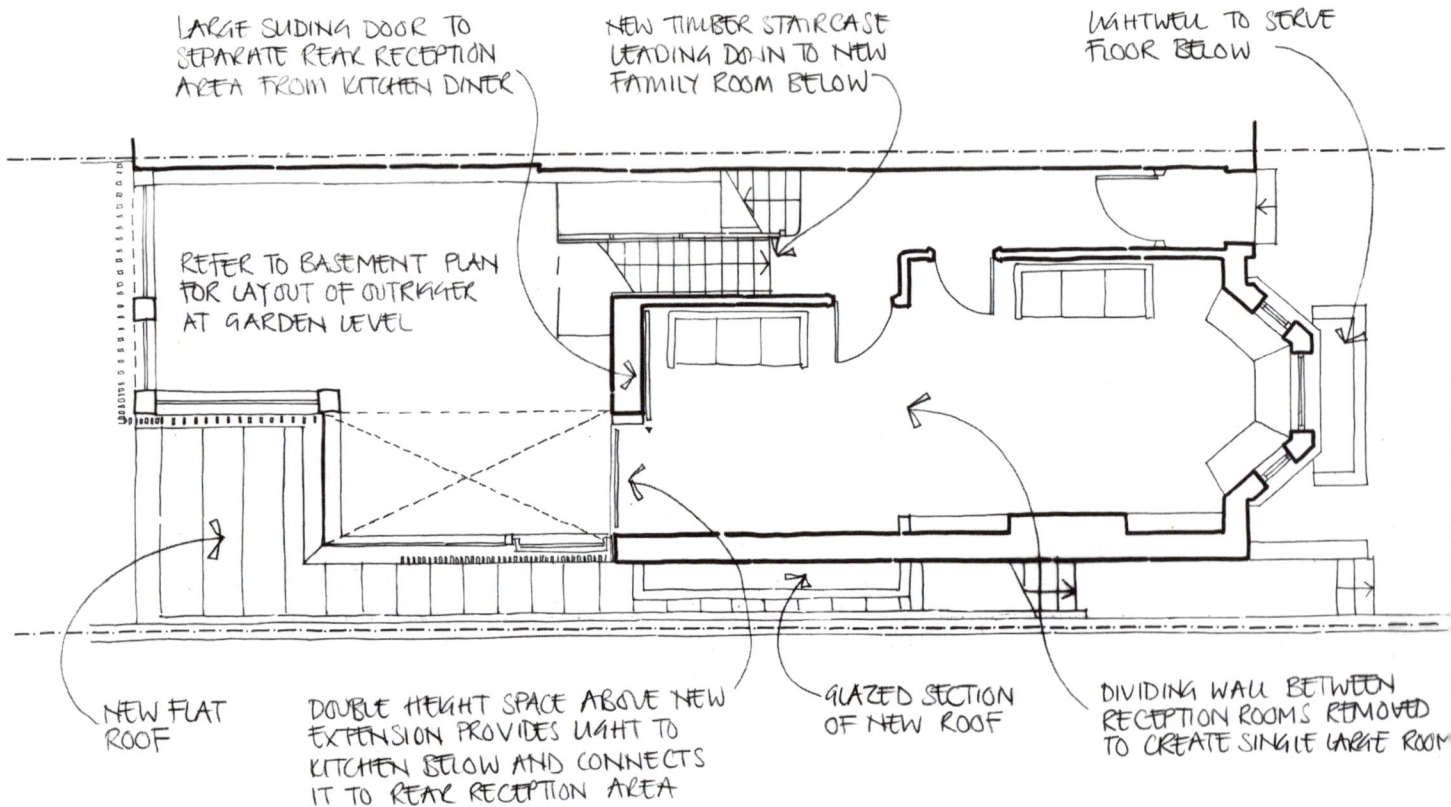

LARGE SLIDING DOOR TO SEPARATE REAR RECEPTION AREA FROM KITCHEN DINER

NEW TIMBER STAIRCASE LEADING DOWN TO NEW FAMILY ROOM BELOW

LIGHTWELL TO SERVE FLOOR BELOW

REFER TO BASEMENT PLAN FOR LAYOUT OF OUTRIGGER AT GARDEN LEVEL

NEW FLAT ROOF

DOUBLE HEIGHT SPACE ABOVE NEW EXTENSION PROVIDES LIGHT TO KITCHEN BELOW AND CONNECTS IT TO REAR RECEPTION AREA

GLAZED SECTION OF NEW ROOF

DIVIDING WALL BETWEEN RECEPTION ROOMS REMOVED TO CREATE SINGLE LARGE ROOM

Power House by Paul Archer Design, Islington, London, 2012. Views down from living-room balcony.

Next page. Power House by Paul Archer Design, Islington, London, 2012. Rear reception room can be used as a performance space, or closed off using the sliding pocket door.

FIRST FLOOR

This floor is typical of a Victorian terraced house of this size. It accommodates two double bedrooms in the main section of the house and a third in the outrigger, together with a bathroom and separate WC.

OPTION 1

This option uses the middle bedroom to accommodate a spacious bathroom serving the front bedroom, although its separate entrance provides flexibility of use. The door of this bedroom has been relocated to allow the bed to be positioned opposite the fireplace without privacy being compromised. The bathroom and corridor at the rear have been rearranged to create an en-suite shower room and dressing area to serve the rear bedroom.

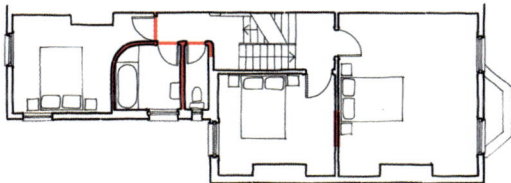

EXISTING BATHROOM AND CORRIDOR SPACE REARRANGED TO CREATE ENSUITE AND DRESSING AREA

DOOR TO FRONT BEDROOM BLOCKED TO GIVE PRIVACY TO BED IF POSITIONED OPPOSITE FIRE PLACE

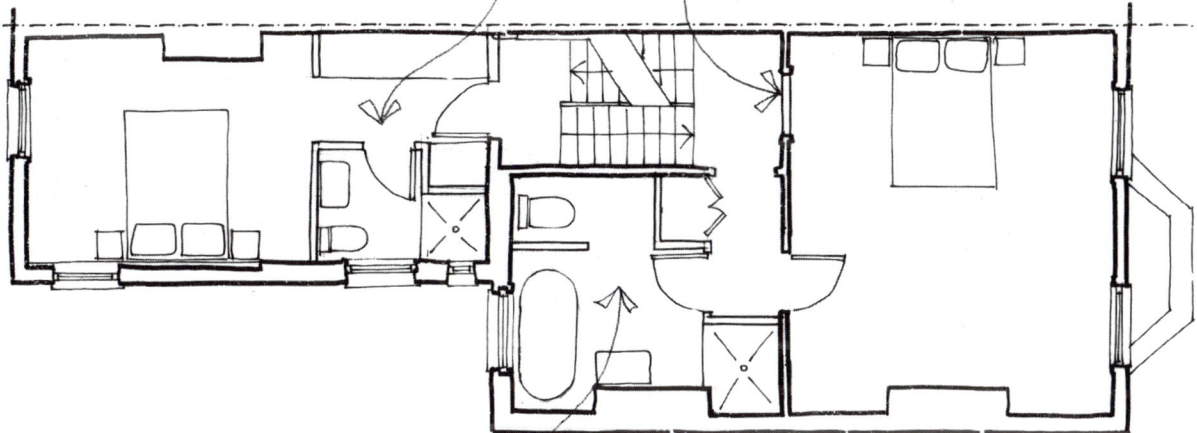

MIDDLE BEDROOM USED TO CREATE SPACIOUS BATHROOM

OPTION 2

This option creates an en-suite shower room in the large front bedroom and relocates the WC to within the existing rear bathroom. The floor of the original WC is removed to create a vertical connection with the floor below, as shown in Ground-floor Option 9. This should be enclosed with fire-rated glazing to comply with fire regulations.

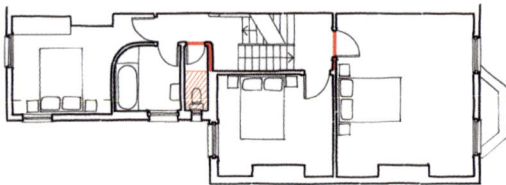

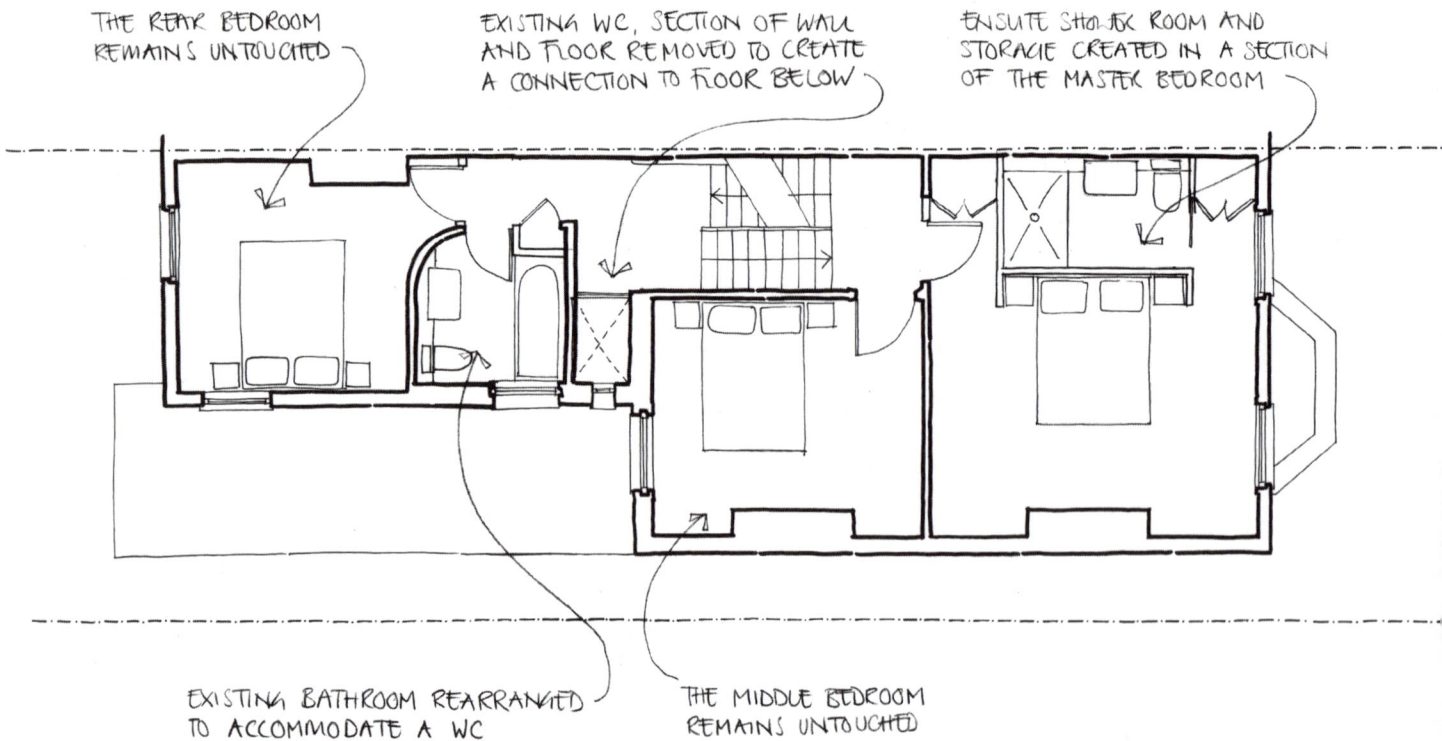

THE REAR BEDROOM
REMAINS UNTOUCHED

EXISTING WC, SECTION OF WALL
AND FLOOR REMOVED TO CREATE
A CONNECTION TO FLOOR BELOW

ENSUITE SHOWER ROOM AND
STORAGE CREATED IN A SECTION
OF THE MASTER BEDROOM

EXISTING BATHROOM REARRANGED
TO ACCOMMODATE A WC

THE MIDDLE BEDROOM
REMAINS UNTOUCHED

OPTION 3

An en-suite and dressing area has been created to serve the front bedroom in this option. The middle bedroom remains as existing, as does the rear bedroom. The bathroom and separate WC have been amalgamated to create a larger family bathroom with separate shower.

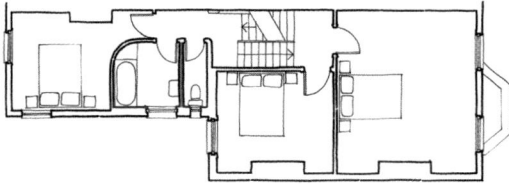

NEW SHOWER ROOM CREATED IN SECTION OF FRONT BEDROOM ACCESSED FROM LANDING AND FROM FRONT BEDROOM

NEW DRESSING AREA CREATED TO SERVE FRONT BEDROOM

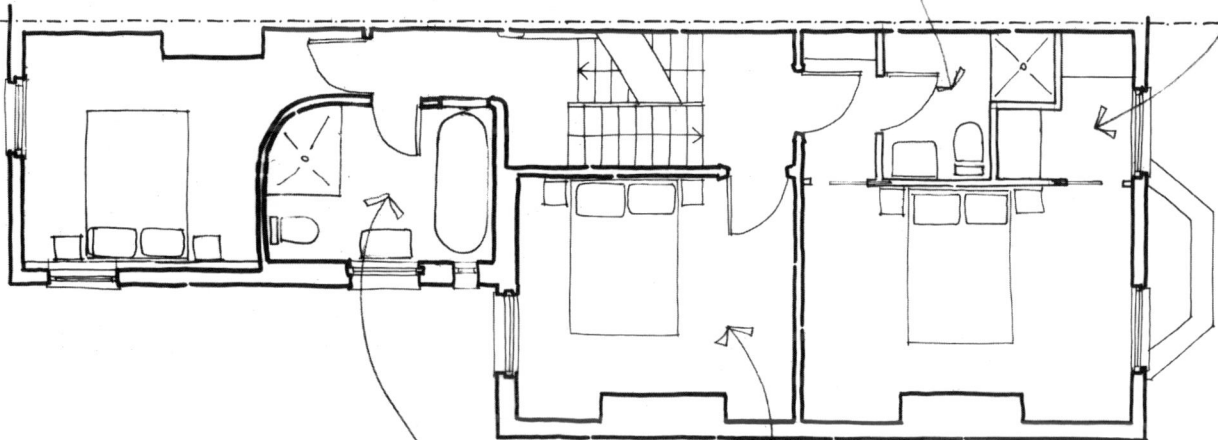

SEPARATE WC AND BATHROOM AMALGAMATED TO CREATE ONE LARGE FAMILY BATHROOM

MIDDLE BEDROOM REMAINS UNTOUCHED

SECOND FLOOR

The existing second floor accommodates two double bedrooms and a small bathroom that appears to have been previously carved out of the original front room. There is also a bathroom and third bedroom accommodated in the outrigger. The loft space in this house is too low to be converted, so none of the options for this floor includes stairs up to a loft conversion – although Second-floor Option 4 does show a small mezzanine level.

OPTION 1

The existing bathroom at the front of the house has been relocated in between the front and middle bedrooms. This serves the front bedroom while still maintaining two good-sized double bedrooms. The bathroom in the outrigger has been slightly enlarged and reconfigured to enable the addition of a roll-top bath and separate shower.

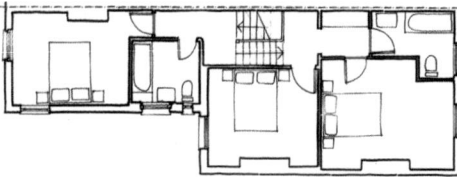

BATHROOM ENLARGED TO CREATE SPACE FOR A SEPARATE SHOWER AND BATH

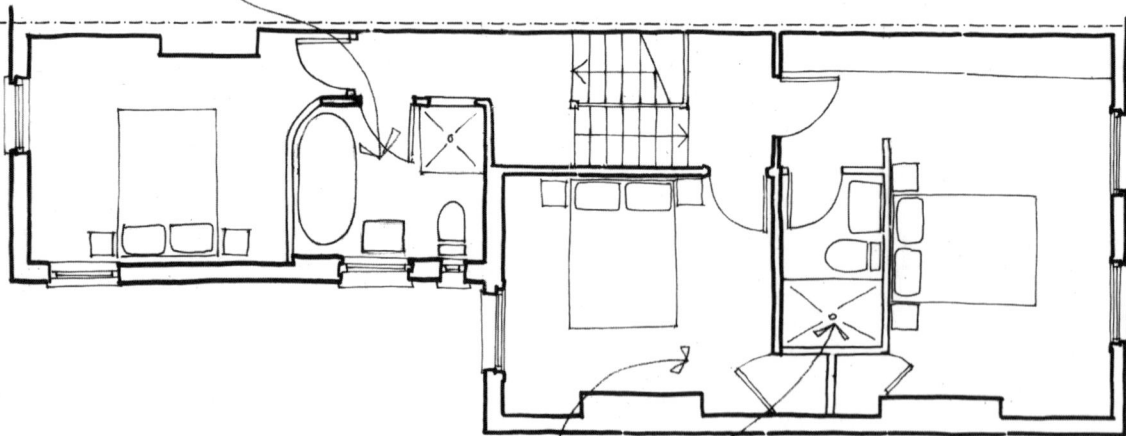

REAR BEDROOM REMAINS UNCHANGED EXCEPT FOR A DOOR TO ACCESS STORAGE

ENSUITE SHOWER AND STORAGE CREATED TO SERVE FRONT BEDROOM

OPTION 2

In this option, the existing bathroom has been enlarged by taking a little more space from the front bedroom. The bathroom in the outrigger has been reconfigured to create an en-suite shower room and dressing area to serve the rear bedroom.

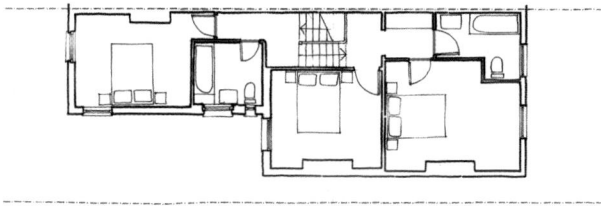

BATHROOM REDUCED TO CREATE ENSUITE SHOWER ROOM AND DRESSING AREA

LARGE FAMILY BATHROOM CREATED IN SECTION OF FRONT BEDROOM

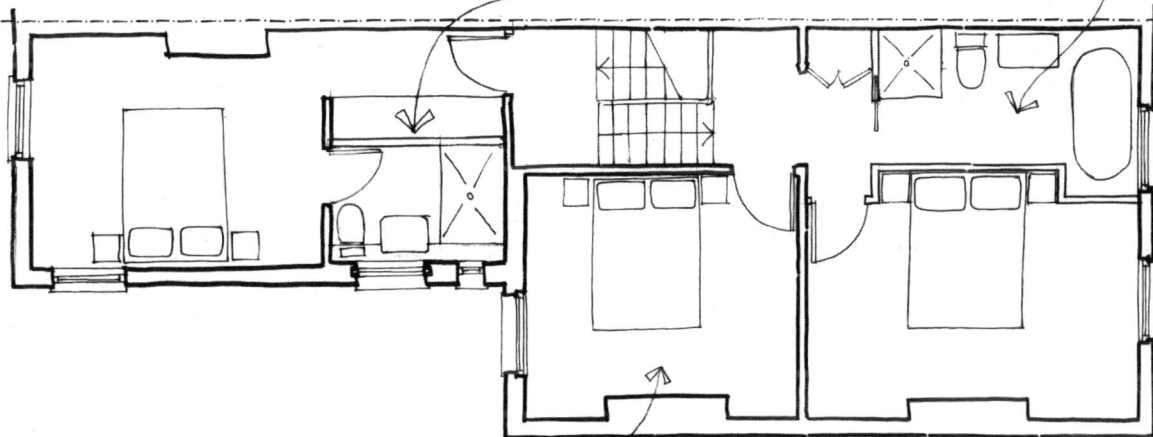

REAR BEDROOM REMAINS UNTOUCHED

OPTION 3

(Based on the Chelsea House project by Studio 30 Architects)

The ceiling and most of the walls have been removed in this option to create a grand, double-height master bedroom with en-suite bathroom. This option assumes either that the stairs are enclosed at the bottom of the flight or the installation of a sprinkler system, but there is room to lobby this stair at the top if preferred. Large skylights bring additional light into the already airy room.

The doors and wall of the outrigger have also been removed to increase a sense of connection between the two spaces. This is used as a living room and study that could serve the master bedroom independently.

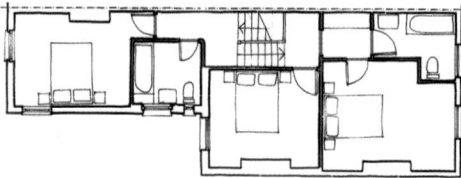

LOBBY DOORS REMOVED TO CREATE FREER FLOW BETWEEN ROOMS

INTERNAL WALLS AND CEILINGS REMOVED ON SECOND FLOOR TO CREATE SPACIOUS MASTER BEDROOM

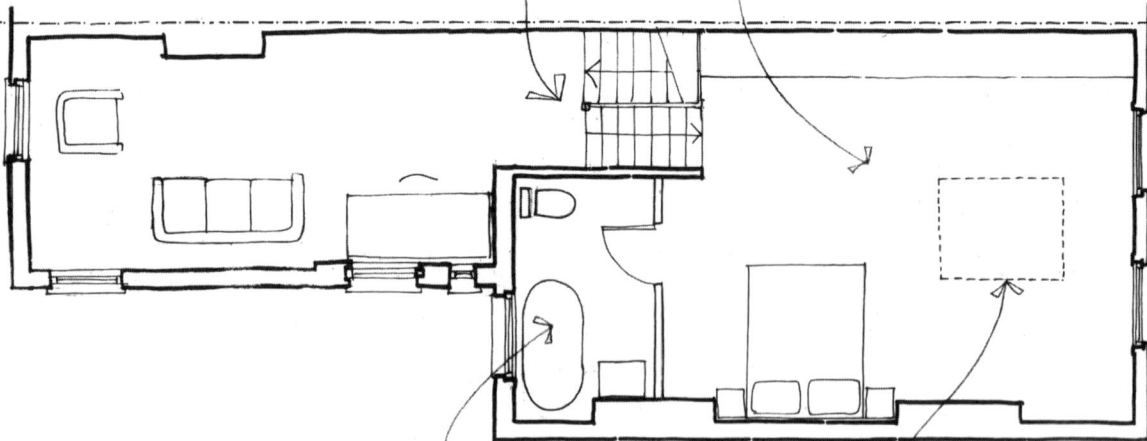

REAR ROOM USED HERE AS A LIVING ROOM AND STUDY TO SERVE MASTER BEDROOM

ENSUITE BATHROOM SLOTTED IN BESIDE STAIRS WITH DOUBLE ENDED BATH WITH VIEW OVER GARDEN

LARGE SKYLIGHT INSERTED INTO FRONT SLOPE OF ROOF

Chelsea House by Studio 30 Architects, Chelsea, London, 2016. All walls and ceiling removed to create a grand master bedroom. Image mirrored to reflect plan.

OPTION 4

(Based on my mother in law's house in Tufnell Park)

In this option the ceiling and walls have been removed to create a grand, double-height space that accommodates living, dining and study areas. Stairs lead up to a small mezzanine level under the eaves. This assumes that the bedrooms are located on the lower floors, creating an upside-down house.

The outrigger accommodates a kitchen/diner, which would serve the grand open-plan living room half a flight up. The door to this room has been moved over slightly to allow kitchen cabinets to be positioned against the party wall. The cooker has been slotted into the chimneybreast.

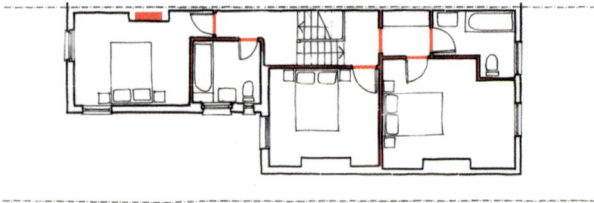

KITCHEN ACCOMMODATED IN REAR ROOM ADJACENT TO UPSTAIRS LIVING DINING ROOM

EXTENT OF NEW MEZZANINE LEVEL LOCATED UNDER EAVES

STAIRS UP TO NEW MEZZANINE LEVEL

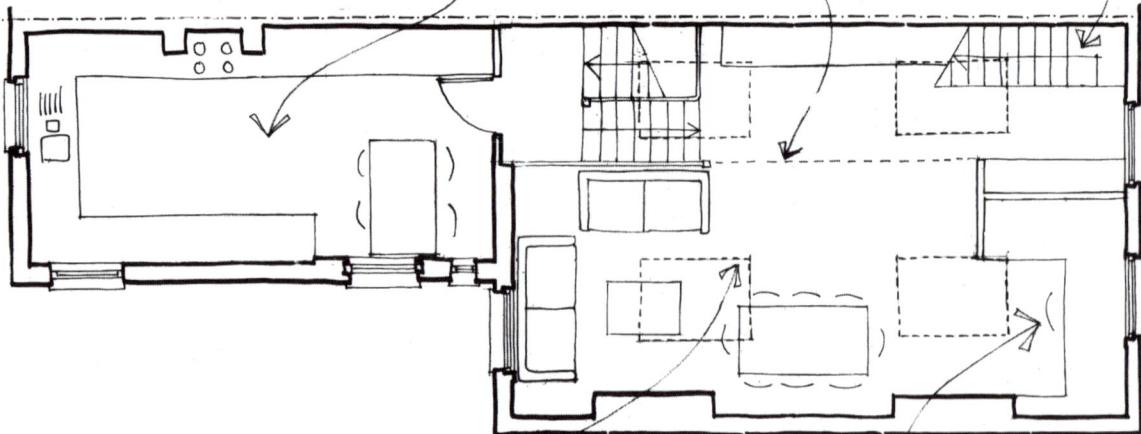

INTERNAL WALLS AND CEILINGS REMOVED TO CREATE GRAND LIVING DINING ROOM

BUILT IN STUDY AREA CREATED AT FRONT OF LIVING ROOM

Small mezzanine under the eaves.

CONCLUSION

I hope that you have found inspiration within these pages. The aim was to set you on the path to making your house a home that works for you. As you can see, there are many more ways of rearranging and extending a Victorian terraced house than first meet the eye.

To further personalise your house, it is important that you have a good understanding of your own taste before embarking on your project. Do your research. Begin compiling a scrapbook of things that you like, and before long a pattern will begin to emerge that reveals your taste. At the same time, evaluate what you like about your house. Retaining original elements will not only keep costs down but, by adding your own taste to the property, will also layer styles that give your house a depth of character and charm. Find images that convey the style of extensions that you prefer. Don't be hasty when choosing materials, furnishings or colours. Start early with the elements that you will need to include in the construction phase, such as external materials, windows, doors, flooring, lighting, kitchen, sanitary ware and ironmongery. Furnishings and colours can come later, and are easier to change than these more permanent components. Try not to be influenced by what is in fashion, as elements chosen purely with this in mind will surely date long before you plan to replace them. If you consider your house holistically rather than as a series of separate rooms, even if you do not intend to tackle everything at once, the result will be more coherent.

If you adhere to these simple guidelines, you should be able to make a positive, informed changes to your house to create the home that you want.

INDEX

IMAGE CREDITS

vi	French + Tye
viii	Thomas Teggin
4	Jacqueline Green
13	Alan Williams
15	Jacqueline Green
16	Jacqueline Green
18 top	Andy Spain
18 middle	Andy Stag
18 bottom	Jacqueline Green
19 top	Chris Snook
19 middle	Jacqueline Green
19 bottom	Adam Scott
20	Jack Hobhouse
31	Jack Hobhouse
32	Jack Hobhouse
33	Jack Hobhouse
35	Matt Clayton
36	Matt Clayton
41	Jacqueline Green
45	Agnese Sanvito
46	Agnese Sanvito
48	French + Tye
53	French + Tye
55	French + Tye
59	Jacqueline Green
66	Jacqueline Green
70	Agnese Sanvito
75	Richard Chivers
77	Agnese Sanvito
78	Agnese Sanvito
79	Agnese Sanvito
81	Agnese Sanvito
82	Agnese Sanvito
87	Jacqueline Green
94	Richard Chivers
96	Emanuelis Stasaitis
100	Anna Pamphilon
103	Jacqueline Green
105	Jacqueline Green
106	Jacqueline Green
109 (both)	Sigrun Sverrisdottir
111	Jacqueline Green
113	Chris Snook
114	Chris Snook

116	Ben Blossom
117	Ben Blossom
119	Emanuelis Stasaitis
120	Emanuelis Stasaitis
121	Emanuelis Stasaitis
129	Salt Productions
130	Salt Productions
133	Amy Barclay
134	Amy Barclay
142	Alexander James
146	Troy Hodgdon
147	Alan Williams
149	Alan Williams
151	Jacqueline Green
152	Jacqueline Green
153	Chris Snook
155	Chris Snook
157	Will Pryce
158	Will Pryce
159	Will Pryce
161 (both)	Jacqueline Green
163	Alexander James
164	Alexander James
165	Alexander James
167	Alexander James
168	Alexander James
169	Richard Chivers
171	Richard Chivers
173	Damian Griffiths
175	Jacqueline Green
177	Chris Snook
179	Alexander James
181	Alexander James
185	Callum Teggin Wickerman Photography
186	Chris Snook
194	Chris Snook
196	Jacqueline Green
200	French + Tye
207	Jacqueline Green
208	French + Tye
210	French + Tye
211	MW Architects
213	Matt Clayton

214	Matt Clayton
219	French + Tye
221	French + Tye
223	Matt Clayton
224	Matt Clayton
228	French + Tye
230	Matt Clayton
233	Martin Swatton Design
235	Martin Swatton Design
237	Will Pryce
239	Will Pryce
240	Andy Stag
244	Jacqueline Green
249	Andy Stag
251	Andy Stag
253	Andy Stag
257	Alexander James
259	Sarah Blee
261	Sarah Blee
263	Megan Taylor
265	David Butler
266	David Butler
269	Will Pryce
270	Will Pryce
273	Andy Stag
274	Andy Stag
281	Salt Productions
283	Callum Teggin Wickerman Photography
All plans	Jacqueline Green

288